GACE
001
002

Early Childhood Education
Teacher Certification Exam

By: Sharon Wynne, M.S
Southern Connecticut State University

"And, while there's no reason yet to panic, I think it's only prudent that we make preparations to panic."

XAMonline, INC.
Boston

XAMonline, Inc.
21 Orient Ave.
Melrose, MA 02176
Toll Free 1-800-509-4128
Email: info@xamonline.com
Web www.xamonline.com
Fax: 1-781-662-9268

Library of Congress Cataloging-in-Publication Data

Wynne, Sharon A.
    GACE: Early Childhood Education Teacher Certification / Sharon A. Wynne. -2nd ed.
    ISBN: 978-1-58197-537-6
    1. Early Childhood Education   2. Study Guides.   3. GACE
    4. Teachers' Certification & Licensure.   5. Careers

Disclaimer:
The opinions expressed in this publication are the sole works of XAMonline and were created independently from the National Education Association, Educational Testing Service, or any State Department of Education, National Evaluation Systems or other testing affiliates.

Between the time of publication and printing, state specific standards as well as testing formats and website information may change that is not included in part or in whole within this product. Sample test questions are developed by XAMonline and reflect similar content as on real tests; however, they are not former tests. XAMonline assembles content that aligns with state standards but makes no claims nor guarantees teacher candidates a passing score. Numerical scores are determined by testing companies such as NES or ETS and then are compared with individual state standards. A passing score varies from state to state.

Printed in the United States of America   œ-1

GACE: Early Childhood Education
ISBN: 978-1-58197-537-6

TEACHER CERTIFICATION STUDY GUIDE

Project Manager: Sharon Wynne, MS

Project Coordinator: Victoria Anderson, MS

Content Coordinators/Authors:
Rennell Brunclik, BS
Susan Andres, MS
Frances Stanford, MS
Natalie Arnett, BS
Janis Petersen, PhD
David White, MS
Ted Purinton, PhD
Christina Forsyth, MS
Barbara Casey, PhD
Kelley Eldredge, MS
Vickie Pittard, MS
James Stark, MS
Don Rogerson, BS
Michele Di Amico, BS

Sample test:
Shelley Wake, MS
Deborah Harbin, MS
Christina Godard, BS
Kim Putney, BS
Carol Moore, BS
Vickie Pittard, MS

Editors: Managing
Proof reader
Dr. Harte Weiner
Heather Sugioka, MS
Cathi Evans, AA
Beth Anderson, PhD
Donna Quesinberry; MS
Paul Giacomelli, MS
Vickie Pittard, MS
Mary Arena, BS
Christina Forsyth, MS
Don Rogerson, BS
Bonnie Snyder, PhD
Jane Carter, MS
Deborah Harbin, MS

Copy editor
Sample test
Pre-Flight
Production
Tamara Brewer, MS
Christina Forsyth, MS
Mary Collins, BS
David Aronson

Graphic Artist Jenna Hamilton

Table of Contents

Great Study and Testing Tips!

What to study in order to prepare for the subject assessments is the focus of this study guide, but equally important is *how* you study.

You can increase your chances of truly mastering the information by taking some simple but effective steps.

Study Tips:

1. Some foods aid the learning process. Foods such as milk, nuts, seeds, rice, and oats help your study efforts by releasing natural memory enhancers called CCKs (*cholecystokinin*) composed of *tryptophan*, *choline*, and *phenylalanine*. All of these chemicals enhance the neurotransmitters associated with memory. Before studying, try a light, protein-rich meal of eggs, turkey, and fish. All of these foods release the memory enhancing chemicals. The better the connections, the more you comprehend.

Likewise, before you take a test, stick to a light snack of energy-boosting and relaxing foods. A glass of milk, a piece of fruit, or some peanuts will release various memory-boosting chemicals and help you to relax and focus on the subject at hand.

2. Learn to take great notes. A by-product of our modern culture is that we have grown accustomed to getting our information in short doses (e.g., TV news sound bites or newspaper articles styled after USA Today).

Consequently, we've subconsciously trained ourselves to assimilate information in neat little packages. If your notes are scrawled all over the paper, it fragments the flow of the information. Strive for clarity. Newspapers use a standard format to achieve clarity. Your notes can be much clearer through the use of proper formatting. A very effective format is called the *"Cornell Method."*

> Take a sheet of loose-leaf lined notebook paper and draw a line all the way down the paper about 1-2" from the left-hand edge.

> Draw another line across the width of the paper about 1-2" up from the bottom. Repeat this process on the reverse side of the page.

Look at the highly effective result. You have ample room for notes, a left hand margin for special emphasis items or inserting supplementary data from the textbook, a large area at the bottom for a brief summary, and a little rectangular space for just about anything you want.

3. Get the concept, then the details. Too often we focus on the details and don't gather an understanding of the concept. However, if you simply memorize only dates, places, or names, you may well miss the whole point of the subject.

A key way to understand things is to put them in your own words. If you are working from a textbook, automatically summarize each paragraph in your mind. If you are outlining text, don't simply copy the author's words.

Rephrase them in your own words. You remember your own thoughts and words much better than someone else's, and subconsciously tend to associate the important details with the core concepts.

4. Ask Why? Pull apart written material paragraph by paragraph and don't forget the captions under the illustrations.

Example: If the heading is "Stream Erosion," flip it around to read "Why do streams erode?" Then answer the questions.

If you train your mind to think in a series of questions and answers, not only will you learn more, but it will also help to lessen test anxiety because you are used to answering questions.

5. Read for reinforcement and future needs. Even if you only have 10 minutes, put your notes or a book in your hand. Your mind is similar to a computer; you have to input data in order to have it processed. *By reading, you are creating the neural connections for future retrieval.* The more times you read something, the more you reinforce the learning of ideas.

Even if you don't fully understand something on the first pass, *your mind stores much of the material for later recall.*

6. Relax to learn; go into exile. Our bodies respond to an inner clock called biorhythms. Burning the midnight oil works well for some people, but not everyone.

If possible, set aside a particular place to study that is free of distractions. Shut off the television, cell phone, and pager, and exile your friends and family during your study period.

If you really are bothered by silence, try background music. Light classical music at a low volume has been shown to aid in concentration over other types of music. Music that evokes pleasant emotions without lyrics is highly suggested. Try just about anything by Mozart. It relaxes you.

7. <u>Use arrows, not highlighters</u>. At best, it's difficult to read a page full of yellow, pink, blue, and green streaks. Try staring at a neon sign for a while and you'll soon see that the horde of colors obscure the message.

A quick note, a brief dash of color, an underline, or an arrow pointing to a particular passage is much clearer than a horde of highlighted words.

8. <u>Budget your study time</u>. Although you shouldn't ignore any of the material, *allocate your available study time in the same ratio that topics may appear on the test.*

By setting your personal study topics in much the same way that the test will be patterned, you will be better equipped to answer all of the test questions.

Testing Tips:

1. <u>Get smart, play dumb</u>. *Don't read anything into the question.* Don't make an assumption that the test writer is looking for something else than what is asked. Stick to the question as written and don't read extra things into it.

2. <u>Read the question and all the choices *twice* before answering the question</u>. You may miss something by not carefully reading and re-reading both the question and the answers.

If you really don't have a clue as to the right answer, leave it blank on the first time through. Go on to the other questions, as they may provide a clue as to how to answer the skipped questions.

If, later on, you still can't answer the skipped ones . . . *Guess.* The only penalty for guessing is that you *might* get it wrong. Only one thing is certain; if you don't put anything down, you will get it wrong!

3. <u>Turn the question into a statement</u>. Look at the way the questions are worded. The syntax of the question usually provides a clue. Does it seem more familiar as a statement rather than as a question? Does it sound strange?

By turning a question into a statement, you may be able to spot if an answer sounds right, and it may also trigger memories of material you have read.

4. <u>Look for hidden clues</u>. It's actually very difficult to compose multiple-foil (choice) questions without giving away part of the answer in the options presented.

In most multiple-choice questions you can often readily eliminate one or two of the potential answers. This leaves you with only two real possibilities; automatically, your odds go to Fifty-Fifty for very little work.

5. <u>Trust your instincts</u>. For every fact that you have read, you subconsciously retain something of that knowledge. On questions that you aren't really certain about, go with your basic instincts. *Your first impression on how to answer a question is usually correct.*

6. <u>Mark your answers directly on the test booklet</u>. Don't bother trying to fill in the optical scan sheet on the first pass through the test.

Just be very careful not to mismark your answers when you eventually transcribe them to the scan sheet.

7. <u>Watch the clock</u>! You have a set amount of time to answer the questions. Don't get bogged down trying to answer a single question at the expense of ten questions you can more readily answer.

COMPETENCY 1.0 UNDERSTAND CONCEPTS OF PRINT AND PHONOLOGICAL AWARENESS

Skill 1.1   Recognizing developmental stages in learning to write and read

In 2000, the National Reading Panel released its now well-known report on teaching children to read. In a way, this report slightly put to rest the debate between phonics and whole language. It argued, essentially, that word-letter recognition was as important as understanding what the text means. The report's "big 5" critical areas of reading instruction are as follows:

- **Phonemic Awareness:** This is the acknowledgement of sounds and words (for example, a child's realization that some words rhyme). Onset and rhyme are two of the skills that might help students learn that the sound of the first letter "b" in the word "bad" can be changed with the sound "d" to make it "dad." The key in phonemic awareness is that when you teach it to children, it can be taught with the students' eyes closed. In other words, it's all about sounds, not about ascribing written letters to sounds.

- **Phonics:** As opposed to phonemic awareness, the study of phonics must be done with the eyes open. It is the connection between the sounds and letters on a page. In other words, students who are learning phonics might see the word "bad" and sound each letter out slowly until they recognize that they just said the word.

- **Comprehension:** Comprehension simply means that the reader can ascribe meaning to text. Even though students may be good with phonics and even know what many words on a page mean, some of them are not good with comprehension because they do not know the strategies that would help them to comprehend. For example, students should know that stories often have structures (beginning, middle, and end). They should also know that when they are reading something and it does not make sense, they will need to employ "fix-up" strategies where they go back into the text they have just read and look for clues. Teachers can use many strategies to teach comprehension, including questioning, asking students to paraphrase or summarize, utilizing graphic organizers, and focusing on mental images.

- **Fluency:** Fluency is the ability to read in much the same manner as speaking, with fluidity and smoothness. Students who are fluent readers are more likely to be successful with comprehension, as they are less focused on individual words and more focused on what is actually being read.

- **Vocabulary:** Vocabulary demonstrates the strong ties between oral and written language. Students who are learning to read are just beginning to realize the link between the words they say and the words they read. Increasing vocabulary—whether by listening to others, reading to themselves, or being read to—will help students with both comprehension and fluency.

Methods used to teach these skills are often featured in a "balanced literacy" curriculum that focuses on the use of skills in various instructional contexts. For example, with independent reading, students independently choose books that are at their reading levels; with guided reading, teachers work with small groups of students to help them with their particular reading problems. With whole group reading, the entire class reads the same text, and the teacher incorporates activities to help students learn phonics, comprehension, fluency, and vocabulary. In addition to these components of balanced literacy, teachers incorporate writing so that students can learn the structures of communicating through text.

Skill 1.2 Demonstrating knowledge of characteristics and purposes of printed information and developmentally appropriate strategies for promoting students' familiarity with concepts of print

Development of the Understanding that Print Carries Meaning

This understanding is demonstrated every day in the elementary classroom when a teacher holds up a selected book to read it aloud to the class. The teacher is explicitly and deliberately thinking about how to hold the book, how to focus the class on looking at its cover, where to start reading, and in what direction to begin.

Even in writing the morning message on the board, the teacher is targeting the children by placing the message at its proper place at the top of the board and following it by additional activities and a schedule for the rest of the day.

When the teacher challenges children to make posters of items that begin with a single letter by using the items in the classroom, their home, or their general knowledge base, the children are making concrete the understanding that print carries meaning.

Strategies for Promoting Awareness of the Relationship between Spoken and Written Language

- Write down what the children are saying on a chart.
- Highlight and celebrate the meanings and uses of print products found in the classroom. These products include: posters, labels, yellow sticky pad notes, labels on shelves and lockers, calendars, rule signs, and directions.
- Intentionally read big-print and oversized books to teach print conventions such as directionality.
- Practice exercises in reading to others (for K-1-2) through which young children practice how to handle a book: how to turn pages, how to find tops and bottoms of pages, and how to tell the difference between the front and back covers of a book.
- Search and discuss adventures in word awareness and close observation through which children are challenged to identify and talk about the length, appearance, boundaries of specific words, and the letters which comprise them.
- Have children match oral words to printed words by forming an echo chorus (where children echo the reading) as the teacher reads the story aloud. This often works best with poetry or rhymes.
- Have the children combine, manipulate, switch, and move letters to change words and spelling patterns.
- Work with letter cards to create messages and respond to the messages that they create.

The Role of Environmental Print in Developing Print Awareness

An environmental print book can be created for the children, initially by the teacher, that contains collaged symbols of the labels from their favorite lunch or breakfast foods. The teacher can ask students to bring in their labels and alphabetically arrange the cut and clipped symbols from the packaging of these foods into the book. The book can then be added to by the students as they clip and place symbols and logos from additional sources of environmental print.

Newspapers are an excellent source of environmental print that are accessible every day. With food ads, clothing ads, and other child-centered products and personalities, i lends itself wonderfully for developing print awareness. Supermarket circulars and coupons distributed in chain drug stores are also excellent for engaging children in using environmental print as a reading device.

What is particularly effective in using environmental print is that it immediately transports the child from an ELL background into print awareness through the familiarity of commercial logos and packaging symbols used on a daily basis.

Development of Book Handling Skills

Have the children identify the front cover, back cover, and title page of a specific book.

Model storytelling by holding the book so that the members of the audience can see the illustrations shown to them. Then have them demonstrate the skills for their peers.

Have children search through the class libraries for special features on the fronts or backs of books as they help return the books to their bins. Have the children display and talk about the special symbols they found.

Review with the children, in an age and grade appropriate format, additional parts of the book as they emerge through the mini-lessons and read alouds. These additional parts of the book can include: title pages, dedication page, foreword, appendix, credits, copyright date, table of contents, etc.

Techniques for Promoting the Ability to Track Print in Connected Texts

Model directionality and one-to-one word matching by pointing to words while using a big book, pocket chart, or poem written out on a chart. As you repeatedly lead the children in this reading, they can follow along and eventually track the print, and also make one-to-one matches on the connected text independently. They can also practice by using a pointer (most children love to use the pointer because then pleasure becomes associated with the reading) or their fingers to follow the words. In general, children will happily vie to be the point person. Even before Vanna White, the joy of "signifying letters" existed and has tremendous appeal for children.

Copy down a brief, familiar rhyme (perhaps from a favorite book or song) and post it in the room at a child's eye level, so the child can independently walk around and read it.

Copy down a brief or familiar rhyme or a poem on individual word cards. You can challenge the children in small groups or independently to reassemble and display them on a pocket chart. As children "play" with constructing and reconstructing this pocket chart, they will develop an awareness of directionality, one-on-one matching of print to spoken words, spacing, and punctuation.

Model interactive emergent writing with the class. While discussing and writing down the weather, deliberately ask and have the children suggest where the first word in that report should go: the top or the bottom of the felt board? Will the first letter be upper case or lower case? What goes at the end of the sentence?

Create with the children sing-song repetitions/rules for using capitals, periods, commas, etc. Encourage the children to begin reciting these sing-songs as soon as they identify specific concepts of print in connected texts.

Model for children how, when pointing at words, they can start at the top and move from left to right. Tell the children that if there are more words to the sentence they are reading under the first line of print, they must go back to the left and under the previous line. Young children enjoy practicing this kinesthetic "return sweep." You might want to teach them to identify the need to do this by saying "don't fall asleep at the page" or "time to get to the 'return sweep' stage!!" Post this saying and encourage them to sing-song as they joyously take ownership of their reading.

Have even beginning readers "read" through the text to find letters they recognize in the story. Share some of the text that includes these specific letters to whet their appetite for more reading.

Strategies for Promoting Letter Knowledge and Letter Formation

Engage the children in a "tale trail" game. Use a story they have already heard or read. Ask the children to circle certain letters and then re-read the story, sharing the letters they have circled.

Give the children plenty of opportunities to do letter sorts. Pass out word cards which have the targeted letter on them. Ask the children to come up and display their answers to questions about the letter. As an example, consider the letter "R."

- R as the first letter—rose, rise, ran,
- R as the last letter—car, star, far,
- R with a t after it—start, heart, part, smart
- Two Rs in the middle of a word—carry, sorry, starry

Play "What's in a Name?" Select a student's name. As an example, consider "William." Copy the name down on a sentence strip. Have the children count the number of letters in the name and how many of them appear twice. Allow them to talk about which letter is upper case and which letters are lower case. Have the students chant the name. Then rewrite the name on another sentence strip. Have the strip cut into separate letters and see if someone from the class can put the name back together correctly.

As you read a book with or to the children, ask them to show you specific letters or lower case or upper case letters. Read the text first and encourage as many children as possible to come up and identify the letters. Use a big book and have felt letters available for display as well. If grade-, age-, and developmentally-appropriate, have the children write the letter they identified themselves. (Or, for even more fun, construct the letter using pipe cleaners, craft sticks, or colored markers, using different colors for upper and lower case letters.)

Play "letter leap" with the children and have them look carefully at the room to identify labeled items that begin with a specific letter by "leaping" over to them and placing a large lettered placard next to them. Children who have advanced in letter formation can then be challenged to "leap" through the classroom when called upon to literally "letter" unlabeled objects.

Use of Reading and Writing Strategies for Teaching Letter-Sound Correspondence

Provide children with a sample of a single letter book (or create one from environmental sources, newspapers, coupons, circulars, magazines, or your own text ideas). Make sure that your selected or created sample includes a printed version of the letter in both upper and lower case forms. Make certain that each page contains a picture of something that starts with that specific letter and also has the word for the picture. The book you select or create should be a predictable one in that when the picture is identified, the word can be read.

Once the children have been provided with your sample and have listened to it being read, challenge them to each make a single letter book. It is often best to focus on familiar consonants or the first letter of the child's first name. Use of the first letter of a name invites children to develop a book that tells about themselves and the words that they find. This is an excellent way for the reading workshop aspect of teaching alphabetic principles to complement and enhance the writing workshop.

Encourage children to be active writers and readers by finding words for their book on the classroom word wall, in alphabet books in the special alphabet book bin, and in grade- and age-appropriate pictionaries (dictionaries for younger children that are filled with pictures).

Of course, the richest resource within the reading and writing workshop classroom for teaching and fostering the alphabetic principle lies in the use of alphabet books as anchor books for inspiring students' writing. While young children in grades K-1 will do better with the single letter book authoring activity, children in grades 2 and beyond can truly be inspired and motivated by alphabet books that enhance their own reading, writing, and alphabetic skills. Furthermore, use of these books—which have and are being produced in a variety of formats to enhance social studies, science, and mathematical themes—provide an opportunity for even young children to create a meaningful product that authenticates their content study while enhancing alphabetic skills and, of course, print awareness.

An annotated bibliography of some of the newest alphabet books has been provided in the bibliography section of this guide. It was limited by space considerations, but educators can catch up on the latest titles and identify those most appropriate for their grades by visiting a bookstore. Consider selecting an alphabet book that has a particularly inviting concept, art style, or adaptable format within the children's capacity to use as a model.

For example, author Tana Hoban uses actual color photographs of letters in her *26 letters and 99 cents*. Children may want to make clay letters or create letter sculptures that develop their own "in style of" alphabet book similar to Hoban's. If nutrition is the science topic, children might want to examine Lois Ehlert's very accessible *Eating the Alphabet: Fruits and Vegetables from A to Z*. This, combined with an examination of the fruits and vegetables in a local store (perhaps a pleasant walk from the school and a quick break from the routine local outing) can yield a wonderful alphabet book on fruits and vegetables that can also include those fruits and vegetables eaten in various cultures (e.g., mangos, plantains, pomegranates, etc).

The alphabet book can also offer the class a chance to work collaboratively within a template created by the teacher. Completion of this collaborative work can be shared with peers in another class and parents. It can also be kept as a model for the following year's class (of course, with the recognition and acceptance of the authors!).

Skill 1.3   Demonstrating knowledge of phonological awareness (i.e., awareness that oral language includes units such as spoken words and syllables)

Phonics is a widely used method for teaching students to read. This method includes studying the rules and patterns found in language. By age five or six, children can typically begin to use phonics to begin to understand the connections between letters, their patterns, vowel sounds (e.g., short vowels or long vowels), and the collective sounds they all make.

The study of phonics is one that involves sound as well as sight. It is defined by the connection between hearing the sounds and seeing the letters on a page. In the beginning stages of phonics, students may use sight to see the word "cat," but they use sound to break the word down to its letter components. It may require slowly speaking each letter before the students recognize that they actually said the word.

Phonological awareness means the ability of the reader to recognize the sound of spoken language. This recognition includes how these sounds can be blended together, segmented (divided up), and manipulated (switched around). This awareness then leads to phonics, a method for teaching children to read. It helps them "sound out words."

Development of phonological skills may begin during pre-K years. Indeed, by the age of five, a child who has been exposed to rhyme can recognize a rhyme. Such a child can demonstrate phonological awareness by filling in the missing rhyming word in a familiar rhyme or rhymed picture book.

Children are taught phonological awareness when they are taught the sounds made by the letters, the sounds made by various combinations of letters, and how to recognize individual sounds in words.

Phonological awareness skills include:
1. Rhyming and syllabification
2. Blending sounds into words (such as pic-tur-bo-k)
3. Identifying the beginning or starting sounds of words and the ending or closing sounds of words
4. Breaking words down into sounds (also called "segmenting" words)
5. Recognizing other smaller words in the bigger word by removing starting sounds (recognizing the word "ear" in "hear")

Explicit and Implicit Strategies for Teaching Phonics

Professor Uta Frith has done work on the sequence of children's phonic learning. Frith has identified three phases that describe the progression of children's phonic learning from ages four through eight. These are:

Logographic Phase: Children recognize whole words that have significance for them, such as their own names, the names of stores they frequent, or products that their parents buy.

Strategies that nurture development in this phase can include explicit labeling in the classroom using the children's names and the names of classroom objects, components, furniture, and materials. In addition, during snack time and lunch-time, explicit attention and talk can be focused on new brands of foods and drink.

Toward the end of this phase children start to notice initial letters in words and the sounds that they represent.

Analytic Phase: During this phase, the children make associations between the spelling patterns in the words they know and the new words they encounter.

Orthographic Phase: In this phase, children recognize words almost automatically. They can rapidly identify an increasing number of words because they know a good deal about the structure of words and how they're spelled.

To best support these phases and the development of emergent and early readers, teachers should focus on elements of phonics learning, which help children analyze words for their letters, spelling patterns, and structural components. The children need to be involved in activities where they can use what they know about words in order to learn new ones. For example, the teacher can build on what the children know to introduce new spelling patterns, vowel combinations, and short and long vowel investigations. The teacher must do this and be aware that these will be reintroduced again and again as needed.

Keep in mind that children's learning of phonics and other key components of reading is not linear, but rather falls back to review and then flows forward to build new understandings.

Sorting Words

This activity allows children to focus closely on the specific features of words and begin to understand the basic elements of letter-sound relationships.

Start with monosyllabic words. Have the children group them by their length, common letters, sound, and/or spelling pattern.

Prepare for the activity by writing ten to fifteen words on oak-tag strips and placing them randomly on the sentence strip holder. These words should come from a book previously shared in the classroom or a language experience chart.

Next, begin to sort out the word with the children, perhaps by focusing on where a particular letter appears in a word. While the children sort the place of a particular letter in a given word, they should also be coached (or facilitated) by the teacher to recognize that sometimes a letter in the middle of the word can still be the last sound that we hear, and that some letters at the end of a word are silent (such as "e").

Children should be encouraged to make their own categories for word sorts and to share their own discoveries as they do the word sorts. The children's discoveries should be recorded and posted in the rooms with their names so they have ownership of their phonics learning.

Assessment of Phonological Awareness

These skills can be assessed by having the child listen to the teacher say two words. The child should then be asked to decide if these two words are the same word repeated twice or two different words. When you make this assessment, if you do use two different words, make certain that they only differ by one phoneme, such as /d/ and /g/. Children can be assessed on words that are not real words or that are not familiar to them. The words used can be make-believe.

Skill 1.4   **Demonstrating knowledge of phonemic awareness (i.e., ability to perceive and discriminate among the component sounds in a spoken word)**

Phonemic awareness is the ability to break down and hear separate and/or different sounds and distinguish between the sounds one hears. The terms "phonics" and "phonemic awareness" are different; however, they are interdependent on each other. Phonemic awareness is required to begin the study of phonics, in which students will need the ability to break down words into the smalls units of sound, known as phonemes, and to later identify syllables, blends, and patterns.

Phonemic awareness is based in a child's ability to acknowledge sounds and words. Unlike phonics, which uses both sight and sound, phonemic awareness can be done with the student's eyes closed.

Phonemic awareness deals with sounds in words that are spoken. To be phonemically aware means that the reader and listener can recognize and manipulate specific sounds in spoken words. The majority of phonemic awareness tasks, activities, and exercises are *oral*.

Since the ability to distinguish between individual sounds or phonemes within words is a prerequisite for the association of sounds with letters and also for manipulating sounds to blend words—a fancy way of saying "reading"—the teaching of phonemic awareness is crucial to emergent literacy (early childhood K-2 reading instruction). Children need a strong background in phonemic awareness in order for phonics instruction (sound-spelling relationship printed materials) to be effective.

Theorist Marilyn Jager Adams, who researches early reading, has outlined five basic types of phonemic awareness tasks.

Task 1-Ability to hear rhymes and alliteration

For example, the children may listen to a poem, rhyming picture book, or song and identify the rhyming words that are heard. The teacher then records or lists these words on an experiential chart.

Task 2-Ability to do oddity tasks (recognize the member of a set that is different [odd] among the group)

For example, the children may look at pictures of a blade of grass, a garden, and a rose and then determine which picture starts with a different sound.

Task 3-Ability to orally blend words and split syllables

For example, the children can say the first sound of a word and then separately vocalize the rest of the word. They can then put it together as a single word.

Task 4-Ability to orally segment words

For example, the children may focus on their abilities to count sounds. The children could be asked as a group to count the sounds in "hamburger."

Task 5-Ability to do phonics manipulation tasks

For example, the children may make sound replacements in common words. The teacher can ask them to replace the "r" sound in rose with a "p" sound.

Assessment of Phonemic Awareness

Teachers can maintain ongoing logs and rubrics for assessment throughout the year of Phonemic Awareness for individual children. Such assessments would identify particular stated reading behaviors or performance standards, the date of observation of the child's behavior (in this context, phonemic activity or exercise), and comments.

The rubric or legend for assessing these behaviors might include the following descriptors: demonstrates or exhibits reading behavior consistently, making progress/strides toward this reading behavior, and/or has not yet demonstrated or exhibited this behavior.

Depending on the particular phonemic task you are modeling, the performance task might include:

- Saying rhyming words in response to an oral prompt
- Segmenting a word spoken by the teacher into its beginning, middle, and ending sounds
- Correctly counting the number of syllables in a spoken word

The Difference Between Phonological and Phonemic Awareness

Phonological awareness involves recognizing that spoken words are comprised of a set of smaller units—including syllables and sounds.

Phonemic awareness is a specific type of phonological awareness that focuses on the ability to distinguish, manipulate, and blend specific sounds or phonemes within a given word.

Think of phonological awareness as an umbrella and phonemic awareness as a specific spoke under this umbrella.

Phonics deals with printed words and the learning of sound-spelling correlations, while phonemic awareness activities are for the most part oral.

If you were, or are, a science or mathematics major, you need to remember in reviewing reading theory that the distinctions are not hard, fast, and absolute as those in the mathematical and scientific fields. Many times they are semantic, and sometimes they are accepted and respected theories that change over time. The information and definitions in this guide are those accepted in the year of its publication and at the time of its authoring and updating. As changes occur in accepted theories, they will be made in the study guides and in the certification exams.

Skill 1.5   Analyzing the significance of phonological and phonemic awareness in reading acquisition

The Role of Phonemic Awareness in Reading Development

Children who have problems with phonics generally have not acquired, nor have been exposed to, phonemic awareness activities, which are usually fostered at home and in preschool. Examples of these activities include extensive songs, rhymes, and read–alouds.

Instructional Methods

Instructional methods that may be effective for teaching phonemic awareness can include:

- Clapping syllables in words
- Distinguishing between a word and a sound
- Using visual cues and movements to help children understand when the speaker moves from one sound to another
- Incorporating oral segmentation activities that focus on easily distinguished syllables rather than sounds
- Singing familiar songs (e.g., Happy Birthday, Knick Knack Paddy Whack) and replacing key words in them with words that have a different ending or middle sound (oral segmentation)
- Dealing children a deck of picture cards and having them sound out the words of the pictures on their cards, or calling for a picture by asking for its first and second sound.

Consideration for ELL Learners

Given the demographics of our country, which is becoming increasingly pluralistic and has burgeoning numbers of citizens who are from ELL (English Language learner) backgrounds, the likelihood that you will be teaching at least one, if not more, children who are from a non-native English speaking background (even though they may not be officially classified as ELL students), is at least 75 percent. Therefore, as a conscientious educator, it is important that you understand the special factors involved in supporting their literacy development, including fostering progress in native language literacy as a perquisite for second language (English) reading progress.

Not all English phonemes are present in various ELL native languages. Some native language phonemes may, and do, conflict with English phonemes.

It is recommended that all teachers of reading—particularly those who are working with ELL students—use meaningful, student-centered, and culture-customized activities. These activities may include: language games, word walls, and poems. Some of these activities might also, if possible, be initiated in the child's first language and then reiterated in English.

Reading and the ELL Learner

Research has shown that there is a positive and strong correlation between a child's literacy in his or her native language and his or her learning of English. The degree of native language proficiency and literacy is a strong predictor of English language development. Children who are literate and engaged readers in their native language can better transfer their skills to a second language (e.g., English).

What this means is that educators should not approach the needs of ELL learners in reading in the same manner that they would approach native English speaking students. Those whose families are not from a focused oral literacy and reading culture in the native language will need additional oral language rhymes, read-alouds, and singing as support for reading skills development in both their native and the English language.

The Role of Phonological Processing in the Reading Development of Individual Students

English Language Learners (ELL)

Children who are raised in homes where English is not the first language and/or standard English is not spoken may have difficulty with hearing the difference between similar sounding words like "send" and "sent." Any child who is not in a home, day care, or preschool environment where English phonology operates may have difficulty perceiving and demonstrating the differences between English language phonemes. If children cannot hear the difference between words that sound the same like "grow" and "glow," they will be confused when these words appear in a print context. This confusion is likely to impact their comprehension.

Considerations for teaching phonological processing to ELL children include recognition by the teacher that what works for the English language speaking child from an English language speaking family does not necessarily work with students who speak other primary languages.

Research recommends that ELL children initially learn to read in their first language. It has also been found that a priority for ELL should be learning to speak English before being taught to read English. Research supports oral language development, since it lays the foundation for phonological awareness.

All phonological instruction programs must be tailored to the children's learning backgrounds. Rhymes and alliteration introduced to ELL children should be read or shared with them in their first language, if possible. If you do not speak the student's first language, get a paraprofessional or pull out an ELL educator to support your instruction in the first language.

Struggling Readers

Among the causes that make reading a struggle for some children (and adults) is auditory trauma or ear infections that affect the ability to hear speech. Such children need one-on-one support with articulation and perception of different sounds. When a child says a word such as "parrot" incorrectly, repeat it back as a question with the correct pronunciation of the sounds. If the child "gets" the sound correctly after your question, this type of extra support was all that was needed. If the child still has difficulty with pronunciation, it may be necessary to consult with a speech therapist or audiologist. Early identification of medical conditions that affect hearing is crucial to reading development. Therefore, as an educator, you need to make the time to sit with struggling readers and play games such as "same or different" in order to identify those children who may be struggling due to a hearing difficulty.

Points to Ponder:
- Phonological awareness is auditory
- It does not involve print
- It must start before children have learned letter-sound correlations
- It is the basis for the successful teaching of phonics and spelling
- It can and must be taught and nurtured

Skill 1.6   Recognizing developmentally appropriate strategies for promoting students' phonological and phonemic awareness (e.g., identifying rhyming words, segmenting words, and blending phonemes)

Using Phonics to Decode Words in Connected Text

Identifying New Words

Some strategies to share with children during conferences or as part of shared reading include the following prompts:

Look at the beginning letter/s. What sound do you hear?

Stop to think about the text or story. What word with this beginning letter would make sense here?

Look at the book's illustrations. Do they provide you with help in figuring out the new word?

Think of which word would make sense, sound right, and match the letters that you see. Start the sentence over, making your mouth ready to say that word.

Skip the word, read to the end of the sentence, and then come back to the word. How does what you've read help you with the word?

Listen to whether what you are reading makes sense and matches the letters (this is asking the child to self-monitor). If it doesn't make sense, see if you can correct it on your own.

Look for spelling patterns you know from the spelling pattern wall.

Look for smaller words you might know within the larger word.

Think of any place you may have seen this word before in a story read to you or read by you, or where you may have met up with this word before.

Read on a little, and then return to the part that confused you.

Use of Semantic and Syntactic Cues

Semantic Cues

Prompts that the teacher can use to alert the children to semantic cues include:

You said (the child's statement and incorrect attempt). Does that make sense to you?

If someone said (repeat the child's attempt), would you know what he or she meant?

You said (child's incorrect attempt). Would you write that?

Children need to use meaning to predict what the text says so that the relevant information can prompt the correct words to surface as they identify the words. If children come to a word they can't immediately recognize, they need to try to figure it out by using their past reading (or being read to) experiences, background knowledge, and what they can deduce so far from the text itself.

Syntactic Cues

Prompts that the teacher can use to alert the children to syntactic cues include:

You said (child's incorrect attempt). Does that sound right?

You said (child's incorrect attempt). Can we say it like that?

Development of Phonics Skills in Individual Students

English Language Learners

In *On Solid Ground* (2000), researcher and educator Sharon Taberski said that it is much harder for children from ELL backgrounds, and children from homes where other English dialects are spoken, to use syntactic cues to attempt to self-correct.

These children, through no fault of their own, do not have sufficient experience hearing Standard English spoken to use this cueing system as they read. These children need a teacher who is sensitive to their linguistic or cultural background to guide them through these issues.

Highly Proficient Readers

Highly proficient readers can be paired as buddy tutors for ELL or special needs classroom members, or they can be used to assist the resource room teacher during their reading time. They can use the CVC Game developed by Jacki Montierth (explained in detail at the end of this skill) to support their peers, and can even modify the game to meet the specific needs of classroom peers. This offers the highly proficient reader the opportunity to do a service learning project while still in elementary school. It also introduces the learner to another dimension of reading, the role of the reader as trainer and recruiter of other peers into the circle of readers and writers!

If the highly proficient readers are so motivated or if their teachers so desire, the peer tutors can also maintain an ongoing reading progress journal for their tutees. This will be a wonderful way to realize the goals of the reading and writing workshop.

Blending Letter Sounds

A good strategy to use in working with individual children is to have them explain how they finally correctly identified a word that was troubling them. If prompted and habituated through one-on-one teacher/tutoring conversations, they can be quite clear about what they did to "get" the word. Some promptings you can use include:

You said (the child's incorrect attempt). Does that match the letters you see?

If it were the word you just said, (the child's incorrect attempt), what would it have to start with?

If it were the word you just said (the child's incorrect attempt), what would it have to end with?

Look at the first letter/s . . . look at the middle letter/s
. . . the last letter. . What could it be?

If you were writing (the child's incorrect attempt), what letter would you write first?
What letters would go in the middle?
What letters would go last?

If the children are already writing their own stories, the teacher might say to them: "When you write your own stories, you know you would never write any story that did not make sense. You wouldn't, and probably this writer didn't either. If you read something that doesn't make sense and doesn't match the letters, then it's probably not what the author wrote. This is the author's story, not yours right now, so go back to the work and see if you can find out the author's story. Later on, you might write your own story."

Letter-Sound Correspondence and Beginning Decoding

Use this procedure for letter-sound investigations that support beginning decoding.

First, focus on the particular letter/s that you want the child to investigate. It is good to choose one from a shared text that the children are familiar with. Make certain that the teachers' directions to the children are clear and either focus them on looking for a specific letter or listening for sounds.

Next, begin a list of words that meet the task given to the children. Use chart paper to list the words that the children identify. This list can be continued into the next week as long as the children's focus is maintained on the list. This can be done by challenging the children with identifying a specific number of letters or sounds and "daring" them as a class team to go beyond those words or sounds.

Third, continue to add to the list. Focus the children at the beginning of the day on their goal of individually adding to the list. Give them an adhesive note (sticky pad sheet) on which they can individually write down the words they find. Then they can attach their newly found words with their names on them to the chart. This provides the children with a sense of ownership and pride in their letter-sounding abilities. During shared reading, discuss the children's proposed additions and have the group decide if these meet the directed category. If all the children agree that they do meet the category, include the words on the chart.

Fourth, do a word sort from all the words generated and have the children put the words into categories that demonstrate similarities and differences. They can be prompted to see if the letter appeared at the beginning of the word, or in the middle of the word. They might also be prompted to see that one sound can have two different letter representations. The children can then "box" the word differences and similarities by drawing colors established in a chart key.

Finally, before the children go off to read, ask them to look for new words in the texts that they can now recognize because of the letter-sound relationships on their chart. During shared reading, make certain that they have time to share the words they were able to decode because of their explorations.

Strategies for Helping Students Decode Single Syllable Words that Hollow Common Patterns and Multi-syllable Words

This activity is presented in detail so it can actually be implemented with children in a classroom and also to provide detail for a potential constructed response question on a certification examination.

The CVC Phonic Card game was developed by Jackie Montierth, a computer teacher in South San Diego for use with fifth and sixth grade students. It is a good activity to adapt to the needs of any group with appropriate modifications for age, grade level, and language needs.

To play, the children use the vehicle of the card game to practice and enhance their use of consonants and vowels. Their fluency in this will increase their ability to decode words.

Potential uses beyond whole classroom instruction include use as part of the small group word work component of the reading workshop and as part of cooperative team learning.

This particular strategy is also particularly helpful for grade four and beyond English Language learners who are in a regular English Language classroom setting.

The card game works well because the practice of the content is implicit for transfer as the children continue to improve their reading skills. In addition, the card game format allows "instructional punctuation" using a student-centered high interest exploration.

Card Design: The teacher can use the computer, 5"x 8" index cards, or actual card deck sized oak-tag cards to create a deck. For repeated use and durability, it is recommended that the deck be laminated.

The deck should consist of the following:
44 consonant cards (including the blends)
15 vowel cards (including 3 of each vowel)
5 wild cards (which can be used as any vowel)
6 final "e" cards

The design of this project can also focus on particular CVC words that are part of a particular book, topic, theme, or genre format (e.g., study of American history, grade four appropriate or U.S. Geography, Canada and Latin America, grades five through six). In advance of playing the game, children can also be directed to review the words on the word wall or other words on a word map.

Procedure:

The game is best introduced first as part of a mini-lesson in which the teacher reads the rules and a pair of children demonstrate the game step-by-step before the class plays the game for the first time.

Have the children divide into pairs or small groups of no more than four per group. Each group needs one deck of CVC cards,

Have each group choose a dealer. The dealer shuffles the deck of cards. The dealer deals five cards to each player. The remaining cards are placed face down for drawing during the play. One card is turned over to form the discard pile.

Players may not show their cards to the other players.

The first player to the left of the dealer looks at his/her cards and if possible, puts down three cards that make a consonant-vowel-consonant word.

For more points, four cards forming a consonant-vowel-consonant word can be placed down. The player must then say the word and draw the number of cards he or she laid down.

If he or she is unable to form a word, he or she draws a card from either the draw pile or the discard pile. The player then discards one card. All players must have five cards at all times.

The next player to the left now takes his or her turn. That player puts down any cards forming a C-V-C word. That player must then say the word and draw the number of cards that he or she laid down. Should the player not be able to say the word he or she draws from the pile, he or she draws a card from the discard or the draw pile.

The game continues until one or more of the following happens:
1. There are no more cards in the draw pile
2. All players run out of cards.
3. All players cannot form a word

The winner is the player who has laid down the most cards during the game.
Players may only lay down words at the beginning of their turn.
Proper names may not be counted as words.
Other ways the game may be played:

The game can be played with teams of individuals in a small group of four or fewer competing against one another (excellent for special needs or resource room students). It can also be done as a whole class activity where all the students are divided into cooperative teams or small groups that compete against one another. This second approach will work well with a heterogeneous classroom that includes special needs and/or ELL children.

Teachers of ELL learners can do this game in the native language first and then transition it into English, which will facilitate native language reading skills and second language acquisition. They can develop their own appropriate decks to meet the vocabulary needs of their children and to complement the curricula.

COMPETENCY 2.0 UNDERSTAND WORD IDENTIFICATION STRATEGIES, INCLUDING PHONICS

Skill 2.1   **Recognizing how beginning writers and readers learn to apply knowledge of the relationship between letters and letter combinations of written words and the sounds of spoken words**

Alphabetic Principle

The Alphabetic Principle is sometimes called Graphophonemic Awareness. This multi-syllabic technical reading foundation term details the understanding that written words are composed of patterns of letters that represent the sounds of spoken words.

There are basically two parts to the alphabetic principle:
- An understanding that words are made up of letters and that each of these letters has a specific sound
- An understanding that the correspondence between sounds and letters leads to phonological reading. This consists of reading regular and irregular words as well as doing advanced analysis of words.

Since the English language is dependent on the alphabet, being able to recognize and sound out letters is the first step for beginning readers. Simply relying on memorization for word recognition is not feasible as a way for children to learn to recognize words. Therefore, decoding is essential. The most important goal of beginning reading teachers is to teach students to decode text so that they can read fluently and with understanding.

There are four basic features of the alphabetic principle:
1. Students need to be able to take spoken words apart and blend different sounds together to make new words
2. Students need to apply letter sounds to all their reading
3. Teachers need to use a systematic, effective program in order to teach children to read
4. The teaching of the alphabetic principle usually begins in kindergarten

It is important to keep in mind that some children already know the letters and sounds before they come to school. Others may catch on to this quite quickly; still others need to have one-on-one instruction in order to learn to read.

Critical skills that students need to learn are:
- Letter-sound correspondence
- How to sound out words
- How to decode text to make meaning

Assessment Throughout the Year of Graphophonemic Awareness

The teacher will want to maintain individual records of children's reading behaviors demonstrating alphabetic principle/graphophonemic awareness.

The following performance standards should be part of a record template form for each child in grades K-1 and beyond, as needed (depending on ELL or special needs):

- Match all consonant and short vowel sounds
- Read one's own name
- Read one syllable words and high frequency words
- Demonstrate the ability to read and understand that as letters in words change, so do the sounds
- Generate the sounds from all letters, including consonant blends and long vowel patterns, and blend those different sounds into recognizable words
- Read common sight words
- Read common word families
- Recognize and use knowledge of spelling patterns when reading (run/running, hop/hopping)
- Decode (sound out) regular words with more than one syllable (vacation, graduation).
- Recognize regular abbreviations (Feb., Mr., P.S.)

Any record kept of an individual child's progress should include each date of observation and some legend or rubric detailing the level of performance, standard acquisition, or mastery.

Some teachers use Y for "exhibits the reading behavior consistently," M for "making progress toward the standard," and N for "has not yet exhibited the behavior." Beyond this objective legend for the assessment, the teacher may want and should include any other comments that detail the child's progress in this awareness.

Development of Alphabetic Knowledge in Individual Students: English Language Learners, Struggling Readers, and Highly Proficient Readers

Researchers Laura M. Justice and Helen K. Ezell of the University of Virginia did a study in 2002 that evaluated alphabetic knowledge and print awareness in pre-school children from low income households. Their research findings offer potential insights for educators who seek to foster the skills and capabilities of all their students.

In their post-testing of children in the experimental group who had participated in shared reading sessions that emphasized a print focus, they found that the at-risk children outperformed their control group peers (other Head Start children) on three measures of print awareness (Words In Print, Print Recognition, and Alphabetic Knowledge).

Other researchers, including Chaney (1994), have demonstrated a statistically significant and inverse relationship between household income and children's performance on measures of print awareness and alphabetic principle.

A study by Lonigan (1999) found that substantial group differences existed on a variety of pre-literacy tasks administered to eighty-five preschool children from lower and middle income households. Measures of print awareness used included environmental print, print and book reading conventions, and alphabet knowledge. Results showed that preschool children from middle income households showed significantly higher levels of skill across all print awareness tasks in comparison with preschoolers from low income households.

Obviously this data highlights the importance of extensive alphabetic knowledge activities and print awareness opportunities for children from low income households in grades K-1 and, when necessary, beyond.

Two other studies undertaken by Ezell and Justice (in the year 2000) suggested that structuring adult-child shared book reading interactions to include an explicit print awareness and alphabetic principle focus resulted in a substantial increase in children's verbal interactions with print.

This work highlights the importance of not only classroom and preschool emphases on print awareness and alphabetic principle routines, but also the need for teachers to reach out to parents to model for them these shared reading experiences so that family life can parallel the classroom experiences. Many schools currently have parent volunteers and reading buddy programs. Training of these volunteers, particularly in high need, low economic income status communities, is certainly warranted.

David J. Chard and Jean Osborn (1999) have reflected on the guidelines necessary for teachers to use in selecting supplemental phonics and word-recognition materials for addressing students with learning disabilities.

They note that an important part of helping children with reading disabilities to figure out the system underlying the printed word is to lead them to understand the alphabetic principle. Children with learning disabilities (LD) particularly benefit from organized instruction that centers on letters, sounds, and the relations between sounds and letters. They also benefit from word-recognition patterns instruction that offers practice with, for example, word families that share similar letter patterns.

Children who are LD also benefit from opportunities to apply what they are learning to the reading and re-reading of stories and other texts. Such texts contain a high portion of words that reflect the letters, sounds, and spelling patterns the children are learning.

For special needs children, a beginning reading program should include the following elements of Alphabetic Knowledge instruction:

1. A variety of alphabetic knowledge activities in which the children learn to identify and name both upper and lower case letters
2. Games, songs, and other activities that help children to learn to name the letters quickly
3. Writing activities that encourage children to practice the letters they are writing
4. A sensible sequence of letter introduction that can be adjusted to the needs of the children

Skill 2.2 Demonstrating knowledge of phonics skills and their application to decoding unfamiliar words

Word analysis (a.k.a. phonics or decoding) is the process readers use to figure out unfamiliar words based on written patterns. Word recognition is the process of automatically determining the pronunciation and some degree of the meaning of an unknown word. In other words, fluent readers recognize most written words easily and correctly, without consciously decoding or breaking them down. These elements of literacy are skills readers need for word recognition.

To decode means to change communication signals into messages. Reading comprehension requires that the reader learn the code within which a message is written and be able to decode it to get the message. Encoding involves changing a message into symbols: for example, to encode oral language into writing (spelling), to encode an idea into words, or to encode a mathematical or physical idea into appropriate mathematical symbols.

Word meanings in context are definitions that a reader determines based on information from the surrounding text, such as other words, phrases, sentences, and/or paragraphs.

Readers can also use words they already know to piece together possible meanings. They can use root words, antonyms, and word forms to help determine the meaning of an unfamiliar word.

For more information on phonics, see Skills 1.1, 1.3, and 1.6.

Skill 2.3   Applying knowledge of structural analysis as a word identification strategy (e.g., identifying prefixes, suffixes, and roots)

Students will be better at comprehension if they have a stronger working vocabulary. Research has shown that students learn more vocabulary when it is presented in context, rather than in vocabulary lists. Furthermore, the more students are enabled to use particular words in context, the more they will a) remember each word, and b) utilize the word in the comprehension of sentences that contain the words.

Auditory games and drills during which students recognize and manipulate the sounds of words, separate or segment the sounds of words, take out sounds, blend sounds, add in new sounds, or take apart sound to recombine them in new formations are good ways to foster phonological awareness.

Identification of Common Morphemes, Prefixes, and Suffixes

This aspect of vocabulary development is used to help students look for structural elements within words that they can use independently to help them determine meanings.

The terms listed below are generally recognized as the key structural analysis components.

Root words: A root word is a word from which another word is developed. The second word can be said to have its "root" in the first. This structural component nicely lends itself to an illustration of a tree with roots, which can concretize the meaning for students. Students may also want to literally construct root words using cardboard trees and/or actual roots from plants to create word family models. This is a wonderful way to help students own their root words.

Base words: A base word is a stand-alone linguistic unit which cannot be deconstructed or broken down into smaller words. For example, in the word "re-tell," the base word is "tell."

Contractions: Contractions are shortened forms of two words in which a letter or letters have been deleted. These deleted letters are then replaced by an apostrophe.

Prefixes: These are beginning units of meaning that can be added (the vocabulary word for this type of structural adding is "affixed") to a base word or root word. They cannot stand alone. They are also sometimes known as "bound morphemes," meaning that they can not stand alone as a base word.

Suffixes: These are ending units of meaning which can be "affixed" or added onto the ends of root or base words. Suffixes transform the original meanings of base and root words. Like prefixes, they are also known as "bound morphemes," because they cannot stand alone as words.

Compound words: Compound words occur when two or more base words are connected to form a new word. The meaning of the new word is in some way connected with that of the base word.

Inflectional endings: These are types are suffixes that impart a new meaning to the base or root word. In particular, these endings change the gender, number, tense, or form of the base or root words. Just like other suffixes, these are also termed "bound morphemes."

Word forms: Sometimes a very familiar word can appear as a different part of speech, as in the examples below:

> You may have heard that *fraud* involves a criminal misrepresentation, so when it appears as the adjective form *fraudulent* ("He was suspected of fraudulent activities."), you can make an educated guess as to the meaning.

> You probably know that something out of date is *obsolete;* therefore, when you read about "built-in *obsolescence,*" you can detect the meaning of the unfamiliar word.

Skill 2.4   Demonstrating knowledge of the use of spelling patterns and syllabication as techniques for decoding unfamiliar words

Morphology, Syntax, and Semantics

Morphology is the study of word structure. When readers develop morphemic skills, they are developing an understanding of patterns they see in words. For example, English speakers realize that cat, cats, and caterpillar share some similarities in structure. This understanding helps readers to recognize words at a faster and easier rate, since each word doesn't need individual decoding.

Syntax refers to the rules or patterned relationships that correctly create phrases and sentences from words. When readers develop an understanding of syntax, they begin to understand the structure of how sentences are built, and eventually the beginning of grammar.

Example: "I am going to the movies"
This statement is syntactically and grammatically correct

Example: "They am going to the movies:
This statement is syntactically correct since all the words are in their correct place, but it is grammatically incorrect with the use of the word "They" rather than "I."

Semantics refers to the meaning expressed when words are arranged in a specific way. This is where connotation and denotation of words will eventually have a role with readers.

All of these skill sets are important to eventually develop effective word recognition skills, which help emerging readers to develop fluency.

Use of Syllabification as a Word Identification Strategy

Strategy - Clap Hands, Count those Syllables as They Come!! (Taberski, 2000)

The objective of this activity is for children to understand that every syllable in a polysyllabic word can be studied for its spelling patterns in the same way that monosyllabic words are studied for their spelling patterns.

The easiest way for the K-3 teacher to introduce this activity to the children is to share a familiar poem from the poetry chart (or to write out a familiar poem on a large experiential chart).

First, the teacher reads the poem with the children. As they are reading it aloud, the children clap the beats of the poem, and the teacher uses a colored marker to place a tic (/) above each syllable.

Next, the teacher takes letter cards and selects one of the polysyllabic words from the poem that the children have already "clapped" out.

The children use letter cards to spell the word on the sentence strip holder, or the letter can be placed on a felt board or up against a window on display. Together, the children and teacher divide the letters into syllables and place blank letter cards between the syllables. The children identify spelling patterns they know.

Finally, and as part of continued small group syllabification study, the children identify other polysyllabic words they clapped out from the poem. They make up the letter combinations of these words. Then they separate them into syllables with blank letter cards between the syllables.

Children who require special support in syllabification can be encouraged to use plenty of letter cards to create a large butcher paper syllabic (in letter cards with spaces) representation of the poem or at least a few lines of the poem. They can be told that this is for use as a teaching tool for others. In this way, they authenticate their study of syllabification with a real product that can actually be referenced by peers.

Techniques for Identifying Compound Words

Semantic Feature Analysis

This technique for enhancing vocabulary skills by using semantic cues is based on the research of Johnson and Pearson (1984) and Anders and Bos (1986). It involves young children who are instructed to set up a feature analysis grid of various subject content words. This grid is an outgrowth of their discussion about these words.

For instance, in *Cooper's Literacy-Helping Children Construct Meaning (*2004), the author includes a sample of a Semantic Features Analysis Grid for Vegetables.

Vegetables	Green	Have Peels	Eat Raw	Seeds
Carrots	-	+	+	-
Cabbage	+	-	+	-

Note the use of + for yes, - for no, and possible use of +/- if a vegetable like squash could be both green and yellow. Make this grid very accessible for young readers and very easily done by them on their own as part of their independent word analysis.

Teachers of children in grade one and beyond can design their own semantic analysis grids to meet their students' needs and to align with the topics the kids are learning.

Select a category or class of words (e.g., planets, rodent family members, winter words, weather words).

Use the left side of the grid to list at least three or more items that fit this category. The number of actual items listed will depend on the age and grade level of the children (typically three or four items for K-1 and up to ten or fifteen for grades five and six).

Brainstorm with the children or, if better suited to the class, the teacher may list the features that the items have in common. As in the example excerpted from Cooper (2004), common features such as vegetables' green color, peels, and seeds are usually pretty easy to identify.

Show the children how to insert +, -,or even ? (if they are not certain) notations on the grid. The teacher might also explore with the children the possibility that an item could get both a + and a -. For example, a vegetable like broccoli might be eaten cooked or raw depending on taste and squash can be green or yellow.

Whatever the length of the grid when first presented to the children (perhaps a semantic cue lesson in and of itself tied to a text being read in class), make certain that the grid as presented and filled out is not the end of the activity. Children can use it as a model for developing their own semantic features grids and sharing them during the share time with the whole class. Child-developed grids can become part of a Word Work center in the classroom or even be published in a Word Study Games book by the class as a whole. Such a publication can be shared with parents during open school week and evening visits or with peer classes.

For information on context clues, see Skill 3.3.

Skill 2.5   Applying knowledge of developmentally appropriate instruction and curriculum materials for promoting students' decoding skills and word identification strategies

In the 1960s and 1970s, many reading specialists, most prominently Fries (1962), believed that successful decoding resulted in reading comprehension. This meant that if children could sound out the words, they would then automatically be able to comprehend the words. Many teachers of reading and many reading texts still subscribe to this theory after over thirty years.

This out-of-date teaching leaves no room for the concepts of decoding and encoding to achieve reading comprehension. As mentioned in Skill 2.2, readers do much more than simply create sounds from words. A word is composed of several constituents, each of which requires its own level of comprehension before the word can be understood at more than just the memorization level.

Although effective reading comprehension requires identifying words automatically (Adams, 1990, Perfetti, 1985), children do not have to be able to identify every single word or know the exact meaning of the every word in a text to understand it. Indeed, Nagy (1988) says that children can read a work with a high level of comprehension even if they do not fully know as many as 15 percent of the words within a given text.

For these reasons, it is important to address issues of decoding, encoding, and word recognition at a very early level. These early teachings create a platform for future reading skills and word identification strategies; children then can extend their ability to decode to multi-syllabic words using the same learned abilities without returning to rote memorization or sounding out words.

COMPETENCY 3.0 UNDERSTAND THE DEVELOPMENT OF VOCABULARY KNOWLEDGE AND SKILLS ACROSS THE CURRICULUM

Skill 3.1 Recognizing criteria for selecting appropriate words to increase students' vocabulary knowledge (e.g., synonyms, antonyms, words with multiple meanings, idioms, and classifications)

The simplest method that teachers can use to increase student vocabulary is by exposing students to many new words in the course of frequent reading and writing exercises. Students can also learn many words indirectly through independent reading. Teachers should emphasize the fact that words are not separate, disconnected units that need to be learned in isolation, but are related and interrelated.

Synonyms, antonyms, and root words are only three obvious examples of the connections that exist among words. When words are connected together in sentences, their individual meanings change and are enhanced by each other. However, teaching particular words—especially words with multiple meanings— before reading a text helps students with both vocabulary acquisition and reading comprehension. When providing instruction in the definitions of new vocabulary words, teachers should focus on the words' classification to other words.

Useful Criteria for Selecting Appropriate New Words in Vocabulary Instruction

- Provide opportunities for extensive reading
- Teach words in related clusters
- Teach key vocabulary words before assigning reading from a text
- Have dictionary and glossary resources available for the precise spelling of words

Student readers comprehend and learn when they are able to connect the new information in their reading material to what they already know. Vocabulary instruction, therefore, should help students make the connections between unknown words and the knowledge they already possess.

Skill 3.2   Demonstrating knowledge of developmentally appropriate strategies for promoting and reinforcing students' oral and written vocabulary knowledge

The typical variation in literacy backgrounds that children bring to reading can make teaching difficult. Oftentimes, a teacher has to choose between focusing on the learning needs of a few students at the expense of the group or focusing on the group at the risk of leaving some students behind academically. This situation is particularly critical for children with gaps in their literacy knowledge, as they may be at risk in subsequent grades for becoming "diverse learners."

Areas of Emerging Evidence

1. **Experiences with print (through reading and writing) help preschool children to develop an understanding of the conventions, purposes, and functions of print.** Children learn about print from a variety of sources; through the process, they come to realize that print carries a story. They also learn how text is structured visually (i.e., text begins at the top of the page, moves from left to right, and carries over to the next page when it is turned). While knowledge about the conventions of print enables children to understand the physical structure of language, the conceptual knowledge that printed words convey a message also helps children bridge the gap between oral and written language.

2. **Phonological awareness and letter recognition** contribute to initial reading acquisition by helping children to develop efficient word recognition strategies (e.g., detecting pronunciations and storing associations in memory.) Phonological awareness and knowledge of print-speech relations play an important role in facilitating reading acquisition. Therefore, phonological awareness instruction should be an integral component of early reading programs. Within the emergent literacy research, viewpoints diverge on whether acquisition of phonological awareness and letter recognition are preconditions of literacy acquisition or whether they develop interdependently with literacy activities such as story reading and writing.

3. **Storybook reading affects children's knowledge about, strategies for, and attitudes toward reading.** Of all the strategies intended to promote growth in literacy acquisition, none is as commonly practiced, nor as strongly supported across the emergent literacy literature, as storybook reading. Children in different social and cultural groups have differing degrees of access to storybook reading. For example, it is not unusual for a teacher to have students who have experienced thousands of hours of story reading time alongside other students who have had little or no such exposure.

Instructional Strategies

1. Teacher-guided activities that require students to organize and to summarize information based on the author's explicit intent are pertinent strategies in middle grades. Evaluation techniques include oral and written responses to standardized or teacher-made worksheets.

2. The reading of fiction introduces and reinforces skills in inferring meaning from narration and description. Teaching-guided activities focused on the process of reading for meaning should be followed by cooperative planning of the skills to be studied, and of the selection of reading resources. Many printed reading for comprehension instruments as well as individualized computer software programs exist to monitor the progress of acquiring comprehension skills.

3. Older middle school students should be given opportunities for more student-centered activities such as individual and collaborative reading selection based on student interest, small group discussions of selected works, and greater written expression. Evaluation techniques include teacher monitoring and the observation of discussions and written work samples.

4. Certain students may begin some fundamental critical interpretation activities: recognizing fallacious reasoning in news media, examining the accuracy of news reports and advertising, or explaining their reasons for preferring one author's writing to another's. Development of these skills may require a more learning-centered approach in which the teacher identifies a number of objectives and suggested resources from which the student may choose his or her course of study. Self-evaluation through a reading diary should be stressed. Teacher and peer evaluation for creative projects resulting from such study is encouraged.

5. Reading aloud before the entire class as a formal means of teacher evaluation should be phased out in favor of one-to-one tutoring or peer-assisted reading. The occasional sharing of favored selections by both teacher and willing students is a good oral interpretation basic.

Skill 3.3   Applying knowledge of how context is used to determine the meaning of unfamiliar words

Contextual Redefinition

This strategy supports children to use context more effectively by presenting them with sufficient background *before* they begin reading. It models for the children the use of contextual clues to make informed guesses about word meanings.

To apply this strategy as a teacher, first select unfamiliar words for teaching. No more than two or three words should be selected for direct teaching. Write a sentence in which there are sufficient clues supplied for the child to successfully figure out the meaning. Among the types of context clues the teacher can use are: compare/contrast, synonyms, and direct definition.

The next step is to present the words only on the experiential chart or as letter cards. Have the children pronounce the words. As they pronounce them, challenge them to come up with a definition for each word. After more than one definition is offered, encourage the children to decide as a whole group what the definition is. Write down their agreed upon definition with no comment as to its true meaning.

Share with the children the contexts (sentences written with the words and explicit context clues). Ask that the children read the sentences aloud. Then have them come up with a definition for each word. Make certain not to comment as they present their definitions. Ask that they justify their definitions by making specific references to the context clues in the sentences. As the discussion continues, direct the children's attention to their previously agreed upon definition of the word. Facilitate them in discussing the differences between their guesses about the word when they saw only the word itself and their guesses about the word when they read it in context. Finally, have the children check their use of context skills to correctly define the word by using a dictionary.

This type of direct teaching of word definitions is useful when the children have dictionary skills and the teacher is aware of the fact that there are not sufficient clues about the words in the context to help the students define it. In addition, struggling readers and students from ELL backgrounds may benefit tremendously from being walked through this same process, even though highly proficient and successful readers may apply it automatically.

By using this strategy, the teacher can also "kid watch" and note their students' prior knowledge as they guess the word in isolation. The teacher can also actually witness and hear how various students use context skills.

Through their involvement in this strategy, struggling readers gain a feeling of community as they experience the ways in which their struggles and guesses resonate in other peers' responses to the text. They are also getting a chance to be "walked through" this maze of meaning, and are learning how to use context clues in order to navigate it themselves.

Skill 3.4 **Recognizing ways to help students identify and use references such as dictionaries and thesauri for various purposes (e.g., determining word meanings and pronunciations, finding alternative word choices)**

Content area vocabulary is the specific vocabulary related to the particular concepts of various academic disciplines (e.g., social science, science, math, and art). While teachers tend to think of content area vocabulary as something that should only be a focus at the secondary level (middle and high school); students go to separate teachers with separate subjects, thus making content area vocabulary very important. However, even elementary school-aged students studying various subjects will understand concepts better when the vocabulary used to describe them is explicitly explained.

Some educators also believe that vocabulary should only be taught in Language Arts classes, not realizing that a) there is not enough time for students to learn all the necessary vocabulary in order to be successful with a standards-based education, and b) that teaching vocabulary, related to a particular subject, is a very good way to help students understand the subject better.

So how do content area teachers teach vocabulary? First and foremost, content area teachers help students to learn strategies to figure out the meanings of difficult vocabulary words when the students encounter them on their own. All teachers can do this by teaching students how to identify the meanings of words in context (usually through activities where the word is taken out and the students have to figure out a way to make sense of the sentence). In addition, dictionary skills must be taught in all subject areas. Teachers should also consider that teaching vocabulary is not just the teaching of words: rather, it is the teaching of complex concepts, each with histories and connotations.

When teachers explicitly teach vocabulary, it is best when they connect new words to ideas, other words, and experiences that students are already familiar with. This helps to reduce the strangeness of the new words. Furthermore, the more concrete the examples are, the more likely students will know how to use the word in context.

Finally, students need plenty of exposure to the new words. They need to be able to hear and use the new words in numerous naturally-produced sentences. The more one hears and uses a sentence in context, the more the word is solidified in the person's long-term vocabulary.

Like a dictionary, a thesaurus is an excellent resource to use when writing. Students can use a thesaurus to find appropriate synonyms, antonyms, and other related words to enhance their writing. However, it is important for teachers to model and instruct students in using a thesaurus so that students do not simply replace words. Students need to learn about word connotations and the "between the lines" meanings of words to effectively use a thesaurus.

COMPETENCY 4.0 UNDERSTAND READING FLUENCY AND COMPREHENSION ACROSS THE CURRICULUM

Skill 4.1 **Demonstrating knowledge of the concepts of rate, accuracy, expression, and phrasing in reading fluency and recognizing factors that affect fluency**

When students practice fluency, they practice reading connected pieces of text. In other words, instead of looking at a word as just a word, they might read a sentence straight through. The point of this is that in order for the student to comprehend what he or she is reading, it is necessary to "fluently" and quickly piece words in a sentence together. If a student is *not* fluent in reading, he or she sounds each letter or word out slowly and pays more attention to the phonics of each word. A fluent reader, on the other hand, might read a sentence out loud using appropriate intonations. The best way to test for fluency is to have a student read something out loud, preferably a few or more sentences in a row. Most students just learning to read will probably not be very fluent right away; however, with practice, they will increase their fluency. Even though fluency is not the same as comprehension, it is said that fluency is a good predictor of comprehension. Think about it: If you're focusing too much on sounding out each word, you're not going to be paying attention to the meaning behind them.

Accuracy

One of the best ways to evaluate reading fluency is to look at student accuracy. One method of accomplishing this involves keeping running records of students during oral reading. Calculating the reading level lets teachers know if the book is at a level where the child can read it independently or comfortably with guidance, or if the book is at a level where reading it frustrates the child.

As part of the informal assessment of primary grade reading, it is important to record the child's word insertions, omissions, requests for help, and attempts to get the word. In informal assessment, the rate of accuracy can be estimated from the ratio of errors to total words read.

The results of keeping a running record informal assessment can be used for teaching based on text accuracy. For example, if a child reads from 95 to 100 percent correctly, the child is ready for independent reading. If the child reads from 92 to 97 percent correctly, the child is ready for guided reading. A score below 92 percent indicates that the child needs a read-aloud or shared reading activity.

Automacity

Fluency in reading is dependent on automatic word identification, which assists the student in achieving comprehension of the material. Even slight difficulties in word identification can significantly increase the time it takes a student to read material, as the difficulties may therefore require re-reading parts or passages of the material and reduce the level of comprehension expected. If the student experiences reading as a constant struggle or an arduous chore, he or she may avoid reading whenever possible and consider it a negative experience. Obviously, the ability to read for comprehension, and learning in general, will suffer if all aspects of reading fluency are not presented to the student as acquirable skills that will be readily accomplished with the appropriate effort.

Automatic reading involves the development of strong orthographic representations, which allows fast and accurate identification of whole words made up of specific letter patterns. Most young students move easily from the use of alphabetic strategies to the use of orthographic representations that can be accessed automatically.

Initially, word identification is based on the application of phonic word accessibility strategies (letter-sound associations). These strategies are in turn based on the development of phonemic awareness, which is necessary to learn how to relate speech to print.

One of the most useful devices for developing automacity in young students is through the visual pattern provided in the six syllable types.

EXAMPLES OF THE SIX SYLLABLE TYPES

1. **NOT** (CLOSED)
   Closed in by a consonant—vowel makes its **short** sound
2. **NO** (OPEN)
   Ends in a vowel—vowel makes its **long** sound
- **NOTE** (SILENT "E")
   Ends in vowel consonant "e"—vowel makes its **long** sound
1. **NAIL** (VOWEL COMBINATION)
   Two vowels together make the sound
5. **BIRD** ("R" CONTROLLED)
   Contains a vowel plus "r"—vowel sound is changed
6. **TABLE** (CONSONANT "L"-"E")
   Applied at the end of a word

These orthographic (letter) patterns signal vowel pronunciation to the reader. Students must be able to apply their knowledge of these patterns to recognize the syllable types, as well as to see these patterns automatically. This will ultimately allow students to read words as wholes. The move from decoding letter symbols and identifying recognizable terms to automatic word recognition is a substantial move toward fluency. A significant aid for helping students move through this phase was developed by Anna Gillingham when she incorporated the Phonetic Word Cards activity into the Orton-Gillingham lesson plan (Gillingham and Stillman, 1997). This activity involves asking the students to practice reading words (and some non-words) on cards as wholes, beginning with simple syllables and moving systematically through the syllable types to complex syllables and two-syllable words. The words should be divided into groups that correspond to the specific sequence of skills being taught.

The students' developments of the elements necessary to automacity continually move through stages. One of the next important stages involves the automatic recognition of single graphemes as a step toward the development of the letter patterns that make up words or word parts. English orthography is made up of four basic word types:

1. Regular, for reading and spelling (e.g., cat, print)
2. Regular, for reading but not for spelling (e.g., float, brain - could be spelled "flote" or "brane," respectively)
3. Rule based (e.g., canning - doubling rule, faking - drop e rule)
4. Irregular (e.g., beauty)

Students must be taught to recognize all four types of words automatically in order to be effective readers. Repeated practice in pattern recognition is often necessary. Practice techniques for student development can include speed drills in which students read lists of isolated words with contrasting vowel sounds that are signaled by the syllable type. For example, several closed syllable and vowel-consonant-"e" words containing the vowel "a" can be arranged randomly on pages containing about twelve lines and read for one minute. Individual goals are established and charts should be kept of the number of words read correctly in successive sessions. The same word lists are then repeated in sessions until the goal has been achieved for several succeeding sessions. When selecting words for these lists, the use of high-frequency words within a syllable category increases the likelihood of generalization to text reading.

True automacity should be linked with prosody and anticipation to acquire full fluency. Concepts such as which syllable is accented or how word structure can be predictive are necessary to true automacity and essential to complete fluency.

A student whose reading rate is slow, halting, or inconsistent is exhibiting a lack of reading fluency. According to an article by Mastropieri, Leinart, and Scruggs (1999), some students have developed accurate word pronunciation skills but read at a slow rate. They have not moved to the phase where decoding is automatic, and their limited fluency may affect performance in the following ways:

1. They read less text than peers and have less time to remember, review, or comprehend the text
2. They expend more cognitive energy than peers trying to identify individual words
3. They may be less able to retain text in their memories and less likely to integrate those segments with other parts of the text

The simplest means of determining a student's reading rate is to have the student read aloud from a prescribed passage (which should be at the appropriate reading level for age and grade and contain a specified number of words). The passage should not be too familiar for the student (some will try to memorize or "work out" difficult bits ahead of time), and should not contain more words than can be read comfortably and accurately by a normal reader in one or two minutes. Count only the words pronounced *correctly* on first reading, and divide this word count into elapsed time to determine the student's reading rate. To determine the student's standing and progress, compare this rate with the norm for the class and the average for all students who read fluently at that specific age/grade level.

The following general guidelines can be applied for reading lists of words with a speed drill and a 1-minute timing: 30 correct wpm for first and second grade children; 40 correct wpm for third grade children; 60 correct wpm for mid-third grade; and 80 wpm for students in fourth grade and higher.

Various techniques are useful with students who have acquired some proficiency in decoding skill but whose levels of skill are lower than their oral language abilities. Such techniques have certain, common features:

1. Students listen to text as they follow along with the book
2. Students follow the print using their fingers as guides
3. Reading materials are used that students would be unable to read independently.

Experts recommend that a beginning reading program should incorporate partner reading, practice in reading difficult words prior to reading the text, timings for accuracy and rate, opportunities to hear books read, and opportunities to read to others.

Prosody concerns the versification of text and involves such matters as which syllable of a word is accented. As regards fluency, it is that aspect that translates reading into the same experience within the reader's mind as listening. Prosody involves intonation and rhythm through such devices as syllable accent and punctuation.

In their article for *Perspectives* (Winter, 2002), Pamela Hook and Sandra Jones proposed that teachers can begin to develop awareness of the prosodic features of language by introducing a short three-word sentence with each of the three different words underlined for stress (e.g., *He is sick. He is sick. He is sick.*) The teacher can then model the three sentences while discussing the possible meaning for each variation. The students can practice reading them with different stresses until they are fluent. These simple three-word sentences can be modified and expanded to include various verbs, pronouns, and tenses. (e.g., *You are sick. I am sick. They are sick.*) This strategy can also be used while increasing the length of phrases and emphasizing the different meanings (e.g., *Get out of bed. Get out of bed. Get out of bed now.*). Teachers can also practice fluency with common phrases that frequently occur in text.

Prepositional phrases are also good syntactic structures for this type of work (e.g., *on the _____, in the _____, over the _____*). Teachers can pair these printed phrases with oral intonation patterns that include variations of rate, intensity, and pitch. Students can infer the intended meaning as the teacher presents different prosodic variations of a sentence. For example, when speakers want to stress a concept they often slow their rate of speech and may speak in a louder voice (e.g., *Joshua, get-out-of-bed-NOW!*). Often, the only text marker for this sentence will be the exclamation point (!) but the speaker's intent will affect the manner in which it is delivered.

Practicing oral variations and then mapping the prosodic features onto the text will assist students in making the connection when reading. This strategy can also be used to alert students to the prosodic features present in punctuation marks. In the early stages, using the alphabet helps to focus a student on the punctuation marks without having to deal with meaning. The teacher models for the students and then has them practice the combinations using the correct intonation patterns to fit the punctuation mark (e.g., ABC. DE? FGH! IJKL? or ABCD! EFGHI? KL.). Teachers can then move to simple two-word or three-word sentences. The sentences are punctuated with a period, question mark, and exclamation point, and the differences in meaning that occur with each different punctuation mark (e.g., *Chris hops. Chris hops? Chris hops!*) are discussed. It may help students to point out that the printed words convey the fact that someone named Chris is engaged in the physical activity of hopping, but the intonation patterns get their cue from the punctuation mark. The meaning extracted from an encounter with a punctuation mark is dependent upon the students' ability to project an appropriate intonation pattern onto the printed text.

Keeping the text static while changing the punctuation marks helps students to attend to prosodic patterns. Students who read word-for-word may benefit initially from practicing phrasing with the alphabet rather than words, since letters do not tax the meaning system. This is similar to using the alphabet to teach intonation patterns. To accomplish this task, letters are grouped, an arc is drawn underneath, and students recite the alphabet in chunks (e.g., ABC DE FGH IJK LM NOP QRS TU VW XYZ). Once students understand the concept of phrasing, it is recommended that teachers help students chunk text into syntactic (noun phrases, verb phrases, and prepositional phrases) or meaning units until they are proficient themselves. There are no hard and fast rules for chunking, but syntactic units are most commonly used.

For better readers, teachers can mark the phrasal boundaries with slashes for short passages. Eventually, the slashes will be used only at the beginning of long passages, and students will be asked to continue "phrase reading" even after the marks end. Marking phrases can be done together with students, or those on an independent level may divide passages into phrases themselves.

Comparisons can be made to clarify reasons for differences in phrasing. Another way to encourage students to focus on phrase meaning and prosody (in addition to word identification) is to provide tasks that require them to identify or supply a paraphrase of an original statement.

Skill 4.2   Analyzing the relationship between reading fluency and comprehension

Reading fluency refers to a student's speed, smoothness, and ease of oral reading. Fluent readers read rapidly and smoothly, allowing their minds to focus on comprehension of the text, thereby gaining meaning from the text they read. Because reading fluency leads to reading comprehension, fluent readers typically enjoy reading more than students who apply all their energy to just sounding out the words. Struggling readers often labor to identify each word on the page, becoming so occupied in the process of identifying words that they are unable to devote any attention to comprehending the text they are reading.

Strategies to Improve Reading Fluency

- Repeated oral reading with guidance
- Graphing the student's reading rate over repeated readings
- Buddy reading
- Instructor modeling of fluent reading followed by student re-reading

Reading Comprehension skills

- Using prior knowledge and making connections
- Determining the main idea, summarizing, and drawing conclusions
- Analyzing, evaluating, and predicting
- Distinguishing facts and opinions
- Determining the author's purpose

In order to develop fluent readers, knowledgeable teachers should devote substantial instructional time to enhancing the reading fluency of students.

Skill 4.3   Recognizing the effects of various factors (e.g., prior knowledge, context, vocabulary knowledge, graphic cues) on reading comprehension

Conspicuous Strategies

As an instructional priority, conspicuous strategies are a sequence of teaching events and teacher actions used to help students to learn new literacy information and relate it to their existing knowledge. Conspicuous strategies can be incorporated in beginning reading instruction to ensure that all learners have basic literacy concepts. For example, during storybook reading, teachers can show students how to recognize the fronts and backs of books, locate titles, or look at pictures and predict the story, rather than assume children will learn this through incidental exposure. Similarly, teachers can teach students a strategy for holding a pencil appropriately or checking the form of their letters against an alphabet sheet on their desks or the classroom wall.

Mediated Scaffolding

Mediated scaffolding can be accomplished in a number of ways to meet the needs of students with diverse literacy experiences. To link oral and written language, for example, teachers may use texts that simulate speech by incorporating oral language patterns or children's writing. Teachers can use daily storybook reading to discuss book-handling skills and directionality concepts that are particularly important for children who are unfamiliar with printed texts. Teachers can also use repeated readings to give students multiple exposures to unfamiliar words, extend opportunities to look at books with predictable patterns, and provide support by modeling the behaviors associated with reading. Teachers can act as *scaffolds* during these storybook reading activities by adjusting their demands (e.g., asking increasingly complex questions or encouraging children to take on portions of the reading) or by reading more complex text as students gain knowledge of beginning literacy components.

Strategic Integration

Many children with diverse literacy experiences have difficulty making connections between old and new information. Strategic integration can be applied to help link old and new learning. For example, in the classroom, strategic integration can be accomplished by providing access to literacy materials in classroom writing centers and libraries. Students should also have opportunities to integrate and extend their literacy knowledge by reading aloud, listening to other students read aloud, and listening to tape recordings and videotapes in reading corners.

Primed Background Knowledge

All children bring some level of background knowledge (e.g., how to hold a book, awareness of directionality of print) to beginning reading. Teachers can utilize children's background knowledge to help children link their personal literacy experiences with beginning reading instruction, while also closing the gap between those students with rich and those students with impoverished literacy experiences. Activities that draw upon background knowledge include incorporating oral language activities (which discriminate between printed letters and words) into daily read-alouds as well as providing frequent opportunities to re-tell stories, look at books with predictable patterns, write messages with invented spellings, and respond to literature through drawing.

Emergent Literacy

Emergent literacy research examines early literacy knowledge and the contexts and conditions that foster that knowledge. Despite differing viewpoints on the relation between emerging literacy skills and reading acquisition, there is strong support that early childhood exposure to oral and written language is linked to the facility with which children learn to read.

Reading for comprehension of factual material (e.g., content area textbooks, reference books, and newspapers) is closely related to study strategies in the middle/junior high setting. Organized study models, such as the SQ3R method, a technique that makes it possible to learn the content of even large amounts of text (Survey, Question, Read, Recite, and Review Studying), teach students to locate main ideas and supporting details, to recognize sequential order, to distinguish fact from opinion, and to determine cause and effect relationships.

Skill 4.4   Distinguishing among literal, inferential, and evaluative comprehension

Literal comprehension is the understanding of the basic facts of a given passage. This level of comprehension is the priority for the reader so that he or she can maintain coherence and a general understanding of what is being read.

Inferential comprehension is the ability to create or infer a hypothesis for a given statement based on collected facts and information. Research suggests that students must mentally "highlight" relevant information they might need later in order to relate and connect ideas from the passage. Understandings of concepts such as syntax, morphology, discourse, and pragmatics are all needed for students to effectively make inferences while reading.

Evaluative comprehension is the ability to understand and sort facts, opinions, assumptions, persuasive elements, and the validity of a passage. Students with excellent evaluative comprehension skills can not only infer meaning from the text, but also compare, contrast, and apply what is read.

Skill 4.5   Identifying strategies for promoting students' literal, inferential, and evaluative comprehension

There are five key strategies to increase children's abilities to read informational/expository texts.

1. Inferencing is an evaluative process that involves the reader in making a reasonable judgment based on the information given and engages children in literally constructing meaning. In order to develop and enhance inferencing in children, a teacher may consider having a mini-lesson in which this key skill is demonstrated by reading an expository book aloud (e.g., one on skyscrapers for young children) and then demonstrating for them the following reading habits: looking for clues, reflecting on what the reader already knows about the topic ("activating" prior knowledge), and using the clues in the expository text to figure out what the author means.

2. Identifying main ideas in an expository text can be improved when children have an explicit strategy for identifying important information. They can be included in making this strategy part of their everyday reading style by being focused and "walked" through exercises as a part of a series of guided reading sessions. The child should read a passage so that the topic is readily identifiable to him or her.

3. The child should be asked to be on the lookout for a sentence within the expository passage that summarizes the key information in the paragraph or in the lengthier excerpt. The child should then read the rest of the passage or excerpt in light of this information and also note which information in the paragraph is not important. The important information the child has identified in the paragraph can be used by the child reader to formulate the author's main idea. The child reader may even want to use some of the author's own language in formulating that idea.

4. Monitoring means self-clarifying: As students read, they often realize that what are reading is not making sense. The reader then has to have a plan for making sensible meaning out of the excerpt. Cooper and other balanced literacy advocates have a "stop and think" strategy that they use with children. The child is asked to reflect, "does this make sense to me?" When the child concludes that it does not, he or she then either: re-reads, reads ahead in the text, looks up unknown words, or asks for help from the teacher.

What is important about monitoring is that some readers ask these questions and try these approaches without ever being explicitly taught them in school by a teacher. However, the key philosophy of the reading theorists mentioned here is that these strategies need to be explicitly modeled and practiced under the guidance of the teacher by most, if not all child readers.

5. Summarizing engages the reader in pulling the essential bits of information within a longer passage or excerpt of text into a cohesive whole. Children can be taught to summarize informational or expository text by following these guidelines. First, they should look at the topic sentence of the paragraph or the text and delete the trivia. They should then search for information that has been mentioned more than once and make sure it is included only once in their summary. Students should find related ideas or items and group them under a unifying heading; they can then search for and identify a main idea sentence. Finally, they can put the summary together using all of these guidelines.

Generating questions can motivate and enhance children's comprehension of reading, in that they become actively involved in generating their own questions and then answer these questions based on their reading. In order to generate meaningful questions that trigger constructive reading in expository texts, children should preview the text by reading the titles and subheads (they should also look at the illustrations and the pictures). Students may then begin to read the first paragraph. These first previews should yield an impressive batch of specific questions.

Next, children should get into their "Dr. Seuss mode" by asking themselves a "think" question. For younger children, having a "think" silly hat in the classroom might be effective as well, as the children could actually go over and put it on. Teachers should make certain that the children write down the "think" question and encourage them to read to find important information to answer it. The children should be asked to write down the answer they found and to copy the sentence or sentences where they found the answer. Also, children should be encouraged to consider whether, in light of their further reading through the text, their original question was a good one or not.

The teacher should ask the students to be prepared to explain why their original question was a good one or not. Once the children have answered their original "think" question, they can generate additional ones.

Skill 4.6 Applying knowledge of strategies (e.g., predicting, re-reading, re-telling) that facilitate comprehension before, during, and after reading

Making Predictions

One theory/approach to the teaching of reading that gained currency in the late 1960s and the early 1970s involved asking inferential and critical thinking questions of the reader that would challenge and engage the children in the text. This approach to reading went beyond the literal level of what was stated in the text to an inferential level of using text clues to make predictions, and extended further to a critical level of involving the child in evaluating the text. While asking engaging and thought-provoking questions is still viewed as part of the teaching of reading, it is currently viewed only as one component of the teaching of reading.

Prior Knowledge

Prior knowledge can be defined as all of an individual's prior experiences, education, and development that precede his or her entrance into a specific learning situation or his or her attempts to comprehend a specific text. At times, prior knowledge can be erroneous or incomplete. If there are misconceptions in a child's prior knowledge, these must be corrected so that the child's overall comprehension skills can continue to progress. Prior knowledge even at the Kindergarten level includes accumulated positive and negative experiences both in and out of school.

Prior knowledge might range from family travels, watching television, and visiting museums and libraries to visiting hospitals, prisons, and struggling with poverty. Whatever the prior knowledge the child brings to the school setting, the independent reading and writing the child does in school immeasurably expands his or her prior knowledge, hence broadening his or her reading comprehension capabilities.

Literary response skills are also dependent on schemata. Schemata (the plural of schema) are those structures that represent generic concepts stored in the memory. Effective textual comprehension, whether done by adults or children, uses schemata and prior knowledge in addition to the ideas from the printed text for reading comprehension; graphic organizers help to organize this information.

Graphic Organizers

Graphic organizers solidify in a chart format a visual relationship among various reading and writing ideas. These ideas include: sequence, timelines, character traits, fact and opinion, main ideas and details, differences, and likenesses (generally done using a VENN DIAGRAM of interlocking circles, KWL Chart, etc.). These charts and formats are essential for providing scaffolding for instruction by activating pertinent prior knowledge.

KWL (Know, Want, Learn) charts are exceptionally useful for reading comprehension, as they outline what children _know_, what they _want_ to know, and what they've _learned_ after reading. Students are asked to activate prior knowledge about a topic and further develop their knowledge about a topic using this organizer. Teachers often opt to display and maintain KWL charts throughout a classroom to continually record pertinent information about students' reading.

When the teacher first introduces the KWL strategy, the children should be allowed sufficient time to brainstorm in response to the first question: what all of them in the class or small group actually know about the topic. The children should have a three-columned KWL worksheet template for their journals, and there should be a chart to record the responses from class or group discussions. The children can write under each column in their own journal, and should also help their teacher with notations on the chart. This strategy involves the children in actually gaining experience in note-taking and in creating a concrete record of new data and information gleaned from the passage about the topic.

Depending on the grade level of the participating children, the teacher may also want to channel them into considering categories of information they hope to find out from the expository passage. For instance, they may be reading a book on animals to find out more about the animal's habitats during the winter or about the animal's mating habits.

When children are working on the middle column—what they want to know about the reading—the teacher may want to help them to express it in question format.

KWL is a useful tool and can even be introduced as early as second grade with extensive teacher discussion and support. It not only serves to support the child's comprehension of a particular expository text, but also models for children a format for note-taking. In addition, when the teacher wants to introduce report writing, the KWL format provides excellent outlines and question introductions for at least three paragraphs of a report.

Cooper (2004) recommends this strategy for use with thematic units and with reading chapters in required science, social studies, or health text books.

In addition to its usefulness with thematic unit study, KWL is wonderful for providing the teacher with a concrete format to assess how well children have absorbed pertinent new knowledge within the passage (by looking at the third L section). Ultimately, it is hoped that students will learn to use this strategy, not only under explicit teacher direction with templates of KWL sheets, but also on their own by informally writing questions they want to find out about in their journals and then going back and answering them after the reading.

Note Taking

Older children should take notes in their reading journals, while younger children and those more in need of explicit teacher support may contribute their ideas and responses as part of the discussion in class. Their responses should be recorded on the experiential chart.

Connecting Texts

The concept of readiness is generally regarded as a developmentally-based phenomenon. Various abilities, whether cognitive, affective, or psychomotor, are perceived to be dependent upon the mastery or development of certain prerequisite skills or abilities. Readiness, then, implies that prior to accomplishing the knowledge, experience, and readiness prerequisites, children should not yet engage in the new task.

Readiness for subject area learning is dependent not only on prior knowledge, but also on affective factors such as interest, motivation, and attitude. These factors are often more influential on student learning than the pre-existing cognitive base.

When texts relate to a student's life or other reading materials or areas of study, they become more meaningful and relevant to students' learning. Students typically enjoy seeing reading material that connects to their lives, other subject areas, and other reading material.

Discussing the Text

Discussion is an activity in which the children (this activity works well from grades three through six and beyond) conclude a particular text. Among the prompts, the teacher-coach might suggest that the children focus on words of interest they encountered in the text. These can also be words that they heard if the text was read aloud. Children can be asked to share something funny, upsetting, or unusual about the words they have read. Through this focus on children's responses to words as the center of the discussion circle, peers become more interested in word study.

Furthermore, in the current teaching of literacy, reading, writing, thinking, listening, viewing, and discussing are not viewed as separate activities or components of instruction, but rather as simultaneous and interactive elements of reading comprehension.

COMPETENCY 5.0 UNDERSTAND COMPREHENSION STRATEGIES FOR LITERARY AND INFORMATIONAL TEXTS ACROSS THE CURRICULUM

Skill 5.1 Recognizing types and characteristics of literary and informational texts

Fiction vs. Nonfiction

Students often misrepresent the differences between fiction and nonfiction. They mistakenly believe that stories are always examples of fiction. The simple truth is that stories are both fiction and nonfiction. The primary difference is that fiction is made up by the author and nonfiction is generally true (or an opinion). It is harder for students to understand that non-fiction entails an enormous range of material, from textbooks and true stories to newspaper articles and speeches. Fiction, on the other hand, is fairly simple—made-up stories, novels, etc. However, it is also important for students to understand that most of fiction throughout history has been based on true events. In other words, authors use their own life experiences to help them create works of fiction.

In understanding fiction, it is important to recognize the artistry in telling a story to convey a point. When students see that an author's choice in a work of fiction is for the sole purpose of conveying a viewpoint, they can make better sense of the specific details in the work of fiction.

In understanding nonfiction, it is important to realize what is truth and what is perspective. Often, a nonfiction writer will present an opinion, and that opinion may be very different from the truth. Knowing the difference between the two is very crucial.

In comparing fiction to nonfiction, students need to learn about the conventions of each. In fiction, students can generally expect to see plot, characters, setting, and themes. In nonfiction, students may see a plot, characters, settings, and themes, but they will also experience interpretations, opinions, theories, research, and other elements.

Over time, students may begin to see patterns that identify fiction from nonfiction. Oftentimes, the more fanciful or unrealistic a story is, the more likely it is fiction. On the other hand, the saying "truth is stranger than fiction" is reinforced by the outrageous true events that sometimes comprise the basis of nonfiction. Therefore, it is vital for students to have a strong framework of understanding for the literary conventions that separate the two genres.

Skill 5.2   Identifying characteristics and functions of literary elements and devices (e.g., plot, point of view, setting)

Most works of fiction contain a common set of elements that make them come alive to readers. In a way, even though writers do not consciously think about each of these elements when they sit down to write, all stories essentially contain these "markers" that make them the stories that they are. However, even though all stories share these elements, they are a lot like fingerprints: Each story's elements are different.

Let's look at a few of the most commonly discussed elements. The most commonly discussed story element in fiction is plot. Plot is the series of events in a story. Typically, but not always, plot moves in a predictable fashion:

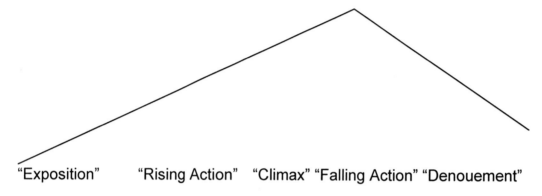

"Exposition"   "Rising Action"   "Climax" "Falling Action" "Denouement"

Exposition is when characters and their situations are introduced. **Rising action** is the point at which conflict starts to occur. **Climax** is the highest point of conflict, often a turning point. **Falling action** is the result of the climax. **Denouement** is the final resolution of the plot.

Character is another commonly studied story element. In stories, we often find heroes, villains, comedic characters, dark characters, etc. When we examine the characters of a story, we look to see who they are and how their traits contribute to the story. Often, because of their characteristics, plot elements become more interesting. For example, authors may pair unlikely characters together in a way that creates specific conflict.

The setting of a story is the place or location where it occurs. Oftentimes, the specific place is not as important as some of the specifics about the setting. For example, the setting of *The Great Gatsby*, New York, is not as significant as the fact that it takes place amongst incredible wealth. Conversely, *The Grapes of Wrath*, although taking place in Oklahoma and California, has a more significant setting of poverty. In fact, as the story takes place *around* other migrant workers, the setting is even more significant. In a way, the setting serves as a reason for various conflicts to occur.

Themes of stories are the underlying messages, above and beyond all plot elements, that writers want to convey. Very rarely will one find that good literature is without a theme—or a lesson, message, or ideal. The best writers in the English language all seem to want to convey something about human nature or the world, and they turn to literature in order to do that. Common themes in literature are jealousy, money, love, and human against corporation or government. These themes are never explicitly stated; rather, they are the result of the portrayal of characters, settings, and plots. Readers get the message even if the theme is not directly mentioned.

Finally, the mood of a story is the atmosphere or attitude the writer conveys through descriptive language. Often, mood fits nicely with theme and setting. For example, in Edgar Allen Poe's stories, we often find a mood of horror and darkness. We get that from the descriptions of characters and the setting, as well as from specific plot elements. Mood simply helps us better understand the writer's theme and intentions through descriptive, stylistic language.

Skill 5.3 Applying strategies for developing students' literary response skills (e.g., making connections between texts and personal experiences)

While literature is a vehicle for teaching reading comprehension and writing, it is often overlooked that a very important reason for teaching literature is to help students understand how to appreciate written text, complex ideas, poetic language and ideas, and unique perspectives. However, just presenting good literature to students is not enough. They need active involvement with the literature. They also need to have a chance to respond to the literature in a variety of ways. Response helps students to personalize the literature (in other words, it helps students to understand that the literature comes from human instincts and issues), it helps them as they make sense of meaning, and it helps them to appreciate it more.

Appropriate responses to literature come in many forms. There are really too many forms to mention here, but we will provide a good overview of possible responses. Many students learn quite a bit by responding with additional works of art—whether it is further literature (poetry, fiction, etc.), visual art, or music. For example, students can write a poem expressing the mood of a character. They can also draw a picture that portrays a scene in a novel. They can even be asked to re-write the ending of a story. Giving students the opportunity to be creative in these ways help them to "enter" into the literature more fully. It gives them a real opportunity to interact with the ideas, characters, setting, and author.

Analytic writing is another good way to respond to literature. Of course, this may not seem as much fun from the student perspective, but analytic writing allows students to see that there is not just one way to view literature. They often learn best when they understand that their possibly unconventional ways of understanding literature must be defended with clear examples from the text. Drama is another very effective tool for responding to literature. When students act out scenes from a novel, for example, they begin to understand character motives more clearly.

As you can see, the list of appropriate responses to literature could go on and on. It is important for teachers to match up appropriate responses with the literature and their students. Not every type of response will work well for all students and for all pieces of literature, so careful selection is important.

Skill 5.4 Demonstrating knowledge of genres, themes, authors, and works of literature written for children

The major literary genres include allegory, ballad, drama, epic, epistle, essay, fable, legend, myth, novel, poem, romance, and the short story.

Allegory: A story in verse or prose with characters representing virtues and vices. There are two meanings, symbolic and literal. John Bunyan's *The Pilgrim's Progress* is the most renowned of this genre.

Ballad: An *in medias res* (Latin for "in the middle of things") story told or sung, usually in verse and accompanied by music. Literary devices found in ballads include the refrain, or repeated section, and incremental repetition, or anaphora, for effect. The earliest forms were anonymous folk ballads. Later forms include Coleridge's Romantic masterpiece, "The Rime of the Ancient Mariner."

Drama: Plays – comedy, modern, or tragedy - typically conducted in five acts. Traditionalists and neoclassicists adhere to Aristotle's unities of time, place, and action. Plot development is advanced through dialogue. Literary devices include asides, soliloquies, and the chorus representation of public opinion. William Shakespeare is considered by many to be the greatest of all dramatists/playwrights. Other notable dramaturges include: Ibsen, Williams, Miller, Shaw, Stoppard, Racine, Moliére, Sophocles, Aeschylus, Euripides, and Aristophanes.

Epic: A long poem usually of book length reflecting values inherent in the generative society. Epic devices include an invocation to a Muse for inspiration, an overall purpose for writing, a universal setting, a protagonist and antagonist who possess supernatural strength and acumen, and the interventions of a God or the gods. Overall, there are very few epics. Of the most notable are: Homer's *Iliad* and *Odyssey*, Virgil's *Aeneid*, Milton's *Paradise Lost*, Spenser's *The Fairie Queene*, Barrett Browning's *Aurora Leigh*, and Pope's mock-epic, *The Rape of the Lock*.

Epistle: A letter that is not always originally intended for public distribution, but due to the fame of the sender and/or recipient, becomes public domain. For example, the apostle Paul wrote epistles that were later placed in the Bible.

Essay: Typically a limited length prose work focusing on a topic and propounding a definite point-of-view through an authoritative tone. Great essayists include Carlyle, Lamb, DeQuincy, Emerson, and Montaigne, who is credited with defining this genre.

Fable: A terse tale offering up a moral or exemplum. Chaucer's "The Nun's Priest's Tale" is a fine example of a bête fabliau (beast fable) in which animals speak and act characteristically human, illustrating human foibles.

Legend: A traditional narrative or collection of related narratives, popularly regarded as historically factual but actually a mixture of fact and fiction.

Myth: Stories that are more or less universally shared within a culture to explain its history and traditions.

Novel: The longest form of fictional prose containing a variety of characterizations, settings, local color, and regionalism. Most have complex plots, expanded descriptions, and attention to detail. Some of the great novelists include Austen, the Brontës, Twain, Tolstoy, Hugo, Hardy, Dickens, Hawthorne, Forster, and Flaubert.

Poem: A work in which the only requirement is rhythm. Sub-genres include fixed types of literature such as the: sonnet, elegy, ode, pastoral, and villanelle. Unfixed types of literature include blank verse and dramatic monologue.

Romance: A highly imaginative tale set in a fantastical realm dealing with the conflicts between heroes and villains and/or monsters. "The Knight's Tale" from Chaucer's Canterbury Tales, *Sir Gawain and the Green Knight*, and Keats' "The Eve of St. Agnes" are prime examples.

Short Story: Typically a terse narrative, with less developmental background about characters, but which may still include description, point-of-view, and tone. Poe emphasized that a successful short story should create one focused impact. Considered among the great short story writers are: Hemingway, Faulkner, Twain, Joyce, Jackson, O'Connor, de Maupassant, Saki, Poe, and Pushkin.

Children's literature is a genre of its own that emerged as a distinct and independent form in the second half of the eighteenth century. *The Visible World in Pictures* by John Amos Comenius, a Czech educator, was one of the first printed works and the first picture book. For the first time, educators acknowledged that children are different from adults in many respects. Modern educators acknowledge that introducing elementary students to a wide range of reading experiences plays an important role in their mental, social, and psychological developments. Some of the most common forms of literature specifically for children follow:

- **Traditional Literature:** Traditional literature opens up a world where right wins out over wrong, where hard work and perseverance are rewarded, and where helpless victims find vindication—all worthwhile values that children identify with even as early as Kindergarten. In traditional literature, children are introduced to fanciful beings, humans with exaggerated powers, talking animals, and heroes who will inspire them. For younger elementary children, these stories in Big Book format are ideal for providing predictable and repetitive elements that can be easily grasped.

- **Folktales/Fairy Tales:** Some examples include: "The Three Bears," "Little Red Riding Hood," "Snow White," "Sleeping Beauty," "Puss-in-Boots," "Rapunzel," and "Rumpelstiltskin." Adventures of animals or humans and the supernatural characterize these stories. The hero is usually on a quest and is aided by other-worldly helpers. More often than not, the story focuses on good and evil and reward and punishment.

- **Fables:** Animals that act like humans are featured in these stories; they usually reveal human foibles or sometimes teach a lesson. Example: *Aesop's Fables.*

- **Myths:** These stories about events from the earliest times, such as the origin of the world, are considered true in their own societies.

- **Legends:** These are similar to myths except that they tend to deal with events that happened more recently. Example: Arthurian legends.

- **Tall tales:** Examples: Paul Bunyan, John Henry, and Pecos Bill. These are purposely exaggerated accounts of individuals with superhuman strength.

- **Modern Fantasy:** Many of the themes found in these stories are similar to those in traditional literature. The stories start out based in reality, which makes it easier for the reader to suspend disbelief and enter worlds of unreality. Little people live in the walls in *The Borrowers* and time travel is possible in *The Trolley to Yesterday*. Including some fantasy tales in the curriculum helps elementary-grade children to develop their senses of imagination. Fantasy literature often appeals to ideals of justice and issues having to do with good and evil; because children tend to identify with the characters, the message is more likely to be retained.

- **Science Fiction:** Robots, spacecraft, mystery, and civilizations from other ages often appear in these stories. Most presume advances in science on other planets or in a future time. Most children like these stories because of their interest in space and the "what if" aspect of the stories. Examples: *Outer Space and All That Junk*, and *A Wrinkle in Time*.

- **Modern Realistic Fiction:** These stories are about real problems that real children face. By finding that their hopes and fears are shared by others, young children can find insight into their own problems. Young readers also tend to experience a broadening of interests as the result of this kind of reading. It's good for them to know that a child can be brave and intelligent and can solve difficult problems.

- **Historical Fiction:** *Rifles for Watie* by Harold Keith is an example of this kind of story. Presented in a historically-accurate setting, it's about a young boy (sixteen years old) who serves in the Union army. He experiences great hardship but discovers that his enemy is an admirable human being. It provides a good opportunity to introduce younger children to history in a beneficial way.

- **Biography:** Reading about inventors, explorers, scientists, political and religious leaders, social reformers, artists, sports figures, doctors, teachers, writers, and war heroes helps children to see that one person can make a difference. They also open new vistas for children to think about when they choose an occupation to consider for their own futures.

- **Informational Books:** These are ways to learn more about something you are interested in or something that you know nothing about. Encyclopedias are good resources, of course, but a book like *Polar Wildlife* by Kamini Khanduri shows pictures and facts that capture the imaginations of young children.

Skill 5.5   Recognizing common patterns of organization in informational texts (e.g., chronological, cause-and-effect)

Main Idea

A **topic** of a paragraph or story is what the paragraph or story is about. The **main idea** of a paragraph or story states the important idea(s) that the author wants the reader to know about a topic. The topic and main idea of a paragraph or story are sometimes directly stated. There are times, however, when the topic and main idea are not directly stated, but simply implied.

For example, look at this paragraph below:

> Henry Ford was an inventor who developed the first affordable automobile. The cars that were being built before Mr. Ford created his Model-T were very expensive. Only rich people could afford to have cars.

The topic of this paragraph is Henry Ford. The main idea is that Henry Ford built the first affordable automobile.

The **topic sentence** indicates what the passage is about. It is the subject of that portion of the narrative. The ability to identify the topic sentence in a passage enables the student to focus on the concept being discussed and to better comprehend the information provided.

You can find the main ideas by looking at the way in which paragraphs are written. A paragraph is a group of sentences about one main idea. Paragraphs usually have two types of sentences: a topic sentence, which contains the main idea, and two or more detail sentences that support, prove, provide more information, explain, or give examples.

You can only tell if you have a detail or topic sentence by comparing the sentences with each other.

Look at this sample paragraph:

> Fall is the best of the four seasons. The leaves change colors to create a beautiful display of golds, reds, and oranges. The air turns crisp and windy. The scent of pumpkin muffins and apple pies fill the air. Finally, Halloween marks the start of the holiday season. Fall is my favorite time of year!

Breakdown of these sentences:

Fall is the best of the four seasons. (TOPIC SENTENCE)
The leaves change colors to create a beautiful display of golds, reds, and oranges. (DETAIL)
The air turns crisp and windy. (DETAIL)
The scent of pumpkin muffins and apple pies fill the air. (DETAIL)
Finally, Halloween marks the start of the holiday season. (DETAIL)
Fall is my favorite time of year! (CLOSING SENTENCE – Often a restatement of the topic sentence)

Tips for Finding the Topic Sentence

1. The topic sentence is usually first, although it could be in any position in the paragraph.

2. A topic is usually more "general" than the other sentences, that is, it addresses many things and looks at the big picture. Sometimes it refers to more that one thing. Plurals and the words "many," "numerous," or "several" often signal a topic sentence.

3. Detail sentences are usually more "specific" than the topic, that is, they usually address one single or side of an idea. Also, the words "for example," "i.e.," "that is," "first," "second," "third," and "finally" often signal a detail.

4. Most of the detail sentences support, give examples, prove, talk about, or point toward the topic in some way.

How can you be sure that you have a topic sentence? Try this trick: switch the sentence you think is the topic sentence into a question. If the other sentences seem to "answer" the question, then you've got it.

For example:

Reword the topic sentence "Fall is the best of the four seasons" in one of the following ways:

"Why is fall the best of the four seasons?"
"Which season is the best season?"
"Is fall the best season of the year?"

Then, as you read the remaining sentences (the ones you didn't pick), you will find that they answer (support) your question.

If you attempt this with a sentence other than the topic sentence, it won't work

For example:

Suppose you select "Halloween marks the start of the holiday season," and you reword it in the following way:

"Which holiday is the start of the holiday season?"

You will find that the other sentences fail to help you answer (support) your question.

Summary Statements

The introductory statement should be at the beginning of the passage. An introductory statement provides a bridge between any previous, relevant text and the content to follow. It provides information about the text and also sets the tone and parameters. The old axiom regarding presenting a body of information suggests that you should always "tell them what you are going to tell them; tell it to them; tell them what you just told them." In accordance with this, the introductory statement is where the writer "tell[s] them what [he or she is] going to tell them," the content portion (the main body of the narrative) is where the writer "tell[s] it to them," and the summary statement is where the writer "tell[s] them what [he or she] just told them." In short, the summary statement should be at or near the end of the passage; it is a concise presentation of the essential data from that passage.

Restating the Main Idea

An accurate restatement of the main idea from a passage will usually summarize the concept in a concise manner; it will often present the same idea from a different perspective. A restatement should always demonstrate complete comprehension of the main idea.

To select an accurate restatement, identifying the main idea of the passage is essential (see Skill 5.2). Once a reader comprehends the main idea of a passage, it is important to evaluate the choices to see which statement restates the main idea while eliminating statements that only restate a supporting detail.

Walk through the steps below the sample paragraph from Skill 5.2 to see how to select the accurate restatement.

Sample Paragraph:

Fall is the best of the four seasons. The leaves change colors to create a beautiful display of golds, reds, and oranges. The air turns crisp and windy. The scent of pumpkin muffins and apple pies fill the air. Finally, Halloween marks the start of the holiday season. Fall is my favorite time of year!

<u>Steps</u>:
1. Identify the main idea (answer: "Fall is the best of the four seasons.")
2. Decide which statement below restates the topic sentence:
   A. The changing leaves turn gold, red and orange.
   B. The holidays start with Halloween.
   C. Of the four seasons, Fall is the greatest of them all.
   D. Crisp wind is a fun aspect of Fall.

The answer is C because it rewords the main idea of the first sentence (the topic sentence).

Supporting Details

The **supporting details** are sentences that give more information about the topic and the main idea. The supporting details in the aforementioned paragraph about Henry Ford include: a) that he was an inventor, and b) that before he created his Model-T, only rich people could afford cars because they were too expensive.

Organization

The organization of a written work includes two factors: the order in which the writer has chosen to present the different parts of the discussion or argument, and the relationships he or she constructs between these parts.

Written ideas need to be presented in a **logical order** so that a reader can follow the information easily and quickly. There are many different ways in which to order a series of ideas, but they all share one thing in common: to lead the reader along a desired path while avoiding backtracking or skipping around. The goal is to give a clear, strong presentation of the writer's main idea. *Some* of the ways in which a paragraph may be organized:

Sequence of events – In this type of organization, the details are presented in the order in which they have occurred. One idea is connected or depends on the next based on how they fit together in a chronological sequence. Paragraphs that describe a process or procedure, give directions, or outline a given period of time (such as a day or a month) are often arranged chronologically.

Statement support – In this type of organization, the main idea is stated and the rest of the paragraph explains or proves it. This is also referred to as relative importance. There are four ways in which this type of order is organized: most to least, least to most, most-least-most, and least-most-least.

Comparison-Contrast – In this type of organization, the compare-contrast pattern is used when a paragraph describes the differences or similarities of two or more ideas, actions, events, or things. The topic sentence usually describes the basic relationship between the ideas or items, and the rest of the paragraph explains this relationship.

Classification – In this type of organization, the paragraph presents grouped information about a topic. The topic sentence usually states the general category and the rest of the sentences show how various elements of the category have a common base as well as how they differ from the common base.

Cause and Effect – This pattern describes how two or more events are connected. The main sentence usually states the primary cause(s) and the primary effect(s) and how they are basically connected. The rest of the sentences explain the connection: how one event caused the next.

Many times, all of these organizations follow the basic P.I.E sequence:
P – The point, or main idea, of the paragraph
I – The information (e.g., data, details, facts) that supports the main idea
E – The explanation or analysis of the information and how it proves, is related to, or is connected to the main idea

Even if the sentences that make up a given paragraph or passage are arranged in logical order, the document as a whole can still seem choppy or the various ideas disconnected. **Transitions**, words that signal relationships between ideas, can help to improve the flow of a document. Transitions can help to achieve clear and effective presentation by establishing connections between sentences, paragraphs, and sections of a document. With transitions, each sentence builds on the ideas in the last, and each paragraph has clear links to the preceding one. As a result, the reader receives clear directions on how to piece together the writer's ideas in a logically coherent argument. By signaling how to organize, interpret, and react to information, transitions allow writers to effectively and elegantly explain their ideas.

Logical Relationship	Transitional Expression
Comparison	also, in the same way, just as, so too, likewise, similarly
Exception/Contrast	but, however, in spite of, on the one hand, on the other hand, nevertheless, nonetheless, notwithstanding, in contrast, on the contrary, still, yet
Sequence/Order	first, second, third, next, then, finally
Time	after, afterward, at last, before, currently, during, earlier, immediately, later, meanwhile, now, recently, simultaneously, subsequently, then

Example	for example, for instance, namely, specifically, to illustrate
Emphasis	even, indeed, in fact, of course, truly
Place/Position	above, adjacent, below, beyond, here, in front, in back, nearby, there
Cause and Effect	accordingly, consequently, hence, so, therefore, thus
Additional Support or Evidence	additionally, again, also, and, as well, besides, equally important, further, furthermore, in addition, moreover, then
Conclusion/Summary	finally, in a word, in brief, in conclusion, in the end, in the final analysis, on the whole, thus, to conclude, to summarize, in sum, in summary

Skill 5.6   **Applying knowledge of strategies for promoting comprehension of informational texts (e.g., identifying the main idea and explicit and implicit supporting details, using a glossary, using a graphic organizer)**

The point of comprehension instruction is not necessarily to focus just on the text(s) students are using at the very moment of instruction, but rather to help them to learn the strategies that they can use independently with any other text.

Some of the most common methods of teaching instruction are as follows:

- Summarization: This is where, either in writing or verbally, students go over the main point of the text, along with strategically chosen details that highlight the main point. This is not the same as paraphrasing, which is saying the same thing in different words. Teaching students how to summarize is very important, as it will help them to look for the most critical areas in a text. For example, it will help them distinguish between main arguments and examples. In fiction, it helps students to learn how to focus on the main characters and events and to distinguish those from the lesser characters and events.

- Question answering: While this tends to be over-used in many classrooms, it is still a valid method of teaching students to comprehend. As the name implies, students answer questions regarding a text, either out loud, in small groups, or individually on paper. The best questions are those that cause students to have to think about the text (rather than just find an answer within the text).

- Question generating: This is the opposite of question answering, although students can then be asked to answer their own questions or the questions of peer students. In general, students should constantly question texts as they read. This is important because it causes students to become more critical readers. To teach students to generate questions helps them to learn the types of questions they can ask, and it gets them thinking about how best to be critical of texts.

- Graphic organizers: Graphic organizers are graphical representations of content within a text. For example, Venn Diagrams can be used to highlight the difference between two characters in a novel or two similar political concepts in a Social Studies textbook. A teacher can also use flow-charts with students to talk about the steps in a process (for example, the steps of setting up a science experiment or the chronological events of a story). Semantic organizers are similar in that they graphically display information. The difference, however, is that semantic organizers focus on words or concepts. For example, a word web can help students to make sense of a word by mapping from the central word all the similar and related concepts to that word.

Text structure: In non-fiction, particularly in textbooks (and sometimes in fiction), text structures often give important clues to readers about what to look for. Often, students do not know how to make sense of all the types of headings in a textbook and do not realize that, for example, the side-bar story about a character in history is not the main text on a particular page in the history textbook. Teaching students how to interpret text structures gives them tools in which to tackle other similar texts.

- Monitoring comprehension: Students need to be aware of their comprehension, or lack of it, in particular texts. As such, it is important to teach students what to do when text suddenly stops making sense. For example, students can go back and re-read the description of a character, or they can go back to the table of contents or the first paragraph of a chapter to see where they are headed.

- Textual marking: This is where students interact with the text as they read. For example, armed with sticky notes, students can insert questions or comments regarding specific sentences or paragraphs within the text. This helps students to focus on the importance of the small things, particularly when they are reading larger works (such as novels in high school). It also gives students a reference point on which to go back into the text when they need to review something.

- Discussion: Small group or whole-class discussion stimulates thoughts about texts and gives students a larger picture of the impact of those texts. For example, teachers can strategically encourage students to discuss related concepts to the text. This helps students to learn to consider texts within larger societal and social concepts. Teachers can also encourage students to provide personal opinions during discussions. By listening to various students' opinions, all students in a class are encouraged to see the wide range of possible interpretations and thoughts regarding one text.

Many people mistakenly believe that the terms "research-based," "research-validated," or "evidence-based" relate mainly to specific programs, such as early reading textbook programs. While research does validate that some of these programs are effective, much research has been conducted regarding the effectiveness of particular instructional strategies. In reading, many of these strategies have been documented in the report from the National Reading Panel (2000). However, just because a strategy has not been validated as effective by research does not necessarily mean that it is not effective with certain students in certain situations. The number of strategies out there are much greater than researchers' ability to test their effectiveness. Some of the strategies listed above have been validated by rigorous research, while others have been shown consistently to help improve students' reading abilities in localized situations. There simply is not enough space to list all the strategies that have been proven effective; it is important to just know that the above strategies are very commonly cited ones that work in a variety of situations.

COMPETENCY 6.0   UNDERSTAND SKILLS AND STRATEGIES INVOLVED IN WRITING FOR VARIOUS PURPOSES ACROSS THE CURRICULUM

Skill 6.1   Recognizing developmental stages of writing, including the use of pictures and developmental spelling

See Skill 6.3 for the Writing Process

Developmental Spelling

Spelling instruction should include learning words misspelled in daily writing, generalizing spelling knowledge, and mastering objectives in progressive phases of development. The developmental stages of spelling include:

1)   **Pre-phonemic spelling**—Children know that letters stand for a message, but they do not know the relationship between spelling and pronunciation.

2)   **Early phonemic spelling**—Children are beginning to understand spelling. They usually write the beginning letter correctly, while the rest of the word is composed of consonants or long vowels.

3)   **Letter-name spelling**—Some words are consistently spelled correctly. The student is developing a sight vocabulary and a stable understanding of letters as representing sounds. Long vowels are usually used accurately, but silent vowels are omitted. Unknown words are spelled by the child attempting to match the name of the letter to the sound.

4)   **Transitional spelling**—This phase is typically entered in late elementary school. Short vowel sounds are mastered and some spelling rules are known. Students are developing a sense of which spellings are correct and which are not.

5)   **Derivational spelling**—This is usually reached from high school to adulthood. This is the stage where spelling rules are being mastered.

Skill 6.2   Analyzing factors to consider in writing for various audiences and purposes, and in writing materials in various genres, formats (e.g., essay, poem), and modes (e.g., descriptive, persuasive, evaluative)

Discourse, whether in speaking or writing, falls naturally into four different forms: narrative, descriptive, expository, and persuasive. The first question to be asked when reading a written piece, listening to a presentation, or writing is "What's the point?" This is usually called the thesis. Whey finished reading an essay, the reader should be able to say something along the lines of, "The point of this piece is that the foster-care system in America is a disaster." If it's a play, readers should also be able to say, "The point of that play is that good overcomes evil." The same is true of any written document or performance. If it doesn't make a point, the reader/listener/viewer may become confused and feel that it's not worth the effort. Knowing this is very helpful when sitting down to write a document, be it essay, poem, or speech, as these forms have been the structure of Western thinking since the Greek Rhetoricians.

Persuasion is a piece of writing, a poem, a play, or a speech whose purpose is to change the minds of the audience members or to get them to do something. This is achieved in many ways:

1) The credibility of the writer/speaker might lead the listeners/readers to a change of mind or a recommended action

2) Reasoning is important in persuasive discourse. No one wants to believe that he or she accepts a new viewpoint or goes out and takes action just because he or she likes and trusts the person who recommended it. Logic comes into play in reasoning that is persuasive.

3) The third and most powerful force that leads to acceptance or action is emotional appeal. Even if a person has been persuaded logically and reasonably that he or she should believe in a different way, the person is unlikely to act on it unless he or she is moved emotionally. A person with resources might be convinced that people suffered in New Orleans after Katrina, but he or she is not likely to do anything about it until he or she is moved emotionally. Sermons are good examples of persuasive discourse.

Exposition is discourse whose only purpose is to inform. Expository writing is not interested in changing anyone's mind or getting anyone to take a certain action. It exists to give information. Some examples include driving directions to a particular place or the directions for putting together a toy. The writer doesn't care whether the readers do or do not follow the directions. The writer only wants to be sure that the information is available in case they do decide to use.

Narration is discourse that is arranged chronologically—something happened, and then something else happened, and then something else happened. It is also called a story. News reports are often narrative in nature, as are records of trips.

Description is discourse whose purpose is to make an experience available through one of the five senses—seeing, smelling, hearing, feeling (as with the fingers), and tasting. Descriptive words are used to make it possible for the reader to "see" with his or her own mind's eye, hear through his or her own mind's ear, smell through his or her own mind's nose, taste with his or her own mind's tongue, and feel with his or her own mind's fingers. This is how language moves people. Only by experiencing an event can the emotions become involved. Poets are experts in descriptive language.

Persuasive writing often uses all forms of discourse. The introduction may be a history or a background of the idea being presented—exposition. Details supporting some of the points may be stories—narrations. Descriptive writing is used to make sure that the point is established emotionally.

Paraphrase is the rewording of a piece of writing. The result is not necessarily shorter than the original, as it uses different vocabulary and possibly a different arrangement of details. Paraphrases are sometimes written to clarify a complex piece of writing. Sometimes, material is paraphrased because it cannot be copied for purposes of copyright restraints.

Summary is a distilling of the elements of a piece of writing or speech. It is much shorter than the original. To write a good summary, the writer must determine what the "bones" of the original piece are. What is its structure? What is the thesis and what are the sub-points? A summary does not make judgments about the original; it simply reports the original in condensed form.

Letters are often expository in nature—their purpose is to give information. However, letters are also often persuasive—the writer wants to persuade or get the recipient to do something. They are also sometimes descriptive or narrative—the writer may share an experience or tell about an event.

Research reports are a special kind of expository writing. A topic is researched—explored by some appropriate means such as searching literature, interviewing experts, or even conducting experiments—and the findings are written up in such a way that the audience may know what was discovered. They can be very simple, such as delving into the history of an event, or very complex, such as a report on a scientific phenomenon that requires complicated testing and reasoning to explain. A research reports often reports possible conclusions but puts forth one as the best answer to the question that inspired the research in the first place, which is what becomes the thesis of the report.

Skill 6.3   Demonstrating knowledge of the writing process (e.g., prewriting, drafting, revising, editing) and strategies for promoting students' writing skills

Writing is a recursive process. As students engage in the various stages of writing, they develop and improve not only their writing skills, but their thinking skills as well. The stages of the writing process are as follows:

Prewriting

Students gather ideas before writing. Prewriting may include clustering, listing, brainstorming, mapping, free writing, and charting. Providing many ways for a student to develop ideas on a topic will increase his or her chances for success.

Writing

Students compose the first draft.

Revising

Students examine their work and make changes in sentences, wording, details, and ideas. Revise comes from the Latin word *revidere,* meaning "to see again."

Editing

Students proofread the draft for punctuation and mechanical errors.

Publishing

Students may have their work displayed on a bulletin board, read aloud in class, or printed in a literary magazine or school anthology. It is important to realize that these steps are recursive; as a student engages in each aspect of the writing process, he or she may begin with prewriting, writing, revising, writing, revising, editing, and publishing. They do not engage in this process in a lockstep manner; it is more circular.

Teaching The Composing Process

Prewriting Activities
1. Have a class discussion of the topic.
2. Map out ideas, questions, and graphic organizers on the chalkboard.
3. Break into small groups to discuss different ways of approaching the topic, develop an organizational plan, and create a thesis statement.
4. Research the topic, if necessary.

Drafting/Revising

1. Students write a first draft in class or at home.
2. Students engage in peer response and class discussion.
3. Using checklists or a rubric, students critique each other's writing and make suggestions for revising the writing.
4. Students revise the writing.

Editing and Proofreading

1. Students, working in pairs, analyze sentences for variety.
2. Students work in groups to read papers for punctuation and mechanics.
3. Students perform final edit.

Skill 6.4 **Demonstrating knowledge of the use of writing strategies and language to achieve various effects (e.g., creating a point of view, showing author's voice, persuading, establishing setting, describing sensory details)**

See also Skill 5.5

Fact and Opinion

A **fact** is something that is true and can be proved. An **opinion** is something that a person believes, thinks, or feels.

Examine the following examples:
> Joe DiMaggio, a Yankees' center-fielder, was replaced by Mickey Mantle in 1952.

This is a fact. If necessary, evidence can be produced to support this.

> First year players are more ambitious than seasoned players.

This is an opinion. There is no proof to support that everyone feels this way.

Author's Purpose

An author may have more than one purpose in writing. An author's purpose may be to entertain, to persuade, to inform, to describe, or to narrate.

There are no tricks or rules to follow in attempting to determine an author's purpose. It is up to the reader to use his or her judgment.

Consider the following paragraph:

> Charles Lindbergh had no intention of becoming a pilot. He was enrolled
> in the University of Wisconsin until a flying lesson changed the entire
> course of his life. He began his career as a pilot by performing daredevil
> stunts at fairs.

The author wrote this paragraph primarily to:

(A) Describe
(B) Inform
(C) Entertain
(D) Narrate

Since the author is simply telling us or informing us about the life of Charles
Lindbergh, the correct answer here is (B).

Author's Tone and Point of View

The author's tone is his or her attitude as reflected in the statement or passage.
His or her choice of words helps the reader to determine the overall tone of a
statement or passage.

Read the following paragraph:

> I was shocked by your article, which said that sitting down to breakfast
> was a thing of the past. Many families consider breakfast time to be family
> time. Children need to realize the importance of having a good breakfast.
> It is imperative that they be taught this at a young age. I cannot believe
> that a writer with your reputation has difficulty comprehending this.

The author's tone in this passage is one of:

(A) concern
(B) panic
(C) excitement
(D) disbelief

Since the author directly states that he "cannot believe" that the writer feels this
way, the answer is (D) disbelief.

Inferences and Conclusions

In order to draw **inferences** and make **conclusions**, a reader must use prior
knowledge and apply it to the current situation. A conclusion or inference is never
stated. The reader must rely on his or her common sense.

Read the following passage:

> The Smith family waited patiently around carousel number seven for their luggage to arrive. They were exhausted after their five hour trip and were anxious to get to their hotel. After about an hour, they realized that they no longer recognized any of the other passengers' faces. Mrs. Smith asked the person who appeared to be in charge if they were at the right carousel. The man replied, "Yes, this is it, but we finished unloading that baggage almost half an hour ago."

From the man's response we can infer that:

(A) The Smiths were ready to go to their hotel.
(B) The Smith's luggage was lost.
(C) The man had their luggage.
(D) They were at the wrong carousel.

Since the Smiths were still waiting for their luggage, we know that they were not yet ready to go to their hotel. From the man's response, we know that they were not at the wrong carousel and that he did not have their luggage. Therefore, though not directly stated, it appears that their luggage was lost. Choice (B) is the correct answer.

Figurative Language

Figurative language is present in both fiction and non-fiction. Figurative language is language that utilizes creative or poetic methods to convey points. Figurative language is used for effect and to make a point stand out. The most common examples of figurative language include hyperbole, metaphor, personification, simile, and idiom. Each is explained below:

Hyperbole: The term, hyperbole, is the literary version of exaggeration. When authors exaggerate in their text, they are using hyperbole. Hyperbole is often used as irony, many times to over-emphasize a point.

Metaphor: A metaphor is any time one thing is used in place of something else in text, signifying some sort of resemblance. For example, we might say that "it is raining cats and dogs." Hopefully, this is not literally true—ever! Instead, we use this to signify heavy rain. Authors use metaphor for emphasis, creativity, and often clarity. Sometimes, metaphors provide a better picture than accurate language.

Personification: Whenever an author gives human life to an inanimate item, personification is used. For example, we might say that the wind is whistling. Authors use personification to provide a more poetic look at common events.

Simile: Similes are comparisons between two objects (or between a person and an object). Similes are like metaphors; however, they typically use "like" or "as" to identify the similarities. A simile is found in the phrase "love is like a rose."

Idiom: Idioms are phrases or words used only in specific locations or cultures. For example, a common American idiom, found anywhere in the country, is "break a leg," which is a wish for good luck. However, each region of the country has its own distinctive idioms as well. Idioms are generally used in writing to spice the language with local flavor. Often, idioms are used to make characters seem more real, or even to indicate where in the country the action is taking place.

Skill 6.5 Applying revision strategies to improve the unity, organization, clarity, precision, and effectiveness of written materials

Revision is probably the most important step for the writer in the writing process. Here, students examine their work and make changes in wording, details, and ideas. So many times, students write a draft and then feel they're done. On the contrary—students must be encouraged to develop, change, and enhance their writing once they've completed the draft as well as during initial composition.

Effective teachers realize that revision and editing go hand-in-hand. They also know that students often move back and forth between these two stages during the course of one written work. These stages are often best practiced in small groups or pairs in addition to on an individual basis. Students must learn to analyze and improve their own work as well as the works of their peers. Some methods to use include:

1. Students working in pairs to analyze sentences for variety.
2. Students working in pairs or groups to ask questions about unclear areas or to help in adding details, information, etc.
3. Students performing their final edit.

Many teachers introduce a Writer's Workshop to their students to maximize learning about the writing process. Writer's Workshops vary across classrooms, but the main idea is for students to become comfortable with the writing process. A basic Writer's Workshop includes a block of classroom time committed to writing various projects (e.g., narratives, memoirs, book summaries, fiction, book reports, etc). Students use this time to write, meet with others to review/edit writing, make comments on writing, revise their own work, proofread, meet with the teacher, and publish their work.

Teachers who facilitate effective Writer's Workshops are able to meet with students one at a time and can guide each student in his or her individual writing needs. This approach allows the teacher to differentiate instruction for each student's writing level.

Clarifying Writing

Writing Introductions

It is important to remember that in the writing process, the introduction should be written last. Until the body of the paper has been determined, including the thesis and its development, it is difficult to make strategic decisions regarding the introduction. The Greek rhetoricians called this part of a discourse *exordium*, or "leading into." The basic purpose of the introduction, then, is to lead the audience into the discourse. It can let the reader know what the purpose of the discourse is, and it can condition the audience to be receptive to what the writer wants to say. It can be very brief or it can take up a large percentage of the total word count. Aristotle said that the introduction can be compared to the flourishes that flute players make before their performance—an overture in which the musicians display what they can play best in an attempt to gain the favor and attention of the audience for the main performance.

In order to do this, the writer must first know what to say; who the readership is likely to be; what the social, political, and economic climate is; what preconceived notions the audience is likely to have regarding the subject; and how long the discourse is going to be.

There are many ways to do this:
- Show that the subject is important.
- Show that although the points being presented may seem improbable, they are true.
- Show that the subject has been neglected, misunderstood, or misrepresented in the past.
- Explain an unusual mode of development.
- Forestall any misconception of the purpose.
- Apologize for a deficiency.
- Arouse interest in the subject with an anecdotal lead-in.
- Ingratiate oneself with the readership.
- Establish one's own credibility.

The introduction often ends with the thesis—the point or purpose of the paper. However, this is not set in stone. The thesis may open the body of the discussion, or it may conclude the discourse. The most important thing to remember is that the purpose and structure of the introduction should be deliberate if it is to serve the purpose of "leading the reader into the discussion."

Writing Conclusions

It is easier to write a conclusion after the decisions regarding the introduction have been made. Aristotle taught that the conclusion should strive to do five things:
1. Inspire the reader with a favorable opinion of the writer.
2. Amplify the force of the points made in the body of the paper.
3. Reinforce the points made in the body.
4. Rouse appropriate emotions in the reader.
5. Restate in a summary way what has been said.

The conclusion may be short or it may be long, depending on its purpose in the paper. Recapitulation, a brief restatement of the main points (or of the thesis) is the most common form of effective conclusion writing. A good example is the closing argument in a court trial.

Text Organization

In studies of professional writers and how they produce their successful works, it has been revealed that writing is a process that can be clearly defined (although, in practice, it must have enough flexibility to allow for creativity). The teacher must be able to define the various stages that a successful writer goes through in order to make a statement that has value. There must be a discovery stage when ideas, materials, and supporting details are deliberately collected. These may come from many possible sources: the writer's own experience and observations, deliberate research of written sources, interviews of live persons, television presentations, or the internet.

The next stage is organizing where the purpose, thesis, and supporting points will be. Most writers will put forth more than one possible thesis; in the next stage, the writing of the paper, they will then settle on one as the result of trial and error. Once the paper is written, the editing stage is probably the most important stage. This is not just the polishing stage. At this point, decisions must be made regarding whether the reasoning is cohesive—does it hold together? Is the arrangement the best possible one, or should the points be rearranged? Are there holes that need to be filled in? What form will the introduction take? Does the conclusion lead the reader out of the discourse, or is it inadequate or too abrupt?

It is important to remember that the best writers engage in all of these stages recursively. They may go back to discovery at any point in the process. They may go back and rethink the organization even once they have almost finished. To help students become effective writers, teachers need to give them adequate practice in the various stages. Students must be encouraged to engage deliberately in the creative thinking that makes writers successful.

Assessing Writing

Students need to be trained to become effective at proofreading, revising, and editing strategies. Begin by training them using both desk-side and scheduled conferences. Listed below are some strategies to use to guide students through the final stages of the writing process (and these can easily be incorporated into the Writer's Workshop).

- Provide some guide sheets or forms for students to use during peer responses
- Allow students to work in pairs and limit the agenda
- Model the use of the guide sheet or form for the entire class
- Give students a time limit or number of written pieces to be completed in a specific amount of time
- Have the students read their partners' papers, and ask at least three who, what, when, why, how questions (the students should answer the questions and use them as a place to begin discussing the piece)
- At this point in the writing process, a mini-lesson that focuses on some of the problems students are having is appropriate

To help students revise, provide them with a series of questions that will assist them in revising their writing. For example:

1. Do the details give a clear picture? Add details that appeal to more than just the sense of sight.

2. How effectively are the details organized? Reorder the details if necessary.

3. Are the thoughts and feelings of the writer included? Add personal thoughts and feelings about the subject.

As teachers discuss revision, they should begin by discussing the definition of "revise." Also, it is important to state that all writing must be revised to improve it. After students have revised their writing, it is time for the final editing and proofreading.

Skill 6.6   Demonstrating knowledge of the use of research skills and computer technology to support writing

Students must be able to research effectively in order to write about a specific assignment. Students need the skills to collect information, sort data, and make a decision as to what facts they will incorporate into their assignment or project.

Student Research Skills
- Learn to generate questions about a topic
- Form a research plan using a variety of strategies
- Restate factual information in the student's own words
- Collect and organize information on various topics
- Write grade-level-appropriate research drafts

Computer technology, in the form of word processing programs, with the capability to add, delete, and rearrange text, are supportive of writing programs. The use of computer technology can lead to better writing outcomes.

Positive Outcomes Associated with the Use of Word Processors in Writing
- Longer written samples
- Greater variety of word usage
- More variety of sentence structure
- More accurate mechanics and spelling
- Better understanding of the writing process
- Better attitudes toward writing

(Batey 1986; Bialo and Sivin 1990)

Computer Technology

Teachers should evaluate and select educational software based on problem solving, critical thinking, and curriculum standards. In so doing, they can create an environment where students are encouraged to research and write effectively while applying a variety of technology processes.

Locating information for research projects and compiling research sources using both print and electronic resources are vital steps in the construct of written documents. The resources that are available in today's school communities include a large database of Internet resources and World Wide Web access, both of which provide individual navigation for print and electronic information. Research sources include looking at traditional commercial databases and using the Electronic Library to print and cite a diversity of informational resources.

One vital aspect of the research process includes learning to analyze the applicability and validity of the massive amounts of accessible information in cyberspace. Verifying and evaluating electronic resources should be a part of the writing process, as should sorting through the downloaded hardcopies or scrolling through the electronic databases. In using a diversity of research sources, the user must be able to discern authentic sources of information from the mass collections of websites and information databases with less-than-reputable sources.

In primary research, selecting a topic and setting up an outline for research information precedes using the secondary research of both print and electronic resources. Using conceptual Venn diagrams to center the topic and brainstorm the peripheral information pertaining to the topic clarifies the purpose of the research. There are two aspects of the secondary research:

1. Using print sources
2. Using electronic research tools

Print sources provide guides on locations for specific or general information resources. Libraries have floors or designated areas dedicated to the collection of encyclopedias, specific resource manuals, card catalogs, and periodical indexes that provide information on the projected topic. Electronic research tools includes a listing of the latest and most effective search engines like Goggle, Microsoft, AOL, Infotrac, and Yahoo to find the topic of research, along with peripheral support information. Electronic databases that contain extensive resources help the user with selecting resources, choosing effective keywords, and constructing search strategies. The world of electronic research opens up a global library of resources for both print and electronic information.

Major online services such as Microsoft, Prodigy, and CompuServe provide users with specialized information that is either free or has a minimal charge assessed for that specific service or website. Online resources teach effective ways to bookmark sites of interest and provide information on how to cut and paste relevant information onto word documents for citation and reference.

Bookmarking favorite Internet searches that contain correct sources for reference can save a lot of research time. On AOL, bookmarking is known as "favorites"; with one click of the mouse, a user can type in the email address on the browser's location bar and create instant access to that location. Netscape uses the terminology of "bookmarks" to save browser locations for future research.

Online search engines and web portals create avenues of navigating the World Wide Web. Web portals provide linkages to other websites and are typically subdivided into other categories for searching. Portals are also specific to certain audience interests that index parts of the web. Search engines can provide additional strategic site searches.

COMPETENCY 7.0 UNDERSTAND THE CONVENTIONS OF STANDARD ENGLISH GRAMMAR, USAGE, AND MECHANICS

Skill 7.1 Demonstrating knowledge of the parts of speech

English grammar, in conventional use, classifies words based on the following eight parts of speech:

- **Verb**: Essential to a sentence, a verb asserts something about the subject of the sentence and expresses an action, event, or state of being. The verb is the critical element of the predicate of a sentence.

- **Noun**: A word used to name/identify a person, animal, place, thing, or abstract idea. Within the structure of a sentence, a noun can function as a subject, a direct or indirect object, a subject or object complement, an appositive, an adjective, or an adverb.

- **Pronoun**: This can be substituted for a noun or another pronoun. Pronoun classifications include the personal pronoun, the demonstrative pronoun, the interrogative pronoun, the indefinite pronoun, the relative pronoun, the reflexive pronoun, and the intensive pronoun. The appropriate use of pronouns (e.g., he, which, none, you) can make sentences less cumbersome and less repetitive (and, therefore, more readable).

- **Adjective**: A word that modifies a noun or a pronoun by describing, identifying, or quantifying other words. An adjective usually precedes the noun or the pronoun that it modifies.

- **Adverb**: A part of a sentence that can modify a verb, an adjective, another adverb, a phrase, or a clause. An adverb indicates manner, time, place, cause, or degree; it answers questions such as "how," "when," "where," or "how much." While some adverbs can be identified by the characteristic "ly" suffix, most adverbs must be identified by analyzing the grammatical relationships within the sentence or clause as a whole. Unlike the adjective, the adverb can be found in various places within the sentence.

- **Preposition**: This word links nouns, pronouns, and phrases to other words in a sentence. The word or phrase that the preposition introduces is the *object* of the preposition. A preposition usually indicates the temporal, spatial, or logical relationship of its object to the rest of the sentence (e.g., on, beneath, against, beside, over, during).

- **Conjunction**: This is used to link words, phrases, or clauses. For independent clauses, phrases, and individual words, **coordinating conjunctions (**e.g., and, but, or, nor, for, so, yet) are used. To introduce a dependent clause and indicate the nature of a relationship between the independent clause and dependent clause, a **subordinating conjunction** (e.g., after, although, as, because, before, how, if, once, since, than, that, though, until, when, where, whether, while) is used. Equivalent sentence elements are linked with **correlative conjunctions**, which always appear in pairs (e.g., both...and, either...or, neither...nor, not...only, but...also, so...as, whether...or). Strictly speaking, correlative conjunctions consist simply of a coordinating conjunction linked to an adjective or adverb.

- **Interjection**: A word added to a sentence to convey emotion, it usually compels the sentence to be closed with an exclamation mark. It is not grammatically related to any other part of the sentence. Some examples include "ouch," "hey," "wow," and "oh no!"

It is important to remember that each part of speech explains not what the word is, but how the word is used. For example, in some instances, the same word can be used as a noun in one sentence and as a verb or adjective in the next.

Skill 7.2   Demonstrating knowledge of elements of appropriate grammar and usage (e.g., subject verb agreement, noun-pronoun agreement, verb tense, correct pronoun usage in prepositional phrases)

Subject-Verb Agreement

A verb agrees in number with its subject. Making the two agree relies on the ability to properly identify the subject.

- <u>One</u> of the boys <u>was playing</u> too rough.
- <u>No one</u> in the class, not the teacher nor the students, <u>was listening</u> to the message from the intercom.
- The <u>candidates,</u> including a grandmother and a teenager, <u>are debating</u> some controversial issues.

If two singular subjects are connected by *and*, the verb must be plural.

- A man *and* his dog <u>were jogging</u> on the beach.

If two singular subjects are connected by *or* or *nor,* a singular verb is required.

- Neither Dot *nor* Joyce <u>has missed</u> a day of school this year.
- Either Fran *or* Paul <u>is</u> missing.

If one singular subject and one plural subject are connected by *or nor,* the verb agrees with the subject nearest to the verb.

- Neither the coach *nor* the <u>players</u> <u>were</u> able to sleep on the bus.

If the subject is a collective noun, its sense of number in the sentence determines the verb: singular if the noun represents a group or unit, and plural if the noun represents individuals.

- The <u>House of Representatives</u> <u>has adjourned</u> for the holidays.
- The<u> House of Representatives</u> <u>have failed</u> to reach an agreement on the subject of adjournment.

Pronoun-Antecedent Agreement

A noun is any word that names a person, place, thing, idea, animal, quality, or activity. A pronoun is a word that is used in place of a noun or more pronouns. The word or word group that a pronoun stands for (or refers to) is called its antecedent.

We use pronouns in many of the sentences that we write. Pronouns add variety to writing by enabling the writer to avoid a monotonous repetition of nouns. Pronouns also help to maintain coherence within and among sentences. Pronouns must agree with their antecedents in number and person. Therefore, if the antecedent is plural, a plural pronoun must be used; if the antecedent is feminine, a feminine pronoun must be used. The pronouns must show a clear reference to their antecedents as well.

The following are the nine different types of pronouns: *personal, possessive, indefinite, reflexive, reciprocal, intensive, interrogative, relative, and demonstrative.*

In order to aid students in revising their texts to correct errors, teachers should have them complete the following steps:

- Read with a focus only on pronouns.
- Circle each pronoun and draw an arrow to its antecedent.
- Replace the pronoun with a noun to eliminate a vague pronoun reference.
- Supply missing antecedents where needed.
- Place the pronoun so that the nearest noun is its antecedent.

Once the students focus on pronoun antecedent agreement a few times, they will progress from correcting errors to avoiding errors. The only way to develop a student's skill with pronoun reference is to focus clear attention on pronouns until it becomes a habit of his or her writing.

Other Agreement

Possessive nouns are used in context to show that something is owned and belongs within a contextual framework of the sentence or the passage. Nouns have common usages in describing people, places, or things; they also provide the collective thought and meaning of the sentence. Nouns provide singular or plural contextual identity to the subject matter being addressed in sentences. The specificity of nouns can describe a diversity of familiar names, places, and things: New York, Statue of Liberty, Coca-Cola, Pacific Ocean, Mom, Dad, student, teacher, life, and America. Nouns provide a common language for the reader in understanding the context of information.

In contrast, pronouns are supportive descriptors that take the place of nouns in a sentence. Pronouns, like nouns, can either be singular or plural in usage. The first person pronoun in a sentence that can take the place of a name in the singular sense include "I," "me," or "my"; in the plural sense, the pronoun descriptor becomes "we," "us," or "our." In second person, pronoun terms include "you" or "yours" (singular and plural, respectively), whereas in the third-person usage, the singular words, "he/she," "him/her," or "his/hers," become "they," "them," or "their." Pronouns can become subjects in sentences and direct or indirect objects in sentences. For example, "I work with a great Professor, and I like her."

Adjectives modify (or help to describe) people, places, or things. They are typically located in front of the noun or pronoun they describe in a sentence. For example, "The sick child stayed in the bed."

As an adjective works as in connection with nouns and pronouns, adverbs work as descriptors of verbs, adjectives, or other adverbs. For example, "Mary barely gets to work on time each day."

Adjectives and adverbs can be either comparative forms or superlative forms when comparisons occur in sentences "This book is lighter than the last book" or "She is the funniest sister in the family."

There are various forms of verbs that show action and the state of being in sentences. Verb forms can be present, present participle, past, or past participle. For example, in the sentence "She eats," the verbs become (respectively) "She is eating," "She ate," and "She has eaten." There are also irregular verbs used in sentences commonly containing "is," "were," and "been."

The importance of using the correct usage of possessive nouns, pronouns, verbs, adjectives, and adverbs is crucial in conveying meaning in written text. In connecting the reader with the written information, understanding how the information is presented creates an access to understanding the contextual aspect of the words. Using correct forms of support words is crucial in creating informative and accessible text.

Use of Verbs (Tense)

Present tense is used to express an action that is currently happening or is always true.

> Randy is playing the piano.
> Randy plays the piano like a pro.

Past tense is used to express an action that occurred in a past time.

> Randy learned to play the piano when he was six
> years old.

Future tense is used to express an action or a condition of future time.

> Randy will probably earn a music scholarship.

Present perfect tense is used to express an action or a condition that started in the past and is continued to or completed in the present.

> Randy has practiced piano every day for the last ten
> years.
> Randy has never been bored with practice.

Past perfect tense expresses an action or a condition that occurred as a precedent to some other action or condition.

> Randy had considered playing clarinet before he
> discovered the piano.

Future perfect tense expresses action that started in the past or the present and will conclude at some time in the future.

> By the time he goes to college, Randy will have
> been an accomplished pianist for more than half
> of his life.

Use of Verbs (Mood)

Indicative mood is used to make unconditional statements; *subjunctive mood* is used for conditional clauses or wish statements that pose untrue conditions. Verbs in subjunctive mood are plural for both singular and plural subjects.

> If I were a bird, I would fly.
> I wish I were as rich as Donald Trump.

Verb Conjugation

The conjugation of verbs follows the patterns used in the discussion of tense above. However, the most frequent problems in verb use stem from the improper formation of past and past participial forms.

> Regular verb: believe, believed, (have) believed
> Irregular verbs: run, ran, run; sit, sat, sat; teach, taught, taught

Other problems arise from the use of verbs that are the same in some tense but have different forms and different meanings in other tenses.

> I lie on the ground. I lay on the ground yesterday. I have lain down.

> I lay the blanket on the bed. I laid the blanket there yesterday. I have laid the blanket every night.

> The sun rises. The sun rose. The sun has risen.

> He raises the flag. He raised the flag. He had raised the flag.

> I sit on the porch. I sat on the porch. I have sat in the porch swing.

> I set the plate on the table. I set the plate there yesterday. I had set the table before dinner.

Two other verb problems often stem from misusing the preposition *of* for the verb auxiliary *have* and misusing the verb *ought* (now rare).

> Incorrect: I should of gone to bed.
> Correct: I should have gone to bed.

> Incorrect: He hadn't ought to get so angry.
> Correct: He ought not to get so angry.

Use of Pronouns

A pronoun used as a subject of predicate nominative occurs in the nominative case.

> She was the drum majorette. The lead trombonists were Joe and he. The band director accepted whoever could march in step.

A pronoun used as a direct object, an indirect object, or as the object of a preposition occurs in the objective case.

> The teacher praised him. She gave him an "A" on the test. Her praise of him was appreciated. The students whom she did not praise will work harder next time.

Common pronoun errors typically occur from the misuse of reflexive pronouns:

> Singular: myself, yourself, herself, himself, itself
> Plural: ourselves, yourselves, themselves

> Incorrect: Jack cut hisself shaving.
> Correct: Jack cut himself shaving.

> Incorrect: They backed theirselves into a corner.
> Correct: They backed themselves into a corner.

Use of Adjectives

An adjective should agree with its antecedent in number.

> Those apples are rotten. This one is ripe. These peaches are hard.

Comparative adjectives end in -er and superlatives in -est, with some exceptions like *worse* and *worst*. Some adjectives that cannot easily make comparative inflections are preceded by *more* and *most*.

> Mrs. Carmichael is the <u>better</u> of the two basketball coaches.

> That is the <u>hastiest</u> excuse you have ever contrived.

Avoid Double Comparisons

> Incorrect: This is the worstest headache I ever had.

Correct: This is the worst headache I ever had.

When comparing one thing to others in a group, exclude the thing under comparison from the rest of the group.

> Incorrect: Joey is larger than any baby I have ever seen. (Since you have seen him, he cannot be larger than himself.)
> Correct: Joey is larger than <u>any other</u> baby I have ever
> seen.

Include all necessary words to make a comparison clear in meaning.

> I am as tall as my mother. I am as tall as she (is).

> My cats are better behaved than those of my neighbor.

Plurals

The multiplicity and complexity of spelling rules based on phonics, letter doubling, and exceptions to rules—not mastered by adulthood—should be replaced by a good dictionary. As spelling mastery is also difficult for adolescents, the recommendation is the same. Learning the use of a dictionary and thesaurus is, overall, a rewarding use of time.

Most plurals of nouns that end in hard consonants or hard consonant sounds followed by a silent *e* are made by adding *s*. Some words ending in vowels only add *s*. For example:

> fingers, numerals, banks, bugs, riots, homes, gates, radios, bananas

For nouns that end in soft consonant sounds *s, j, x, z, ch,* and *sh,* add *es*. Some nouns ending in *o* also add *es*.

> dresses, waxes, churches, brushes, tomatoes

For nouns ending in *y* and preceded by a vowel, just add *s*.

> boys, alleys

For nouns ending in *y* and preceded by a consonant, change the *y* to *i* and add *es*.

> babies, corollaries, frugalities, poppies

Some nouns' plurals are formed irregularly or remain the same.

> sheep, deer, children, leaves, oxen

Some nouns derived from foreign words, especially Latin, may make their plurals in two different ways—one of them Anglicized. Sometimes, the meanings are the same; other times, the two plurals are used in slightly different contexts. It is always wise to consult the dictionary.

> appendices, appendixes   criterion, criteria
> indexes, indices   crisis, crises

Make the plurals of closed (solid) compound words in the usual way except for words ending in *ful*, which make their plurals on the root word.

> timelines, hairpins, cupsful

Make the plurals of open or hyphenated compounds by adding the change in inflection to the word that changed in number.

> fathers-in-law, courts-martial, masters of art, doctors of medicine

Make the plurals of letters, numbers, and abbreviations by adding *s*.

> fives and tens, IBMs, 1990s, *p*s and *q*s (Note that letters are italicized.)

Possessives

Make the possessives of singular nouns by adding an apostrophe followed by the letter *s* (´s).

> baby's bottle, father's job, elephant's eye, teacher's desk,
> sympathizer's protests, week's postponement

Make the possessive of singular nouns ending in *s* by adding either an apostrophe or an (´s) depending upon common usage or sound. When making the possessive causes difficulty, use a prepositional phrase instead. Even with the sibilant ending, it is advisable to use the (´s) construction (with a few exceptions).

> dress's color, species' characteristics or characteristics of the
> species, James' hat or James's hat, Delores's shirt.

Make the possessive of plural nouns ending in *s* by adding the apostrophe after the *s*.

> horses' coats, jockeys' times, four days' time

Make possessives of plural nouns that do not end in *s* the same as singular nouns by adding ´s.

> children's shoes, deer's antlers, cattle's horns

Make possessives of compound nouns by adding the inflection at the end of the word or phrase.

> the mayor of Los Angeles' campaign, the mailman's new truck, the mailmen's new trucks, my father-in-law's first wife, the keepsakes' values, several daughters-in-law's husbands

Note: Because a gerund functions as a noun, any noun preceding it and operating as a possessive adjective must reflect the necessary inflection. However, if the gerundive following the noun is a participle, no inflection is added.

> The general was perturbed by the private's sleeping on duty. (The word *sleeping* is a gerund, the object of the preposition *by*.

> *but*

> The general was perturbed to see the private sleeping on duty. (The word *sleeping* is a participle modifying private.)

Skill 7.3   Demonstrating knowledge of appropriate mechanics in writing (e.g., capitalization, punctuation)

The candidate should be cognizant of proper rules and conventions of punctuation, capitalization, and spelling. Competency exams will generally test the ability to apply more advanced skills; thus, a limited number of more frustrating rules are presented here. Rules should be applied according to the American style of English, i.e. spelling *theater* instead of *theatre* and placing terminal marks of punctuation almost exclusively within other marks of punctuation.

Capitalization

Capitalize all proper names of persons (including specific organizations or agencies of government); places (countries, states, cities, parks, and specific geographical areas); things (political parties, structures, historical and cultural terms, and calendar and time designations); and religious terms (any deity, revered person or group, sacred writings).

> Percy Bysshe Shelley, Argentina, Mount Rainier National Park, Grand Canyon, League of Nations, the Sears Tower, Birmingham, Lyric Theater, Americans, Midwesterners, Democrats, Renaissance, Boy Scouts of America, Easter, God, Bible, Dead Sea Scrolls, Koran

Capitalize proper adjectives and titles used with proper names.

California gold rush, President John Adams, Homeric epic, Romanesque architecture, Senator John Glenn

Note: Some words that represent titles and offices are not capitalized unless used with a proper name.

Capitalized	Not Capitalized
Congressman McKay	the congressman from Florida
Commander Alger	commander of the Pacific Fleet
Queen Elizabeth	the queen of England

Capitalize all main words in titles of works of literature, art, and music. (See "Using Italics" in the Punctuation section.)

Punctuation

Using Terminal Punctuation in Relation to Quotation Marks

In a quoted statement that is either declarative or imperative, place the period inside the closing quotation marks.

"The airplane crashed on the runway during takeoff."

If the quotation is followed by other words in the sentence, place a comma inside the closing quotation marks and a period at the end of the sentence.

"The airplane crashed on the runway during takeoff," said the announcer.

In most instances in which a quoted title or expression occurs at the end of a sentence, the period is placed before either the single or double quotation marks.

"The middle school readers were unprepared to understand Bryant's poem 'Thanatopsis.'"

Early book-length adventure stories like *Don Quixote* and *The Three Musketeers* were known as "picaresque novels."

There are instances in which the final quotation mark does precede the period— for example, if the content of the sentence is about a speech or quote in which the meaning could be confused by the placement of the period.

The first thing out of his mouth was "Hi, I'm home."
but

The first line of his speech began "I arrived home to an empty house".

In sentences that are interrogatory or exclamatory, the question mark or exclamation point should be positioned outside the closing quotation marks if the quote itself is a statement, command, or cited title.

Who decided to lead us in the recitation of the "Pledge of Allegiance"?
Why was Tillie shaking as she began her recitation, "Once upon a midnight dreary..."?
I was embarrassed when Mrs. White said, "Your slip is showing"!

In sentences that are declarative but the quotation is a question or an exclamation, place the question mark or exclamation point inside the quotation marks.

The hall monitor yelled, "Fire! Fire!"
"Fire! Fire!" yelled the hall monitor.

Cory shrieked, "Is there a mouse in the room?" (In this instance, the question supersedes the exclamation.)

Using Periods with Parentheses or Brackets

Place the period inside the parentheses or brackets if they enclose a complete sentence, independent of the other sentences around it.

Stephen Crane was a confirmed alcohol and drug addict. (He admitted as much to other journalists in Cuba.)

If the parenthetical expression is a statement inserted within another statement, the period in the enclosure is omitted.

Mark Twain used the character Indian Joe (who also appeared in *The Adventures of Tom Sawyer*) as a foil for Jim in *The Adventures of Huckleberry Finn*.

When enclosed matter comes at the end of a sentence requiring quotation marks, place the period outside the parentheses or brackets.

"The secretary of state consulted with the ambassador [Albright]."

Using Commas

Separate two or more coordinate adjectives modifying the same word and three or more nouns, phrases, or clauses in a list.

Maggie's hair was dull, dirty, and lice-ridden.

Dickens portrayed the Artful Dodger as skillful pickpocket, loyal follower of Fagin, and defendant of Oliver Twist.

Ellen daydreamed about getting out of the rain, taking a shower, and eating a hot dinner.

In Elizabethan England, Ben Johnson wrote comedy, Christopher Marlowe wrote tragedies, and William Shakespeare composed both.

Use commas to separate antithetical or complimentary expressions from the rest of the sentence.

The veterinarian, not his assistant, would perform the delicate surgery.

The more he knew about her, the less he wished he had known.

Randy hopes to, and probably will, get an appointment to the Naval Academy.

His thorough, though esoteric, scientific research could not easily be understood by high school students.

Using Double Quotation Marks with Other Punctuation

Quotations—whether words, phrases, or clauses—should be punctuated according to the rules of the grammatical function they serve in the sentence.

The works of Shakespeare, "the bard of Avon," have been contested as originating with other authors.

"You'll get my money," the old man warned, "when 'Hell freezes over'."

Sheila cited the passage that began "Four score and seven years ago...." (Note the ellipsis followed by an enclosed period.)

"Old Ironsides" inspired the preservation of the U.S.S. Constitution.

Use quotation marks to enclose the titles of shorter works: songs, short poems, short stories, essays, and chapters of books. (See "Using Italics" for punctuating longer titles.)

"The Tell-Tale Heart" "Casey at the Bat"   "America the Beautiful"

Using Semicolons

Use semicolons to separate independent clauses when the second clause is introduced by a transitional adverb. (These clauses may also be written as separate sentences, preferably by placing the adverb within the second sentence.)

> The Elizabethans modified the rhyme scheme of the sonnet; thus, it was called the English sonnet.
> *or*
> The Elizabethans modified the rhyme scheme of the sonnet. It was thus called the English sonnet.

Use semicolons to separate items in a series that are long and complex or have internal punctuation.

> The Italian Renaissance produced masters in the fine arts: Dante Alighieri, author of the *Divine Comedy;* Leonardo da Vinci, painter of *The Last Supper;* and Donatello, sculptor of the *Quattro Coronati*, the four saints.

> The leading scorers in the WNBA were: Zheng Haixia, averaging 23.9 points per game; Lisa Leslie, 22; and Cynthia Cooper, 19.5.

When using a semicolon in conjunction with quotation marks, the semicolon falls outside the final quotation mark (even when a period applied in the same situation falls inside the final quotation mark).

> Jane Austen's final novel was "Persuasion."
> *but*
> Jane Austen's final novel was "Persuasion"; some critics consider it her best work.

Using Colons

Place a colon at the beginning of a list of items. (Note its use in the sentence about Renaissance Italians on the previous page.)

> The teacher directed us to compare Faulkner's three symbolic novels: *Absalom, Absalom; As I Lay Dying;* and *Light in August.*

Do **not** use a colon if the list is preceded by a verb.

> Three of Faulkner's symbolic novels are *Absalom, Absalom; As I Lay Dying,* and *Light in August.*

Using Dashes

Place dashes to denote sudden breaks in thought.

> Some periods in literature—the Romantic Age, for example—spanned different time periods in different countries.

Use dashes instead of commas if commas are already used elsewhere in the sentence for amplification or explanation.

> The Fireside Poets included three Brahmans—James Russell Lowell, Henry David Wadsworth, Oliver Wendell Holmes— and John Greenleaf Whittier.

Use italics to punctuate the titles of long works of literature, names of periodical publications, musical scores, works of art and motion picture television, and radio programs. (When unable to write in italics, students should be instructed to underline in their own writing where italics would be appropriate.)

The Idylls of the King	*Hiawatha*	*The Sound and the Fury*
Mary Poppins	*Newsweek*	*The Nutcracker Suite*

Skill 7.4 Identifying appropriate corrections of errors in sentence structure (e.g., run-on sentences, misplaced modifiers, sentence fragments)

Fragments

Fragments occur 1) if word groups standing alone are missing either a subject or a verb, and 2) if word groups containing a subject, containing a verb, and standing alone are actually made dependent because of the use of subordinating conjunctions or relative pronouns.

Error: The teacher waiting for the class to complete the assignment.

Problem: This sentence is not complete because an -ing word alone does not function as a verb. When a helping verb is added (for example, was waiting), it will become a sentence.

Correction: The teacher was waiting for the class to complete the assignment.

Sentence Completeness

Avoid fragments and run-on sentences. Recognizing sentence elements necessary to make a complete thought, properly using independent and dependent clauses (see *Use Correct Coordination and Subordination*), and using correct punctuation will amend such errors.

Sentence Structure

Recognize simple, compound, complex, and compound-complex sentences. Use dependent (subordinate) and independent clauses correctly to create these sentence structures.

Simple	Joyce wrote a letter.
Compound	Joyce wrote a letter, and Dot drew a picture.
Complex	While Joyce wrote a letter, Dot drew a picture.
Compound/Complex	When Mother asked the girls to demonstrate their new-found skills, Joyce wrote a letter, and Dot drew a picture.

Note: *Do not* confuse compound sentence elements with compound sentences.

Simple sentence with compound subject:

> Joyce and Dot wrote letters.
> The girl in row three and the boy next to her were passing notes across the aisle.

Simple sentence with compound predicate:

> Joyce wrote letters and drew pictures.
> The captain of the high school debate team graduated with honors and studied broadcast journalism in college.

Simple sentence with compound object of preposition:

> Colleen graded the students' essays for style and mechanical accuracy.

Parallelism

Recognize parallel structures using phrases (prepositional, gerund, participial, and infinitive) and omissions from sentences that create the lack of parallelism.

Prepositional Phrase/Single Modifier

Incorrect: Colleen ate the ice cream with enthusiasm and hurriedly.
Correct: Colleen ate the ice cream with enthusiasm and in a hurry.
Correct: Colleen ate the ice cream enthusiastically and hurriedly.

Participial Phrase/Infinitive Phrase

Incorrect: After hiking for hours and to sweat profusely, Joe sat down to rest and drinking water.
Correct: After hiking for hours and sweating profusely, Joe sat down to rest and drink water.

Recognition of Dangling Modifiers

Dangling phrases are attached to sentence parts in a way that create ambiguity and incorrectness of meaning.

Participial Phrase

Incorrect: Hanging from her skirt, Dot tugged at a loose thread.
Correct: Dot tugged at a loose thread hanging from her skirt.

Incorrect: Relaxing in the bathtub, the telephone rang.
Correct: While I was relaxing in the bathtub, the telephone rang.

Infinitive Phrase

Incorrect: To improve his behavior, the dean warned Fred.
Correct: The dean warned Fred to improve his behavior.

Prepositional Phrase

Incorrect: On the floor, Father saw the dog eating table scraps.
Correct: Father saw the dog eating table scraps on the floor.

Recognition of Syntactical Redundancy or Omission

These errors occur when superfluous words have been added to a sentence or key words have been omitted from a sentence.

Redundancy

Incorrect: Joyce made sure that when her plane arrived that she retrieved all of her luggage.

Correct: Joyce made sure that when her plane arrived she retrieved all of her luggage.

Incorrect: He was a mere skeleton of his former self.
Correct: He was a skeleton of his former self.

Omission

Incorrect: Dot opened her book, recited her textbook, and answered the teacher's subsequent question.

Correct: Dot opened her book, recited from the textbook, and answered the teacher's subsequent question.

Avoidance of Double Negatives

This error occurs from positioning two negatives that, in fact, cancel each other in meaning.

Incorrect: Dot didn't have no double negatives in her paper.
Correct: Dot didn't have any double negatives in her paper.

Skill 7.5 Demonstrating knowledge of various types of sentence structures (e.g., declarative, interrogative)

Teachers can instruct students to classify a sentence structure according to its purpose. Have the students ask themselves, "Why did the writer write this sentence this way?" The answer is then likely to lead them to the function of the sentence classification. Students can then classify sentences based on their purpose.

There are four types of sentences: *declarative, interrogative, imperative,* and *exclamatory*.

1. A **declarative sentence** makes a statement and ends with a period. Declarative sentences consist of a subject and a predicate.

2. An **interrogative sentence** asks a question and ends with a question mark, in addition to having a different tonal pattern (often a raised tone near the end of the sentence).

3. An **imperative sentence** gives a command or makes a request. Sometimes the subject of an imperative sentence (you) is understood without being written.

4. An **exclamatory sentence** emphasizes a statement (either declarative or imperative), shows strong feeling, and ends with an exclamation mark.

Declarative, imperative, or interrogative sentences can be made into exclamatory sentences by punctuating them with an exclamation point.

Students should be taught to utilize the various sentence types in their writing in order to create and combine diverse sentences for writing effective paragraphs.

COMPETENCY 8.0   UNDERSTAND SKILLS AND STRATEGIES INVOLVED IN SPEAKING, LISTENING, AND VIEWING ACROSS THE CURRICULUM

Skill 8.1   Applying knowledge of conventions of one-on-one and group verbal interactions (e.g., turn taking, responding to questions with appropriate information)

Listening is not a skill that is talked about much, except when someone clearly does not listen. The truth is, however, that listening is a very specific skill for very specific circumstances. There are two aspects to listening that warrant attention. The first is comprehension. This is simply understanding what someone says, the purposes behind the message, and the context in which it is said. The second is purpose. While someone may completely understand a message, what is the listener supposed to do with it? Just nod and smile? Go out and take action? While listening comprehension is indeed a significant skill in itself that deserves a lot of focus in the classroom (much in the same way that reading comprehension does), we will focus on purpose here. Often, when we understand the purpose of listening in various contexts, comprehension will be much easier. Furthermore, when we know the purpose of listening, we can better adjust our comprehension strategies.

First, when complex or new information is provided to us orally, we must analyze and interpret that information. What is the author's most important point? How do the figures of speech impact meaning? How are conclusions made? Often, making sense of this information can be tough when presented orally—first, because we have no place to go back and review material already stated; second, because oral language is so much less predictable than written language. However, when we focus on extracting the meaning, message, and speaker's purpose (rather than just "listening" and waiting for things to make sense for us—in other words, when we are more "active" in our listening), we have greater success in interpreting speech.

Second, listening is often done for the purpose of enjoyment. We like to listen to stories; we enjoy poetry; we like radio dramas and theater. Listening to literature can also be a great pleasure. The problem today is that students have not learned to extract great pleasure on a wide-spread scale from listening to literature, poetry, or language read aloud. Perhaps that is because we have not done a good job of showing students how listening to literature (or other oral communications) can indeed be more interesting than television or video games. In the classrooms of exceptional teachers, we will often find that students are captivated by the reading aloud of good literature. It is refreshing and enjoyable to just sit and soak in the language, story, and poetry of literature when it is read to us. Therefore, we must teach students *how* to listen and enjoy such work. We do this by making it fun and giving many possibilities and alternatives to capture the wide array of interests in each classroom.

Finally, we will discuss listening in large and small group conversations. The difference here is that conversation requires more than just listening: it involves feedback and active involvement. This can be particularly challenging, as in our culture, we are trained to move conversations along, to discourage silence in a conversation, and to always get the last word in. In a discussion, for example, when we are preparing our next response—rather than listening to what others are saying—we do a large disservice to the entire discussion. Students need to learn how listening carefully to others in discussions actually promotes better responses on the part of subsequent speakers. One way teachers can encourage this in both large and small group discussions is to expect students to respond *directly* to the previous student's comments before moving ahead with their new comments. This will encourage them to pose their new comments in light of the comments that came just before them.

Skill 8.2   Analyzing ways in which verbal cues (e.g., word choice, tone, volume) and nonverbal cues (e.g., body language, eye contact) affect communication in various situations

Analyzing the speech of others is a very good technique for helping students to improve their own public speaking abilities. In most circumstances, because students cannot view themselves as they give speeches and presentations, they begin to learn what works and what doesn't work in effective public speaking when they get the opportunity to critique, question, and analyze others' speeches. However, a very important word of warning: DO NOT have students critique each others' public speaking skills. It could be very damaging to a student to have his or her peers point out what did not work in a speech. Instead, video is a great tool teachers can use. Any appropriate source of public speaking can be used in the classroom for students to analyze and critique.

Some of the things students can pay attention to include the following:

- **Volume:** A speaker should use an appropriate volume—not too loud to be annoying, but not too soft to be inaudible.
- **Pace:** The rate at which words are spoken should be appropriate—not too fast to make the speech incomprehensible, but not too slow so as to put listeners to sleep.
- **Pronunciation**: A speaker should make sure words are spoken clearly. Listeners do not have a text to go back to, and they cannot re-read things they didn't catch.
- **Body language:** While animated body language can help a speech, too much of it can be distracting. Body language should help to convey the message, not detract from it.
- **Word choice:** The words speakers choose should be consistent with their intended purpose as well as the audience.
- **Visual aids:** Visual aids, like body language, should enhance a message. Many visual aids can be distracting, which can detract from the message.

Overall, instead of telling students to keep these above factors in mind when presenting information orally, it may be beneficial to have them view speakers who do these things both well and poorly. Witnessing other speakers first-hand will help students to remember the "rules" the next time they give a speech.

Skill 8.3   Demonstrating knowledge of strategies for promoting effective listening skills

Oral speech can be very difficult to follow, as listeners typically have no written record in which to "re-read" things they didn't hear or understand. In addition, oral speech can be much less structured than written language. At the same time, many of the skills and strategies that help students in reading comprehension can help them in listening comprehension. For example, as soon as we start listening to something new, we should tap into our prior knowledge in order to attach new information to what we already know. This will not only help in understanding, but it will also assist in remembering the material.

We can also look for transitions between ideas. Sometimes, in oral speech, this is fairly simple to find (such as when voice tone or body language change). Although we don't have the luxury of looking at paragraphs in oral language, we do have the animation that comes along with live speech. Human beings have to try very hard to be completely non-expressive in their speech. Listeners should take advantage of this and notice how the speaker changes character and voice to signal a transition of ideas.

Listeners can also better comprehend the underlying intent of a speaker when they notice nonverbal cues. For example, looking to see an expression on the face of a speaker that signals irony is often simpler than trying to extract irony from written words.

One good way to follow oral speech is to take notes and outline major points. Because oral speech can be more circular (as opposed to linear) than written text, it can be of great assistance to keep track of an author's message. Students can practice this strategy in many ways in the classroom, including taking notes during the teacher's oral messages as well as other students' presentations and speeches.

Additional classroom methods can help students to learn good listening skills. For example, teachers can have students practice following complex directions. They can also have students orally re-tell stories—or re-tell (in writing or in oral speech) oral presentations of stories or other materials. These activities give students direct practice in the very important skills of listening. They provide students with outlets in which they can slowly improve their abilities to comprehend oral language; they also allow students to take decisive action based on oral speech.

Skill 8.4 **Recognizing types, characteristics, and roles of visual and oral media (e.g., television, radio, film, electronic media)**

The use of the media, television, radio, film, internet resources, and other electronic sources has become an asset in teaching, as they encourage students to practice critical thinking. The use of media offers new ways of engaging students in learning and in making connections among themselves, between school and life, and between educators and the outside world. Teachers should utilize a variety of media, as it is through the media that our culture largely expresses itself.

Media literacy is an informed, critical understanding gleaned from verbal and visual symbols that are experienced every day through television, radio, computers, and other electronic sources. Teachers should be aware of the need for students to develop critical *viewing* abilities along with critical *thinking* abilities when viewing various types of media. Critical viewing involves examining the techniques and characteristics that are involved in media production, critically analyzing media messages, and recognizing the roles that audiences play in deriving meaning from those messages.

When listening to a radio program, viewing a film, or watching a television program, students should ask themselves some key questions:

- What is this program's point of view?
- What persuasive techniques are used?
- What evidence is used to support the program's argument?
- Is there a media stereotyping, or are there correct representations of gender, race, and ethnicity?

Teachers should have an understanding of how to select, evaluate, and use information from television, radio, film, and electronic media sources. The key component of media literacy is understanding the symbols, information, ideas, values, and messages that emanate from the media. Teachers should choose appropriate media selection by analyzing the various instructional media programs available. This will help them to achieve learning goals, which, after all, is the motivation for the use of technology.

Skill 8.5   Demonstrating knowledge of the structures and elements of oral, visual, and multimedia presentations for diverse audiences and for various purposes

The media's impact on today's society is immense and ever-increasing. As children, we watch programs on television that are amazingly fast-paced and visually rich. Parents' roles as verbal and moral teachers are diminishing in response to the much more stimulating guidance of the television set. Adolescence, which used to be the time for going out and exploring the world first-hand, is now consumed by the allure of MTV, popular music, and video games.

At the same time, the media's effect on society is also beneficial and progressive. In particular, its effect on education provides special challenges and opportunities for teachers and students.

Thanks to satellite technology, instructional radio and television programs can be received by urban classrooms and rural villages. CD-ROMs allow students to learn information through a virtual reality experience. The Internet allows instant access to unlimited data and connects people across cultures. Educational media, when used in a productive way, enriches instruction and makes it more individualized, accessible, and economical.

Multimedia Teaching Model

Step 1. Diagnose
- Figure out what students need to know.
- Assess what students already know.

Step 2. Design
- Design tests of learning achievement.
- Identify effective instructional strategies.
- Select suitable media.
- Sequence learning activities within the program.
- Plan introductory activities.
- Plan follow-up activities.

Step 3. Procure
- Secure materials at hand.
- Obtain new materials.

Step 4. Produce
- Modify existing materials.
- Craft new materials.

Step 5. Refine

- Conduct a small-scale test of the program.
- Evaluate procedures and achievements.
- Revise the program accordingly.
- Conduct a classroom test of the program.
- Evaluate procedures and achievements.
- Revise the program in anticipation of the next school term.

Tips for Using Print Media and Visual Aids

- Use pictures over words whenever possible.
- Present one key point per visual.
- Use no more than three to four colors per visual to avoid clutter and confusion.
- Use contrasting colors such as dark blue and bright yellow.
- Use a maximum of twenty-five to thirty-five numbers per visual aid.
- Use bullets instead of paragraphs whenever possible.
- Make sure it is student-centered, not media-centered. The delivery is just as important as the media presented.

Tips for Using Film and Television

- Study the programs in advance.
- Obtain supplementary materials such as printed transcripts of the narrative or study guides.
- Provide students with background information, explain unfamiliar concepts, and anticipate outcomes.
- Assign outside readings based on the students' viewing.
- Ask cuing questions.
- Watch along with the students.
- Observe the students' reactions.
- Follow up the viewing with discussions and related activities.

The Media and Culture

Research is beginning to document the ways in which cultural minority parents interact with their children to support learning. The research mostly focuses on how these interactions differ from more mainstream or middle-class approaches.

One recent study explored the non-traditional ways in which Hispanic parents are involved in their children's education; ways that are not necessarily recognized by educators as parent involvement. However, further research is needed to delve more deeply into the connections that diverse families create, as traditional indicators do not always recognize effective interactions. More studies are also needed to consider the reasons why some diverse families might not be involved in the more traditional ways. Building a body of knowledge about the specific practices of various cultural groups may support the validation of those practices by school personnel, and this research may even support sharing effective practices across cultural groups.

Interactive Homework Assignments

The development of interactive homework assignments (homework that requires parent-child interaction as part of the activity) has shown promise as a way of supporting parent involvement and student achievement. Homework activities that are explicitly designed to be interactive have shown positive results for increasing achievement in several subject areas, including science and the language arts. Well-designed interactive assignments can have a number of positive outcomes: they can help students to practice study skills, to prepare for class, to participate in learning activities, and to develop personal responsibility for homework. These assignments may also promote parent-child relations, develop parent-teacher communication, and fulfill policy directives from administrators.

School Support of Parental Homework Help

Although parents express positive feelings about homework, many have concerns about their children's homework, including their personal limitations in subject-matter knowledge and effective helping strategies. More research is needed on how school personnel can effectively support parental homework help.

Teachers have a critical role to play in encouraging multicultural experiences. They have an opportunity to incorporate activities that reflect our nation's increasing diversity by allowing students to share their similarities, to develop a positive cultural identity, and to appreciate the unique contributions of all cultures. For example, one of the best ways to incorporate multicultural literature (depicting African American, Asian, Arabic, Native American, and Hispanic heritage) is to integrate it into the established reading program rather than to teach it as a separate or distinct area of study.

COMPETENCY 9.0   UNDERSTAND IMPORTANT EVENTS, CONCEPTS, AND METHODS OF INQUIRY RELATED TO GEORGIA, U.S., AND WORLD HISTORY

Skill 9.1   Recognizing chronological relationships among historical events

Chronology is the ordering of events through time. Chronologies are often listed along a timeline or in a list by date.

Chronologies allow for an easy visualization of a wide expanse of history. Information condensed this way allows a student to quickly get an overview of the major events and changes over time. By focusing on important related events, the causes and effects of major developments can be emphasized. In addition, in placing chronologies for different societies parallel to one another, comparisons in relative development can be quickly interpreted, providing material for further historical exploration.

Historic causation is the concept that events in history are linked to one another by and endless chain of cause and effect. The root causes of major historical events cannot always be seen immediately; they are often only apparent when looking back from many years later.

When Columbus landed in the New World in 1492, the full effect of his discovery could not have been measured at that time. By opening the Western Hemisphere to economic and political developments from Europeans, Columbus changed the face of the world. The Native populations that had existed before Columbus arrived were fairly quickly decimated by disease and warfare. Over the following century, the Spanish conquered most of South and Central America; English and French settlers arrived in North America, eventually displacing the Native people. This gradual displacement took place over many years and could not have been foreseen by those early explorers. Nevertheless, looking back, it can be said that Columbus caused a series of events that greatly impacted world history.

In some cases, individual events do have an immediate, clear effect. In 1941, Europe was embroiled in war. On the Pacific Rim, Japan was engaged in a military occupation of Korea and other Asian countries. The United States took a position of isolation, choosing not to become directly involved with the conflicts. This position changed rapidly, however, on the morning of December 7, 1941, when Japanese forces launched a surprise attack on a U.S. naval base at Pearl Harbor in Hawaii. The United States immediately declared war on Japan and became involved in Europe shortly afterwards. The entry of the United States into the Second World War undoubtedly contributed to the eventual victory of the Allied forces in Europe and the defeat of Japan after two atomic bombs were dropped there by the United States. The surprise attack on Pearl Harbor affected the outcome of the war and the shape of the modern world.

Interactions between cultures—either by exploration, migration, or war—often contribute directly to major historical events; however, other forces can influence the course of history as well. Religious movements, such as the rise of Catholicism in the Middle Ages, created social changes throughout Europe and culminated in the Crusades and the expulsion of Muslims from Spain. Technological developments can also lead to major historical events, as in the case of the Industrial Revolution, which was driven by the replacement of water power with steam power.

Social movements can also cause major historical shifts. Between the Civil War and the early 1960s in the United States, racial segregation was practiced legally in many parts of the country through "Jim Crow" laws. Demonstrations and activism opposing segregation began to escalate during the late 1950s and early 1960s, eventually leading to the passage in the U.S. Congress of the Civil Rights Act of 1964, effectively ending legal segregation in the United States.

Even now, all of these examples of historical occurrences can be changed by the passage of time. Viewed in light of the entire scope of U.S. history, the events of fifty years ago are still incredibly pertinent to today's society. Viewed in light of the entire scope of world history, the events of 500 years ago may have less of an overall impact than those changes wrought 5,000 years ago. Chronology, like time, is relative. Students must have a grasp of how events relate to one another and to history as a whole in order to understand what the events mean in a greater context.

Skill 9.2 **Demonstrating knowledge of the importance and lasting influence of diverse people, events, issues, and developments in Georgia, U.S., and world history (e.g., slavery, roots of democracy, westward expansion, the Civil War, World Wars I and II, the Cold War, civil rights movement)**

History is the study of the past, especially aspects of human past: political incidents, economic events, and cultural and social conditions. Students study history through textbooks, research, field trips to museums and historical sights, and other hands-on methods. Most nations set requirements in history around the study of their own country's heritage, usually to develop an awareness and feeling of loyalty and patriotism.

For better comprehension, history can be divided into the three main classifications: *a) time periods, b) nations* (in terms of a group of peoples sharing political and social boundaries, not necessarily nations as we know them today), and *c) specialized topics*. In the following pages, all of the provided historical information for study falls into one of these three divisions. Note that the three categories can and do overlap in some of their content; this is a natural outcome of the complex details that make up our world's history. For example, Imperial and Feudal Japan can fall under the categories of both time period and nation. It is a time period in that there were definite years when Imperialism and Feudalism were common forms of government. At the same time, the provided information deals only with those forms of government in Japan. In order to understand history in a greater context, the reader must grasp that with history, all things are relative; comparisons and chronologies can be manipulated to provide evidence for any line of reasoning the reader wishes to take.

Examples of Time Periods

Prehistory

Prehistory is defined as the period of mankind's achievements before the development of writing. In the Stone Age cultures, there were three different periods. They include the *Lower Paleolithic Period*, which is characterized by the use of crude tools; the *Upper Paleolithic Period*, which exhibited a greater variety of more intricate tools and implements, the adoption of wearing clothing, a highly organized group life, and skills in art; and finally, the *Neolithic Period*, during which time the people domesticated animals; formalized food production; practiced the arts of knitting, spinning, and weaving cloth; started fires through friction; built domestic shelters; and developed the institutions of family, religion, and government.

Tang Dynasty

The *Tang Dynasty* extended from 618 to 907 CE. Its capital was the most heavily populated of any city in the world at the time. Buddhism was adopted by the imperial family (Li) and became an integral part of Chinese culture. The emperor, however, feared the monasteries and began to take action against them in the tenth century. Confucianism experienced a rebirth during the time of this dynasty as an instrument of state administration.

Following a civil war, the central government lost control of local areas. Warlords arose in 907, and China was divided into North and South. These areas came to be ruled by short-lived minor dynasties. A major political accomplishment of this period was the creation of a class of career government officials who functioned between the populace and the government. This class of "scholar-officials" continued to fulfill this function in government and society until 1911.

The period of the Tang Dynasty is generally considered a pinnacle of Chinese civilization. Through contact with the Middle East and India, the period was marked by great creativity in many areas. Block printing was invented; it made much information and literature available to wide audiences. In science, astronomers calculated the paths of the sun and the moon as well as the movements of the constellations. This facilitated the development of the calendar. In agriculture, such technologies as land cultivation by setting it on fire, the curved-shaft plow, separate cultivation of seedlings, and sophisticated irrigation systems increased productivity. Hybrid breeds of horses and mules were created to strengthen the labor supply. In medicine, there were achievements like the understanding of the circulatory and digestive systems as well as great advances in pharmacology.

Ceramics was another area in which great advances were made. A new type of glazing was invented; it gave the dynasty's porcelain and earthenware its unique appearance through three-colored glazing.

In literature, the poetry of the period is generally considered the best in the entire history of Chinese literature. The rebirth of Confucianism led to the publication of many commentaries on his classical writings. Encyclopedias on several subjects were produced, as well as histories and philosophical works.

Middle Ages

In Europe, the system of *feudalism* was one of loyalty and protection. The strong and wealthy protected the weak, who, in turn, provided services in farm labor, military service, and lifelong allegiances. Life was typically lived on a vast estate, owned by a nobleman and his family, called a "manor." It was a complete village supporting a few hundred people, mostly peasants. Improved tools and farming methods made life more bearable, although most people never left the manor or traveled from their village during their entire lifetimes.

In feudal societies, a very small number of people owned land. Instead, they held it as a hereditary trust from some social or political superior in return for services. The superiors were a small percentage of the people; they were a fighting and ruling aristocracy. The vast majority of the people were simply workers. One of the largest landowners of the time was the Roman Catholic Church. It was estimated that during the twelfth and thirteenth centuries, the Church controlled one-third of the useable land in Western Europe.

In addition to the tremendous influence of the Church, the era of knighthood and its code of chivalry also came into importance at this time. Until the period of the Renaissance, the Church was the only place where people could be educated. The Bible and other books were hand-copied by monks in the monasteries. Cathedrals were built and decorated with art depicting religious subjects.

With the increase in trade and travel, cities sprang up and began to grow. Craft workers in the cities developed their skills to a high degree, eventually organizing guilds to protect the quality of the work and to regulate the buying and selling of their products. City government, centered on strong town councils, developed and flourished. The wealthy businessmen who made up the rising middle class were the most active in city government and town councils.

The end of the feudal manorial system was sealed by the outbreak and spread of the infamous *Black Death*, which killed over one-third of the total population of Europe. Those who survived and were skilled in any job or occupation were in demand; for the first time, many serfs and peasants found freedom and (for that time period) a decidedly improved standard of living. Strong *nation-states* became powerful, and people developed a renewed interest in life and learning.

Imperial and Feudal Japan

From its beginnings, Japan operated under an Imperial form of government. The divine emperor was believed to do no wrong and, therefore, served for his entire life. *Kyoto*, the capital, became one of the largest and most powerful cities in the world. As in Europe, however, the rich and powerful landowners—the nobles—grew powerful over time. Eventually, the nobles had more power than the emperor, which required a change in attitude in the minds of the Japanese people.

The nobles of Japan were lords of great lands; they were called *Daimyos*. They were of the highest social class, and people of lower social classes worked for them. The workers included the lowly peasants, who had few privileges other than being allowed to work for the great men that the Daimyos told everyone they were. Serving them, the Daimyos had warriors known as *Shogun,* who were answerable only to the Daimyo. The Shogun code of honor was an exemplification of the overall Japanese belief that every man was a soldier and a gentleman. The contradiction that the emerging social classes identified didn't seem to get noticed much, nor did the needs of women.

The main economic difference between Imperial and Feudal Japan was that the money that continued to flow into the country from trade with China, Korea, and other Asian countries (and from good old-fashioned plundering on the high seas) made its way into the pockets of the Daimyos rather than the emperor's coffers.

Feudalism developed in Japan later than it did in Europe, and it lasted longer as well. Japan dodged one huge historical bullet when a huge Mongol invasion was driven away by the famed *kamikaze*, or "divine wind," in the twelfth century. Japan was thus free to continue to develop itself as it saw fit and to refrain from interacting with the West. This isolation lasted until the nineteenth century.

Scientific Revolution

The *Scientific Revolution* was characterized by a shift in scientific approaches and ideas. Near the end of the sixteenth century, *Galileo Galilei* introduced a radical approach to the study of motion. He moved from attempts to explain the general reasons why objects move the way they do and began to use experiments to describe precisely how they move. He also used experimentation to describe how forces affect non-moving objects. Other scientists continued in the same approach.

Outstanding scientists of the period also included: *Johannes Kepler, Evangelista Torricelli, Blaise Pascal, Isaac Newton*, and *Gottfried Wilhelm Leibniz*. This was the period when experiments dominated scientific study. This method was particularly applied to the study of physics.

Agricultural Revolution

The *Agricultural Revolution* occurred first in England. It was marked by experimentation that resulted in the increased production of crops as well as a new and more technical approach to the management of agriculture. This revolution was hugely enhanced by the Industrial Revolution and the invention of the steam engine. The introduction of steam-powered tractors greatly increased crop production and significantly decreased labor costs. Developments in agriculture were also enhanced by the Scientific Revolution and the process of learning from experimentation (which ultimately led to philosophies of crop rotation and soil enrichment). Improved systems of irrigation and harvesting also contributed to the growth of agricultural production.

Industrial Revolution

The *Industrial Revolution*, which began in Great Britain and spread elsewhere, was the development of power-driven machinery (fueled by coal and steam). This revolution led to the accelerated growth of industry, with large factories replacing homes and small workshops as work centers. The lives of people changed drastically, and a largely agricultural society changed to an industrial one. In Western Europe, the period of colonialism began. The industrialized nations seized and claimed parts of Africa and Asia in an effort to control and provide the raw materials needed to feed the industries and machines in the "mother country." Later developments included power based on electricity and internal combustion, replacing coal and steam.

1920s America

Many refer to the decade of the 1920s as the *Jazz Age*. The decade was a time of optimism and of exploring new boundaries. In many ways, it was a clear movement away from conventionalism. Jazz music, uniquely American, was the country's popular music at the time. Jazz is essentially free-flowing improvisation on a simple theme with a four-beat rhythm; this musical style perfectly typified the mood of society. Jazz originated in the poor districts of New Orleans as an outgrowth of the Blues. The leading jazz musicians of the time included: Buddy Bolden, Joseph "King" Oliver, Duke Ellington, Louis Armstrong, and Jelly Roll Morton.

As jazz grew in popularity and in intricacy of the music, it gave birth to swing and the era of big band jazz. Some of the most notable musicians of the Big Band era were: Bing Crosby, Frank Sinatra, Don Redman, Fletcher Henderson, Count Basie, Benny Goodman, Billie Holiday, Ella Fitzgerald, and the Dorsey Brothers.

Information Revolution

The *Information Revolution* refers to the sweeping changes during the latter half of the twentieth century as a result of technological advances and a new respect for the knowledge provided by trained, skilled, and experienced professionals in a variety of fields. This approach to understanding a number of social and economic changes in global society arose from the ability to make computer technology both accessible and affordable. In particular, the development of the computer chip led to such technological advances as the Internet, the cell phone, Cybernetics, wireless communication, and the related ability to disseminate and access a massive amount of information quite readily.

In terms of economic theory and segmentation, it is now very much the norm to think of three basic economic sectors: agriculture and mining, manufacturing, and "services." Indeed, labor is now often divided between manual labor and informational labor. The fact that businesses are involved in the production, distribution, processing, and transmission of information has, according to some, created a new business sector.

The Information Revolution has clearly changed modern life in many ways, including by creating devices and processes that actually control much of the world as it is experienced by the average person. It has most certainly revolutionized the entertainment industry, as well as influenced the way people spend their time. In education, new technology has made information on virtually any subject instantly accessible. It has also thoroughly altered the minute-to-minute knowledge persons have of world events. Sixty years ago, news from the war front became available by radio for the first time. Visual images, however, were primarily available through the weekly newsreels shown in motion picture theaters. Today, live pictures from the battlefield are instantly available to people, no matter where they are. This technology has also made it possible for "smart wars" to be fought, reducing the number of civilian casualties.

Examples of Nations

Ancient civilizations were those nations and cultures that developed to a greater degree and were considered "advanced." These included the following sixteen civilizations and their accomplishments:

Egypt made numerous significant contributions, including constructing the Great Pyramids; developing hieroglyphic writing; preserving bodies after death; making paper from papyrus; contributing to developments in arithmetic and geometry; inventing the method of counting in groups of 1-10 (the decimal system); completing a solar calendar; and laying the foundation for science and astronomy.

The ancient civilization of the **Sumerians** invented the wheel; developed irrigation through use of canals, dikes, and devices for raising water; devised the system of cuneiform writing; learned to divide time; and built large boats for trade. The Babylonians devised the famous *Code of Hammurabi*, a code of laws.

The ancient **Assyrians** were warlike and aggressive due to a highly organized military. They also used horse-drawn chariots.

The **Hebrews**, also known as the ancient Israelites, instituted "monotheism," which is the worship of one God, Yahweh.

The **Minoans** had a system of writing using symbols to represent syllables in words. They built palaces with multiple levels that contained many rooms, water and sewage systems with flush toilets, bathtubs, hot and cold running water, and bright paintings on the walls.

The **Mycenaeans** changed the Minoan writing system to aid their own language and used symbols to represent syllables.

The **Phoenicians** were sea traders well-known for their manufacturing skills in glass and metals. They also developed their famous purple dye. They became so proficient in the skill of navigation that they were able to sail by the stars at night. Further, they devised an alphabet using symbols to represent single sounds, which was an improved extension of the Egyptian principle and writing system.

In **India**, the caste system was developed, the principle of zero in mathematics was discovered, and the major religion of Hinduism began. Industry and commerce developed along with extensive trading with the Near East. Outstanding advances in the fields of science and medicine were made, and the civilization was one of the first to be active in navigation and maritime enterprises.

China began building the Great Wall, practiced crop rotation and terrace farming, increased the importance of the silk industry, and developed caravan routes across Central Asia for extensive trade. Also, they increased proficiency in rice cultivation and developed a written language based on drawings or pictographs (no alphabet symbolizing sounds, as each word or character had a form different from all others). China is considered by some historians to be the oldest, uninterrupted civilization in the world; it was in existence around the same time as the ancient civilizations founded in *Egypt, Mesopotamia*, and the *Indus Valley*. The Chinese studied nature and weather; stressed the importance of education, family, and a strong central government; followed the religions of Buddhism, Confucianism, and Taoism; and invented such things as gunpowder, paper, printing, and the magnetic compass.

The ancient **Persians** developed an alphabet; contributed the religions/philosophies of *Zoroastrianism, Mithraism,* and *Gnosticism*; and allowed conquered peoples to retain their own customs, laws, and religions.

The classical civilization of **Greece** reached the highest levels in mankind's achievements based on the foundations already laid by such ancient groups as the *Egyptians, Phoenicians, Minoans*, and *Mycenaeans*.

Among the more important contributions of Greece were the Greek alphabet derived from the Phoenician letters. The Greek alphabet formed the basis for the Roman alphabet and our present-day alphabet. Extensive trading and colonizing resulted in the spread of the Greek civilization. The love of sports, with emphasis on a sound body, led to the tradition of the Olympic Games. Greece was responsible for the rise of strong, independent city-states.

Other important areas that the Greeks are credited with influencing include drama, epic and lyric poetry, fables, myths centered on their many gods and goddesses, science, astronomy, medicine, mathematics, philosophy, art, architecture, and records of historical events. The conquests of Alexander the Great spread Greek ideas and brought to the Greek world many ideas from Asia. Some of these ideas included the values of wisdom and curiosity as well as the desire to learn as much about the world as possible.

A most interesting and significant characteristic of the Greek, Hellenic, and Roman civilizations was "secularism," in which emphasis shifted away from religion to the state. Men were not absorbed in or dominated by religion as had been the case in Egypt and the nations located in Mesopotamia.

The civilization in **Japan** appeared around the same time as the Greeks, having borrowed much of its culture from China. It was the last of the classical civilizations to develop. Although they used, accepted, and copied Chinese art, law, architecture, dress, and writing, the Japanese refined these into their own unique way of life, including incorporating the religion of Buddhism into their culture.

The nations in **Africa** south of the Sahara developed systems of refining and using iron, especially for farm implements (and later for weapons). Trading was done by land using camels as well as overseas from important seaports. The Arab influence was extremely important, as was the Arabs' later contact with Indians, Christian Nubians, and Persians. In fact, their trading activities were probably the most important factor in the spread of and assimilation of different ideas and stimulation of cultural growth in Africa.

The **Vikings** had a lot of influence at this time through spreading their ideas and their knowledge of trade routes and sailing. Most of this was accomplished first through their conquests and later through trade.

In other parts of the world were the **Byzantine** and **Saracenic** (or Islamic) civilizations, both dominated by religion. The major contributions of the Saracens were in the areas of science and philosophy. Included were accomplishments in astronomy, mathematics, physics, chemistry, medicine, literature, art, trade and manufacturing, agriculture, and a marked influence on the Renaissance period of history. The Byzantines (Christians) made important contributions in art and in the preservation of Greek and Roman achievements, including architecture (especially in Eastern Europe and Russia) as well as the Code of Justinian and Roman law.

The ancient empire of **Ghana** occupied an area that is now known as Northern Senegal and Southern Mauritania. There is no absolute certainty regarding the origin of this empire. Oral history dates the rise of the empire to the seventh century BCE. Most believe, however, that the date should be placed much later. Many believe that the nomads who were herding animals on the fringes of the desert posed a threat to the early *Soninke* people, who were an agricultural community. In times of drought, it is believed that the nomads raided the agricultural villages for water and places to pasture their herds. To protect themselves, these farming communities formed a loose confederation that eventually became the empire of ancient Ghana.

The empire's economic vitality was determined by geographic location. It was situated midway between the desert, which was a major source of salt, and the gold fields. This location along the trade routes of the camel caravans provided exceptional opportunities for economic development. The caravans brought copper, salt, dried fruit, clothing, and manufactured goods. For these goods, the people of Ghana traded kola nuts, leather products, gold, hides, ivory, and slaves. In addition, the empire collected taxes on every trade item that entered its boundaries. With the revenue from the trade goods tax, the empire supported a government, an army that protected the trade routes and the borders, and maintained the capital and primary market centers.

However, it was control of the gold fields that gave the empire political power and economic prosperity. The location of the gold fields was a carefully guarded secret. By the tenth century, Ghana was very rich and controlled an area about the size of the state of Texas. Demand for this gold sharply increased in the ninth and tenth centuries as the Islamic states of Northern Africa began to mint coins. As the gold trade expanded, so did the empire. The availability of local iron ore enabled the early people of the Ghana kingdom to make more efficient farm implements and effective weapons.

United States

The *Industrial Revolution* had spread from Great Britain to the United States. Before 1800, most manufacturing activities were done in small shops or in homes. However, starting in the early 1800s, factories with modern machines were built to make it easier to produce goods faster. The eastern part of the country became a major industrial area (although some developed in the west as well). At about the same time, improvements began to be made in building roads, railroads, canals, and steamboats. The increased ease of travel facilitated the westward movement; it also boosted the economy with a faster and cheaper shipment of goods and products. One of the notable innovations of the time included the construction of the Erie Canal, which connected the interior of the country and the Great Lakes with the Hudson River and the coastal port of New York.

Westward expansion occurred for a number of reasons, most notably those reasons founded in economics. Cotton had become the most important crop to most of the people who lived in the southern states. The effects of the Industrial Revolution, which began in England, were now being felt in the United States. With the invention of power-driven machines, the demand for cotton fibers was greatly increased along with the need for the yarn for spinning and weaving. Eli Whitney's cotton gin made the separation of the seeds from the cotton much more efficient and faster. This, in turn, increased the demand for cotton; more and more farmers became involved in raising and selling cotton plants.

The innovations and developments of better methods of long-distance transportation moved the cotton in greater quantities to textile mills in England (as well as the areas of New England and the Middle Atlantic States in the Unitd States). As prices increased along with increased demand, southern farmers began expanding by clearing increasingly more land to grow cotton. Movement, settlement, and farming headed west to utilize the fertile soils. This, in turn, demanded increased need for a large supply of cheap labor. The system of slavery expanded, both in numbers and in the movement to lands "west" of the South.

Cotton farmers and slave owners were not the only ones heading west. Many individuals in other fields of economic endeavor also began the migration: trappers, miners, merchants, and ranchers were among those seeking their fortunes. The Lewis and Clark expedition stimulated the westward push. Fur companies hired men, known as "Mountain Men," to go westward, searching for animal pelts to supply the market and meet the demands of the East and Europe. These men, in their own way, explored and discovered the many passes and trails that would eventually be used by settlers in their trek to the west. The California Gold Rush also had a very large influence on the westward movement.

In the American Southwest, the results were exactly the opposite. Spain had claimed this area since the 1540s, had spread northward from Mexico City and, in the 1700s, had established missions, forts, villages, towns, and very large ranches. After the purchase of the *Louisiana Territory in 1803*, Americans began moving into Spanish territory. A few hundred American families in what is now Texas were allowed to live there but had to agree to become loyal subjects to Spain. In 1821, Mexico successfully revolted against Spanish rule, won independence, and chose to be more tolerant toward the American settlers and traders. The Mexican government encouraged and allowed extensive trade and settlement, especially in Texas. Many of the new settlers were Southerners who brought their slaves with them. Slavery was outlawed in Mexico and was technically illegal in Texas; however, the Mexican government adopted a system of "looking the other way."

The *Red River Cession* was the next acquisition of land; it came about as part of a treaty with Great Britain in 1818. It included parts of North and South Dakota and Minnesota. In 1819, Florida was ceded to the United States by Spain, along with parts of Alabama, Mississippi, and Louisiana. Texas was annexed in 1845, and after the war with Mexico in 1848, the government paid $15 million for what would become the states of California, Utah, Nevada and parts of four other states. In 1846, the Oregon Country was ceded to the United States, which effectively extended the western border to the Pacific Ocean. The northern U.S. boundary was established at the 49th parallel. The states of Idaho, Oregon, and Washington were formed from this territory. In 1853, the *Gadsden Purchase* rounded out the present boundary of the forty-eight conterminous states through a payment to Mexico of $10 million for land that makes up the present states of New Mexico and Arizona.

The election of Andrew Jackson as president signaled a swing of the political pendulum from government influence of the wealthy, aristocratic Easterners to the interests of the Western farmers and pioneers—a time also known as the era of the "common man." Jacksonian democracy was a policy of equal political power for all. Many of his policies dealt with making changes to policies created after the War of 1812, when Henry Clay and supporters favored economic measures that came to be known as the *American System*. This system involved creating tariffs that protected American farmers and manufacturers from having to compete with foreign products, stimulating industrial growth, and increasing employment opportunities. The goal was that with more people working, more farm products would be consumed, prosperous farmers would be able to buy more manufactured goods, and the additional monies from tariffs would make it possible for the government to make the needed internal improvements. To get this going, Congress not only passed a high tariff in 1816, but it also chartered a second Bank of the United States. Upon becoming president, Jackson fought to get rid of the bank.

Many *social reform movements* began during this period, including those dealing with education, women's rights, working conditions, temperance, prisons, and insane asylums. Among the most intense and controversial was the abolitionists' efforts to end slavery, an effort that alienated and split the country, hardening the Southern defense of slavery and leading to four years of bloody civil war. The abolitionist movement had a political fallout, affecting the admittance of states into the Union and the government's continued efforts to keep a balance between the total number of free and slave states. Congressional legislation after 1820 reflected this.

Robert Fulton's "*Clermont*," the first commercially successful steamboat, led the way in developing an efficient method to ship goods. Later, steam-powered railroads became the biggest rival of the steamboat as a means of shipping, eventually becoming the most important transportation method (also effectively opening the West). With expansion into the interior of the country, the United States became the leading agricultural nation in the world. The hardy pioneer farmers produced a vast surplus of goods, and emphasis went to producing products with a high-sale value. These implements, such as the cotton gin and reaper, improved production. Travel and shipping were greatly assisted in areas not yet touched by railroad or by improved or new roads, such as the National Road in the eastern portions of the United States and the Oregon and Santa Fe Trails in the West.

With better communication and travel, people were exposed to greater numbers of works of literature, art, newspapers, drama, live entertainment, and political rallies. In addition, more information was desired about previously unknown areas of the country, especially the West. The discovery of gold and other mineral wealth resulted in a literal surge of settlers and even greater interest.

Public schools were established in many of the states, allowing more and more children to become educated. With greater literacy and more participation in literature and the arts, the young nation was developing its own unique culture—becoming less and less influenced by and dependent on Europe.

More industries and factories required more labor. Women, children, and, at times, entire families worked incredibly long hours and days to make ends meet until the 1830s. By that time, factories were getting even larger and employers began hiring the immigrants who were coming to America in huge numbers. Before then, efforts were made to organize a labor movement to improve working conditions and increase wages. It never really caught on until after the Civil War, but the seed had been sown in these early years.

Between the growing economy, the westward expansion of the population, and improvements in travel and mass communication, the federal government did face periodic financial depressions. Contributing to these downward spirals were land speculations, the availability and soundness of money and currency, failed banks, failing businesses, and unemployment. Sometimes, conditions outside the nation would help to trigger the problems; at other times, domestic politics and presidential elections did. The growing strength and influence of two major political parties with opposing philosophies and methods of conducting government did not ease matters.

As 1860 began, the nation had extended its borders north, south, and west. Industry and agriculture were flourishing. Although the United States did not involve itself actively in European affairs, the relationship with Great Britain was much improved, and other nations that dealt with the young nation accorded it more respect and admiration. Nevertheless, war was on the horizon. The country was deeply divided along political lines concerning slavery and the election of *Abraham Lincoln.*

As **African Americans** left the rural South and migrated to the North in search of opportunities, many settled in Harlem in New York City. By the 1920s, Harlem had become a center of life and activity for people of color. The music, art, and literature of this community gave birth to a cultural movement known as the *Harlem Renaissance.* The artistic expressions that emerged from this community in the 1920s and 1930s celebrated the Black experience, Black traditions, and the voices of Black America. Major writers and works of this movement included: Langston Hughes (The Weary Blues), Nella Larsen (Passing), Zora Neale Hurston (Their Eyes Were Watching God), Claude McKay, Countee Cullen, and Jean Toomer.

Hispanic Americans have contributed to American life and culture since before the Civil War. Hispanics have distinguished themselves in every area of society and culture. Mexicans taught Californians to pan for gold and introduced the technique of using mercury to separate silver from worthless ores. Six state names are of Hispanic origin.

Native Americans have made major contributions to the development of the nation and have been contributors, either directly or indirectly, in almost every area of political and cultural life. In the early years of European settlement, Native Americans were both teachers and neighbors. Even during periods of extermination and relocation, their influence was profound.

Numerous conflicts, often called the *Indian Wars*, broke out between the U.S. army and many different Native tribes during the nineteenth century. Many treaties were signed with the various tribes, but most were broken by the government for a variety of reasons. Two of the most notable battles were the Battle of Little Bighorn in 1876, in which the Native people defeated General Custer and his forces, and the massacre of Native Americans in 1890 at Wounded Knee. In 1876, the U.S. government ordered all surviving Native Americans to move to reservations.

Asian Americans, particularly in the West and in large cities, have made significant contributions despite immigration bans, mistreatment, and confinement. Asians were particularly important in constructing the trans-continental railroad, mining metals, and providing other kinds of labor and services.

Examples of Specialized Topics

Nationalism

During the eighteenth and especially the nineteenth centuries, *nationalism* emerged as a powerful force in Europe and elsewhere in the world. Strictly speaking, nationalism was a belief in one's own nation, country, and people. The people of the European nations began to think economically, socially, and politically in terms of a group of people who had similar beliefs, concerns, and needs. This was partly a reaction to a growing discontent with the autocratic governments of the day and partly a general realization that there was more to life than the individual. People could feel a part of something bigger (their nation), making themselves more than just an insignificant soul struggling to survive.

Nationalism precipitated several changes in government, most notably in France; it also brought large groups of people together, as with the unifications of Germany and Italy. What it didn't do, however, was provide sufficient outlets for this sudden rise in national fervor. During the 1700s and 1800s in particular, European powers and peoples began looking to Africa and Asia to find colonies: rich sources of goods, trade, and cheap labor. Africa especially suffered at the hands of European Imperialists, bent on expanding their reach outside the borders of Europe. Asia also suffered colonial expansion, most notably in India and Southeast Asia.

This colonial expansion would come back to haunt the European Imperialists in a very big way, as colonial skirmishes spilled over into alliances that dragged the European powers into World War I. Some of these colonial battles were still being fought as late as the start of World War II.

Nineteenth Century Contributors to the United States

The following is just a partial list of well-known Americans who contributed their leadership and talents in various fields and reforms throughout history:

- *Lucretia Mott* and *Elizabeth Cady Stanton* for women's rights
- *Emma Hart Willard, Catharine Esther Beecher,* and *Mary Lyon* for the education for women
- *Dr. Elizabeth Blackwell*, the first female to graduate from an American medical school
- *Antoinette Louisa Blackwell*, the first female minister
- *Dorothea Lynde Dix* for reforms in prisons and insane asylums
- *Elihu Burritt* and *William Ladd* for peace movements
- *Robert Owen* for a Utopian society
- *Horace Mann, Henry Barnard, Calvin E. Stowe, Caleb Mills*, and *John Swett* for public education
- *Benjamin Lundy, David Walker, William Lloyd Garrison, Arthur* and *Lewis Tappan, Theodore Weld, Frederick Douglass, Harriet Tubman, James G. Birney, Henry Highland Garnet, James Forten, Robert Purvis, Harriet Beecher Stowe, Wendell Phillips*, and *John Brown* for the abolition of slavery and the *Underground Railroad*
- *Louisa May Alcott, James Fenimore Cooper, Washington Irving, Walt Whitman, Henry David Thoreau, Ralph Waldo Emerson, Herman Melville, Richard Henry Dana, Nathaniel Hawthorne, Henry Wadsworth Longfellow, John Greenleaf Whittier, Edgar Allan Poe,* and *Oliver Wendell Holmes*, famous writers
- *John C. Fremont, Zebulon Pike,* and *Kit Carson*, explorers
- *Henry Clay, Daniel Webster, Stephen Douglas,* and *John C. Calhoun*, American statesmen
- *Robert Fulton, Cyrus McCormick,* and *Eli Whitney*, inventors
- *Noah Webster*, American Dictionary and Speller

U.S. Civil Rights

In 1957, the formation of the *Southern Christian Leadership Conference* by Martin Luther King, Jr., John Duffy, Rev. C. K. Steele, Rev. T. J. Jemison, Rev. Fred Shuttlesworth, Ella Baker, A. Philip Randolph, Bayard Rustin, and Stanley Levison provided training and assistance to local efforts fighting segregation. Non-violence was its central doctrine as well as its major method of fighting segregation and racism—a belief or doctrine that biological differences determine success or cultural achievement and that one's own race is superior, thereby possessing the right to rule over others.

American Political Parties

During the colonial period, political parties, as the term is now understood, did not exist. The issues, which divided the people, were centered on the relations of the colonies to the mother country. There was initially little difference of opinion on these issues. About the middle of the eighteenth century, after England began to develop a harsher colonial policy, two factions arose in America. One favored the attitude of home government and the other declined to obey and demanded a constantly increasing level of self-government. The former came to be known as *Tory* party, the latter as *Whigs*. During the course of the American Revolution, a large number of Tories left the country either to return to England or to move into Canada.

From the beginning of the Confederation, there were differences of opinion about the new government. One faction favored a loose confederacy in which the individual state would retain all powers of sovereignty except the absolute minimum required for the limited cooperation of all the states. The other faction, which steadily gained influence, demanded that the central government be granted all the essential powers of sovereignty and that states could only possess limited powers of local self-government. The inadequacy of the Confederation demonstrated that the latter were promoting a more effective point of view.

The first real party organization developed soon after the inauguration of George Washington as President. His cabinet included people of both factions. Alexander Hamilton was the leader of the *Nationalists* (also known as the *Federalist Party*) and Thomas Jefferson was the spokesman for the Anti-Federalists, later known as *Republicans*, *Democratic-Republicans*, and finally *Democrats*. Several other parties formed over the years, including the Anti-Masonic Party and the Free Soil Party (who existed for the 1848 and 1852 elections only). The Liberty Party of this period was abolitionist.

The American Party was called the "Know Nothings." They lasted from 1854 to 1858 and were opposed to Irish-Catholic immigration. The *Constitution Union Party* was formed in 1860. It was made up of entities from other extinguished political powers. They claimed to support the Constitution above all and thought this would do away with the slavery issue. The *National Union Party* of 1864 was formed only for the purpose of the Lincoln election. Although these parties provide a good sampling of those that have been in existence throughout American history, there were many more to follow.

Religion

Religion has always been a factor in American life. Many early settlers came to America in search of religious freedom. Religion, particularly Christianity, was an essential element of the value and belief structure shared by the Founding Fathers. Yet the Constitution prescribes a separation of Church and State.

The *First Great Awakening* was a religious movement within American Protestantism in the 1730s and 1740s. This was primarily a movement among Puritans seeking the return to a strict interpretation of morality and values as well as an emphasis on the importance and power of personal religious or spiritual experience. Many historians believe the First Great Awakening unified the people of the original colonies and supported the independence of the colonists.

The *Second Great Awakening* (the Great Revival) was a broad movement within American Protestantism that led to several kinds of activities distinguished by region and denominational tradition. In general terms, the Second Great Awakening, which began in the 1820s, was a time of recognition that "awakened religion" to weed out sin on both a personal and a social level. It inspired a wave of social activism. In New England, the Congregationalists established missionary societies to evangelize the West. Publication and education societies arose, most notably the American Bible Society. This social activism gave rise to the temperance movement, prison reform efforts, and help for the handicapped and mentally ill. This period was particularly notable for the abolition movement. In the Appalachian region, the camp meeting was used to revive religion. The camp meeting became a primary method of evangelizing new territory.

The *Third Great Awakening* (the Missionary Awakening) gave rise to the Social Gospel Movement. This period (1858 to 1908) resulted in a massive growth in membership of all major Protestant denominations, largely through their missionary activities. This movement was partly a response to claims that the Bible was fallible. Many churches attempted to reconcile or change biblical teachings to fit scientific theories and discoveries. Colleges associated with Protestant churches began to appear rapidly throughout the nation. In terms of social and political movements, the Third Great Awakening was the most expansive and profound. Coinciding with many changes in production and labor, it won battles against child labor and stopped the exploitation of women in factories. Compulsory elementary education for children came from this movement, as did the establishment of a set work day. Much was also done to protect and rescue children from abandonment and abuse, to improve the care of the sick, to prohibit the use of alcohol and tobacco, as well as numerous other "social ills."

History of Georgia

During the seventeenth century, the east coast of North America was rapidly being settled by European colonists in the north and by the Spanish in the south. In 1670, the British colony of South Carolina was founded directly north of Spanish-controlled Florida, creating a tense frontier in what is now *Georgia*. Military conflict followed until the Spanish missions were withdrawn in 1704 and the area occupied by Yamasee Native Americans became more friendly to the British.

However, relations grew sour between the Yamasee and the British in 1715 over the fur trade, and the Yamasee began attacking British colonists. The colonists responded with force and the Yamasee were driven out of the area toward Florida. This largely depopulated the coastal region between Charleston, the capital of British Carolina, and St, Augustine, the capital of Spanish Florida.

In the early 1730s, James Oglethorpe, a British Member of Parliament, was engaged in a campaign of prison reform in England. English citizens who fell into debt could be thrown into debtor's prisons under deplorable conditions, where they were usually mistreated and often died. Oglethorpe presented a plan to colonize the newly available land in North America with some of these debtors to give them an opportunity to escape the horrors of prison and start over in the New World.

King George II approved Oglethorpe's scheme, and on June 9, 1732, he granted a royal charter to Oglethorpe and a group of twenty other philanthropists to found a colony in North America. These twenty-one trustees called the new colony "Georgia" in honor of the king.

In the end, the first people chosen to go to the new colony were not debtors, but were individuals chosen by the trustees based on their skills, professions, and potential usefulness in the new colony. The first group of 114 people, including Oglethorpe, sailed from England on the *Anne* in November 1732 and arrived in Charleston two months later. Oglethorpe scouted ahead into the Georgia region and selected a bluff on the Savannah River to build the first settlement, which became called Savannah.

Oglethorpe and the trustees wished to avoid duplicating England's strict class system in the new colony, as they felt it had led to the practice of imprisoning debtors. They implemented a series of rules in the colony that prohibited slavery and required each man to work his own land. Identical houses were built on equal-sized lots to emphasize the equality of all.

The peaceful agrarian community that was envisioned by Oglethorpe grew happily for a time, but positioned as it was on the British frontier with the Spanish, the realities of potential warfare occupied the colony's attentions. Oglethorpe successfully petitioned the British government to grant him military authority in the area and to provide him with a regiment of British troops to defend the frontier. Oglethorpe unsuccessfully attempted to capture St. Augustine, spurring a series of battles between the Spanish and the British allied troops under Oglethorpe. The British emerged victorious after holding the line at the Battle of Bloody Marsh in 1742, after which the Spanish did not try to invade Georgia again.

As dissatisfaction with taxation increased in the northern colonies, similar rumblings began in Georgia, which joined the other colonies in 1765 in renouncing the Stamp Act. Georgia had prospered under its royal charter, however, and many Georgians believed that they needed British protection from neighboring Native Americans.

When news of the Battle of Lexington and Concord reached Georgia, patriotic resolve was strengthened; in May of 1775, a group of patriots raided the arsenal at Savannah and took a supply of British gunpowder. Georgian colonists set up their own government shortly thereafter and joined the association of colonies in enforcing a ban on trade with the British. While British Governor James Wright was still the official authority in Georgia, the provincial government founded in July 1775 gave executive authority to Council of Safety, which held the real power.

Wright was eventually expelled in 1776, after being held hostage by the colonists once British warships approached Savannah. Without a governor, provincial congress was convened at Augusta in April 1776, and a set of Rules and Regulations was adopted outlining a simple structure of government. Three delegates were sent to the Second Continental Congress in Philadelphia in time to sign the Declaration of Independence in July.

Three months later, a convention was called in Savannah to provide for a more permanent form of government in Georgia. The result of this convention was Georgia's first constitution, the Constitution of 1777. The new constitution created a single elected assembly that, in turn, chose a governor. The constitution was remarkable for its time in granting voting rights to a wide group of citizens, although only white men were allowed to vote. The Georgia Constitution also provided for future amendments by state convention. This provision, which was not included in all state constitutions at the time, eventually became common practice throughout the United States. However, the Constitution of 1777 lacked many of the internal balances of political power that would be included in the United States Constitution, and serious movements began in 1788 to redraft it.

Following the American victory in the Revolutionary War, Georgia engaged with the rest of the new states in the debate over a federal constitution. Along with its southern neighbors, Georgia opposed a strong central government advocated by the Federalists, fearing the concentration of political power in the northern states. The Bill of Rights, the first ten amendments to the U.S. Constitution that spell out limits on governmental authority, were included in the proposed Constitution to ensure the rights of the states. In this way, Georgia and the other southern states greatly influenced the shape of the Constitution. Georgia ratified the U.S. Constitution in January 1788.

"New South" is a term sometimes used to describe the South after the Civil War; it refers to a South no longer dependent on slave labor and based on industry instead. In Georgia, Henry Grady is closely associated with the New South movement of the 1880s. This movement sought to bring northern investments and industry to the state, particularly in the Atlanta region.

The New South was more of an ideal than a reality for Georgia farmers, who found themselves stressed by falling cotton prices after the Civil War. The growing Populist movement in the 1890s blamed the entrenched Democratic Party for many of the farmer's woes and mounted a challenge to the party. Georgia populists sought to include Blacks in the movement and called for prison reform. By the turn of the century, Populism as a movement had largely faded from Georgia politics, although it did have lasting effects.

Jim Crow laws were laws enacted after the Civil War that resulted in the segregation of Whites and Blacks, with Blacks being forced to use inferior facilities. During Reconstruction, southern states were forced to adopt protections for free Black citizens. Once the Reconstruction governments were replaced with "Redeemer" governments, laws were enacted that required separate schools and public facilities for Blacks and Whites, thereby replacing the Black Codes that had been in effect prior to the Civil War.

Jim Crow laws had the effect of denying voting rights to many Black citizens by requiring the payment of a poll tax. The Democratic Party also discouraged Black participation in politics and elections.

Despite these prejudices, many Blacks prospered following the war, especially in the growing industrial center of Atlanta. As the White elite witnessed the emergence of a Black economic elite in Atlanta, some argued that allowing Blacks to vote had caused them to think of themselves as equal to Whites, and that the vote should be taken away from them.

Tension grew between the races, eventually erupting in violence in Atlanta in 1906. Unsubstantiated reports circulated that Black men had attacked four White women. A mob of White men and boys gathered and raided Black neighborhoods, destroying businesses and killing several people. The state militia was called in to control the mob, which eventually subsided. As a result of the riot, even further restrictions were placed on Black voting rights.

World War I greatly impacted Georgia, which became the location of several military training camps. Thousands of troops from all over the country passed through Georgia on their way to war. In 1918, the troop ship *Otranto* sunk tragically, killing almost 400 men. One hundred and thirty of them were from Georgia.

When President Wilson instituted the draft, many White Georgians (especially landowners who employed Black sharecroppers) tried to prevent Black men from being called into service. Not wanting to lose their labor force, they would sometimes not deliver draft notices and prevent Blacks from registering. Many Blacks were arrested and jailed for evading the draft as a result.

Agriculture during this time was threatened by more than just the potential loss of farm labor. The boll weevil is an insect that affects cotton. It began its spread northward from Mexico in the late nineteenth century and reached Georgia around 1915. Within ten years, the number of acres planted in cotton in Georgia halved because of the pest. The boll weevil forced farmers to diversify their crops, leading to the rise of peanut farming, which became an important agricultural product.

Eugene Talmadge began his career in state politics as the Commissioner of Agriculture in 1926. Outspoken and opinionated, Talmadge won popular support from the rural community and rapidly became a polarizing influence in the Democratic Party. He was elected governor in 1932 and re-elected in 1934. After unsuccessful bids for the U.S. Senate, Talmadge was again elected governor in 1940.

Talmadge was a forceful leader who bypassed legislative action and removed appointees who disagreed with his views. Talmadge undertook to remove faculty members from the state University system who he thought wanted to integrate the schools or held the belief of racial equality. As a result of his raid on the system, the University lost its accreditation. The more moderate Ellis Arnall challenged Talmadge in the gubernatorial race of 1942, promising to restore accreditation, and won. Talmadge was re-elected governor in 1946, but died before taking office.

Talmadge was a major opponent of President Franklin Roosevelt's New Deal, a series of public programs beginning in 1933 designed to assist Depression-wracked Americans and to promote economic recovery. Talmadge and others saw the New Deal as federal interference with local affairs, but the program, which provided farm subsidies, built new infrastructure, and provided direct assistance to poor Georgians was popular among the people. President Roosevelt himself was popular in Georgia, having adopted Warm Springs as a second home during his time in office.

The New Deal did help many poor Southerners, although it failed to bring the dramatic turnaround that had been hoped for in the South. It was World War II and the related boom in the war industry that transformed Georgia's economy. Defense contractors found a large and willing labor force in Georgia, and shipbuilding and aircraft manufacturing became important industries that employed hundreds of thousands of people. With many men away in the military, women entered the workforce in large numbers for the first time. Black workers also benefited from the labor shortage, entering positions that had formerly been reserved for White men. Segregation, however, was still enforced.

New methods of agriculture made farming a viable endeavor once again, but Georgia was no longer entirely dependent on agriculture. The city of Atlanta made an early commitment to develop air travel when it establishment an airfield in 1925. The airfield grew throughout the twentieth century; under the administration of Mayor Maynard Jackson, it was transformed into the Hartsfield International Airport, a huge building project that opened in 1980. Later named the Hartsfield-Jackson International airport, the facility is currently the busiest airport in the world.

Ellis Arnall was elected as the governor of Georgia in 1942 at the age of thirty-five. Arnall made several significant reforms, including eliminating poll taxes and lowering the voting age. He also proposed checks to the power of the governor, feeling that Eugene Talmadge had previously abused his power. Arnall left office in 1947, although he ran again in 1966 against the segregationist Lester Maddox. Maddox emerged the victor in that race and served as governor until 1971.

Herman Talmadge was the only son of former Governor Eugene Talmadge. He ran his father's successful campaign for governor in 1946 and was briefly appointed to the position by the legislature when his father died before taking office. Herman Talmadge was himself elected governor in 1948. Talmadge supported segregation and worked to bring industry to Georgia. He served as Governor until 1954, when he ran for the U.S. Senate and was elected. Talmadge served in the Senate until 1981.

Between Reconstruction and the 1960s, the Democratic Party dominated Georgia politics. Republicans had been installed by the federal government during Reconstruction, but they were quickly replaced by Democrats after the federal troops that supported the Republican state governments were withdrawn. The civil rights era began drawing sharp lines between old-line Democrats and more moderate Democrats, sometimes splitting the vote and allowing Republicans to gain footholds.

Another change in Georgia politics in the 1960s was the end of the county unit system of conducting state primaries. Under this system, all of a county's unit votes were awarded to the candidate that received the most individual votes within that county. This system favored rural counties, and allowed for the election of candidates who had actually lost the popular vote, as was the case in 1946 when Eugene Talmadge won the primary for Governor. Primary politics were important in Georgia. Because of the dominance of the Democratic Party, winning the primary virtually ensured winning the general election. The U.S. Supreme Court declared the county unit system illegal in 1963.

In 1962, Jimmy Carter was elected to the Georgia legislature after challenging fraudulent returns in his election. He went on to serve as the governor of Georgia and was elected President of the United States in 1976, defeating President Gerald Ford.

Skill 9.3 Demonstrating knowledge of early Native American cultures in North America and their interactions with early explorers

Native American tribes lived throughout what we now call the United States in varying degrees of togetherness. They had established cultures long before Columbus or any other European explorer arrived on the scene. The tribes adopted different customs, pursued different avenues of agriculture and food gathering, and made slightly different weapons. They also fought among themselves and with other groups.

Perhaps the most famous of the Native American tribes is the *Algonquians*. Historians know much about this tribe because it was one of the first to interact with the newly arrived English settlers in Plymouth (and elsewhere). The Algonquians lived in wigwams and wore clothing made from animal skins. They were proficient hunters, gatherers, and trappers who also knew quite a bit about farming.

Beginning with a brave man named Squanto, the Algonquians shared their agricultural knowledge with the English settlers, including how to plant and cultivate corn, pumpkins, and squash. Other famous Algonquians include Pocahontas and her father, Powhatan—both of whom are immortalized in English literature—and Tecumseh and Black Hawk—known foremost for their fierce fighting abilities. To the overall Native American culture, they were responsible for contributing wampum and dream catchers.

Another group of tribes who lived in the Northeast were the *Iroquois*, who were fierce fighters but also forward thinkers. They lived in long houses and wore clothes made of buckskin. They, too, were expert farmers, growing the "Three Sisters" (corn, squash, and beans). Five of the Iroquois tribes formed a Confederacy, which functioned as a shared form of government. The Iroquois also formed the False Face Society, a group of medicine men who shared their medical knowledge with others but kept their identities secret while doing so. The masks they wore are one of the enduring symbols of the Native American era.

Among those living in the Southeast were the *Seminoles* and *Creeks*, a huge collection of people who lived in chickees (open, bark-covered houses) and wore clothes made from plant fibers. They were expert planters and hunters; they were also proficient at making and paddling dugout canoes. The beaded necklaces they created were some of the most beautiful on the continent. They are best known, however, for their struggles against Spanish and English settlers, especially those struggles led by the great Osceola.

The *Cherokee* also lived in the Southeast. They were one of the most advanced tribes, living in domed houses and wearing deerskin and rabbit furs. Accomplished hunters, farmers, and fishermen, the Cherokee were known the continent over for their intricate and beautiful basketry and clay pottery. They also played a game called lacrosse, which survives to this day in countries around the world.

In the middle of the continent lived the Plains tribes such as the *Sioux, Cheyenne, Blackfeet, Comanche,* and *Pawnee.* These peoples lived in teepees and wore buffalo skins and feather headdresses. (It is this image of the Native American that has made its way into most movies depicting the period.) They hunted wild animals on the Plains, especially the buffalo. They were well-known for their many ceremonies, including the Sun Dance, and for the peace pipes that they smoked. Famous Plains people include Crazy Horse and Sitting Bull, authors of the Custer Disaster; Sacagawea, leader of the Lewis and Clark expedition; and Chief Joseph, the famous Nez Perce leader.

Dotting the deserts of the Southwest were a handful of tribes, including the famous *Pueblo*, who lived in houses that bear their tribe's name, wore clothes made of wool and woven cotton, farmed crops in the middle of desert land, created exquisite pottery and Kachina dolls, and had one of the most complex religions of all the tribes. They are perhaps best known for the challenging vista-based villages that they constructed out of the sheer faces of cliffs and rocks as well as for their *adobes*, which were mud-brick buildings that housed their living and meeting quarters. Theirs was perhaps one of the oldest representative governments in the world; the Pueblos chose their own chiefs.

Another well-known Southwestern tribe included the *Apache*, with their famous leader Geronimo. The Apache lived in homes called wickiups, which were made of bark, grass, and branches. They wore cotton clothing and were excellent hunters and gatherers. Adept at basketry, the Apache believed that everything in nature had special powers and that they were honored just to be part of it all.

The *Navajo,* also residents of the Southwest, lived in hogans (round homes built with forked sticks) and wore clothes of rabbit skin. Their major contribution to the overall culture of the continent was in sand painting, weapon making, silversmithing, and weaving. Some of the most beautiful woven rugs were crafted by Navajo hands.

Living in the Northwest were the *Inuit*, who lived in tents made from animal skins or, in some cases, igloos. They wore clothes also made from animal skins, usually seals or caribou. They were excellent fishermen and hunters; they crafted efficient kayaks and umiaks to take them through waterways as well as harpoons with which to hunt animals. The Inuit are perhaps best known for the great carvings that they built. Among these are ivory figures and tall totem poles.

Colonists from England, France, Holland, Sweden, and Spain all settled in North America on lands once frequented by Native Americans. Spanish colonies were mainly in the south, French colonies were mainly in the extreme north and in the middle of the continent, and the rest of the European colonies were in the northeast and along the Atlantic coast. These colonists got along with their new neighbors with varying degrees of success.

Of all of them, the French colonists seemed the most willing to work with the Native Americans. Even though their pursuit of animals to fill the growing demand for the fur trade was overpowering, they managed to find a way to keep their new neighbors happy. The French and Native Americans even fought on the same side of the war against England.

The Dutch and Swedish colonists were mainly interested in surviving in their new homes. However, they didn't last long in their struggles against England.

The English and Spanish colonists had the worst relations with the Native Americans, mainly because the Europeans made a habit of taking land, signing and then breaking treaties, massacring, and otherwise abusing their new neighbors. The Native Americans were only too happy to share their agriculture and jewel-making secrets with the Europeans; what they got in return was grief and deceit. The term "Manifest Destiny" meant nothing to the Native Americans, who believed that they lived on land granted access to them by the gods above.

The conflicts between Europeans and the various Native American groups carved an incredibly large portion of early U.S. history; the repercussions of many of these conflicts are still evident in society today.

Skill 9.4   **Analyzing various perspectives, interpretations, and implications of events, issues, and developments in Georgia, U.S., and world history**

The practice of dividing time into a number of discrete periods or blocks of time is called "periodization." Because history is continuous, all systems of periodization are, to some extent, arbitrary. However, dividing time into segments helps to facilitate an understanding of the changes that occur over time as well as the ability to identify similarities between events, knowledge, and experiences within the defined period.

Divisions of time may be determined by date, by cultural advances or changes, by historical events, by the influence of particular individuals or groups, or by geography. For example, the World War II era is defined as a particular period of time in which key historical, political, social, and economic events occurred throughout the entire world. However, the Jacksonian Era only has meaning in terms of American history. In that same vein, defining the "Romantic period" is only applicable in England, Europe, and countries under their direct influence.

Many of the commonly used divisions of time are open to controversy and discussion. For example, the use of BC and AD dating has clear reference only in societies that account time according to the Christian calendar. Similarly, speaking of "the year of the pig" has the greatest meaning in China.

An example of the kind of questions that can be raised about designations of time periods can be understood in the context of "Victorian." For example, is it possible to speak of a Victorian era beyond England? Is literature written in the style of the English poets and writers "Victorian" if it is written beyond the borders of England? Time designations can also carry both positive and negative connotations. For example, the term "Victorian" is often used to refer to class conflict, sexual repression, and heavy industry. These can be construed with negative connotations or positive connotations depending on the issue at hand.

Sometimes, several designations can be applied to the same period. The period known as the "Elizabethan Period" in English history is also called "the English Renaissance." In some cases, the differences in designation refer primarily to the specific aspect of history that is being considered. For example, one designation may be applied to a specific period of time when analyzing cultural history, while a different designation can be applied to the same period of time when considering military history.

Discussions of wars are especially susceptible to periodization. Because war histories are typically written by the "winners," the viewpoint is often skewed in favor of the victors. How the victors define the era, then, is typically how the information is relayed. Even more periodization occurs when the war is discussed in relation to a specific geographical location, such as Georgia. Consider the discussion of various wars below. How has periodization impacted what we, as readers, know about each war?

Civil War

In 1833, Congress lowered tariffs at a level acceptable to South Carolina. Although President Jackson believed in states' rights, he also firmly believed in and was determined to keep the preservation of the Union. A constitutional crisis had been averted, but sectional divisions were getting deeper and more pronounced. The abolition movement was growing rapidly, becoming an important issue in the North. The slavery issue was at the root of almost every problem, crisis, event, decision, and struggle from then on.

For example, the next major crisis involved Texas. By 1836, Texas was an independent republic with its own constitution. During its fight for independence, Americans were sympathetic to and supportive of the Texans, and some recruited volunteers who crossed into Texas to help the struggle. Problems arose when the state petitioned Congress for statehood. Texas wanted to allow slavery, but Northerners in Congress opposed admission to the Union because it would disrupt the balance between free and slave states and give Southerners in Congress increased influence.

A few years later, Congress took up consideration of new territories between Missouri and present-day Idaho. Again, a heated debate over permitting slavery in these areas flared up. Those opposed to slavery used the *Missouri Compromise* to prove their point by demonstrating that the land being considered for territories had already been designated as banned to slavery. On May 25, 1854, Congress passed the infamous *Kansas-Nebraska Act,* which nullified the provision creating the territories of Kansas and Nebraska. This provided for the people of these two territories to decide for themselves whether or not to permit slavery to exist there. Feelings were so deep and divided that any further attempts to compromise met with little, if any, success.

Political and social turmoil swirled everywhere. Kansas was called "Bleeding Kansas" because of the extreme violence and bloodshed due to the two governments that existed there—one pro-slavery and the other anti-slavery.

In 1857, the Supreme Court handed down a decision guaranteed to cause explosions throughout the country. Dred Scott was a slave whose owner had taken him from the slave state of Missouri, to free-state Illinois, into Minnesota Territory (a free territory under the provisions of the Missouri Compromise), and finally back to slave-state Missouri. Abolitionists pursued the dilemma by presenting a court case stating that because Scott had lived in a free state and free territory, he was in actuality a free man. Two lower courts ruled before the Supreme Court became involved, one ruling in favor and one against. The Supreme Court decided that residing in a free state and free territory did not make Scott a free man because Scott (and all other slaves) was not a U.S. citizen or a state citizen of Missouri. Therefore, he did not have the right to sue in state or federal courts.

The Court went a step further and ruled that the old Missouri Compromise was now unconstitutional because Congress did not have the power to prohibit slavery in the Territories.

In 1858, Abraham Lincoln and Stephen A. Douglas were both running for the office of U.S. Senator from Illinois. They participated in a series of debates that directly affected the outcome of the 1860 Presidential election. Douglas, a Democrat, was up for re-election and knew that if he won this race, he had a good chance of becoming President in 1860. Lincoln, a Republican, was not an abolitionist but he believed that slavery was morally wrong; he also firmly believed in and supported the Republican Party principle that slavery must not be allowed to extend any further.

The final straw came with the election of Lincoln to the Presidency the next year. Due to a split in the Democratic Party, there were four candidates from four political parties. With Lincoln receiving a minority of the popular vote and a majority of electoral votes, the Southern states, one by one, voted to secede from the Union, as they had promised they would do if Lincoln and the Republicans were victorious. The die was cast.

South Carolina was the first state to secede from the Union, and the first shots of the war were fired on Fort Sumter in Charleston Harbor. Both sides quickly prepared for war. The North had quite a bit in its favor: a larger population; superiority in finances and transportation facilities; and more manufacturing, agricultural, and natural resources. The North possessed most of the nation's gold, had about 92 percent of all industries, and almost all known supplies of copper, coal, iron, and various other minerals. Most of the nation's railroads were in the North and mid-West, men and supplies could be moved wherever needed, and food could be transported from the farms of the mid-West to workers in the East and soldiers on the battlefields. Trade with nations overseas could go on as usual due to the North's control of the navy and the merchant fleet. The Northern states numbered twenty-four and included western (California and Oregon) and border (Maryland, Delaware, Kentucky, Missouri, and West Virginia) states. The Southern states numbered eleven and included South Carolina, Georgia, Florida, Alabama, Mississippi, Louisiana, Texas, Virginia, North Carolina, Tennessee, and Arkansas, making up the Confederacy. Although outnumbered in population, the South was completely confident of victory. They knew that all they had to do was to fight a defensive war and protect their own territory; the North had to invade and defeat an area almost the size of Western Europe.

Another advantage of the South was that a number of its best officers had graduated from the U.S. Military Academy at West Point and had had long years of army experience. Many had exercised varying degrees of command in the Indian Wars and the war with Mexico. Men from the South were conditioned to living outdoors and were more familiar with horses and firearms than men from northeastern cities. Since cotton was such an important crop, Southerners felt that British and French textile mills were so dependent on them that they would be forced to help the Confederacy in the war.

The South won decisively until the Battle of Gettysburg, July 1 - 3, 1863. Until Gettysburg, Lincoln's main commanders, McDowell and McClellan, were less than desirable, and Burnside and Hooker were not what was needed. Lee, on the other hand, had many able officers; Stonewall Jackson and J.E.B. Stuart were depended on heavily by him. Jackson died at Chancellorsville and was replaced by Longstreet. Lee decided to invade the North and depended on Stuart and his cavalry to keep him informed of the location of Union troops and their strengths.

The day after Gettysburg, on July 4, Vicksburg, Mississippi surrendered to Union General Ulysses Grant, thus severing the western Confederacy from the eastern part. In September 1863, the Confederacy won its last important victory at Chickamauga. In November, the Union victory at Chattanooga made it possible for Union troops to go into Alabama and Georgia, splitting the eastern Confederacy in two. Lincoln gave Grant command of all Northern armies in March of 1864. Grant led his armies into battles in Virginia while Phil Sheridan and his cavalry did as much damage as possible. In a skirmish at a place called Yellow Tavern, Virginia, Sheridan's and Stuart's forces met; Stuart was fatally wounded.

The Civil War took more American lives than any other war in history, the South losing one-third of its soldiers in battle compared to about one-sixth for the North. More than half of the total deaths were caused by disease and the horrendous conditions of field hospitals. Both sides paid a tremendous economic price, but the South suffered more severely from direct damages. Destruction was pervasive, as towns, farms, trade, industry, and the lives and homes of men, women, and children were all destroyed and an entire Southern way of life was lost.

The South had no voice in the political, social, and cultural affairs of the nation, lessening to a great degree the influence of the more traditional Southern ideals. The Northern Yankee Protestant ideals of hard work, education, and economic freedom became the standard of the United States and helped to influence the development of the nation into a modem, industrial power.

The effects of the Civil War were tremendous. It changed the methods of waging war and has been called the first modern war. It was considered this because of the vast destruction and because it involved the use of all the resources of the opposing sides. There was no way it could have ended other than total defeat and unconditional surrender of one side or the other. It introduced weapons and tactics that, when improved later, were used extensively in the wars of the late 1800s and 1900s. Civil War soldiers were the first to fight in trenches, first to fight under a unified command, and the first to wage a tactic known as the "major cordon defense," a strategy of advance on all fronts. They were also the first to use repeating and breech-loading weapons. Observation balloons were first used during the war along with submarines, ironclad ships, and mines. Telegraphy and railroads were also put to use in the Civil War.

By executive proclamation and constitutional amendment, slavery was officially ended, although deep prejudice and racism remained. The Union was preserved and the states were finally truly united. Sectionalism, especially in the area of politics, remained strong for another 100 years but not to the degree and with the same amount of violence that existed before 1861. It has been noted that the Civil War may have been American democracy's greatest failure because, from 1861 to 1865, calm reason (which is basic to democracy) fell to human passion. Yet, democracy did survive.

The victory of the North established that no state has the right to end or leave the Union. Because of this unity, the United States became a major global power. It is important to remember that Lincoln never proposed to punish the South. He was mostly concerned with restoring the South to the Union in a program that was flexible and practical rather than rigid and unbending. In fact, he never really felt that the states had succeeded in leaving the Union, but that they had left the 'family circle" for a short time.

Twentieth Century Wars

The American isolationist mood was given a shocking and lasting blow in 1941 with the Japanese attack on Pearl Harbor. The nation arose and forcefully entered the international arena as never before. Declaring itself "the arsenal of democracy," it entered the Second World War and emerged not only victorious, but also as the strongest power on the earth. From that point on, the nation would have a permanent and leading place in world affairs.

In the aftermath of World War II, with the Soviet Union having emerged as the second strongest power on Earth, the United States embarked on a policy known as "Containment" of the communist menace. This involved what came to be known as the "Marshall Plan" and the "Truman Doctrine." The Marshall Plan involved the economic aid that was sent to Europe in the aftermath of the war; it aimed at preventing the spread of communism. To that end, the United States devoted an increasingly large share of its foreign policy making, diplomacy, and economic and military might to combat it.

The Truman Doctrine offered military aid to those countries that were in danger of communist upheaval. This led to the era known as the *Cold War*, in which the United States took the lead (accompanied by the Western European nations) against the Soviet Union and the Eastern Bloc countries. It was also at this time that the United States finally gave up on George Washington's advice against "European entanglements" and joined the North Atlantic Treaty Organization (NATO). This was formed in 1949 and was comprised of the United States and several Western European nations for the purposes of opposing communist aggression.

The United Nations was also formed at this time (1945) to replace the defunct League of Nations for the purposes of ensuring world peace. Even with American involvement, this organization would prove largely ineffective in maintaining world peace. In the 1950s, the United States embarked on what was called the "Eisenhower Doctrine," named after the then president, Dwight D. Eisenhower. This policy aimed at trying to maintain peace in a troubled area of the world, the Middle East. However, unlike the Truman Doctrine in Europe, it would have little success.

The United States became involved in a number of world conflicts in the ensuing years. At the core, each was a struggle against communist expansion. Among these were the *Korean War* (1950-1953), *the Vietnam War* (1965-1975), and various continuing entanglements in Central and South America and the Middle East. By the early 1970s, under the leadership of then Secretary of State Henry Kissinger, the United States and its allies embarked on a policy that came to be known as "Détente." This was aimed at easing the tensions between the United States and its allies as well as between the Soviet Union and its allies.

By the 1980s, the United States embarked on what some saw as a renewal of the Cold War. This was owed to the fact that the United States was becoming more involved in trying to prevent communist insurgency in Central America. A massive expansion of its armed forces and the development of space-based weapons systems were undertaken at this time. As this occurred, the Soviet Union, with a failing economic system and a risky adventure in Afghanistan, found itself unable to compete. By 1989, events had come to a head; they ended with the breakdown of the Communist Bloc, the virtual end of the monolithic Soviet Union, and the collapse of the communist system by the early 1990s.

Skill 9.5   Demonstrating knowledge of strategies (e.g., formulating research questions) and resources for historical inquiry

Historical Data

Historical data can come from a wide range of sources, including libraries—small local ones or very large university libraries. Records and guides are almost universally digitally organized and available for instant searching by era, topic, event, personality, or area. Libraries offer resources such as survey information from various departments and bureaus of the federal and state governments; magazines and periodicals in a wide range of topics; artifacts; encyclopedias and other reference materials; and usually, access to the Internet.

Although all these sources offer incredible possibilities for finding even the most obscure information, few things are more valuable than a visit to the site being researched. This can include a visit to historical societies, local libraries, and sometimes even local schools. For example, a historian who is searching for an answer to the question of why his or her great-great-grandfather enlisted in the Union army even though he lived in the Deep South may find that going to the site where the ancestor grew up and looking in the historical records stored in the local school house is a better source than anything found in his or her city library. In this situation, the residents of the town may also be better able to answer the question. The historian may never have find the pertinent historical information without a physical visit to the site.

The same things could be said about geographical data. It is possible to find a map of almost any area online; however, the best maps are often available locally along with first-hand knowledge and information about the development of the area. For example, a courthouse that had been moved from one small town to another in a county in Tennessee for no apparent reason may actually have a detailed history. Perhaps the local residents can relate the tale of a railroad company that wanted to come through the town. The farmers in the area surrounding the previous courthouse didn't want to raise the $100,000 it would take to prevent the railroad from coming through; it was actually more cost effective to uproot the entire community to a new county. This information is not in a history book, yet it would be very important to a study of the geography of the area to get all of the facts.

Scientific Method

The **scientific method** is the process by which researchers can, over time, endeavor to construct an accurate (reliable, consistent, and non-arbitrary) representation of the world. Recognizing that personal and cultural beliefs influence both our perceptions and our interpretations of natural phenomena, standard procedures, and criteria can minimize those influences when developing a theory.

The scientific method has four steps:

1. Observation and description of a phenomenon or group of phenomena
2. Formulation of a hypothesis to explain the phenomena
3. Use of the hypothesis to predict the existence of other phenomena or to predict quantitatively the results of new observations
4. Performance of experimental tests of the predictions by several independent experimenters (as well as the use of properly-performed experiments)

While the researcher may bring certain biases to the study, it is important that bias not be permitted to enter into the interpretation. It is also important that data that doesn't fit the hypothesis not be ruled out. This is unlikely to happen if the researcher is open to the possibility that the hypothesis might turn out to be null. Another important caution is to be certain that the methods for analyzing and interpreting are flawless. Abiding by these mandates is important if the discovery is to make a contribution to human understanding.

The phenomena that interest social scientists are usually complex. Capturing that complexity more fully requires the assessment of simultaneous co-variations along the following dimensions: the units of observation, their characteristics, and time. This is how behavior occurs. For example, to obtain a richer and more accurate picture of the progress of school children means measuring changes in their attainment over time together with changes in the school over time. This acknowledges that changes in one arena of behavior are usually contingent on changes in other areas. Models used for research in the past were inadequate to handle the complexities suggested by multiple co-variations. However, the evolution of computerized data processing has taken away that constraint.

While descriptions of a research project as well as the presentation of outcomes and analyses must be a part of every report, graphs, charts, and sometimes maps are necessary to make the results clearly understandable.

Demography

Demography is the branch of science of statistics most concerned with the social well being of people. Demographic tables may include:

1) Analysis of the population on the basis of age, parentage, physical condition, race, occupation, and/or civil position, giving the actual size and the density of each separate area
2) Changes in the population as a result of birth, marriage, and death
3) Statistics on population movements and their effects/relations to given economic, social, and political conditions
4) Statistics of crime, illegitimacy, and suicide
5) Levels of education and economic and social statistics

Such information is also similar to the area of science known as **vital statistics**; as such, it is indispensable in studying social trends and making important legislative, economic, and social decisions.

Demographic information is typically gathered from census and registrar reports as well as state laws. Such information, especially that from vital statistics, is kept by physicians, attorneys, funeral directors, member of the clergy, and similar professional people. In the United States, demographic information is compiled, kept, and published by the Public Health Services of the United States Department of Health, Education, and Welfare.

The most important element of this information is the **crude rate**, which customarily represents the average of births and deaths for a unit of population of 1000 people over a given calendar year. These can also be sub-divided into categories of sex, color, age, occupation, locality, etc. They are then known as **refined rates**.

Statistics

In examining **statistics** and the sources of statistical data, it is important to be aware of the methods of gathering statistical information. For instance, there are many good sources of raw statistical data. Books such as *The Statistical Abstract of the United States*, published by the United States Chamber of Commerce, *The World Fact Book*, published by the Central Intelligence Agency, or *The Monthly Labor Review* published by the United States Department of Labor are excellent examples that contain a quantity raw data. Many similar yearbooks on various topics are readily available from any library or from the government itself.

However, knowing how that data and information were gathered is at least as equally important as the figures themselves. Only by having knowledge of statistical language and methodology can a reader be truly able to gauge the usefulness of any given piece of data presented. Thus it is important to first understand just what statistics are and what they can and cannot tell us.

Simply put, statistics is a mathematical science that deals with the collection, organization, presentation, and analysis of various forms of numerical data as well as the issues of interpreting and understanding such data. The raw materials of statistics are sets of numbers obtained from enumerations or measurements collected by various methods of extrapolation, such as census taking, interviews, and observations.

In collecting any such statistical information and data, care and adequate precautions must always be taken to assure that the knowledge obtained is complete and accurate. It is also important to be aware of just how much data is necessary to collect in order to establish the idea that is being formulated. One important idea to understand is that statistics usually deal with a specific **model**, **hypothesis**, or **theory** that is being attempted to be proven.

There are several limitations to bear in mind when working with these ideas. For example, a theory can never actually be proven correct; it can only really be corroborated. (**Corroboration** means that the data presented is more consistent with one particular theory than with any other theory.) Additionally, **correlation**, the joint movement of various data points, does not infer **causation** (which occurs when a change in one of those data points causes the other data points to change). It is important to take these aspects into account to be in a better position to appreciate what the collected data is really saying.

Once collected, data must then be arranged, tabulated, and presented. This will permit a ready and meaningful analysis and interpretation. Oftentimes, tables, charts, or graphs can be used to present the information in a concise and easy-to-see manner (the information is sometimes presented in raw numerical order as well). **Tests of reliability** are then used, bearing in mind the manner in which the data has been collected and the inherent biases of any artificially created model, to explain real world events. Indeed, the methods used, as well as the inherent biases and reasons for doing the study, must never be discounted.

Conducting a research project once involved the use of punch cards, microfiche, and other manual means of storing data in a retrievable fashion. Those methods are no more. With high-powered computers available to anyone who chooses to conduct research, organizing data has become revolutionized. Creating multi-level folders, copying and pasting into the folders, making ongoing additions to the bibliography at the exact moment a source is consulted, and using search-and-find functions make this stage of the research process much faster. The results of these new sorting methods equal less frustration and a decrease in the likelihood that important data might be overlooked.

Serious research requires high-level analytical skills. A degree in statistics (or at least a graduate-level concentration) is very useful. A team approach to a research project typically includes a statistician in addition to those members who are knowledgeable in the social sciences.

COMPETENCY 10.0 UNDERSTAND MAJOR CONCEPTS, PRINCIPLES, AND METHODS OF INQUIRY RELATED TO GEOGRAPHY

Skill 10.1 Applying knowledge of basic concepts of geography (e.g., location, movement of people, interaction among peoples)

Geography

Geography involves studying location and how living things and the earth's features are distributed. It includes where animals, people, and plants live as well as the effects of their relationships with earth's physical features. Geographers also explore the locations of earth's features, how they got there, and why they are so important.

Geographical studies are divided into:

- **Regional**: Elements and characteristics of a place or region
- **Topical**: One earth feature or one human activity occurring throughout the entire world
- **Physical**: Earth's physical features, what creates and changes them, and their relationships to each other as well as to human activities
- **Human**: Human activity patterns and how they relate to the environment including political, cultural, historical, urban, and social geographical fields of study

Two of the most important terms in the study of geography are *absolute* and *relative location*. Knowing the location is important in order to determine where something is and where it can be found. To be able to point to a spot on a map and say, "That is where we are" or "That is where we want to be" is very important in geography. It is also important to know where something is in comparison to other things. It is very difficult for many people to describe something without referring to something else. This kind of associative reasoning is a powerful way to think.

Absolute location is the exact whereabouts of a person, place, or thing, according to any kind of geographical indicators. Indicators can include latitude and longitude or GPS. For example, Paris is at 48 degrees north longitude and 2 degrees east latitude. It cannot get much more exact than that. If a person had a map that showed every degree of latitude and longitude, he or she could pinpoint exactly where Paris was and have absolutely no doubt that the geographical depiction was accurate.

Relative location, on the other hand, is always a description that involves more than one thing. When describing a relative location, something is located by describing what is around it. For example, the description of where the nearest post office is in terms of relative location might be "down the street from the supermarket, on the right side of the street, next to the dentist's office."

Ecology

Ecology is the study of how living organisms interact with the physical aspects of their surroundings (their environment), including soil, water, air, and other living things. **Biogeography** is the study of how the surface features of the earth—form, movement, and climate—affect living things.

There are three critical levels of environmental understanding:

1. An **ecosystem** is a community (of any size) consisting of a physical environment and the organisms that live within it.

2. A **biome** is a large area of land with characteristic climate, soil, and mixtures of plants and animals. Biomes are made up of groups of ecosystems. The major biomes include: desert, chaparral, savanna, tropical rain forest, temperate grassland, temperate deciduous forest, taiga, and tundra.

3. A **habitat** is the set of surroundings within which members of a species normally live. Elements of the habitat include soil, water, predators, and competitors.

Within habitats, interactions between members of the species occur. These interactions tend to be of three types:

1. **Competition** occurs between members of the same species or between members of different species for resources required to continue life, to grow, or to reproduce. For example, competition for acorns can occur between squirrels, or it can occur between squirrels and woodpeckers. One species can either push out or cause the demise of another species if it is better adapted to obtain the resource. When a new species is introduced into a habitat, the result can be a loss of the native species and/or significant changes to the habitat. For example, the introduction of the Asian plant Kudzu into the American South has resulted in the destruction of several species because Kudzu grows and spreads very quickly, often smothering everything in its path.

2. **Predation** occurs when predators, which are organisms that live by hunting and eating others, consume the organisms in an area. The species best suited for hunting other species in the habitat will be the species that survives. Larger species that have better hunting skills reduce the amount of prey available for smaller and/or weaker species. This affects both the amount of available prey and the diversity of species that are able to survive in the habitat.

3. **Symbiosis** is a condition in which two organisms of different species are able to live in the same environment over an extended period of time without harming one another. In some cases, one species may benefit without harming the other. In other cases, both species benefit.

Biodiversity refers to the variety of species and organisms on the earth, as well as the variety of available habitats for them. Biodiversity provides the life-support system for all the earth's habitats and species. The greater the degree of biodiversity, the more species and habitats will continue to survive.

When human and other population and migration changes, climate changes, or natural disasters disrupt the delicate balance of a habitat or an ecosystem, species either adapt or become extinct.

Natural changes (e.g., floods, volcanoes, storms, and earthquakes) can occur to alter habitats. These changes can affect the species that exist within the habitat, either by causing extinction or by changing the environment in a way that will no longer support the life systems. **Climate changes** can have similar effects. Inhabiting species can also alter habitats, particularly through migration. Human civilization, population growth, and efforts to control the environment often have a negative effect on various habitats. Humans change their environments to suit their particular needs and interests, which can result in the extinction of species or changes to the habitat itself. For example, deforestation damages the stability of mountain surfaces. One particularly devastating example was in the removal of the grasses of the Great Plains for agriculture. Tilling the ground and planting crops left the soil unprotected. Sustained drought dried out the soil into dust. When windstorms occurred, the topsoil was stripped away and blown all the way to the Atlantic Ocean.

Skill 10.2   Demonstrating knowledge of major physical and human-constructed features of the earth

The six themes of geography are:

Location. This includes relative and absolute location. Remember, a relative location refers to the surrounding geography, such as "on the banks of the Mississippi River," and absolute location refers to a specific point, such as 41 degrees North latitude, 90 degrees West longitude, or 123 Main Street.

Spatial Organization. This is a description of how things are grouped in a given space. In geographical terms, this can describe people, places, and environments anywhere and everywhere on Earth. The most basic form of spatial organization for people is where they live. The vast majority of people live near other people, in villages, towns, cities, or settlements. Oftentimes, these people live near others in order to take advantage of the goods and services that naturally arise from cooperation. Villages, towns, cities, and settlements are, to varying degrees, near bodies of water. Water is a staple of survival for every person on the planet, is a good source of energy for factories and other industries, and is a form of transportation for people and goods. For example, in a city, where are the factories and heavy industry buildings? Are they near airports or train stations? Are they on the edge of town, near major roads? What about housing developments? Are they near these industries, or are they far away? Where are the other industry buildings? Where are the schools and hospitals and parks? What about the police and fire stations? How close are homes to each of these things? Towns, and especially cities, are routinely organized into neighborhoods so that each house or home is near to most things that its residents might need on a regular basis. This means that large cities have multiple schools, hospitals, grocery stores, fire stations, etc.

Place. A place has both human and physical characteristics. Physical characteristics include features such as mountains, rivers, deserts, etc. Human characteristics are the features created by humans' interaction with their environment, such as canals and roads.

Human-Environmental Interaction. The theme of human-environmental interaction has three main concepts: humans adapt to the environment (wearing warm clothing in a cold climate), humans modify the environment (planting trees to block a prevailing wind), and humans depend on the environment (for food, water, and raw materials).

Movement. The theme of movement covers how humans interact with one another through trade, communications, emigration, and other forms of contact.

Region. A region is an area that has some kind of unifying characteristic, such as a common language or a common government. There are three main types of regions: **formal regions** are areas defined by actual political boundaries, such as a city, county, or state; **functional regions** are defined by a common function, such as the area covered by a telephone service; and **vernacular regions** are less formally defined areas that are formed by people's perceptions (e.g., the Middle East or the South).

Human Geography

One way to describe where people live is by the **topography** around them. The vast majority of people on the planet live in areas that are very hospitable. It is true that people live in the Himalayas and in the Sahara, but the populations in those areas are very small when compared to the plains of China, India, Europe, and the United States. People naturally want to live where they won't have to work really hard just to survive, and world population patterns reflect this. However, it is important to remember that these patterns of human distribution took many thousands of years to develop.

Initially, human communities subsisted as gatherers collecting berries, leaves, and other food items. With the invention of tools, it became possible for people to dig for roots, hunt small animals, and catch fish from rivers and oceans. Humans observed their environments and eventually learned to plant seeds and harvest crops. As people migrated to areas in which game and fertile soil were abundant, communities began to develop.

As habitats attracted larger numbers of people, environments became crowded and there was competition for resources. The concept of dividing labor and sharing food began to be realized in more heavily populated areas. Some groups of people focused on growing crops, while others concentrated on hunting. Individual experiences led to the development of skills and of knowledge that made the work easier. Farmers began to develop new plant species, and hunters began to protect animal species from other predators for their own use. This ability to manage the environment led people to settle down and to guard and manage their resources.

Camps soon became villages, and villages became year-round settlements. Animals were domesticated and gathered into herds that met the needs of the village. Along with settled life came a decrease in the need to "travel light"; pottery was developed for storing and cooking food.

By 8000 BCE, culture was beginning to evolve in these villages. Agriculture was developed for the production of grain crops, which led to a decreased reliance on wild plants. Domesticating animals for various purposes decreased the need to hunt wild game. Life became more settled. It was then possible to turn attention to such matters as managing water supplies, producing tools, and making cloth.

From here, there was an increase in both social interaction and the opportunity to reflect upon existence. Mythologies arose alongside various kinds of belief systems. Rituals that re-enacted the mythologies that gave meaning to life were developed.

As farming and animal husbandry skills increased, the dependence upon wild game and food gathering declined. With this change came the realization that a larger number of people could be supported on the produce of farming and animal husbandry.

Two things seem to have come together to produce *cultures* and *civilizations*: a society based on agriculture and centers of the community with literate social and religious structures. The members of the community hierarchies began to manage water supply and irrigation, develop ritual and religious life, and exert their own right to use a portion of the goods produced by the community for their own subsistence in return for their management.

Sharpened skills, the development of more sophisticated tools, commerce with other communities, increasing knowledge of their environment, greater resources available to them, responses to the needs to share an ordered community life, and the protection of their possessions from outsiders led to further division of labor and community development.

As trade routes developed and travel between cities became easier, trade led to specialization. Trade enables a people to obtain the goods they desire in exchange for the goods they are able to produce. This, in turn, leads to increased attention to refinements of technique and the sharing of ideas. As each community learned the value of the goods they produced and improved its ability to produce the goods in greater quantity, industry was born. These concepts continue to prevail in the economic world of today.

Skill 10.3   Analyzing interactions between physical systems and human systems (e.g., economic, cultural, political)

Agricultural Revolution

The **Agricultural Revolution**, initiated by the invention of the plow, led to a thorough transformation of human society by making large-scale agricultural production possible and facilitating the development of agrarian societies. During the period during which the plow was invented, the wheel, numbers, and writing were also invented. Coinciding with the shift from hunting wild game to the domestication of animals, this period was one of dramatic social and economic change.

Numerous changes in lifestyle and thinking accompanied the development of stable agricultural communities. Rather than gathering a wide variety of plants as hunter-gatherers, agricultural communities are dependent on a limited number of plants and crops. Subsistence is vulnerable to the weather and dependent upon planting and harvesting times. Agriculture also required a great deal of physical labor as well as a sense of discipline. Agricultural communities are also more sedentary and stable in terms of location. This made the construction of dwellings possible—especially dwellings relatively close together, creating villages and towns.

Stable communities also freed people from the need to carry everything with them in the move from hunting ground to hunting ground. In addition to pottery, this facilitated the invention of larger, more complex tools. As new tools were envisioned and developed it began to make sense to have some specialization within the society.

In the beginning of the transition to agriculture, the tools that were used for hunting and gathering were adequate to the tasks of agriculture. The initial challenge was in adapting to a new way of life. Once that challenge was met, attention turned to the development of more advanced tools and sources of energy. Six thousand years ago, the first plow was invented in Mesopotamia. This plow was pulled by animals. With this invention, agriculture became possible on a much larger scale. Soon, tools were developed that make such basic tasks as gathering seeds, planting, and cutting grain faster and easier.

It also becomes necessary to maintain social and political stability to ensure that planting and harvesting times are not interrupted by internal discord or a war with a neighboring community. It was also necessary to develop ways to store the crop and to prevent its destruction by the elements and animal (not to mention protection from thieves).

Settled communities that produced the necessities of life were largely self-supporting. Advances in agricultural technology and the ability to produce a surplus of produce created two opportunities: first, the opportunity to trade the surplus goods for other desired goods, and second, vulnerability to others who might steal the goods. Protecting domesticated livestock and surplus crops become an issue for the early communities. This, in turn, led to the construction of walls and other fortifications around the community.

The ability to produce surplus crops also created the opportunity to trade or barter with other communities in exchange for desired goods. Traders and trade routes began to develop between villages and cities. With the expansion of trade and travel between communities came the exchange of ideas and knowledge.

Industrial Revolution

The **Industrial Revolution** of the eighteenth and nineteenth centuries resulted in even greater changes in human civilization, in creating opportunities for trade, in increased production, and in the exchange of ideas and knowledge.

The first phase of the Industrial Revolution (1750-1830) saw the mechanization of the textile industry; vast improvements in mining with the invention of the steam engine; and numerous improvements in transportation with the development and improvement of turnpikes, canals, and the invention of the railroad.

The second phase (1830-1910) resulted in improvements in a number of industries that had already been mechanized through such inventions as the Bessemer steel process and steam ships. New industries arose as a result of the new technological advances, including photography, electricity, and chemical processes. New sources of power were harnessed and applied, including petroleum and hydroelectric power. Precision instruments were developed and engineering was launched. It was during this second phase that the Industrial Revolution spread to other European countries, Japan, and the United States.

The direct results of the Industrial Revolution, particularly as they affected industry, commerce, and agriculture, included:

- Enormous increases in productivity
- Huge increases in world trade
- Specialization and division of labor
- Standardization of parts
- Mass production
- Growth of giant business conglomerates and monopolies
- A new revolution in agriculture facilitated by the steam engine, machinery, chemical fertilizers, processing, canning, and refrigeration

The political results included:

- Growth of complex government by technical experts
- Centralization of government, including regulatory administrative agencies
- Advantages to democratic development, including the extension of franchise to the middle class (and later to all elements of the population), mass education to meet the needs of an industrial society, and the development of media of public communication, including radio, television, and cheap newspapers

- Dangers to democracy, including the risk of media manipulation, the facilitation of dictatorial centralization and totalitarian control, the subordination of the legislative function to administrative directives, greater efforts to achieve uniformity and conformity, and social impersonalization

The economic results included:

- The conflict between free trade and low tariffs and protectionism
- The issue of free enterprise against government regulation
- Struggles between labor and capital, including the trade-union movement
- The rise of socialism
- The rise of the utopian socialists
- The rise of Marxian or scientific socialism

The social results of the Industrial Revolution included:

- Increase of population, especially in industrial centers
- Advances in science applied to agriculture, sanitation, and medicine
- Growth of great cities
- Disappearance of the difference between city dwellers and farmers
- Faster tempo of life and increased stress from the monotony of the work routine
- The emancipation of women
- The decline of religion
- The rise of scientific materialism
- Darwin's theory of evolution

Increased mobility produced a rapid diffusion of knowledge and ideas. Increased mobility also resulted in wide-scale immigration to industrialized countries. Cultures clashed and cultures melded.

Trade Organizations

GATT, NAFTA, WTO, and EU are all forms of trade liberalization. The GATT was founded in 1947; today, as the WTO (established in 1995), it has 147 member nations. It was based on three principles. The first was Most Favored National status for all members. This meant that trade should be based on comparative advantage without tariffs or trade barriers. The second principle was the elimination of quotas. The third was a reduction of trade barriers through multi-lateral trade negotiations. Today, the WTO's object is to promote free trade. As such, it administers trade agreements, settles disputes, and provides a forum for trade discussions and negotiations.

NAFTA and the EU are both forms of regional economic integration. Economic integration is a method of trade liberalization on a regional basis. NAFTA represents the lowest form or first step in the regional trade integration process. Through it, a free trade area exists for two or more countries that abolishes tariffs and other trade barriers but allows the countries to maintain their own trade barriers against the rest of the world. It allows for specialization and trade on the basis of comparative advantage within the area.

The next stage in the integration process is a customs union, which is a free trade area that has common external tariffs against non-members. The third stage is a common market, which is a customs union with free factor mobility within the area. Factors migrate where they find the best payment within the area. The fourth state is an economic union in which the market members have common or coordinated economic and social policies. The final stage is a monetary union in which the area has a common currency. This is what Europe is working toward. They have a common market with elements of the fourth and fifth stages of integration.

The WTO does not change or blur the significance of political borders and territorial sovereignty in the same way that economic integration does, although the WTO is a way of settling trade disputes that arise from the different integration agreements. In the advanced stages of economic integration, the political borders remain but economic and social policies are common or coordinated. In a monetary union, there is one common currency. Each nation is its own independent entity but they each give up some sovereignty in the interest of having a successful union.

Trade agreements proliferate in the world today. The Smoot Hawley Tariffs and the rounds of retaliation in the 1930s are what laid the basis for today's WTO and EU. The GATT and the beginnings of what is now the EU came into being as organizations trying to undo the effects of the Great Depression and the First World War.

Free trade without trade barriers typically results in the most efficient use of resources, with higher consumption, employment, and income levels for all participants. This is why there are so many free trade agreements being negotiated in today's world.

Skill 10.4 **Applying knowledge of maps (e.g., political, physical, topographic, resource), globes, and other geographic tools (e.g., compass rose, legend, map scale)**

Physical locations of the earth's surface features include the four major hemispheres and the parts of the earth's continents in them. Political locations are the political divisions, if any, within each continent. Both physical and political locations are precisely determined in two ways: 1) surveying is done to determine boundary lines and distance from other features, and 2) exact locations are determined by imaginary lines of **latitude** (parallels) and **longitude** (meridians). The intersection of these lines at right angles forms a grid, making it possible to pinpoint an exact location of any place using two grip coordinates.

The process of putting the features of the earth onto a flat surface is called **projection**. All maps are really map projections. There are many different types—each one deals in a different way with the problem of distortion. Map projections are made in a number of ways; some, for example, are done using complicated mathematics. However, the basic ideas behind map projections can be understood by looking at the three most common types:

1) **Cylindrical Projections** - These are done by taking a cylinder of paper and wrapping it around a globe. A light is used to project the globe's features onto the paper. Distortion is least where the paper touches the globe. For example, suppose that the paper was wrapped so that it touched the globe at the equator, the map from this projection would have just a little distortion near the equator. However, in moving north or south of the equator, the distortion would increase. The best known and most widely used cylindrical projection is the **Mercator Projection**. It was first developed in 1569 by Gerardus Mercator, a Flemish mapmaker.

2) **Conical Projections** - The name for these maps comes from the fact that the projection is made onto a cone of paper. The cone is made so that it touches a globe at the base of the cone only. It can also be made so that it cuts through part of the globe in two different places. Again, there is the least distortion where the paper touches the globe. If the cone touches at two different points, there is some distortion at both of them. Conical projections are most often used to map areas in the middle latitudes. Maps of the United States are most often conical projections (because most of the country lies within the middle latitudes).

3) **Flat-Plane Projections** - These are made with a flat piece of paper. It touches the globe at one point only. Areas near this point show little distortion. Flat-plane projections are often used to show the areas of the north and south poles. One such flat projection is called a **Gnomonic Projection**. On this kind of map, all meridians appear as straight lines. Gnomonic projections are useful because any straight line drawn between points on it forms a **Great-Circle Route**.

Great-Circle Routes can best be described by thinking of a globe. When using a globe, the shortest route between two points can be found by simply stretching a string from one point to the other. However, if the string were extended in reality, so that it took into effect the globe's curvature, it would then make a great-circle. A great-circle is any circle that cuts a sphere, such as the globe, into two equal parts. Because of distortion, most maps do not show great-circle routes as straight lines. Gnomonic projections, however, do show the shortest distance between the two places as a straight line; because of this, they are valuable for navigation. They are also called Great-Circle Sailing Maps.

Reading Maps

To properly analyze a given map, it is important to be familiar with the various parts and symbols that most modern maps use. For the most part, this is standardized. Some common features include:

Title - All maps should have a title, just like all books should. The title tells you what information is to be found on the map.

Legend - Most maps have a legend. A legend tells the reader about the various symbols that are used on that particular map as well as what the symbols represent. (It is also called a **map key**.)

Grid - A grid is a series of lines that are used to find exact places and locations on the map. There are several different kinds of grid systems in use; however, most maps do use the longitude and latitude system, known as the **Geographic Grid System**.

Directions - Most maps have some directional system to show which way the map is being presented. Oftentimes, a small compass will be present with arrows showing the four basic directions: north, south, east, and west.

Scale - This is used to show the relationship between a unit of measurement on the map versus the real world measurement on the earth. Maps are drawn to many different scales. Some maps show a lot of detail for a small area. Others show a greater span of distance. It is important to always be cognizant of the scale. For example, the scale might be something like 1 inch = 10 miles for a small area or, for a map showing the whole world, it might have a scale in which 1 inch = 1,000 miles.

Maps have four main properties. They are:
1) The size of the areas shown on the map
2) The shapes of the areas
3) Consistent scales
4) Straight line directions

A map can be drawn so that it is correct in one or more of these properties. No map can be correct in all of them.

Equal Areas - One property that maps often have is that of equal areas. In an equal area map, the meridians and parallels are drawn so that the areas shown have the same proportions as they do on the earth. For example, Greenland is about 1/18th the size of South America; thus, it will show as 1/18th the size on an equal area map. The **Mercator projection** is an example of a map that does not have equal areas. In it, Greenland appears to be about the same size of South America. This is because the distortion is worst at the poles, and Greenland lies near the North Pole.

Conformal Maps - A second map property is conformal, also known as correct shapes. There are no maps that can show very large areas of the earth in their exact shapes; only globes can do that. However, Conformal **Maps** are as close as possible to true shapes. The United States is often shown by **a** Lambert Conformal Conic Projection Map.

Consistent Scales - Many maps attempt to use the same scale on all parts of the map. Generally, this is easier when maps show a relatively small part of the earth's surface. For example, a map of just Florida could be a Consistent Scale Map. Maps showing large areas are typically not Consistent Scale Maps. This is due to distortion. Often, large area maps will have two scales noted in the key. One scale, for example, might be accurate to measure distances between points along the equator. Another might be then used to measure distances between the north and south poles.

Relief Maps - Maps showing physical features often try to show information about the elevation or **relief** of the land. **Elevation** is the distance above or below the sea level. The elevation is usually shown with colors; for instance, all areas on a map that are at a certain level may be shown in the same color.

Relief Maps specifically show the shape of the land surface: flat, rugged, or steep. They usually give more detail than simply showing the overall elevation of the land's surface. Relief is also sometimes shown with colors, but another way to show relief is by using **contour lines**. These lines connect all points of a land surface that are the same height surrounding the particular area of land.

Thematic Maps - These are used to show more specific information, often on a single theme or topic. Thematic Maps show the distribution or amount of something over a certain given area. This can include things such as population density, climate, economic information, cultural, political information, etc.

Skill 10.5   Demonstrating knowledge of strategies (e.g., interpreting maps) and resources for geographic inquiry

An **atlas** is a collection of maps usually bound into a book that contain geographic features, political boundaries, and perhaps social, religious, and economic statistics. Atlases can be found at most libraries, but they are also widely available on the Internet. The United States Library of Congress holds more than 53,000 atlases; it is most likely the largest and most comprehensive collection in the world.

Statistical **surveys** are used in the social sciences to collect information on a sample of the population. With any kind of information, care must be taken to accurately record information so the results are not skewed or distorted.

Opinion polls are used to represent the opinions of a population by asking a number of people a series of questions about a product, place, person, or event and then using the results to apply the answers to a larger group or population. Polls, like surveys, are subject to errors in the process. Errors can occur based on who is asked the question, where they are asked, the time of day, or the biases one may hold in relevance to the poll being taken.

Illustrations of various sorts are used because it is often easier to demonstrate a given idea visually instead of orally. This is especially true in the areas of education and research because humans tend to be visually stimulated; most ideas presented visually are easier to understand and to comprehend than those presented verbally. Among the more common illustrations used in political and social sciences are various types of maps, graphs, and charts.

Photographs and **globes** are useful as well, but as they are limited in what kind of information that they can show, they are rarely used for statistical purposes unless something like a photograph of a particular political figure is necessary for visualization purposes.

Although maps have advantages over globes and photographs, they do have a major disadvantage. Issues of **distortion** limit the truthfulness of the information that maps relay.

Distance is the measurement between two points of location on a map. Measurement can be in terms of feet, yards, miles, meters, or kilometers (just to name a few). Distance is often correct on equidistant maps only in the direction of latitude.

Another method for measuring curvilinear map distances is to use a mechanical device called an **opisometer**. This device uses a small rotating wheel that records the distance traveled. The recorded distance is measured by this device either in centimeters or inches.

Direction is usually measured relative to the location of the north or south pole. Directions determined from these locations are said to be relative to "true north" or "true south." The magnetic poles can also be used to measure direction. However, these points on the earth are located in spatially different spots from the geographic north and south poles. The north magnetic pole is located at 78.3° north, 104.0° west. In the southern hemisphere, the south magnetic pole is located in Commonwealth Day, Antarctica and has a geographical location of 65° south, 139° east. The magnetic poles are not fixed; over time, they shift their spatial position.

COMPETENCY 11.0 UNDERSTAND MAJOR CONCEPTS, PRINCIPLES, AND METHODS OF INQUIRY RELATED TO U.S. GOVERNMENT AND CIVICS

Skill 11.1 Demonstrating knowledge of the functions of government and the basic principles of the U.S. government as a republic

Many of the core values in the U.S. democratic system can be found in the opening words of the Declaration of Independence. This includes the important beliefs in equality and the rights of citizens to "life, liberty and the pursuit of happiness."

The Declaration was a condemnation of the British King's tyrannical government, and these words emphasized the American colonists' belief that a government received its authority to rule from the people, and its function should not be to suppress the governed, but to protect the rights of the governed, including protection from the government itself. These two ideals, **popular sovereignty** and the **rule of law**, are basic core values of democracy.

Popular sovereignty grants citizens the ability to directly participate in their own government by voting and running for public office. This ideal is based on a belief of equality that holds that all citizens have an equal right to engage in their own governance. The ideal of equality has changed over the years, as women and non-white citizens were not always allowed to vote or bring suit in court. Now, all U.S citizens above the age of 18 are allowed to vote. This expansion of rights since the adoption of the Constitution demonstrates an American value of *respect for minority rights*.

The democratic system of election and representation is based on **majority rule**. In the case of most public elections, the candidate who receives the most votes is awarded the office. Majority rule is also used to pass legislation in Congress. Majority rule is meant to ensure that authority cannot be concentrated in one small group of people.

The rule of law is the ideal that the law applies not only to the governed, but to the government as well. This core value gives authority to the justice system, which grants citizens protection from the government by requiring that any accusation of a crime be proved by the government before a person is punished. This is called **due process**, and it ensures that any accused person will have an opportunity to confront his accusers and provide a defense. Due process follows from the core value of a right to liberty. The government cannot take away a citizen's liberty without reason or without proof. The correlating ideal is also a core value—that someone who does harm to another or breaks a law will receive **justice** under the democratic system. The ideal of justice holds that a punishment will fit the crime, and that any citizen can appeal to the judicial system if he feels he has been wronged.

Central to the ideal of justice is an expectation that citizens will act in a way that promotes the **common good**, meaning that they will treat one another with honesty and respect and will exercise self-discipline in their interactions with others. These are among the basic responsibilities of a citizen of a democracy.

Skill 11.2   Identifying the roles and interrelationships of national, state, and local governments in the United States

<u>Powers delegated to the Federal government:</u>

1. To tax.
2. To borrow and coin money
3. To establish postal service.
4. To grant patents and copyrights.
5. To regulate interstate & foreign commerce.
6. To establish courts.
7. To declare war.
8. To raise and support the armed forces.
9. To govern territories.
10. To define and punish felonies and piracy on the high seas.
11. To fix standards of weights and measures.
12. To conduct foreign affairs.

<u>Powers reserved to the states:</u>

1. To regulate intrastate trade.
2. To establish local governments.
3. To protect general welfare.
4. To protect life and property.
5. To ratify amendments.
6. To conduct elections.
7. To make state and local laws.

<u>Concurrent powers of the Federal government and states.</u>
1. Both Congress and the states may tax.
2. Both may borrow money.
3. Both may charter banks and corporations.
4. Both may establish courts.
5. Both may make and enforce laws.
6. Both may take property for public purposes.
7. Both may spend money to provide for the public welfare.

<u>Implied powers of the Federal government.</u>
1. To establish banks or other corporations to tax, borrow, and regulate commerce.
2. To spend money for roads, schools, health, insurance, etc., to establish post roads, to tax to provide for general welfare and defense, and to regulate commerce.
3. To create military academies to raise and support an armed force.
4. To locate and generate sources of power and sell surplus to dispose of government property, commerce, and war powers.
5. To assist and regulate agriculture to tax and spend for general welfare and to regulate commerce.

Skill 11.3   Recognizing the roles and powers of the executive, legislative, and judicial branches of government

At the United States federal level:

Legislative – Article I of the Constitution established the legislative, or law-making, branch of the government called the Congress. It is made up of two houses, the House of Representatives and the Senate. Voters in all states elect the members who serve in each respective House of Congress. The legislative branch is responsible for making laws, raising and printing money, regulating trade, establishing the postal service and federal courts, approving the president's appointments, declaring war, and supporting the armed forces. The Congress also has the power to change the Constitution itself, and to *impeach* (bring charges against) the president. Charges for impeachment are brought by the House of Representatives, and are then tried in the Senate.

Executive – Article II of the Constitution created the executive branch of the government, headed by the president, who leads the country. This branch recommends new laws and can veto bills passed by the legislative branch. As the chief of state, the president is responsible for carrying out the laws of the country as well as the treaties and declarations of war passed by the legislative branch. The president also appoints federal judges and is commander-in-chief of the military when it is called into service. Other members of the executive branch include the vice-president, also elected, and various cabinet members as the president might appoint: ambassadors, presidential advisors, members of the armed forces, and other appointed and civil servants of government agencies, departments, and bureaus. Though the president appoints them, they must be approved by the legislative branch.

Judicial – Article III of the Constitution established the judicial branch of government headed by the Supreme Court. The Supreme Court has the power to rule that a law passed by the legislature, or an act of the executive branch, is illegal and unconstitutional. Citizens, businesses, and government officials can, in an appeal capacity, ask the Supreme Court to review a decision made in a lower court if they believe that the ruling by a judge is unconstitutional. The judicial branch also includes lower federal courts known as federal district courts that have been established by the Congress. These courts try lawbreakers and review cases referred from other courts.

Skill 11.4   Demonstrating knowledge of the Declaration of Independence, the U.S. Constitution, and the Bill of Rights

Declaration of Independence

The beginnings of civil liberties and the idea of civil rights in the United States go back to the ideas of the ancient Greeks. This was illustrated by the early struggle for civil rights against the British and by the very philosophies that led people to come to the New World in the first place. Religious freedom, political freedom, and the right to live one's life as one sees fit are basic to the American ideal. These were embodied in the ideas expressed in the Declaration of Independence and the Constitution.

The Declaration of Independence was adopted on July 4, 1776. It laid out the reasons and justifications for separating from Britain, but was also used as a founding document to later form the United States of America. It was a joint work created by some of America's most important founding fathers, including John Adams, Benjamin Franklin, Roger Sherman, Robert Livingston, and Thomas Jefferson.

Influences for the Declaration of Independence included the Dutch Oath of Abjuration and philosophies of the Enlightenment period in addition to those of early Greek democratic processes.

U.S. Constitution

The United States Constitution is the supreme law of the United States of America. Its first draft was written in 1787 by the Constitutional Convention in Philadelphia, Pennsylvania.

It is composed of a preamble (a statement of purpose), seven articles, and twenty-seven amendments. The seven articles include information on the following:

Article One: Legislative power   Article Five: Process of Amendments
Article Two: Executive power   Article Six: Federal power
Article Three: Judicial power   Article Seven: Ratification
Article Four: States' powers and limits

Bill Of Rights

The first ten of the twenty-seven amendments to the United States Constitution are known as the Bill of Rights. They outline information on civil liberties and civil rights. James Madison was credited with writing a majority of them.

Skill 11.5   Identifying the rights and responsibilities of U.S. citizenship

The cause of human rights has been advanced significantly since the eighteenth century, both in theory and in fact. Several fundamental statements of human rights in the United States have extended and established human rights throughout the world.

The U.S. Declaration of Independence, ratified in 1776, declared that certain truths are self-evident: all men are created equal, and they are inherently endowed with certain unalienable rights that no government should ever violate. These rights include the right to life, liberty, and the pursuit of happiness. When a government infringes upon those rights or fails to protect those rights, it is both the right and the duty of the people to overthrow that government and to establish in its place a new government that will protect those rights.

The Declaration of the Rights of Man and of the Citizen is a document created by the French National Assembly and issued in 1789. It sets forth the "natural, inalienable and sacred rights of man." It proclaims the following rights:

- Men are born and remain free and equal in rights. Social distinctions may only be founded upon the general good.
- The aim of all political association is the preservation of the natural and imprescriptible rights of man: liberty, property, security, and resistance to oppression.
- All sovereignty resides essentially in the nation. No body or individual may exercise any authority that does not proceed directly from the nation.
- Liberty is the freedom to do everything that injures no one else; hence, the exercise of these rights has no limits except those that assure to the other members of the society the enjoyment of the same rights. These limits can only be determined by law.
- Law can only prohibit such actions as are hurtful to society.
- Law is the expression of the general will. Every citizen has a right to participate in the formation of law. It must be the same for all. All citizens, being equal in the eyes of the law, are equally eligible to all dignities and to all public positions and occupations, according to their abilities.
- No person shall be accused, arrested, or imprisoned except in the cases and according to the forms prescribed by law.
- The law shall provide for such punishments only as are strictly and obviously necessary.
- All persons are held innocent until they have been declared guilty. If it is necessary to arrest a person, all harshness not essential to the securing of the prisoner's person shall be severely repressed by law.
- No one shall be disquieted on account of his opinions, including religious views, provided their manifestation does not disturb the peace.
- The free communication of ideas and opinions is one of the most precious of the rights of man.

- The security of the rights of man and of the citizen requires public military force. These forces are, therefore, established for the good of all and not for the personal advantage of those to whom they shall be entrusted.
- A common contribution is essential for the maintenance of the public forces and for the cost of administration. This should be equitably distributed among all the citizens in proportion to their means.
- All the citizens have a right to decide, either personally or by their representatives, as to the necessity of the public contribution.
- Society has the right to require of every public agent an account of his administration.
- A society in which the observance of the law is not assured, nor the separation of powers defined, has no constitution at all.
- Since property is an inviolable and sacred right, no one shall be deprived thereof except where public necessity, legally determined, shall clearly demand it, and then only on condition that the owner shall have been previously and equitably indemnified.

The United Nations Declaration of Universal Human Rights (1948) opens with these words: "Whereas recognition of the inherent dignity and of the equal and inalienable rights of all members of the human family is the foundation of freedom, justice and peace in the world. Whereas disregard and contempt for human rights have resulted in barbarous acts which have outraged the conscience of mankind, and the advent of a world in which human beings shall enjoy freedom of speech and belief and freedom from fear and want has been proclaimed as the highest aspiration of the common people." It sets out these articles:

1. All human beings are born free and equal in dignity and rights. They are endowed with reason and conscience and should act towards one another in a spirit of brotherhood.
2. Everyone is entitled to all the rights and freedoms set forth in this Declaration, without distinction of any kind.
3. Everyone has the right to life, liberty, and security of person.
4. No one shall be held in slavery or servitude.
5. No one shall be subjected to torture or to cruel, inhuman, or degrading treatment or punishment.
6. Everyone has the right to recognition everywhere as a person before the law.
7. All are equal before the law and are entitled without any discrimination to equal protection of the law.
8. Everyone has the right to an effective remedy by the competent national tribunals for acts violating the fundamental rights granted by the constitution of by law.
9. No one shall be subjected to arbitrary arrest, detention, or exile.
10. Everyone is entitled in full equality to a fair and public hearing by an independent and impartial tribunal, in the determination of rights and obligations and of any criminal charges.

11. All people charged with a penal offence have the right to be presumed innocent until proved guilty according to law in a public trial at which they have had all the guarantees necessary for their defense. No one shall be held guilty of any penal offence on account of any act or omission which did not constitute a penal offence, under national or international law, at the time when it was committed

12. No one shall be subjected to arbitrary interference with privacy, family, home, or correspondence, nor to attacks upon honor and reputation.

13. Everyone has the right to freedom of movement and residence within the borders of each state. All people have the right to leave any country, including their own, and to return to their country.

14. Everyone has the right to seek and to enjoy in other countries asylum from persecution. This right may not be invoked in the case of prosecutions genuinely arising from non-political crimes or from acts contrary to the purposes and principles of the United Nations.

15. Everyone has the right to a nationality. No one shall be arbitrarily deprived of his nationality nor denied the right to change nationality.

16. Men and women of full age have the right to marry and to found a family. They are entitled to equal rights as to marriage, during marriage, and at its dissolution. Marriage shall be entered into only with the free and full consent of the intending spouses. The family is the natural and fundamental group unit of society and is entitled to protection by society and the State.

17. Everyone has the right to own property alone or in association with others. No one shall be arbitrarily deprived of his property.

18. Everyone has the right to freedom of thought, conscience, and religion, including the right to change religion or belief, and freedom to manifest religion or belief in teaching, practice, worship, and observance.

19. Everyone has the right to freedom of opinion and expression.

20. Everyone has the right to freedom of peaceful assembly and association. No one may be compelled to belong to an association

21. Everyone has the right to take part in the government of his or her country, directly or through freely chosen representatives. Everyone has the right of equal access to public service in his or her country. The will of the people shall be the basis of the authority of government.

22. Everyone has the right to social security and is entitled to realization of the economic, social, and cultural rights indispensable for dignity and the free development of personality.

23. Everyone has the right to work. Everyone, without any discrimination, has the right to equal pay for equal work. Everyone who works has the right to just and favorable remuneration. Everyone has the right to form and to join trade unions for the protection of interests.

24. Everyone has the right to rest and leisure, including reasonable limitation of working hours and periodic holidays with pay.

25. All people have the right to a standard of living adequate for the health and well-being of themselves and their families, and the right to security in the event of unemployment, sickness, disability, widowhood, old age, or other lack of livelihood in circumstances beyond their control. Motherhood and childhood are entitled to special care and assistance. All children shall enjoy the same social protection.

26. Everyone has the right to education. Education shall be directed to the full development of the human personality and to the strengthening of respect for human rights and fundamental freedoms. Parents have a prior right to choose the kind of education that shall be given to their children.

27. Everyone has the right to freely participate in the cultural life of the community. All people have the right to the protection of the moral and materials interests resulting from any scientific, literary, or artistic production of which they are the author.

28. Everyone is entitled to a social and international order in which the rights and freedoms set forth in this Declaration can be fully realized.

The United Nations Convention on the Rights of the Child brings together the rights of children as they are enumerated in other international documents. In this document, those rights are clearly and completely stated, along with the explanation of the guiding principals that define the way society views children. The goal of the document is to clarify the environment that is necessary to enable every human being to develop to his or her full potential. The Convention calls for resources and contributions to be made to ensure the full development and survival of all children. The document also requires the establishment of appropriate means to protect children from neglect, exploitation, and abuse. The document also recognizes that parents have the most important role in raising children.

Skill 11.6   Demonstrating knowledge of strategies and resources (e.g., Internet, mass communication) for inquiry related to government and civics

Primary sources are works, records, etc. that were created during the period being studied or immediately after it. Secondary sources are works written significantly after the period being studied; they are based upon primary sources.

Suppose an individual is preparing for a presentation on the Civil War and intends to focus on causes, an issue that has often been debated. If examining the matter of slavery as a cause, a graph of the increase in the number of slaves by area of the country for the previous 100 years would be very useful in the discussion. If focusing on the economic conditions that were driving the politics of the age, graphs of GDP, distribution of wealth geographically and individually, and relationship of wealth to ownership of slaves would be useful.

In that same manner, if discussing the war in Iraq, detailed maps with geopolitical elements would help to clarify not only the day-to-day happenings, but also the historical features that led up to it. A map showing the number of oil fields and where they are situated with regard to the various political factions, and charts showing output of those fields historically, would be useful.

As another example, when teaching the history of space travel, photos of the most famous astronauts can add interest to the discussion. Graphs showing the growth of the industry, and charts showing discoveries and their relationship to the lives of everyday Americans might also be helpful.

Geography and history classes are notoriously labeled by students as dull. With all the visual resources available nowadays, however, those classes have the potential for being the most exciting courses in the curriculum.

COMPETENCY 12.0 UNDERSTAND MAJOR CONCEPTS, PRINCIPLES, AND METHODS OF INQUIRY RELATED TO ECONOMICS

Skill 12.1 **Recognizing basic economic concepts (e.g., scarcity, supply and demand, needs and wants, opportunity cost, productivity, trade) and the purposes and functions of currency**

The fact that resources are scarce is the basis for the existence of economics. Economics is defined as a study of how scarce resources are allocated to satisfy unlimited wants. **Resources** refer to the four factors of production: labor, capital, land, and entrepreneurship. The individual has the right to supply whatever resources he or she wants to the market. The fact that the supply of these resources is finite means that society cannot have as much of everything that it wants. There is a constraint on production and consumption, and on the kinds of goods and services that can be produced and consumed. **Scarcity** means that choices have to be made. If society decides to produce more of one good, this means that there are fewer resources available for the production of other goods.

Assume a society can produce two goods: good A and good B. The society uses resources in the production of each good. If producing one unit of good A results in a reduction of the same amount of resources used to produce three units of good B, then producing one more unit of good A results in a decrease in three units of good B. In effect, one unit of good A "costs" three units of good B. This cost is referred to as opportunity cost. **Opportunity cost** is the value of the sacrificed alternative (the value of what had to be given up in order to have the output of good A). Opportunity cost does not just refer to production. Your opportunity cost of studying with this guide is the value of what you are not doing because you are studying, whether that cost is watching TV, spending time with family, or working. Every choice has an opportunity cost.

The **supply curve** represents the selling and production decisions of the seller; it is based on the costs of production. The costs of production of a product are based on the costs of the resources used in its production. The costs of resources are based on the scarcity of the resource. The scarcer a resource is, relatively speaking, the higher its price. A diamond costs more than paper because diamonds are scarcer than paper is. All of these concepts are embodied in the seller's supply curve. The same thing is true on the buying side of the market. The buyer's preferences, tastes, income—all of his buying decisions—are embodied in the **demand curve**. Where the demand and supply curves intersect is where the buying decisions of buyers are equal to the selling decisions of sellers. At this point, the quantity that buyers want to buy at a particular price is equal to the quantity that sellers want to sell at that particular price. When this occurs, the market is in equilibrium.

What happens when there is a change? Suppose a new big oil field is found. Also suppose there is a technology that allows its recovery and refining at a fraction of the present costs. The result is a big increase in the supply of oil at lower costs, as reflected by a rightward shifting oil supply curve. Oil is used as an input into almost all production. Firms now have lower costs. This means that the firm can produce the same amount of output at a lower cost, or they can produce a larger amount of output at the same cost. The result is a rightward shift of the firm's, and therefore, the industry's supply curve. This means that sellers are willing and able to offer for sale larger quantities of output at each price. Assuming buyers' buying decisions stay the same, there is a new market equilibrium, or new point of intersection of the shifted supply curve with the buyers' demand curve. The result is a lower price with a larger quantity of output. The market has achieved a new equilibrium based on the increase in the quantity of a resource.

Firms in markets tend to grow over time. If there is a market for the firm's product, it experiences economies of scale (lower per unit costs) as it grows. As firms grow, they tend to become larger relative to the market, and the smaller, more inefficient firms tend to go out of business. Larger firms have more market power and are able to influence their price and output. They can become monopolistic. Government counters this reduction in competition in a market by enacting anti-trust legislation to protect the competitive nature of the market.

Skill 12.2   Demonstrating knowledge of the basic structure of the U.S. economy and ways in which the U.S. economy relates to and interacts with the economies of other nations

The **traditional economy** is one based on custom. This term usually describes the situation that exists in many less developed countries, where people tend to do things the way their ancestors did. Since their whole mindset is directed toward tradition, they are typically not very interested in technology, equipment, and new ways of doing things. Technology and equipment are viewed as a threat to the old way and to their traditions; there is usually very little upward mobility.

The model of **capitalism** is based on the private ownership of the means of production. It operates on the basis of free markets, on both the input and output sides. The free markets function to coordinate market activity and to achieve an efficient allocation of resources.

Laissez-faire capitalism is based on the premise of no government intervention in the economy. In it, the market will eliminate any unemployment or inflation that occurs. Government needs only to provide the framework for the functioning of the economy and to protect private property. The role of financial incentives is crucial, as they result in risk-taking and research and development. Capitalist economies tend to have democratic forms of government because the system is based on competition and individual freedoms.

A **command economy** is almost the exact opposite of a market economy. A command economy is based on government ownership of the means of production; it also uses planning to take the place of the market. Instead of the market determining the output mix and the allocation of resources, the bureaucracy fulfills this role by determining the output mix and establishing production target for the enterprises, which are publicly owned. The result is inefficiency. There is little interest in innovation and research because there is no financial reward for the innovator. A command economy tends to have an authoritarian form of government because a planning mechanism that replaces the market requires a planning authority to make decisions, supplementing the freedom of choice of consumers and workers.

A **mixed economy** uses a combination of markets and planning, with the degree of each varying according to country. The real world can be described as a series of mixed economies, each with varying degrees of planning. The use of markets in a mixed economy results in the greatest efficiency because markets direct resources in and out of industries according to changing profit conditions. However, government is needed to perform various functions. The degree of government involvement in the economy can vary in mixed economies. Government is needed to keep the economy stable during periods of inflation and unemployment.

All of the major economies of the world are mixed economies. They use markets but have different degrees of government involvement in the functioning of the markets and in the provision of public goods. For example, in some countries, health care and education are provided by government and are not a part of the private sector. In the United States, most health care and higher education organizations are private at the expense of the consumer.

Skill 12.3   Recognizing the roles and interactions of consumers and producers in the U.S. economy

The U.S. economy consists of the **household** or consumer sector, the **business** sector, and the **government** sector. Households earn their incomes by selling their factors of production in the input market. Businesses hire their inputs in the factor market and use them to produce outputs. Households use their incomes earned in the factor market to purchase the output of businesses. Both households and businesses are active participants in both the input and output market. Households do not spend all of their income; they save some of it in banks. A well-organized, smoothly functioning banking system is required for the operation of the economy.

The function of organized labor is to help obtain a higher factor income for workers. Organized labor negotiates the work agreement, or contract, for their union members. This collective bargaining agreement is a contract between the worker and the employer; it states the terms and conditions of employment for the length of the contract.

Macroeconomics refers to the functioning of the economy on the national level as well as the functioning of the aggregate units that comprise the national economy. Macroeconomics is concerned with a study of the economy's overall economic performance, or what is called the **Gross Domestic Product** (GDP). The GDP is a measure of the economy's output during a specified time period. Tabulating the economy's output can be measured in two ways, both of which give the same result: the expenditures approach and the incomes approach. Basically, what is spent on the national output by each sector of the economy is equal to what is earned producing the national output by each of the factors of production.

The macroeconomy consists of four broad sectors: *consumers, businesses, government,* and the *foreign* sector. In the expenditures approach, GDP is determined by the amount of spending in each sector. GDP is equal to the consumption expenditures of consumers, plus the investment expenditures of businesses, plus the spending of all three levels of government, plus the net export spending in the foreign sector. It can be determined by the equation below:

$$GDP = C + I + G + (X-M)$$

When the economy is functioning smoothly, the amount of national output produced, or the aggregate supply, is just equal to the amount of national output purchased, or aggregate demand. It is at this point that we have an economy in a period of prosperity without economic instability. However, market economies experience the fluctuations of the business cycle (the ups and downs in the level of economic activity). There are four phases: **boom** (period of prosperity), **recession** (a period of declining GDP and rising unemployment), **trough** (the low point of the recession), and **recovery** (a period of lessening unemployment and rising prices). There are no rules pertaining to the duration or severity of any of the phases. The phases result in periods of unemployment and periods of inflation. Inflation results from too much spending in the economy; it occurs when buyers want to buy more than sellers can produce and bid up prices for the available output. Unemployment occurs when there is not enough spending in the economy; sellers have produced more output than buyers are buying, and the result is a surplus situation. Firms faced with surplus merchandise then lower their production levels and lay off workers. The result is unemployment. These are situations that require government policy actions.

The U.S. economy is based on the concepts of individual freedom of choice and competition. Economic agents are free to pursue their own interests. They can choose their occupation and undertake entrepreneurial ventures. If they are successful, they gain in the form of profits. The profit incentive is very important because people and businesses are willing to take risks for the possibility of gaining profit. The U.S. economy is one of the most successful economies in the world, with the highest total GDP. Like any market economy, it is subject to the business cycle and temporary bouts of inflation and/or unemployment. When they do occur, appropriate policies are typically implemented in time to counteract them.

Skill 12.4   Identifying the functions of private business, banks, and the government in the U.S. economy

Households, businesses, and government are related through the **circular flow diagram**. They are all integral parts of the macroeconomy, and they contain two markets. The **input market** exists when factor owners sell their factors and employers hire their inputs. Sometimes, labor is organized into labor unions in the input market. The purpose of the labor union is to negotiate the work contract with the employer and to establish a procedure for grievances. Unions typically hope to acquire a larger share of income for their members. The **output market** exists when firms sell the output they produce with their inputs. It is wherein factors owners spend their incomes on goods and services.

There are two sectors of the macroeconomy: households and businesses. Households sell their factors in the input market and use their income to purchase goods and services in the output market. Therefore, wages, interest, rents, and profits flow from the business sector to the household sector. Because factor incomes are based on the scarcity of the factor as well as the contribution of the factor, there is often an unequal distribution of income; not all factors are equal.

Households that earn their factor incomes in the factor market spend their incomes on goods and services produced by businesses and sold in the output market. Receipts for goods and services flow from households to businesses. The government receives tax payments from households and businesses, and then provides services to businesses and households. Each of these three exchanges of factors is a component of the aggregate sectors of the economy; as such, they all make a contribution to the GDP.

Adding financial institutions to the picture demonstrates how the Federal Reserve implements monetary policy. There are three components of monetary policy: the reserve ratio, the discount rate, and open market operations. Changes in any of these three components affect the amount of money in the banking system and thus, the level of spending in the economy. The **reserve ratio** refers to the portion of deposits that banks are required to hold as vault cash or on deposit with the Federal Reserve. The purpose of this reserve ratio is to give the Federal Reserve a way to control the money supply. These funds can't be used for any other purpose. When the Federal Reserve changes the reserve ratio, it changes the money creation and lending ability of the banking system. When the Federal Reserve wants to expand the money supply, it lowers the reserve ratio, leaving banks with more money to loan. This is one aspect of **expansionary** monetary policy. When the reserve ratio is increased, the result is that banks have less money to make loans with, which is considered a form of **contractionary** monetary policy. This type of policy leads to a lower level of spending in the economy.

Another way in which monetary policy is implemented is by changing the discount rate. When banks have temporary cash shortages, they can borrow from the Federal Reserve. The interest rate on the funds they borrow is called the discount rate. Raising and lowering the discount rate is a way of controlling the money supply. Lowering the discount rate encourages banks to borrow from the Federal Reserve, instead of restricting their lending to deal with the temporary cash shortage. By encouraging banks to borrow, their lending ability is increased; this results in a higher level of spending in the economy. Lowering the discount rate is another form of expansionary monetary policy. Discouraging bank lending by raising the discount rate is another form of contractionary monetary policy. In this way, a well-developed banking system is necessary for capital formation and investment purposes.

Skill 12.5   Identifying the knowledge and skills necessary to make reasoned and responsible financial decisions as a consumer, producer, saver, and borrower in a market economy

Economics is the study of how a society allocates its scare resources to satisfy what are basically unlimited and competing wants. Economics can also be defined as a study of the production, consumption, and distribution of goods and services. Both of these definitions are the same. A fundamental fact of economics is that resources are scarce and that wants are infinite. The fact that scarce resources have to satisfy unlimited wants means that choices have to be made, whether the entity is a consumer, producer, saver, or investor. As mentioned in an example in Skill 12.1, if society uses its resources to produce good A, then it doesn't have those resources to produce good B. More of good A means less of good B.

On the consumption side of the market, consumers buy the goods and services that give them satisfaction, or utility. They want to obtain the most utility they can for their dollar. The quantity of goods and services that consumers are willing and able to purchase at different prices during a given period of time is referred to as demand. Since consumers buy the goods and services that give them satisfaction, this means that, for the most part, they don't buy the goods and services that they don't want or that don't give them satisfaction. Consumers are, in effect, voting for the goods and services that they want with their dollars, or what is called **dollar voting**. Consumers are basically signaling firms as to how they want society's scarce resources used with their dollar votes. A good that society wants acquires enough dollar votes for the producer to experience profits—a situation in which the firm's revenues exceed the firm's costs. The existence of profits indicates to the firm that it is producing the goods and services that consumers want, and that society's scarce resources are being used in accordance with consumer preferences.

This process through which consumers vote with their dollars is called **consumer sovereignty**. Consumers are directing the allocation of scarce resources in the economy with their dollar spending. Firms, who are in business to earn profit, then hire resources, or inputs, in accordance with consumer preferences. This is the way in which resources are allocated in a market economy, with consumers basing their decisions on the utility or satisfaction they receive from buying goods.

Supply is based on production costs. The supply of a good or service is defined as the quantities of a good or service that a producer is willing and able to sell at different prices during a given period of time. Remember, market equilibrium occurs when the buying decisions of buyers are equal to the selling decision of seller, or where the demand and supply curves intersect. At this point, the quantity that sellers want to sell at a price is equal to the quantity the buyers want to buy at that same price. This is the market equilibrium price.

The price of an input or output allocates that input or output to those who are willing and able to transact at the market price. Those who can transact at the market price or better are included in the market; those that can't or won't transact at the market price are excluded from the market.

The fundamental characteristics of the U.S. economic system are the uses of competition and markets. Profit and competition all go together in the U.S. economic system. Competition is determined by market structure. Since the cost curves are the same for all the firms, the only difference comes from the revenue side. Each firm maximizes profit by producing at the point where marginal cost equal marginal revenue. The existence of economic profits, an above normal rate of return, attracts capital to an industry and results in expansion.

Whether or not new firms can enter the market depends on barriers to entry. Firms can enter easily in perfect competition, and the expansion will continue until economic profits are eliminated and firms earn a normal rate of return. The significant barriers to entry in monopoly serve to keep firms out, so the monopolist continues to earn an above normal rate of return. Some firms will be able to enter in monopolistic competition but won't have a monopoly over the existing firm's brand name. The competitiveness of the market structure determines whether new firms or capital can enter in response to profits.

Profit functions as a financial incentive for individuals and firms. The possibility of earning profit is why individuals are willing to undertake entrepreneurial ventures and why firms are willing to spend money on research and development and innovation. Without these kinds of financial incentives, there wouldn't be new product development or technological advancement.

Savings represents delayed consumption. Savers must be paid a price for delaying consumption. This price is called the interest rates. Savers will save more money at higher interest rates than at lower interest rates. The interest rate is the price of borrowing to the investor. Investors will borrow more funds at lower interest rates than at higher interest rates. The equilibrium rate of interest is the rate at which the amount savers want to save is equal to the amount borrowers want to borrow for investment purposes.

Skill 12.6   Demonstrating knowledge of strategies (e.g., interpreting graphs and tables) and resources for inquiry related to economics

In measuring the social significance of an event or issue, one of the first questions to ask is how many people are affected. Wide sweeping events such as wars, natural disasters, and revolutions are significant partly because they can change the way of life for many people in a short time.

However, some significant changes take place over long periods of time, so it is also important to look at the long-term effects of an event or phenomenon, following the chain of causes and effects. In this way, events that seem insignificant at the time they occur, or which affect only a small number of people, can be linked directly to large societal changes.

Participation in self-government is one of the United States' core democratic values. By participating in democratic institutions, citizens become better informed of their rights and responsibilities in a democracy, and thus better citizens. While elementary students are too young to participate directly by voting, classroom activities that simulate elections can help to develop a sense of the importance of participating. Encouraging structured discussions or debates on issues directly affecting the students can help to establish respect for minority viewpoints and the importance of free expression—both core democratic values.

There are many different ways to find ideas for **research problems**. One of the most common ways is through experiencing and assessing relevant problems in a specific field. Researchers are often involved in the fields in which they choose to study, and thus encounter practical problems related to their areas of expertise on a daily basis. They can then use their knowledge, expertise, and research ability to examine their selected research problem. For students, all that this entails is being curious about the world around them. Research ideas can come from one's background, culture, education, or experiences. Another way to get research ideas is by exploring literature in a specific field and coming up with a question that extends or refines previous research.

Once a **topic** is decided upon, a research question must be formulated. A research question is a relevant, researchable, feasible statement that identifies the information to be studied. Once this initial question is formulated, it is a good idea to think of specific issues related to the topic. This will help to create a hypothesis. A research **hypothesis** is a statement of the researcher's expectations for the outcome of the research problem. It is a summary statement of the problem to be addressed in any research document. A good hypothesis states, clearly and concisely, the researchers' expected relationship between the variables that they are investigating. Once a hypothesis is decided, the rest of the research paper should focus on analyzing a set of information or arguing a specific point. Thus, there are two types of research papers: analytical and argumentative.

Analytical papers focus on examining and understanding the various parts of a research topic and reformulating them in a new way to support your initial statement. In this type of research paper, the research question is used as both a basis for investigation as well as a topic for the paper. Once a variety of information is collected on the given topic, it is coalesced into a clear discussion

Argumentative papers focus on supporting the question or claim with evidence or reasoning. Instead of presenting research to provide information, an argumentative paper presents research in order to prove a debatable statement and interpretation.

COMPETENCY 13.0 UNDERSTAND PROCESSES AND APPROACHES FOR EXPLORING MATHEMATICS AND SOLVING PROBLEMS

Skill 13.1   Identifying effective strategies (e.g., determining relevant information, simplifying, estimating) for solving single-step and multi-step problems in mathematical and other contexts

Successful math teachers introduce their students to multiple problem-solving strategies. They create classroom environments where free thought and experimentation are encouraged. Teachers can promote problem-solving among their students by allowing them to make multiple attempts at problems, giving credit for reworking test or homework problems, and encouraging students to share their ideas through class discussion. To maximize efficacy, there are several specific problem-solving skills with which teachers should be familiar.

The **guess-and-check** strategy calls for students to make an initial guess at the solution, check the answer, and use that outcome to guide the next guess. With each successive guess, the student should get closer to the correct answer. Constructing a table from the guesses can help to organize the data.

Example:
There are 100 coins in a jar. 10 are dimes. The rest are pennies and nickels. There are twice as many pennies as nickels. How many pennies and nickels are in the jar?

There are 90 total nickels and pennies in the jar (100 coins – 10 dimes).

There are twice as many pennies as nickels. Students can take guesses that fulfill the criteria and adjust these guesses based on the answer found. They can continue until they find the correct answer: 60 pennies and 30 nickels.

Number of Pennies	Number of Nickels	Total Number of Pennies and Nickels
40	20	60
80	40	120
70	35	105
60	30	90

The **working backwards** strategy requires students to determine a starting point when solving a problem where the final result and the steps to reach the result are given.

Example:
John subtracted 7 from his age, and divided the result by 3. The final result was 4. What is John's age?

Work backward by reversing the operations.
4 x 3 = 12;
12 + 7 = 19
John is 19 years old.

The strategy of **estimation** and testing for **reasonableness** are related skills that students should employ prior to and after solving a problem. These skills are particularly important when students use calculators to find answers.

Example:
Find the sum of 4387 + 7226 + 5893.

4300 + 7200 + 5800 = 17300   Estimation.
4387 + 7226 + 5893 = 17506   Actual sum.

By comparing the estimate to the actual sum, students can determine that their answer is reasonable.

Many times, the description of a problem may contain more information than is needed to solve the problem. Some of the information may actually be irrelevant. It is important to focus on what information is relevant to the problem.

Example:
Jonathan went to the mall and bought a baseball cap for $14, gloves for $10, a stocking cap for $8, a headband for $7, and an umbrella for $15. What was the average price of the headwear that Jonathan bought?

In this problem, we are interested only in the items Jonathan bought that could be worn on the head: a baseball cap, a stocking cap, and a headband. We would not be interested in the gloves or the umbrella. Therefore, we average $14, $8, and $7 to get $9.67.

The strategy of **simplifying** is used when the best way to solve a problem is to break it into a series of simpler problems. This may be most appropriate when:

- A direct solution to the problem is too complicated
- The problem involves numbers that are either too small or too large
- The student needs to better understand the problem
- The computations are too complex
- The problem involves a diagram or a large array

Example:
There are 20 people at a party. If each person shakes hands with every other person, how many handshakes will there be?

> We could take the long approach by determining that the first person shakes hands with 19 other people, the second person has 18 other people with whom to shake hands, the third person has 17 other people with whom to shake hands, etc., and then adding each of these numbers together.

A simpler approach would be to break the problem down into a smaller problem—such as 4 people at a party. We determine that the first person would shake hands with 3 other people, the second would shake hands with 2 other people, and the third person would shake hands with 1 other person. We can represent this as

$$(4-1)+(4-2)+(4-3) = 3+2+1 = 6$$

or

$$(n-1)+(n-2)+(n-3) = 3n-6 = 6$$

where $n =$ the total number of people at the party. If we set the answer equal to x, we can solve for x as follows:

$$(n-1)n - x = x$$
$$(20-1)(20) = 2x$$
$$(19)(20) = 2x$$
$$380 = 2x$$
$$190 = x$$

Skill 13.2 Demonstrating knowledge of strategies for investigating, developing, and evaluating mathematical arguments

Write Simple Proofs in Two-Column Form

In a two-column proof, the left side should be the given information, or statements that could be proven by deductive reasoning. The right column should consist of the methods used to determine that each statement to the left is verifiably true. The right side can identify given information or state theorems, postulates, definitions, or algebraic properties used to prove that each particular line of the proof is true.

Write Indirect Proofs

Assume the opposite of the conclusion. Keep the hypothesis and the given information the same. Proceed to develop the steps of the proof, looking for a statement that contradicts the original assumption or some other known fact. This contradiction indicates that the assumption made at the beginning of the proof was incorrect; therefore, the original conclusion has to be true.

Classify Conclusions as Examples of Inductive or Deductive Thinking

Inductive thinking is the process of finding a pattern from a group of examples. That pattern is the conclusion that this set of examples seemed to indicate. It may be a correct conclusion, or it may be an incorrect conclusion because other examples may not follow the predicted pattern.

Deductive thinking is the process of arriving at a conclusion based on other statements that are all known to be true, such as theorems, axioms postulates, or postulates. Conclusions found by deductive thinking based on true statements will <u>always</u> be true.

Examples:

Suppose:
     On Monday Mr. Peterson eats breakfast at McDonalds.
     On Tuesday Mr. Peterson eats breakfast at McDonalds.
     On Wednesday Mr. Peterson eats breakfast at McDonalds.
     On Thursday Mr. Peterson eats breakfast at McDonalds.
Conclusion:
     On Friday Mr. Peterson will eat breakfast at McDonalds again.

This is a conclusion based on inductive reasoning. Based on several days' observations, it can be concluded that Mr. Peterson will eat at McDonalds. This may or may not be true, but it is a conclusion developed by inductive thinking.

Make Conditional Statements

Conditional statements are frequently written in "if-then" form. The "if" clause of the conditional is known as the **hypothesis**, and the "then" clause is called the **conclusion**. In a proof, the hypothesis is the information that is assumed to be true, while the conclusion is what is to be proven true. A conditional statement often follows a basic form:

If p, then q.
p is the hypothesis and q is the conclusion

Conditional statements can be diagrammed using a **Venn diagram**. This diagram can be drawn with one circle inside another circle. The inner circle represents the hypothesis. The outer circle represents the conclusion. If the hypothesis is taken to be true, then you are located inside the inner circle. If you are located in the inner circle then you are also inside the outer circle, so that proves the conclusion is true.

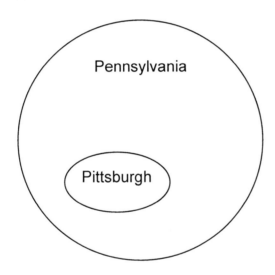

Example:
If you are in Pittsburgh, then you are in Pennsylvania.
In this statement, "you are in Pittsburgh" is the hypothesis.
In this statement, "you are in Pennsylvania" is the conclusion.

Example:
If an angle has a measure of 90 degrees, then it is a right angle.
In this statement, "an angle has a measure of 90 degrees" is the hypothesis.
In this statement, "it is a right angle" is the conclusion.

Conditional: If p, then q.
p is the hypothesis and q is the conclusion

Inverse: If not p, then not q.
Negate both the hypothesis (If p) and the conclusion (then q) from the original conditional.

Converse: If q, then p.
Reverse the two clauses. The original hypothesis becomes the conclusion. The original conclusion then becomes the new hypothesis.

Contrapositive: If not q, then not p.
Reverse the two clauses. The original hypothesis becomes the conclusion and the original conclusion becomes the hypothesis. Then negate both the new hypothesis and the new conclusion.

Example:
Given the *conditional*:
If an angle has 60°, then it is an acute angle.

Its *inverse* form would be:
If an angle doesn't have 60°, then it is not an acute angle.

NOTICE that the inverse is not true, even though the conditional statement was true.

Its *converse* form would be:
If an angle is an acute angle, then it has 60°.

NOTICE that the converse is not necessarily true, even though the conditional statement was true.

Its *contrapositive* form would be:
If an angle isn't an acute angle, then it doesn't have 60°.

NOTICE that the contrapositive is true, assuming the original conditional statement was true.

TIP: If you are asked to pick a statement that is logically equivalent to a given conditional, look for the contrapositive. The inverse and converse are not always logically equivalent to every conditional. The contrapositive is ALWAYS logically equivalent.

Find the inverse, converse, and contrapositive of the following conditional statements. Also, determine if each of the statements is true or false.

Conditional: If $x = 5$, then $x^2 - 25 = 0$.   TRUE

Inverse: If $x \neq 5$, then $x^2 - 25 \neq 0$.   FALSE, x could be $^-5$

Converse: If $x^2 - 25 = 0$, then $x = 5$.   FALSE, x could be $^-5$

Contrapositive: If $x^2 - 25 \neq 0$, then $x \neq 5$.   TRUE

Conditional: If $x = 5$, then $6x = 30$.   TRUE
Inverse: If $x \neq 5$, then $6x \neq 30$.   TRUE
Converse: If $6x = 30$, then $x = 5$.   TRUE
Contrapositive: If $6x \neq 30$, then $x \neq 5$.   TRUE

Sometimes, as in the latter example, all four statements can be logically equivalent; however, the only statement that will always be logically equivalent to the original conditional is the contrapositive.

The use of Venn diagrams (explained above) can help to visualize this process. Suppose that the following statements were given to you, and you were asked to try to reach a conclusion.

1)   All swimmers are athletes.
      All athletes are scholars.

In "if-then" form, these would be:

        If you are a swimmer, then you are an athlete.
        If you are an athlete, then you are a scholar.

Clearly, if you are a swimmer, then you are also an athlete. This includes you in the group of scholars.

2)   All swimmers are athletes.
       All wrestlers are athletes.

In "if-then" form, these would be:

   If you are a swimmer, then you are an athlete.
   If you are a wrestler, then you are an athlete.

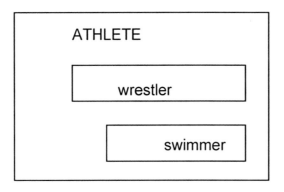

Clearly, if you are a swimmer or a wrestler, then you are also an athlete. This does NOT allow you to come to any other conclusions.

A swimmer may or may NOT also be a wrestler. Therefore, NO CONCLUSION IS POSSIBLE.

3)   All rectangles are parallelograms.
       Quadrilateral ABCD is not a parallelogram.

In "if-then" form, the first statement would be:

   If a figure is a rectangle, then it is also a parallelogram.

Note that this second statement is the negation of the conclusion of statement one. Remember also that the contrapositive is logically equivalent to a given conditional. That is, "If not q, then not p." Since "ABCD is NOT a parallelogram" is like saying "if not q," then you can come to the conclusion "then not p." Therefore, the conclusion is "ABCD is not a rectangle." Looking at the Venn diagram below, if all rectangles are parallelograms, then rectangles are included as part of the parallelograms. Since quadrilateral ABCD is not a parallelogram, it is excluded from anywhere inside the parallelogram box. This allows you to conclude that ABCD cannot be a rectangle either.

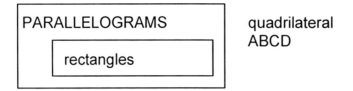

quadrilateral
ABCD

A **counterexample** is an exception to a proposed rule or conjecture that disproves the conjecture. For example, the existence of a single non-brown dog disproves the conjecture "all dogs are brown." Thus, any non-brown dog is a counterexample.

In searching for mathematic counterexamples, one should consider extreme cases near the ends of the domain of an experiment as well as special cases where an additional property is introduced. Examples of extreme cases are numbers near zero and obtuse triangles that are nearly flat. An example of a special case for a problem involving rectangles is a square because a square is a rectangle with the additional property of symmetry.

Example:
Identify a counterexample for the following conjectures.

If n is an even number, then $n + 1$ is divisible by 3.

$n = 4$
$n + 1 = 4 + 1 = 5$
5 is not divisible by 3.

If n is divisible by 3, then $n^2 - 1$ is divisible by 4.

$n = 6$
$n^2 - 1 = 6^2 - 1 = 35$
35 is not divisible by 4.

The **questioning technique** is a mathematic process in which students devise questions to clarify the problem, eliminate possible solutions, and simplify the problem-solving process. By developing and attempting to answer simple questions, students can tackle difficult and complex problems.

Sometimes, the discourse may be teacher-guided though a process in which the teacher asks questions to generate dialogue and lead discussions. Other times, the students might be encouraged to generate their own inquiry discussions by sharing their questions and thoughts among themselves. A third type of discourse can take place in small groups where the students work both independently and collaboratively.

Teachers might ask the following types of questions to encourage higher order thinking:

- Questions that require manipulation of prior knowledge
- Asking students to state ideas or definitions in their own words
- Questions that require students to solve a problem
- Questions that require observations and/or descriptions of an object or event
- Questions that call for comparison and contrast

It is also recommended that teachers give students enough time to attempt to answer the question before calling on another student. When a student is having trouble responding to a question, a teacher should ask probing questions such as:

- Asking for clarification
- Rephrasing the question
- Asking related questions
- Restating the student's ideas

(Ornstein, 1995)

Skill 13.3   Demonstrating knowledge of how the language and vocabulary of mathematics are used to communicate ideas precisely

Mathematical concepts and procedures can take many different forms. Students of mathematics must be able to recognize different forms of equivalent concepts.

For example, the slope of a line can be represented graphically, algebraically, verbally, and numerically. A line drawn on a coordinate plane will show the slope. In the equation of a line, $y = mx + b$, the term m represents the slope. The slope of a line can be defined in several different ways; it is the change in the value of the y divided by the change in the value of x over a given interval. Alternatively, the slope of a line is the ratio of "rise" to "run" between two points. The numeric value of the slope can be calculated by using the verbal definitions and the algebraic representation of the line.

In order to understand mathematics and to solve problems, it is important to know the definitions of basic mathematic terms and concepts. For a list of definitions and explanations of basic math terms, visit the following website: http://home.blarg.net/~math/deflist.html.

Additionally, one must use the language of mathematics correctly and precisely to communicate concepts and ideas.

For example, the statement "minus 10 times minus 5 equals plus 50" is incorrect because "minus" and "plus" are arithmetic operations, not numerical modifiers. The statement should read "negative 10 times negative 5 equals positive 50."

Skill 13.4 **Demonstrating knowledge of the variety of materials, models, and methods used to explore mathematical concepts and solve problems**

Manipulatives

Manipulatives can foster learning for all students. The subject of Mathematics needs to be derived from something that is real to the learner. If the learner can "touch" it, he or she will better understand and remember it. Students can use fingers, ice cream sticks, tiles, and paper folding (as well as commercially available manipulatives) to visualize operations and concepts. The teacher needs to solidify concrete examples into abstract mathematics.

Example:
Use tiles to demonstrate both geometric ideas and number theory.

Give each group of students 12 tiles and instruct them to build rectangles. Students draw their rectangles on paper.

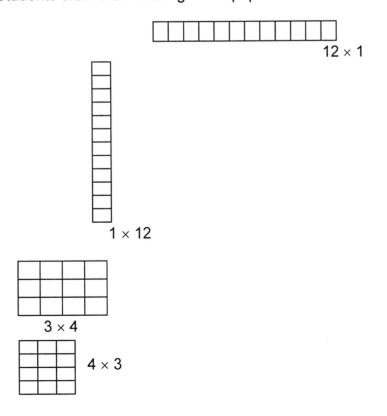

12 × 1

1 × 12

3 × 4

4 × 3

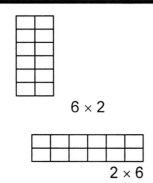

6×2

2×6

Encourage students to describe their reactions. Extend to 16 tiles. Ask students to form additional problems.

Models

Models are another means of representing mathematical concepts by relating them to real-world situations. Teachers must choose wisely when devising and selecting models because, to be effective, models must be applied properly. For example, a building with floors above and below ground is a good model for introducing the concept of negative numbers. It would be difficult, however, to use the building model in teaching subtraction of negative numbers.

When introducing a new mathematical concept to students, teachers should utilize the concrete-to-representational-to-abstract sequence of instruction. The first step of this instructional progression is the introduction of a concept modeled with concrete materials. The second step is the translation of concrete models into representational diagrams or pictures. The third and final step is the translation of representational models into abstract models using only numbers and symbols.

Teachers should first use concrete models to introduce a mathematical concept because they are easiest to understand. For example, teachers can allow students to use counting blocks to learn basic arithmetic. Teachers should give students ample time and many opportunities to experiment, practice, and demonstrate mastery with the concrete materials.

The second step in the learning process allows for a deeper understanding of the first step. For example, students may use tally marks or pictures to represent the counting blocks they used in the previous stage. Once again, teachers should give students ample time to master the concept on the representational level.

The final step in the learning process is necessary for more abstract levels of thought. For example, students represent the processes carried out in the previous stages using only numbers and arithmetic symbols. To ease the transition, teachers should associate numbers and symbols with the concrete and representational models throughout the learning progression.

Sometimes, using a model is the best way to see the solution to a problem, as in the case of fraction multiplication.

<u>Example</u>:

Model $\dfrac{5}{6} \times \dfrac{2}{3}$.

Draw a rectangle. Divide it vertically into 6 equal sections (the denominator of the first number.)

Divide the rectangle horizontally into 3 equal sections (the denominator of the second number).

Color in a number of vertical strips equal to the numerator of the first number.

Use a different color to shade a number of horizontal strips equal to the numerator of the second number.

By describing the area where both colors overlap, we have the product of the two fractions. The answer is $\dfrac{10}{18}$.

Scales

Students need to understand that ratios and proportions are used to create scale models of real-life objects. The also must understand the principles of ratio and proportion, and how to calculate scale using ratio and proportion.

Scaled drawings (maps, blueprints, and models) are used in many real-world situations. Architects make blueprints and models of buildings. These drawings and models are then used by the contractors to build the buildings. Engineers make scaled drawings of bridges, machine parts, roads, airplanes, and many other things. Maps of the world, countries, states, and roads are scaled drawings too. Landscape designers use scale drawings and models of plants, decks, and other structures to show how they should be placed around a building. Models of cars, boats, and planes made from kits are scaled. Automobile engineers construct models of cars before the actual assembly is done. Many museum exhibits are actually scaled models because the real size of the items displayed would be too large.

Examples of real-world problems that students might solve using scaled drawings include:

- Reading road maps and determining the distance between locations by using the map scale
- Creating a scaled drawing (floor plan) of the classroom to determine the best use of space
- Creating an 8 ½" x 11" representation of a quilt to be pieced together
- Drawing blueprints of their rooms and creating models from them

Diagrams

Drawing pictures or diagrams can also help to make relationships in a problem clearer.

For example: In a women's marathon, the first five finishers (in no particular order) were Frieda, Polly, Christa, Betty, and Dora. Frieda finished 7 seconds before Christa. Polly finished 6 seconds after Betty. Dora finished 8 seconds after Betty. Christa finished 2 seconds before Polly. In what order did the women finish the race?

Drawing a picture or diagram will help to demonstrate the answer more easily.

From the diagram, we can see that the women finished in the following order: 1st – Frieda, 2nd – Betty, 3rd – Christa, 4th – Polly, and 5th – Dora.

Technology

Finally, there are many forms of **technology** available to math teachers. For example, students can test their understanding of math concepts by working on skill-specific computer programs and websites. Graphing calculators can help students to visualize the graphs of functions. Teachers can also enhance their lectures and classroom presentations by creating multimedia presentations.

Skill 13.5   Demonstrating knowledge of the interconnections among mathematical concepts

Recognition and understanding of the relationships between concepts and topics is of great value in mathematical problem-solving as well as in the explanation of more complex processes.

For instance, multiplication is simply repeated addition. This relationship explains the concept of **variable addition**. We can show that the expression $4x + 3x = 7x$ is true by rewriting 4 times x and 3 times x as repeated addition, yielding the expression $(x + x + x + x) + (x + x + x)$. Thus, because of the relationship between multiplication and addition, variable addition is accomplished by **coefficient addition**.

In this same way, division and multiplication are also linked. Many students find multiplication to be much more simple to understand than division. Teaching them that they are two sides of the same concept may make all the difference.

For example, knowing that 6 x 8 = 48 off the top one's head makes understanding 48 ÷ 6 = 8 even easier. This is why multiplication charts have always held a place in many elementary education classrooms.

Students will react differently to this type of mathematical breakdown. Some may find that explaining multiplication (or any other complex mathematical concept) in terms of an already mastered concept—in this case, addition—will help to strengthen their ability to understand and even enjoy mathematics. However, others may find difficulty in understanding the basis behind the correlation—either because they don't grasp the connection or because they have moved beyond it.

Although this may make teaching mathematical relationships more difficult for the teacher, it is important to recognize that mathematical concepts and procedures can take many different forms. Students of mathematics must be able to recognize different forms of equivalent concepts. These basic skill sets will relay into a higher level of understanding as the level of difficulty in mathematical concepts increases.

Skill 13.6 Recognizing applications of mathematics in other content areas and in everyday life

Teachers can increase interest in math and promote learning and understanding by relating mathematical concepts to the lives of students. Instead of using only abstract presentations and examples, teachers should relate concepts to real-world situations that then shift the emphasis from memorization and abstract application to understanding and applied problem-solving. In addition, relating math to careers and professions helps to illustrate the relevance of math; it may even aid in the career exploration process.

For example, when teaching a unit on the geometry of certain shapes, teachers can ask students to design a structure of interest using the shapes in question. This exercise serves the dual purpose of teaching students to learn and apply the properties (e.g., area, volume) of shapes while demonstrating the relevance of geometry to architectural and engineering professions.

Artists, musicians, scientists, social scientists, and business people use mathematical modeling to solve problems in their disciplines. These disciplines rely on the tools and symbology of mathematics to model natural events and manipulate data.

Mathematics is a key aspect of visual art. Artists use the geometric properties of shapes, ratios, and proportions in creating paintings and sculptures. For example, mathematics is essential to the concept of perspective. Artists must determine the appropriate lengths and heights of objects to portray three-dimensional distance in two dimensions.

Mathematics is also an important part of music. Many musical terms have mathematical connections. For example, the musical octave contains twelve notes and spans a factor of two in frequency. In other words, the frequency, the speed of vibration that determines tone and sound quality, doubles from the first note in an octave to the last. Thus, starting from any note, we can determine the frequency of any other note with the following formula.

$$\text{Freq} = \text{note} \times 2^{N/12}$$

In this equation, N is the number of notes from the starting point, and *note* is the frequency of the starting note. Mathematical understanding of frequency plays an important role in tuning musical instruments.

In addition to the visual and auditory arts, mathematics is an integral part of most scientific disciplines. The uses of mathematics in science are almost endless. The following are but a few examples of how scientists use mathematics, but it is certainly not a comprehensive list. Physical scientists use vectors, functions, derivatives, and integrals to describe and model the movement of objects. Biologists and ecologists use mathematics to model ecosystems and study DNA. Chemists use mathematics to study the interaction of molecules and to determine proper amounts and proportions of reactants.

Many social science disciplines use mathematics to model and solve problems as well. Economists, for example, use functions, graphs, and matrices to model the activities of producers, consumers, and firms.

COMPETENCY 14.0 UNDERSTAND CONCEPTS AND SKILLS RELATED TO NUMBERS AND MATHEMATICAL OPERATIONS

Skill 14.1   Applying concepts of quantities, numbers, and numeration to compare, order, estimate, and round

Rational numbers can be expressed as the ratio of two integers, $\boxed{}$ where $b \neq 0$, for example $\frac{2}{3}$, $-\boxed{}$, $5 = \frac{5}{1}$.

Rational numbers include integers, fractions, mixed numbers, and terminating and repeating decimals. Every rational number can be expressed as a repeating or terminating decimal and can be shown on a number line.

Integers are positive and negative whole numbers, and zero.
....-6, -5, -4, -3, -2, -1, 0, 1, 2, 3, 4, 5, 6...

Whole numbers are natural numbers and zero.
0, 1, 2, 3, 4, 5, 6...

Natural numbers are the counting numbers.
1, 2, 3, 4, 5, 6...

Irrational numbers are real numbers that cannot be written as the ratio of two integers. These are infinite non-repeating decimals.

Examples:
$\sqrt{5}$ = 2.2360.., pi =π = 3.1415927...

A **fraction** is an expression of numbers in the form of x/y, where x is the numerator and y is the denominator, which cannot be zero.

Example:
$\frac{3}{7}$ 3 is the numerator; 7 is the denominator

If the fraction has common factors for the numerator and denominator, divide both by the common factor to reduce the fraction to its lowest form.

Example:
$$\frac{13}{39} = \frac{1 \times 13}{3 \times 13} = \frac{1}{3}$$ Divide by the common factor 13

A **mixed** number has an integer part and a fractional part.

Example:

$$2\frac{1}{4},\ ^-5\frac{1}{6},\ 7\frac{1}{3}$$

Percent = per 100 (written with the symbol %)

Example:

$$10\% = \frac{10}{100} = \frac{1}{10}$$

Decimals = deci = part of ten
To find the decimal equivalent of a fraction, use the denominator to divide the numerator, as shown in the following example.

Example:

Find the decimal equivalent of $\frac{7}{10}$.

Since 10 cannot divide into 7 evenly

$$\frac{7}{10} = 0.7$$

The **exponent form** is a shortcut method to write repeated multiplication. Basic form: b^n, where b is called the base and n is the exponent. Both b and n are real numbers. The b^n implies that the base b is multiplied by itself n times.

Examples:

$$3^4 = 3 \times 3 \times 3 \times 3 = 81$$

$$2^3 = 2 \times 2 \times 2 = 8$$

$$(^-2)^4 = (^-2) \times (^-2) \times (^-2) \times (^-2) = 16$$

$$^-2^4 = ^-(2 \times 2 \times 2 \times 2) = ^-16$$

Key exponent rules:

For 'a' nonzero, and 'm' and 'n' real numbers:

1) $a^m \cdot a^n = a^{(m+n)}$ Product rule

2) $\dfrac{a^m}{a^n} = a^{(m-n)}$ Quotient rule

3) $\dfrac{a^{-m}}{a^{-n}} = \dfrac{a^n}{a^m}$ Negative rule

When 10 is raised to any power, the exponent tells the numbers of zeroes in the product.

Example:
$$10^7 = 10,000,000$$

Caution: Unless the negative sign is inside the parentheses and the exponent is outside the parentheses, the sign is not affected by the exponent.

$(^-2)^4$ implies that -2 is multiplied by itself 4 times.

$^-2^4$ implies that 2 is multiplied by itself 4 times, then the answer is negated.

Scientific notation is a more convenient method for writing very large and very small numbers. It employs two factors. The first factor is a number between 1 and 10. The second factor is a power of 10. This notation is a "shorthand" for expressing large numbers (like the weight of 100 elephants) or small numbers (like the weight of an atom in pounds).

Recall that:

$10^n = (10)^n$	Ten multiplied by itself n times.
$10^0 = 1$	A nonzero number raised to power of zero is 1.
$10^1 = 10$	
$10^2 = 10 \times 10 = 100$	
$10^3 = 10 \times 10 \times 10 = 1000$ (kilo)	
$10^{-1} = 1/10$ (deci)	
$10^{-2} = 1/100$ (centi)	
$10^{-3} = 1/1000$ (milli)	
$10^{-6} = 1/1,000,000$ (micro)	

Example:
Write 46,368,000 in scientific notation.

1) Introduce a decimal point and decimal places.
46,368,000 = 46,368,000.0000

2) Make a mark between the two digits that give a number between -9.9 and 9.9.
4 ∧ 6,368,000 .0000

3) Count the number of digit places between the decimal point and the ∧ mark. This number is the 'n'-the power of ten.

So, $46,368,000 = 4.6368 \times 10^7$

Example:
Write 0.00397 in scientific notation.

1) Decimal place is already in place.

2) Make a mark between 3 and 9 to get a one number between -9.9 and 9.9.

3) Move decimal place to the mark (3 hops).

0.003 ∧ 97

Motion is to the right, so n of 10^n is negative.

Therefore, $0.00397 = 3.97 \times 10^{-3}$

Rounding numbers is a form of estimation that is very useful in many mathematical operations. For example, when estimating the sum of two three-digit numbers, it is helpful to round the two numbers to the nearest hundred prior to addition. Numbers can be rounded to any place value.

To **round whole numbers**, you first find the place value you want to round to (the rounding digit) and look at the digit directly to the right. If the digit is less than five, do not change the rounding digit and replace all numbers after the rounding digit with zeroes. If the digit is greater than or equal to five, increase the rounding digit by one and replace all numbers after the rounding digit with zeroes.

Example:
Round 517 to the nearest ten.

1 is the rounding digit because it occupies the ten's place.

517 rounded to the nearest ten = 520; because 7 > 5, we add 1 to the rounding digit.

Example:
Round 15,449 to the nearest hundred.

The first 4 is the rounding digit because it occupies the hundred's place.

15,449 rounded to the nearest hundred = 15,400; because 4 < 5 we do not add to the rounding digit.

Rounding decimals is identical to rounding whole numbers except that you simply drop all the digits to the right of the rounding digit.

Example:
Round 417.3621 to the nearest tenth.

3 is the rounding digit because it occupies the tenth place.

417.3621 rounded to the nearest tenth = 417.4; because 6 > 5, we add 1 to the rounding digit.

Skill 14.2   Demonstrating knowledge of the concepts of place value, prime numbers, multiples, and factors

Whole Number Place Value

Consider the number 792. We can assign a place value to each digit.

Reading from left to right, the first digit (7) represents the hundred's place. The hundred's place tells us how many sets of 100 the number contains. Thus, there are 7 sets of 100 in the number 792.

The second digit (9) represents the ten's place. The ten's place tells us how many sets of 10 the number contains. Thus, there are 9 sets of 10 in the number 792.

The last digit (2) represents the one's place. The one's place tells us how many sets of 1 the number contains. Thus, there are 2 sets of 1 in the number 792.

Therefore, there are 7 sets of 100, plus 9 sets of 10, plus 2 sets of 1 in the number 792.

Decimal Place Value

More complex numbers have additional place values to both the left and right of the decimal point. Consider the number 374.8.

Reading from left to right, the first digit (3) is in the hundred's place; it tells us that the number contains 3 sets of 100.

The second digit (7) is in the ten's place and tells us the number contains 7 sets of 10.

The third digit (4) is in the one's place and tells us the number contains 4 sets of 1.

Finally, the number after the decimal (8) is in the tenth's place; it tells us that the number contains 8 tenths.

Place Value for Older Students

Each digit to the left of the decimal point increases progressively in powers of 10. Each digit to the right of the decimal point decreases progressively in powers of 10.

Example:
12345.6789 occupies the following powers of 10 positions:

10^4	10^3	10^2	10^1	10^0	0	10^{-1}	10^{-2}	10^{-3}	10^{-4}
1	2	3	4	5	.	6	7	8	9

Names of power-of-10 positions:

10^0 = ones (note that any non-zero base raised to power zero is 1)

10^1 = tens   (number 1 and 1 zero or 10)

10^2 = hundred   (number 1 and 2 zeros or 100)

10^3 = thousand   (number 1 and 3 zeros or 1000)

10^4 = ten thousand   (number 1 and 4 zeros or 10000)

$10^{-1} = \dfrac{1}{10^1} = \dfrac{1}{10}$ = tenths   (1st digit after decimal point or 0.1)

$10^{-2} = \dfrac{1}{10^2} = \dfrac{1}{100}$ = hundredth   (2nd digit after decimal point or 0.01)

$10^{-3} = \dfrac{1}{10^3} = \dfrac{1}{1000}$ = thousandth   (3rd digit after decimal point or 0.001)

$10^{-4} = \dfrac{1}{10^4} = \dfrac{1}{10000}$ = ten thousandth   (4th digit after decimal point or 0.0001)

Example:
Write 73169.00537 in expanded form.

We start by listing all the powers of 10 positions.

10^4	10^3	10^2	10^1	10^0	.	10^{-1}	10^{-2}	10^{-3}	10^{-4}	10^{-5}

Multiply each digit by its power of ten. Add all the results.

Thus $73169.00537 = (7 \times 10^4) + (3 \times 10^3) + (1 \times 10^2) + (6 \times 10^1)$
$$+ (9 \times 10^0) + (0 \times 10^{-1}) + (0 \times 10^{-2}) + (5 \times 10^{-3})$$
$$+ (3 \times 10^{-4}) + (7 \times 10^{-5})$$

Example:

Determine the place value associated with the underlined digit in 3.16$\underline{9}$5.

10^0	.	10^{-1}	10^{-2}	10^{-3}	10^{-4}
3	.	1	6	9	5

The place value for the digit 9 is 10^{-3} or $\dfrac{1}{1000}$.

Example:

Find the number that is represented by $(7 \times 10^3) + (5 \times 10^0) + (3 \times 10^{-3})$.

$$= 7000 + 5 + 0.003$$
$$= 7005.003$$

Example:

Write 21×10^3 in standard form.

$$= 21 \times 1000 = 21,\!000$$

Example:

Write 739×10^{-4} in standard form.

$$= 739 \times \frac{1}{10000} = \frac{739}{10000} = 0.0739$$

Common Factors

GCF is the abbreviation for the **greatest common factor.** The GCF is the largest number that is a factor of all the numbers given in a problem. The GCF can be no larger than the smallest number given in the problem. If no other number is a common factor, then the GCF is the number 1. To find the GCF, list all possible factors of the smallest number given (include the number itself). Starting with the largest factor (which is the number itself), determine if it is also a factor of all the other given numbers. If so, that is the GCF. If that factor doesn't work, try the same method on the next smaller factor. Continue until a common factor is found. That is the GCF.

Note: There can be other common factors besides the GCF.

Example:
Find the GCF of 12, 20, and 36.

> The smallest number in the problem is 12. The factors of 12 are 1,2,3,4,6 and 12. 12 is the largest factor, but it does not divide evenly into 20. Neither does 6, but 4 will divide into both 20 and 36 evenly.

Therefore, 4 is the GCF.

Example:
Find the GCF of 14 and 15.

> Factors of 14 are 1,2,7 and 14. 14 is the largest factor, but it does not divide evenly into 15. Neither does 7 or 2. Therefore, the only factor common to both 14 and 15 is the number 1.

The GCF is 1.

LCM is the abbreviation for **least common multiple.** The least common multiple of a group of numbers is the smallest number that all of the given numbers will divide into. The least common multiple will always be the largest of the given numbers or a multiple of the largest number.

Example:
Find the LCM of 20, 30 and 40.

> The largest number given is 40, but 30 will not divide evenly into 40. The next multiple of 40 is 80 (2 x 40), but 30 will not divide evenly into 80 either. The next multiple of 40 is 120. 120 is divisible by both 20 and 30, so 120 is the LCM (least common multiple).

Example:
Find the LCM of 96, 16 and 24.

> The largest number is 96. 96 is divisible by both 16 and 24, so 96 is the LCM.

Example:
Elly Mae can feed the animals in 15 minutes. Jethro can feed them in 10 minutes. How long will it take them if they work together?

If Elly Mae can feed the animals in 15 minutes, then she could feed 1/15 of them in 1 minute, 2/15 of them in 2 minutes, $x/15$ of them in x minutes. In the same fashion Jethro could feed $x/10$ of them in x minutes. Together they complete 1 job. The equation is:

$$\frac{x}{15} + \frac{x}{10} = 1$$

Multiply each term by the LCD (least common denominator) of 30:

$$2x + 3x = 30$$
$$x = 6 \text{ minutes}$$

Factors

Composite numbers are whole numbers that have more than 2 different factors. For example, 9 is composite because besides factors of 1 and 9, 3 is also a factor. 70 is composite because besides the factors of 1 and 70, the numbers 2,5,7,10,14, and 35 are also all factors.

Prime numbers are whole numbers greater than 1 that have only 2 factors: 1 and the number itself. Examples of prime numbers are 2,3,5,7,11,13,17, and 19. Note that 2 is the only even prime number. When factoring into prime factors, all the factors must be numbers that cannot be factored again (without using 1). Initially, numbers can be factored into any 2 factors. Check each resulting factor to see if it can be factored again. Continue factoring until all remaining factors are prime. This is the list of prime factors. Regardless of what way the original number was factored, the final list of prime factors will always be the same.

Remember that the number 1 is neither prime nor composite.

Example:
Factor 30 into prime factors.

> Factor 30 into any 2 factors.
> > 5 · 6   Now factor the 6.
> > 5 · 2 · 3   These are all prime factors.

> Factor 30 into any 2 factors.
> > 3 · 10   Now factor the 10.
> > 3 · 2 · 5   These are the same prime factors even though the original factors were different.

Example:
Factor 240 into prime factors.

> Factor 240 into any 2 factors.
> 24 · 10   Now factor both 24 and 10.
> 4 · 6 · 2 · 5   Now factor both 4 and 6.
> 2 · 2 · 2 · 3 · 2 · 5 These are prime factors.

> This can also be written as $2^4 \cdot 3 \cdot 5$.

Skill 14.3   Recognizing equivalent forms of common fractions, decimal fractions, and percentages

If we compare numbers in various forms, we see that:

The integer 400 = $\dfrac{800}{2}$ (fraction) = 400.0 (decimal) = 400% (percent).

From this, you should be able to determine that fractions, decimals, and percents can be used interchangeably within problems.

- To change a percent into a decimal, move the decimal point two places to the left and drop off the percent sign.

- To change a decimal into a percent, move the decimal two places to the right and add on a percent sign.

- To change a fraction into a decimal, divide the numerator by the denominator.

- To change a decimal number into an equivalent fraction, write the decimal part of the number as the fraction's numerator. As the fraction's denominator, use the place value of the last column of the decimal. Reduce the resulting fraction as far as possible.

Example:

J.C. Nickels has Hunch jeans for sale at $1/4$ off the usual price of $36.00. Shears and Roadster have the same jeans for sale at 30% off their regular price of $40. Find the cheaper price.

$1/4$ = .25 so .25(36) = $9.00 off $36 - 9 = $27 sale price

30% = .30 so .30(40) = $12 off $40 - 12 = $28 sale price

The price at J.C Nickels is actually lower.

To convert a fraction to a decimal, as we did in the example above, simply divide the numerator (top) by the denominator (bottom). Use long division if necessary.

If a decimal has a fixed number of digits, the decimal is said to be **terminating**. To write such a decimal as a fraction, first determine what place value the farthest right digit is in (for example: tenths, hundredths, thousandths, ten thousandths, hundred thousands, etc). Then drop the decimal and place the string of digits over the number given by the place value.

If a decimal continues forever by repeating a string of digits, the decimal is said to be **repeating**. To write a repeating decimal as a fraction, follow these steps.

a. Let x = the repeating decimal (ex. $x = .716716716...$)
b. Multiply x by the multiple of ten that will move the decimal just to the right of the repeating block of digits. (ex. $1000x = 716.716716...$)
c. Subtract the first equation from the second (ex. $1000x - x = 716.716.716... - .716716...$)
d. Simplify and solve this equation. The repeating block of digits will subtract out (ex. $999x = 716$ so $x = {}^{716}\!/_{999}$)
e. The solution will be the fraction for the repeating decimal

Skill 14.4   Applying knowledge of the relationships among mathematical operations and strategies for using the basic four operations with variables and numbers

For standardization purposes, there is an accepted order in which operations are performed in any given algebraic expression. The following pneumonic is often used for the order in which operations are performed.

Please	Parentheses	
Excuse	Exponents	
My	Multiply	(Multiply or Divide depending on which
Dear	Divide	operation is encountered first from left to right.)
Aunt	Add	(Add or Subtract depending on which
Sally	Subtract	operation is encountered first from left to right.)

This **Order of Operations** should be followed when evaluating algebraic expressions:

1. Simplify inside grouping characters such as parentheses, brackets, square root, fraction bar, etc.

2. Multiply out expressions with exponents.

3. Do multiplication or division, from left to right.

4. Do addition or subtraction, from left to right.

Samples of simplifying expressions with exponents:

$$(^-2)^3 = -8 \qquad\qquad ^-2^3 = ^-8$$
$$(^-2)^4 = 16 \qquad\qquad ^-2^4 = 16 \qquad \text{Note change of sign.}$$
$$(\tfrac{2}{3})^3 = \tfrac{8}{27}$$
$$5^0 = 1$$
$$4^{-1} = \tfrac{1}{4}$$

Skill 14.5   Demonstrating knowledge of properties of numbers and the number system (e.g., commutative, associative, distributive, identity, and property of zero)

The real number properties are best explained in terms of a small set of numbers. For each property, a given set will be provided.

Axioms of Addition

Closure—For all real numbers a and b, $a + b$ is a unique real number.

Associative—For all real numbers a, b, and c, $(a + b) + c = a + (b + c)$.

Additive Identity—There exists a unique real number 0 (zero) such that $a + 0 = 0 + a = a$ for every real number a.

Additive Inverses—For each real number a, there exists a real number $-a$ (the opposite of a) such that $a + (-a) = (-a) + a = 0$.

Commutative—For all real numbers a and b, $a + b = b + a$.

Axioms of Multiplication

Closure—For all real numbers a and b, ab is a unique real number.

Associative—For all real numbers a, b, and c, $(ab)c = a(bc)$.

Multiplicative Identity—There exists a unique nonzero real number 1 (one) such that $1 \cdot a = a \cdot 1 = a$.

Multiplicative Inverses—For each nonzero real number, there exists a real number $1/a$ (the reciprocal of a) such that $a(1/a) = (1/a)a = 1$.

Commutative—For all real numbers a and b, $ab = ba$.

The Distributive Axiom of Multiplication over Addition

For all real numbers a, b, and c, $a(b + c) = ab + ac$.

Recognizing the Property of Denseness

The **Denseness Property** of real numbers states that if all real numbers are ordered from least to greatest on a number line, there is an infinite set of real numbers between any two given numbers on the line.

Example:

Between 7.6 and 7.7, there is the rational number 7.65 in the set of real numbers.
Between 3 and 4 there exists no other natural number.

Applying Inverse Operations

Subtraction is the inverse of Addition, and vice-versa.
Division is the inverse of Multiplication, and vice-versa.
Taking a square root is the inverse of squaring, and vice-versa.

These inverse operations are used when solving equations.

Skill 14.6   Performing calculations with whole numbers, decimals, and fractions

Addition of Whole Numbers

Example:
At the end of a day of shopping, a shopper had $24 remaining in his wallet. He spent $45 on various goods. How much money did the shopper have at the beginning of the day?

The total amount of money the shopper started with is the sum of the amount spent and the amount remaining at the end of the day.

```
    24
 +  45
    69 ────────▶        The original total was $69.
```

Example:
A race took the winner 1 hr. 58 min. 12 sec. on the first half of the race and 2 hr. 9 min. 57 sec. on the second half of the race. How much time did the entire race take?

```
     1 hr. 58 min. 12 sec.
 +   2 hr.  9 min. 57 sec.     Add these numbers
     3 hr. 67 min. 69 sec.
         + 1 min -60 sec.      Change 60 seconds to 1 min.
     3 hr. 68 min. 9 sec.
 +   1 hr.-60 min.    .        Change 60 minutes to 1 hr.
     4 hr. 8 min.   9 sec.  ← final answer
```

Subtraction of Whole Numbers

Example:
At the end of his shift, a cashier has $96 in the cash register. At the beginning of his shift, he had $15. How much money did the cashier collect during his shift?

The total collected is the difference of the ending amount and the starting amount.

$$\begin{array}{r} 96 \\ -\ \underline{15} \\ 81 \end{array} \longrightarrow$$
The total collected was $81.

Multiplication of Whole Numbers

Multiplication is one of the four basic number operations. In simple terms, multiplication is the addition of a number to itself a certain number of times. For example, 4 multiplied by 3 is the equal to 4 + 4 + 4 or 3 + 3 + 3 +3. Another way of conceptualizing multiplication is to think in terms of groups. For example, if we have 4 groups of 3 students, the total number of students is 4 multiplied by 3. We call the solution to a multiplication problem the **product**.

The basic algorithm for whole number multiplication begins with aligning the numbers by place value with the number containing more places on top.

$$\begin{array}{r} 172 \\ \times\ \underline{43} \end{array} \longrightarrow$$
Note that we placed 172 on top because it has more places than 43 does.

Next, we multiply the one's place of the second number by each place value of the top number sequentially.

(2)
$$\begin{array}{r} 172 \\ \times\ \underline{43} \\ 516 \end{array} \longrightarrow$$
{3 x 2 = 6, 3 x 7 = 21, 3 x 1 = 3}
Note that we had to carry a 2 to the hundred's column because 3 x 7 = 21. Note also that we add, not multiply, carried numbers to the product.

Next, we multiply the number in the ten's place of the second number by each place value of the top number sequentially. Because we are multiplying by a number in the ten's place, we place a zero at the end of this product.

(2)
```
   172
 x  43  ───►  {4 x 2 = 8, 4 x 7 = 28, 4 x 1 = 4}
   516
  6880
```

Finally, to determine the final product, we add the two partial products.

```
    172
  x  43
    516
 + 6880
   7396  ───►  The product of 172 and 43 is 7396.
```

Example:
A student buys 4 boxes of crayons. Each box contains 16 crayons. How many total crayons does the student have?

The total number of crayons is 16 x 4.

```
   16
  x 4
   64  ───►  The total number of crayons equals 64.
```

Division of Whole Numbers

Division, the inverse of multiplication, is another of the four basic number operations. When we divide one number by another, we determine how many times we can multiply the divisor (number divided by) before we exceed the number we are dividing (dividend). For example, 8 divided by 2 equals 4 because we can multiply 2 four times to reach 8 (2 x 4 = 8 or 2 + 2 + 2 + 2 = 8). Using the grouping conceptualization we used with multiplication, we can divide 8 into 4 groups of 2, or 2 groups of 4. We call the answer to a division problem the **quotient**.

If the divisor does not divide evenly into the dividend, we express the leftover amount either as a remainder or as a fraction with the divisor as the denominator. For example, 9 divided by 2 equals 4 with a remainder of 1 or 4 ½.

The basic algorithm for division is long division. We start by representing the quotient as follows.

$$14\overline{)293} \longrightarrow$$

14 is the divisor and 293 is the dividend.

This represents $293 \div 14$.

Next, we divide the divisor into the dividend, starting from the left.

$$\begin{array}{r} 2 \\ 14\overline{)293} \end{array} \longrightarrow$$ 14 divides into 29 two times with a remainder.

Next, we multiply the partial quotient by the divisor, subtract this value from the first digits of the dividend, and bring down the remaining dividend digits to complete the number.

$$\begin{array}{r} 2 \\ 14\overline{)293} \\ -28 \\ \hline 13 \end{array} \longrightarrow 2 \times 14 = 28, \; 29 - 28 = 1, \text{ and bringing down the 3 yields 13.}$$

Finally, we divide again (the divisor into the remaining value) and repeat the preceding process. The number left after the subtraction represents the remainder.

$$\begin{array}{r} 20 \\ 14\overline{)293} \\ -28 \\ \hline 13 \\ -0 \\ \hline 13 \end{array} \longrightarrow$$ The final quotient is 20 with a remainder of 13. We can also represent this quotient as 20 13/14.

Example:
Each box of apples contains 24 apples. How many boxes must a grocer purchase to supply a group of 252 people with one apple each?

The grocer needs 252 apples. Because he must buy apples in groups of 24, we divide 252 by 24 to determine how many boxes he needs to buy.

$$\begin{array}{r} 10 \\ 24\overline{)252} \\ -24 \\ \hline 12 \\ -0 \\ \hline 12 \end{array}$$

→ The quotient is 10 with a remainder of 12.

Thus, the grocer needs 10 boxes plus 12 more apples. Therefore, the minimum number of boxes the grocer can purchase is 11.

Example:
At his job, John gets paid $20 for every hour he works. If John made $940 in a week, how many hours did he work?

This is a division problem. To determine the number of hours John worked, we divide the total amount made ($940) by the hourly rate of pay ($20). Thus, the number of hours worked equals 940 divided by 20.

$$\begin{array}{r} 47 \\ 20\overline{)940} \\ -80 \\ \hline 140 \\ -140 \\ \hline 0 \end{array}$$

→ 20 divides into 940 a total of 47 times with no remainder.

John worked 47 hours.

Addition and Subtraction of Decimals

When adding and subtracting decimals, we align the numbers by place value as we do with whole numbers. After adding or subtracting each column, we bring the decimal down, placing it in the same location as in the numbers added or subtracted.

Example:
Find the sum of 152.3 and 36.342.

$$
\begin{array}{r}
152.300 \\
+\quad 36.342 \\
\hline
188.642
\end{array}
$$

Note that we placed two zeroes after the final place value in 152.3 to clarify the column addition.

Example:
Find the difference of 152.3 and 36.342.

$$
\begin{array}{cc}
2\ 9\ 10 & (4)11(12) \\
152.\cancel{300} & 1\cancel{52.300} \\
-\quad 36.342 \longrightarrow & -\quad 36.342 \\
\hline
58 & 115.958
\end{array}
$$

Note how we borrowed to subtract from the zeroes in the hundredth's and thousandth's place of 152.300.

Multiplication of Decimals

When multiplying decimal numbers, we multiply exactly as with whole numbers, placing the decimal moving in from the left the total number of decimal places contained in the two numbers multiplied. For example, when multiplying 1.5 and 2.35, we place the decimal in the product, 3 places in from the left (3.525).

Example:
Find the product of 3.52 and 4.1.

$$
\begin{array}{r}
3.52 \\
\times\quad 4.1 \\
\hline
352 \\
+\ 14080 \\
\hline
14432
\end{array}
$$

Note that there are 3 total decimal places in the two numbers.

We place the decimal 3 places in from the left.

Thus, the final product is 14.432.

Example:
A shopper has 5 one-dollar bills, 6 quarters, 3 nickels, and 4 pennies in his pocket. How much money does he have?

$$5 \times \$1.00 = \$5.00$$

$$\begin{array}{ccc} \overset{3}{\$0.25} & \$0.05 & \$0.01 \\ \underline{\times\ \ 6} & \underline{\times\ \ 3} & \underline{\times\ \ 4} \\ \$1.50 & \$0.15 & \$0.04 \end{array}$$

Note the placement of the decimals in the multiplication products. Thus, the total amount of money in the shopper's pocket is:

$$\begin{array}{r} \$5.00 \\ 1.50 \\ 0.15 \\ +\ 0.04 \\ \hline \$6.69 \end{array}$$

Division of Decimals

When dividing decimal numbers, we first remove the decimal in the divisor by moving the decimal in the dividend the same number of spaces to the right. For example, when dividing 1.45 into 5.3 we convert the numbers to 145 and 530 and perform normal whole number division.

Example:
Find the quotient of 5.3 divided by 1.45.

Convert to 145 and 530.

Divide.

$$145\overline{)530} \quad\longrightarrow\quad 145\overline{)530.00} \quad\longrightarrow\quad$$

$$\begin{array}{r} 3 \\ 145\overline{)530} \\ \underline{-435} \\ 95 \end{array} \qquad \begin{array}{r} 3.65 \\ 145\overline{)530.00} \\ \underline{-435} \\ 950 \\ \underline{-870} \\ 80 \end{array}$$

Note that we insert the decimal to continue division.

Because one of the numbers divided contained one decimal place, we round the quotient to one decimal place. Thus, the final quotient is 3.7.

Operating with Percents

Example:
5 is what percent of 20?

This is the same as converting $\frac{5}{20}$ to % form.

$$\frac{5}{20} \times \frac{100}{1} = \frac{5}{1} \times \frac{5}{1} = 25\%$$

Example:
There are 64 dogs in the kennel. 48 are collies. What percent are collies?

Restate the problem.   48 is what percent of 64?
Write an equation. $48 = n \times 64$
Solve. $\frac{48}{64} = n$

$n = \frac{3}{4} = 75\%$

75% of the dogs are collies.

Example:
The auditorium was filled to 90% capacity. There were 558 seats occupied. What is the capacity of the auditorium?

Restate the problem.   90% of what number is 558?
Write an equation. $0.9n = 558$
Solve. $n = \frac{558}{.9}$
                        $n = 620$

The capacity of the auditorium is 620 people.

Example:
A pair of shoes costs $42.00. Sales tax is 6%. What is the total cost of the shoes?

Restate the problem.   What is 6% of 42?
Write an equation. $n = 0.06 \times 42$
Solve. $n = 2.52$

Add the sales tax to the cost. $42.00 + $2.52 = $44.52

The total cost of the shoes, including sales tax, is $44.52.

Addition and Subtraction of Fractions

Key Points

1. You need a common denominator in order to add and subtract reduced and improper fractions.

Example:

$$\frac{1}{3} + \frac{7}{3} = \frac{1+7}{3} = \frac{8}{3} = 2\frac{2}{3}$$

Example:

$$\frac{4}{12} + \frac{6}{12} - \frac{3}{12} = \frac{4+6-3}{12} = \frac{7}{12}$$

2. Adding an integer and a fraction of the <u>same</u> sign results directly in a mixed fraction.

Example:

$$2 + \frac{2}{3} = 2\frac{2}{3}$$

Example:

$$^-2 - \frac{3}{4} = {}^- 2\frac{3}{4}$$

3. Adding an integer and a fraction with different signs involves the following steps.

   o get a common denominator
   o add or subtract as needed
   o change to a mixed fraction if possible

Example:

$$2 - \frac{1}{3} = \frac{2 \times 3 - 1}{3} = \frac{6-1}{3} = \frac{5}{3} = 1\frac{2}{3}$$

Example:

Add $7\dfrac{3}{8} + 5\dfrac{2}{7}$

Add the whole numbers, add the fractions, and combine the two results:

$$7\dfrac{3}{8} + 5\dfrac{2}{7} = (7+5) + (\dfrac{3}{8} + \dfrac{2}{7})$$

$$= 12 + \dfrac{(7 \times 3) + (8 \times 2)}{56} \quad \text{(LCM of 8 and 7)}$$

$$= 12 + \dfrac{21+16}{56} = 12 + \dfrac{37}{56} = 12\dfrac{37}{56}$$

Example:
Perform the operation.

$$\dfrac{2}{3} - \dfrac{5}{6}$$

We first find the LCM of 3 and 6 which is 6.

$$\dfrac{2 \times 2}{3 \times 2} - \dfrac{5}{6} \rightarrow \dfrac{4-5}{6} = \dfrac{^-1}{6} \quad \text{(Using method A)}$$

Example:

$^-7\dfrac{1}{4} + 2\dfrac{7}{8}$

$$^-7\dfrac{1}{4} + 2\dfrac{7}{8} = (^-7 + 2) + (\dfrac{^-1}{4} + \dfrac{7}{8})$$

$$= (^-5) + \dfrac{(^-2 + 7)}{8} = (^-5) + (\dfrac{5}{8})$$

$$= (^-5) + \dfrac{5}{8} = \dfrac{^-5 \times 8}{1 \times 8} + \dfrac{5}{8} = \dfrac{^-40 + 5}{8}$$

$$= \dfrac{^-35}{8} = ^-4\dfrac{3}{8}$$

Divide 35 by 8 to get 4, remainder 3.

Caution: A common error would be

$$^-7\frac{1}{4}+2\frac{7}{8}=^-7\frac{2}{8}+2\frac{7}{8}=^-5\frac{9}{8}\qquad\text{Wrong.}$$

It is correct to add -7 and 2 to get -5, but adding $\frac{2}{8}+\frac{7}{8}=\frac{9}{8}$

is wrong. It should have been $\frac{^-2}{8}+\frac{7}{8}=\frac{5}{8}$. Then,

$$^-5+\frac{5}{8}=^-4\frac{3}{8}\quad\text{as before.}$$

Multiplication of Fractions

Using the following example: $3\frac{1}{4}\times\frac{5}{6}$

   1. Convert each number to an improper fraction.

$$3\frac{1}{4}=\frac{(12+1)}{4}=\frac{13}{4}\qquad\qquad\frac{5}{6}\text{ is already in reduced form.}$$

   2. Reduce (cancel) common factors of the numerator and denominator if they exist.

$$\frac{13}{4}\times\frac{5}{6}\qquad\text{No common factors exist.}$$

   3. Multiply the numerators by each other and the denominators by each other.

$$\frac{13}{4}\times\frac{5}{6}=\frac{65}{24}$$

   4. If possible, reduce the fraction back to its lowest term.

$$\frac{65}{24}\quad\text{Cannot be reduced further.}$$

5. Convert the improper fraction back to a mixed fraction by using long division.

$$\frac{65}{24} = 24\overline{)65} \quad\quad = 2\frac{17}{24}$$
$$\quad\quad\quad\;\;\underline{48}$$
$$\quad\quad\quad\;\;17$$

Summary of Sign Changes for Multiplication

    a. $(+) \times (+) = (+)$

    b. $(-) \times (+) = (-)$

    c. $(+) \times (-) = (-)$

    d. $(-) \times (-) = (+)$

Example:

$$7\frac{1}{3} \times \frac{5}{11} = \frac{22}{3} \times \frac{5}{11}$$

    Reduce like terms (22 and 11)

$$= \frac{2}{3} \times \frac{5}{1} = \frac{10}{3} = 3\frac{1}{3}$$

Example:

$$^-6\frac{1}{4} \times \frac{5}{9} = \frac{^-25}{4} \times \frac{5}{9}$$

$$= \frac{^-125}{36} = ^-3\frac{17}{36}$$

Example:

$$\frac{^-1}{4} \times \frac{^-3}{7}$$

    Negative times a negative equals positive.

$$= \frac{1}{4} \times \frac{3}{7} = \frac{3}{28}$$

Division of Fractions

1. Change mixed fractions to improper fractions.

2. Change the division problem to a multiplication problem by using the reciprocal of the number after the division sign.

3. Find the sign of the final product.

4. Cancel if common factors exist between the numerator and the denominator.

5. Multiply the numerators together and the denominators together.

6. Change the improper fraction to a mixed number.

<u>Example</u>:

$$3\frac{1}{5} \div 2\frac{1}{4} = \frac{16}{5} \div \frac{9}{4}$$

$$= \frac{16}{5} \times \frac{4}{9} \qquad \text{Reciprocal of } \frac{9}{4} \text{ is } \frac{4}{9}.$$

$$= \frac{64}{45} = 1\frac{19}{45}$$

<u>Example</u>:

$$7\frac{3}{4} \div 11\frac{5}{8} = \frac{31}{4} \div \frac{93}{8}$$

$$= \frac{31}{4} \times \frac{8}{93} \qquad \text{Reduce like terms.}$$

$$= \frac{1}{1} \times \frac{2}{3} = \frac{2}{3}$$

Example:

$$\left(^-2\frac{1}{2}\right) \div 4\frac{1}{6} = \frac{^-5}{2} \div \frac{25}{6}$$

$$= \frac{^-5}{2} \times \frac{6}{25} \qquad \text{Reduce like terms.}$$

$$= \frac{^-1}{1} \times \frac{3}{5} = \frac{^-3}{5}$$

Example:

$$\left(^-5\frac{3}{8}\right) \div \left(\frac{^-7}{16}\right) = \frac{^-43}{8} \div \frac{^-7}{16}$$

$$= \frac{^-43}{8} \times \frac{^-16}{7} \qquad \text{Reduce like terms.}$$

$$= \frac{43}{1} \times \frac{2}{7} \qquad \text{Negative times a negative equals a positive.}$$

$$= \frac{86}{7} = 12\frac{2}{7}$$

Skill 14.7 Applying methods for making estimations and for evaluating the accuracy of estimated solutions

Estimation and approximation may be used to check the reasonableness of answers.

Example:
Estimate the answer.

$$\frac{58 \times 810}{1989}$$

58 becomes 60, 810 becomes 800 and 1989 becomes 2000.

$$\frac{60 \times 800}{2000} = 24$$

For word problems, an estimate may sometimes be all that is needed to find the solution.

<u>Example</u>:

Janet goes into a store to purchase a CD on sale for $13.95. While shopping, she sees two pairs of shoes priced at $19.95 and $14.50. She only has $50. Can she purchase everything?

Solve by rounding:
$19.95→$20.00
$14.50→$15.00
$13.95→$14.00
$49.00   Yes, she can purchase the CD and the shoes.

COMPETENCY 15.0 UNDERSTAND PRINCIPLES AND SKILLS OF MEASUREMENT AND THE CONCEPTS AND PROPERTIES OF GEOMETRY

Skill 15.1 **Identifying appropriate measurement procedures, tools, and units (e.g., customary and metric) for problems involving length, perimeter, area, capacity, weight, time, and temperature**

Measurements of length (English system)

12 inches (in)	=	1 foot (ft)
3 feet (ft)	=	1 yard (yd)
1760 yards (yd)	=	1 mile (mi)

Measurements of length (Metric system)

kilometer (km)	=	1000 meters (m)
hectometer (hm)	=	100 meters (m)
decameter (dam)	=	10 meters (m)
meter (m)	=	1 meter (m)
decimeter (dm)	=	1/10 meter (m)
centimeter (cm)	=	1/100 meter (m)
millimeter (mm)	=	1/1000 meter (m)

Conversion of length from English to Metric

1 inch	=	2.54 centimeters
1 foot	$\approx$	30 centimeters
1 yard	$\approx$	0.9 meters
1 mile	$\approx$	1.6 kilometers

Measurements of weight (English system)

28 grams (g)	=	1 ounce (oz)	
16 ounces (oz)	=	1 pound (lb)	
2000 pounds (lb)	=	1 ton (t)	(short ton)
1.1 ton (t)	=	1 ton (t)	

Measurements of weight (Metric system)

kilogram (kg)	=	1000 grams (g)
gram (g)	=	1 gram (g)
milligram (mg)	=	1/1000 gram (g)

Conversion of weight from English to metric

1 ounce	≈	28 grams
1 pound	≈	0.45 kilogram (454 grams)

Measurement of volume (English system)

8 fluid ounces (oz)	=	1 cup (c)
2 cups (c)	=	1 pint (pt)
2 pints (pt)	=	1 quart (qt)
4 quarts (qt)	=	1 gallon (gal)

Measurement of volume (Metric system)

kiloliter (kl)	=	1000 liters (l)
liter (l)	=	1 liter (l)
milliliter (ml)	=	1/1000 liters (ml)

Conversion of volume from English to metric

1 teaspoon (tsp)	≈	5 milliliters
1 fluid ounce	≈	15 milliliters
1 cup	≈	0.24 liters
1 pint	≈	0.47 liters
1 quart	≈	0.95 liters
1 gallon	≈	3.8 liters

Measurement of time

1 minute	=	60 seconds
1 hour	=	60 minutes
1 day	=	24 hours
1 week	=	7 days
1 year	=	365 days
1 century	=	100 years

Note: (') represents feet and (") represents inches.

Square Units

Square units can be derived from the knowledge of basic units of length by squaring the equivalent measurements.

> 1 square foot (sq. ft.) = 144 sq. in.
> 1 sq. yd. = 9 sq. ft.
> 1 sq. yd. = 1296 sq. in.

Example:

14 sq. yd. = _____ sq. ft.
14 × 9 = 126 sq. ft.

Weight

Example:
Kathy has a bag of potatoes that weighs 5 lbs., 10 oz. She uses one-third of the bag to make mashed potatoes. How much does the bag weigh now?

1 lb. = 16 oz.
5(16 oz.) + 10 oz.
= 80 oz + 10 oz = 90 oz.
$90 - (\frac{1}{3})90$ oz.
= 90 oz. − 30 oz.
= 60 oz.
60 ÷ 16 = 3.75 lbs.
.75 = 75%
$75\% = \frac{75}{100} = \frac{3}{4}$
$\frac{3}{4}$ x 16 oz = 12 oz

The bag weighs 3 lbs., 12 oz.

Example:
The weight limit of a playground merry-go-round is 1000 pounds. There are 11 children on the merry-go-round. 3 children weigh 100 pounds. 6 children weigh 75 pounds. 2 children weigh 60 pounds. George weighs 80 pounds. Can he get on the merry-go-round?

3(100) + 6(75) + 2(60)
= 300 + 450 + 120
= 870
1000 − 870
= 130
Since 80 is less than 130, George can get on the merry-go-round.

Perimeter and Area

The **perimeter** of any polygon is the sum of the lengths of the sides.

The **area** of a polygon is the number of square units covered by the figure.

FIGURE	AREA FORMULA	PERIMETER FORMULA
Rectangle	LW	$2(L+W)$
Triangle	$\frac{1}{2}bh$	$a+b+c$
Parallelogram	bh	sum of lengths of sides
Trapezoid	$\frac{1}{2}h(a+b)$	sum of lengths of sides

Example:

A farmer has a piece of land shaped as shown below. He wishes to fence this land at an estimated cost of $25 per linear foot. What is the total cost of fencing this property to the nearest foot?

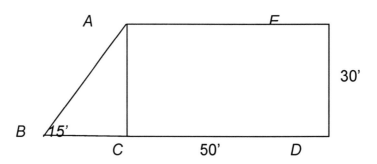

From the right triangle ABC, AC = 30 and BC = 15.

Since $(AB) = (AC)^2 + (BC)^2$
$(AB) = (30)^2 + (15)^2$

So $\sqrt{(AB)^2} = AB = \sqrt{1125} = 33.5410$ feet

To the nearest foot AB = 34 feet.

Perimeter of the piece of land is = $AB + BC + CD + DE + EA$

= 34 + 15 + 50 + 30 + 50 = 179 feet

cost of fencing = $25 x 179 = $4, 475.00

Example:

What will be the cost of carpeting a rectangular office that measures 12 feet by 15 feet if the carpet costs $12.50 per square yard?

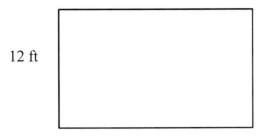

12 ft

15 ft

The problem is asking you to determine the area of the office. The area of a rectangle is *length x width = A*

Substitute the given values in the equation $A = lw$

$A = (12 \text{ ft.})(15 \text{ ft.})$

$A = 180 \text{ ft.}^2$

The problem asked you to determine the cost of carpet at $12.50 per square yard.

First, you need to convert 180 ft.^{2} into yards^2.

1 yd. = 3 ft.
(1 yard)(1 yard) = (3 feet)(3 feet)
$1 \text{ yd}^2 = 9 \text{ ft } 2$

Hence, $\underline{180 \text{ ft}^2}$ $\underline{1 \text{ yd}^2}$ $\underline{20}$

$1 = 9 \text{ ft}^2 = 1 = 20 \text{ yd}^2$

The carpet cost $12.50 per square yard; thus the cost of carpeting the office described is $12.50 x 20 = $250.00.

<u>Example</u>:
Find the area of a parallelogram whose base is 6.5 cm and the height of the altitude to that base is 3.7 cm.

6.5 cm

3.7 cm

$$A_{parallelogram} = bh$$
$$= (3.7)(6.5)$$
$$= 24.05 \text{ cm}^2$$

<u>Example</u>:
Find the area of this triangle.

11.4 cm

9.3 cm   7.1 cm

16.8 cm

$$A_{triangle} = \tfrac{1}{2}bh$$
$$= 0.5\ (16.8)\ (7.1)$$
$$= 59.64 \text{ cm}^2$$

<u>Example</u>:
Find the area of this trapezoid.

17.5 cm

6.4 cm

23.7 cm

The area of a trapezoid equals one-half the sum of the bases times the altitude.

$$A_{trapezoid} = \tfrac{1}{2}h(b_1 + b_2)$$
$$= 0.5\ (6.4)\ (17.5 + 23.7)$$
$$= 131.84 \text{ cm}^2$$

Circles

The distance around a circle is the **circumference**. The ratio of the circumference to the diameter is represented by the Greek letter pi, $\pi \sim 3.14 \sim \dfrac{22}{7}$.

The circumference of a circle is found by the formula $C = 2\pi r$ or $C = \pi d$, where r is the radius of the circle and d is the diameter.

The area of a circle is found by the formula $A = \pi r^2$.

Example:
Find the circumference and area of a circle whose radius is 7 meters.

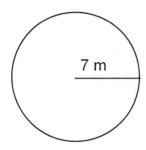

7 m

$C = 2\pi r$
$= 2(3.14)(7)$
$= 43.96$ m

$A = \pi r^2$
$= 3.14(7)(7)$
$= 153.86$ m^2

Reading Instruments

When reading an instrument, students should first determine the interval of scale on that particular instrument. To achieve the greatest accuracy, they should read the scale to the nearest measurement mark.

If they are using a scale with a needle that has a mirrored plate behind it, the scale should be viewed so that the needle's reflection is hidden behind the needle itself. Students should not look at it from an angle. In order to read a balance scale accurately, it is necessary to place the scale on a level surface and make sure that the hand points precisely at 0. Objects should be placed on the plate gently and taken away gently. The dial should be faced straight on to read the graduation accurately. Students should read from the large graduation to smaller graduation. If the dial hand points between two graduations, they should choose the number that is closest to the hand.

When reading inches on a ruler, the student needs to understand that each inch is divided into halves by the longest mark in the middle; into fourths by the next longest marks; into eighths by the next; and into sixteenths by the shortest. When the measurement falls between two inch marks, they can give the whole number of inches, count the additional fractional marks, and give the answer as the number and fraction of inches. Remind students that the convention is always to express a fraction by its lowest possible denominator.

If students are using the metric system on a ruler, have them focus on the marks between the whole numbers (centimeters). Point out that each centimeter is broken into tenths, with the mark in the middle being longer to indicate a halfway mark. Students should learn to measure things accurately to the nearest tenth of a centimeter, then the nearest hundredth, and finally the nearest thousandth. Measurements using the metric system should always be written using the decimal system, for example, 3.756 centimeters.

When reading a thermometer, it should be held vertically at eye level. Students should check the scale of the thermometer to make certain they read as many significant digits as possible. Thermometers with heavy or extended lines that are marked 10, 20, 30 ... should be read to the nearest 0.1 degree. Thermometers with fine lines every two degrees may be read to the nearest 0.5 degree.

In order to get an accurate reading in a liquid measuring cup, students should set the cup on a level surface and read it at eye level. The measurement should be read at the bottom of the concave arc at the liquid's surface (the **meniscus** line). When measuring dry ingredients, dip the appropriately sized measuring cup into the ingredient and sweep away the excess across the top with a straight-edged object.

Protractors measure angles in degrees. To measure accurately, students must find the center hole on the straight edge of the protractor and place it over the vertex of the angle they wish to measure. They should line up the zero on the straight edge with one of the sides of the angle, and find the point where the second side of the angle intersects the curved edge of the protractor. They can then read the number that is written at the point of intersection.

When reading an instrument such as a rain gauge, it is again important to read at eye level and at the base of the meniscus. The measuring tube is divided, marked, and labeled in tenths and hundredths. The greatest number of decimal places there will be is two.

Most numbers in mathematics are "exact" or "counted." Measurements are "approximate." They usually involve interpolation, or figuring out which mark on the ruler is closest. Any measurement acquired with a measuring device is approximate. These variations in measurement are called precision and accuracy.

Precision is a measurement of how exactly a measurement is made, without reference to a true or real value. If a measurement is precise, it can be made again and again with little variation in the result. The precision of a measuring device is the smallest fractional or decimal division on the instrument. The smaller the unit or fraction of a unit on the measuring device, the more precisely it can measure.

The greatest possible error of measurement is always equal to one-half the smallest fraction of a unit on the measuring device.

Accuracy is a measure of how close the result of measurement comes to the "true" value.

If throwing darts, the true value is the bull's eye. If the three darts land on the bull's eye, the dart thrower is both precise (all land near the same spot) and accurate (the darts all land on the "true" value).

The greatest measure of error allowed is called the **tolerance**. The least acceptable limit is called the **lower limit,** and the greatest acceptable limit is called the **upper limit**. The difference between the upper and lower limits is called the **tolerance interval**. For example, a specification for an automobile part might be 14.625 ± 0.005 mm. This means that the smallest acceptable length of the part is 14.620 mm and the largest length acceptable is 14.630 mm. The tolerance interval is 0.010 mm. One can see how it would be important for automobile parts to be within a set of limits in terms of length. If the part is too long or too short it will not fit properly, and vibrations will occur that weaken the part and may eventually cause damage to other parts.

Skill 15.2   Applying knowledge of approaches to direct measurement through the use of standard and nonstandard units and to indirect measurement through the use of algebra or geometry

There are two types of measurement: **direct measurement** and **indirect measurement**. As the name implies, direct measurement is the action of measuring something directly. For example, the length of a boat can be measured with a measuring tape, or elapsed time can be measured with a stop watch.

Indirect measurement is measurement that is not done with a tool such as a ruler or watch. Instead, other mathematical approaches are used to derive the desired measurement. Using similar triangles is an example of indirect measurement. Similar triangles have the same angles and proportionate sides, but they are different sizes. They can be used to determine the distance from one point to another without measuring it directly. In the diagram below, X represents the distance between two points with an unknown length.

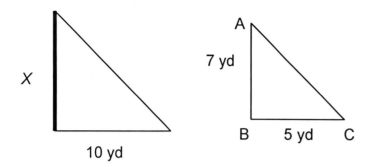

The problem can be determined by setting up the proportion below and solving for *X*.

$$\frac{X}{10 \text{ yd}} = \frac{7 \text{ yd}}{5 \text{ yd}}$$

After cross-multiplying, the equation can be written as 5X = 70; X equals 14 yards. Without actually measuring the distance with a measuring tape or other tools, the distance between the points is determined.

Indirect measurement also occurs in instances other than simply measuring length. The area of a room can be measured using a scale drawing. Measuring the weight of the moon is possible using the measurable effects the moon exerts on the earth, such as the changes in tides. Another familiar indirect measurement is the Body Mass Index (BMI), which indicates body composition. The body composition uses height and weight measurements to measure health risks.

Skill 15.3   Classifying plane and solid geometric figures (e.g., triangle, quadrilateral, sphere, cone)

A **triangle** is a polygon with three sides.

Triangles can be classified by the types of angles or the lengths of their sides.

Classifying By Angles

An **acute** triangle has exactly three acute angles.
A **right** triangle has one right angle.
An **obtuse** triangle has one obtuse angle.

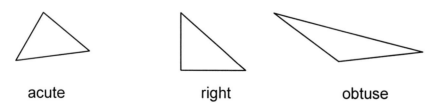

acute   right   obtuse

Classifying By Sides

All three sides of an **equilateral** triangle are the same length.
Two sides of an **isosceles** triangle are the same length.
None of the sides of a **scalene** triangle are the same length.

equilateral   isosceles   scalene

A **quadrilateral** is a polygon with four sides.
The sum of the measures of the angles of a convex quadrilateral is 360°.

A **trapezoid** is a quadrilateral with exactly <u>one</u> pair of parallel sides.

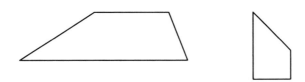

In an **isosceles trapezoid**, the non-parallel sides are congruent.

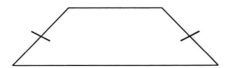

A **parallelogram** is a quadrilateral with <u>two</u> pairs of parallel sides.

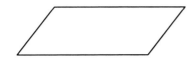

A **rectangle** is a parallelogram with a right angle.

A **rhombus** is a parallelogram with all sides of equal length.

A **square** is a rectangle with all sides of equal length.

The union of all points on a simple closed surface and all points in its interior form a space figure called a **solid**. The five regular solids, or **polyhedra**, are the cube, tetrahedron, octahedron, icosahedron, and dodecahedron. A **net** is a two-dimensional figure that can be cut out and folded up to make a three-dimensional solid. Below are models of the five regular solids with their corresponding face polygons and nets.

Cube		6 squares	
Tetrahedron		4 equilateral triangles	
Octahedron		8 equilateral triangles	
Icosahedron		20 equilateral triangles	
Dodecahedron		12 regular pentagons	

Other examples of solids:

Sphere

Cone

A **sphere** is a space figure having all its points the same distance from the center.

A **cone** is a space figure having a circular base and a single vertex.

Skill 15.4   Applying knowledge of basic geometric concepts (e.g., similarity, congruence, parallelism)

Congruent figures have the same size and shape. If one is placed above the other, they will fit exactly. Congruent lines have the same length. Congruent angles have equal measures.

The symbol for congruent is ≅ .

Polygons (pentagons) *ABCDE* and *VWXYZ* are congruent. They are exactly the same size and shape.

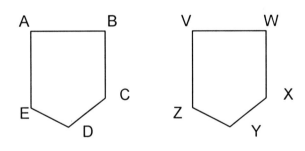

$$ABCDE \cong VWXYZ$$

Corresponding parts are the congruent angles and congruent sides. They are:

corresponding angles	corresponding sides
∠A ↔ ∠V	AB ↔ VW
∠B ↔ ∠W	BC ↔ WX
∠C ↔ ∠X	CD ↔ XY
∠D ↔ ∠Y	DE ↔ YZ
∠E ↔ ∠Z	AE ↔ VZ

Example:
Given two similar quadrilaterals, find the lengths of sides *x, y,* and *z.*

Since corresponding sides are proportional, the scale is:

$$\frac{12}{x} = \frac{3}{5} \qquad\qquad \frac{21}{y} = \frac{3}{5} \qquad\qquad \frac{z}{30} = \frac{3}{5}$$

$$3x = 60 \qquad\qquad 3y = 105 \qquad\qquad 5z = 90$$
$$x = 20 \qquad\qquad\; y = 35 \qquad\qquad\;\; z = 18$$

Similarity

Two figures that have the same shape are **similar**. Polygons are similar if and only if corresponding angles are congruent and corresponding sides are in proportion. Corresponding parts of similar polygons are proportional.

Example:
Tommy draws and cuts out 2 triangles for a school project. One of them has sides of 3, 6, and 9 inches. The other triangle has sides of 2, 4, and 6 inches. Is there a relationship between the two triangles?

Take the proportion of the corresponding sides.

$$\frac{2}{3} \qquad\qquad \frac{4}{6} = \frac{2}{3} \qquad\qquad \frac{6}{9} = \frac{2}{3}$$

The smaller triangle is 2/3 the size of the large triangle.

Example:
Given the rectangles below, compare the area and perimeter.

$A = LW$	$A = LW$	1. write formula
$A = (6)(9)$	$A = (9)(13.5)$	2. substitute known values
$A = 54$ sq. units	$A = 121.5$ sq. units	3. compute
$P = 2(L + W)$	$P = 2(L + W)$	1. write formula
$P = 2(6 + 9)$	$P = 2(9 + 13.5)$	2. substitute known values
$P = 30$ units	$P = 45$ units	3. compute

Notice that the areas relate to each other in the following manner:
Ratio of sides $9/13.5 = 2/3$

Multiply the first area by the square of the reciprocal $(3/2)^2$ to get the second area.
$54 \times (3/2)^2 = 121.5$

The perimeters relate to each other in the following manner:
Ratio of sides $9/13.5 = 2/3$

Multiply the perimeter of the first by the reciprocal of the ratio to get the perimeter of the second.
$30 \times 3/2 = 45$

Skill 15.5   Applying strategies for measuring the component parts of geometric figures (e.g., angles, segments) and computing the volume of simple geometric solids

In geometry, the point, line, and plane are key concepts that can be discussed in relation to each other.

collinear points
are all on the same line

non-collinear points
are not on the same line

coplanar points
are on the same plane

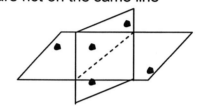

non-coplanar points
are not on the same plane

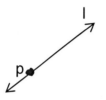

Point p is in line l
Point p is on line l
l contains P
l passes through P

l and m intersect at p
p is the intersection of l and m

l and p are in plane N
N contains p and l
m intersects N at p
p is the intersection
of m and N

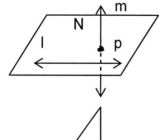

Planes M and N intersect at rq
rq is the intersection of M and N
rq is in M and N
M and N contain rq

The classifying of angles refers to the angle measure. The naming of angles refers to the letters or numbers used to label the angle.

<u>Example:</u>

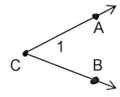

$\overrightarrow{CA}$ (read ray CA) and $\overrightarrow{CB}$ are the sides of the angle.
The angle can be called $\angle ACB$, $\angle BCA$, $\angle C$ or $\angle 1$.

Angles are classified according to their size as follows:

acute: greater than 0 and less than 90 degrees.
right: exactly 90 degrees.
obtuse: greater than 90 and less than 180 degrees.
straight: exactly 180 degrees

Angles can be classified in a number of ways. Some of those classifications are outlined here.

Adjacent angles have a common vertex and one common side but no interior points in common.

Complementary angles add up to 90 degrees.

Supplementary angles add up to 180 degrees.

Vertical angles have sides that form two pairs of opposite rays.

Corresponding angles are in the same corresponding position on two parallel lines cut by a transversal.

Alternate interior angles are diagonal angles on the inside of two parallel lines cut by a transversal.

Alternate exterior angles are diagonal on the outside of two parallel lines cut by a transversal.

Parallel lines or planes do not intersect.

Perpendicular lines or planes form a 90 degree angle to each other.

Intersecting lines share a common point, and intersecting planes share a common set of points or line.

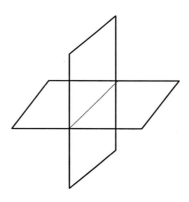

Skew lines do not intersect and do not lie on the same plane.

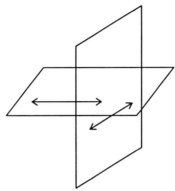

The three undefined terms of geometry are point, line, and plane.

A **plane** is a flat surface that extends forever in two dimensions. It has no ends or edges. It has no thickness to it. It is usually drawn as a parallelogram that can be named either by three non-collinear points (three points that are not on the same line) on the plane, or by placing a letter in the corner of the plane that is not used elsewhere in the diagram.

A **line** extends forever in one dimension. It is determined and named by two points that are on the line. The line consists of every point that is between those two points as well as the points that are on the "straight" extension each way. A line is drawn as a line segment with arrows facing opposite directions on each end to indicate that the line continues in both directions forever.

A **point** is a position in space, on a line, or on a plane. It has no thickness and no width. Only one line can go through any two points. A point is represented by a dot named by a single letter.

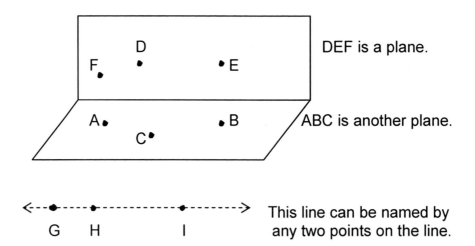

DEF is a plane.

ABC is another plane.

This line can be named by
any two points on the line.

For example, the line could be named $\overleftrightarrow{GH}$, $\overleftrightarrow{HI}$, $\overleftrightarrow{GI}$, $\overleftrightarrow{IG}$, $\overleftrightarrow{IH}$, or $\overleftrightarrow{HG}$. Any two points (letters) on the line can be used, and their order is not important in naming a line.

In the above diagrams, A, B, C, D, E, F, G, H, and I are all locations of individual points.

A **ray** is not an undefined term. A ray consists of all the points on a line starting at one given point and extending in only one of the two opposite directions along the line. The ray is named by naming two points on the ray. The first point must be the endpoint of the ray, while the second point can be any other point along the ray. The symbol for a ray is a ray above the two letters used to name it. The endpoint of the ray MUST be the first letter.

This ray could be named $\overrightarrow{JK}$ or $\overrightarrow{JL}$. It cannot be called $\overrightarrow{KJ}$ or $\overrightarrow{LJ}$ or $\overrightarrow{LK}$ or $\overrightarrow{KL}$, because none of these names starts with the endpoint, J.

The **distance** between two points on a number line is equal to the absolute value of the difference of the two numbers associated with the points.

If one point is located at "a" and the other point is at "b," then the distance between them is found by this formula:

$$\text{distance} = |a - b| \text{ or } |b - a|$$

If one point is located at $^-3$ and another point is located at 5, the distance between them is found by:

$$\text{distance} = |a - b| = |(^-3) - 5| = |^-8| = 8$$

Volume and **surface area** are computed using the following formulas:

FIGURE	VOLUME	TOTAL SURFACE AREA
Right Cylinder	$\pi r^2 h$	$2\pi rh + 2\pi r^2$
Right Cone	$\dfrac{\pi r^2 h}{3}$	$\pi r\sqrt{r^2 + h^2} + \pi r^2$
Sphere	$\dfrac{4}{3}\pi r^3$	$4\pi r^2$
Rectangular Solid	LWH	$2LW + 2WH + 2LH$

FIGURE	LATERAL AREA	TOTAL AREA	VOLUME
Regular Pyramid	1/2Pl	1/2Pl+B	1/3Bh

P = Perimeter
h = height
B = Area of Base
l = slant height

Example:
What is the volume of a shoe box with a length of 35 cm, a width of 20 cm, and a height of 15 cm?

Volume of a rectangular solid
= Length x Width x Height
= 35 x 20 x 15
= 10500 cm^3

Example:

A water company is trying to decide whether to use traditional cylindrical paper cups or to offer conical paper cups, since both cost the same. The traditional cups are 8 cm wide and 14 cm high. The conical cups are 12 cm wide and 19 cm high. The company will use the cup that holds the most water.

Draw and label a sketch of each.

$V = \pi r^2 h$	$V = \dfrac{\pi r^2 h}{3}$	1. write formula
$V = \pi(4)^2(14)$	$V = \dfrac{1}{3}\pi(6)^2(19)$	2. substitute
$V = 703.717 \text{ cm}^3$	$V = 716.283 \text{ cm}^3$	3. solve

The choice should be the conical cup since its volume is more.

Example:

How much material is needed to make a basketball that has a diameter of 15 inches? How much air is needed to fill the basketball?

Draw and label a sketch:

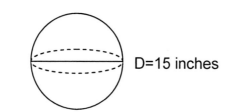

D=15 inches

Total surface area	Volume	
$TSA = 4\pi r^2$	$V = \dfrac{4}{3}\pi r^3$	1. write formula
$= 4\pi(7.5)^2$	$= \dfrac{4}{3}\pi(7.5)^3$	2. substitute
$= 706.858 \text{ in}^2$	$= 1767.1459 \text{ in}^3$	3. solve

Skill 15.6   Applying knowledge of coordinate systems to identify representations of basic geometric figures and concepts

We can represent any two-dimensional geometric figure in the **Cartesian** or **rectangular coordinate system**. The Cartesian or rectangular coordinate system is formed by two perpendicular axes (coordinate axes): the X-axis and the Y-axis. If we know the dimensions of a two-dimensional (planar) figure, we can use this coordinate system to visualize the shape of the figure.

Example:
Represent an isosceles triangle with two sides of length 4.

Draw the two sides along the x- and y- axes and connect the points (vertices).

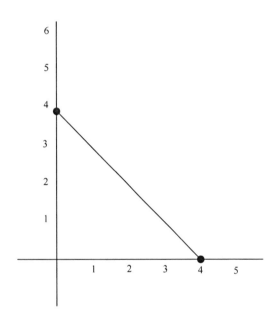

In order to represent three-dimensional figures, we need three coordinate axes (X, Y, and Z) that are all mutually perpendicular to each other. Since we cannot draw three mutually perpendicular axes on a two-dimensional surface, we use oblique representations.

Example:
Represent a cube with sides of 2.

Once again, we draw three sides along the three axes to make things easier.

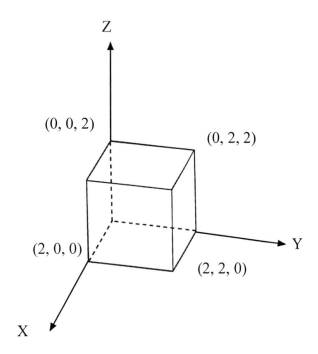

Each point has three coordinates (x, y, z).

Skill 15.7   **Demonstrating knowledge of applications of measurement and geometry in everyday life**

Length

Example:

A car skidded 170 yards on an icy road before coming to a stop. How long is the skid distance in kilometers?

Since 1 yard ≈ 0.9 meters, multiply 170 yards by 0.9.

$$170 \times 0.9 = 153 \text{ meters}$$

Since 1000 meters = 1 kilometer, divide 153 by 1000.

$$\frac{153}{1000} = 0.153 \text{ kilometers}$$

Example:

The distance around a race course is exactly 1 mile, 17 feet, and $9\frac{1}{4}$ inches.

Approximate this distance to the nearest tenth of a foot.

Convert the distance to feet.

1 mile = 1760 yards = 1760 × 3 feet = 5280 feet.

$$9\frac{1}{4} \text{ inches } = \frac{37}{4} \times \frac{1}{12} = \frac{37}{48} \approx 0.77083 \text{ feet}$$

So 1 mile, 17 feet and $9\frac{1}{4}$ inches = $5280 + 17 + 0.77083$ feet

$$= 5297.\underline{7}7083 \text{ feet.}$$

Now, we need to round to the nearest tenth digit. The underlined 7 is in the tenth place. The digit in the hundredth place, also a 7, is greater than 5, the 7 in the tenths place needs to be rounded up to 8 to get a final answer of 5297.8 feet.

Weight

Example:

Zachary weighs 150 pounds. Tom weighs 153 pounds. What is the difference in their weights in grams?

153 pounds – 150 pounds = 3 pounds
1 pound = 454 grams
3(454 grams) = 1362 grams

Capacity

Example:
Students in a fourth grade class want to fill a 3 gallon jug using cups of water. How many cups of water are needed?

1 gallon = 16 cups of water
3 gallons x 16 cups = 48 cups of water are needed.

Time

Example:
It takes Cynthia 45 minutes to get ready each morning. How many hours does she spend getting ready each week?

45 minutes X 7 days = 315 minutes

$$\frac{315 \text{ minutes}}{60 \text{ minutes in an hour}} = 5.25 \text{ hours}$$

Rounding

Depending on the degree of accuracy needed, an object may be measured to different units. For example, a pencil may be 6 inches to the nearest inch, or 6 3/8 inches to the nearest eighth of an inch. Similarly, it might be 15 cm to the nearest cm or 154 mm to the nearest mm.

When given a set of objects and their measurements, it is often helpful to attempt to round to the nearest given unit. When rounding to a given place value, it is necessary to look at the number in the next smaller place. If this number is 5 or more, the number in the place being rounded to is increased by 1, and all numbers to the right are changed to 0. If the number is less than 5, the number in the place being rounded to stays the same, and all numbers to the right are changed to 0.

Some methods of rounding measurements can require an additional step. First, the measurement must be converted to a decimal number. Then the rules for rounding applied.

Example:
Round the measurements to the given units.

MEASUREMENT	ROUND TO NEAREST	ANSWER
1 foot 7 inches	foot	2 ft
5 pound 6 ounces	pound	5 pounds
5 9/16 inches	inch	6 inches

Convert each measurement to a decimal number. Then apply the rules for rounding.

$$\text{foot 7 inches} = 1\frac{7}{12} \text{ ft} = 1.58333 \text{ ft, round up to 2 ft}$$

$$\text{pounds 6 ounces} = 5\frac{6}{16} \text{ pounds} = 5.375 \text{ pound, round to 5 pounds}$$

$$\text{inches} = 5.5625 \text{ inches, round up to 6 inches}$$

Symmetry

There are four basic **transformational symmetries** that can be used: *translation, rotation, reflection,* and *glide reflection.* The transformation of an object is called its image. If the original object was labeled with letters, such as $ABCD$, the image may be labeled with the same letters followed by a prime symbol, $A'B'C'D'$.

A **translation** is a transformation that "slides" an object a fixed distance in a given direction. The original object and its translation have the same shape and size, and they face in the same direction.

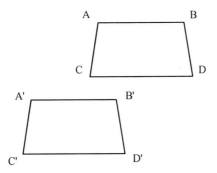

An example of a translation in architecture would be stadium seating. The seats are the same size and the same shape and face in the same direction.

A **rotation** is a transformation that turns a figure about a fixed point called the center of rotation. An object and its rotation are the same shape and size, but the figures may be turned in different directions. Rotations can occur in either a clockwise or a counterclockwise direction.

Rotations can be seen in wallpaper and art, and a Ferris wheel is an example of rotation.

An object and its **reflection** have the same shape and size, but the figures face in opposite directions.

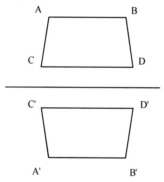

The line (where a mirror may be placed) is called the **line of reflection**. The distance from a point to the line of reflection is the same as the distance from the point's image to the line of reflection.

A **glide reflection** is a combination of a reflection and a translation.

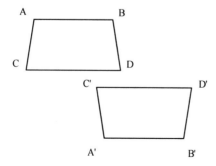

Objects that are **tangent** make contact at a single point or along a line without crossing. Understanding tangency is critical in the construction industry, where architects and engineers must figure out how various elements fit together. An example can be demonstrated by building a stair railing. The architect must determine the points of tangency between the banisters, which might even be curved, and the posts supporting the banisters.

Many types of flooring found in homes are examples of **symmetry**: Oriental carpets, tiling, patterned carpet, etc. The human body is an example of symmetry, even though it is not usually perfect. If you split the torso down the middle, on each half, you will find one ear, one eye, one nostril, one shoulder, one arm, one leg, and so on, in approximately the same place.

COMPETENCY 16.0 UNDERSTAND CONCEPTS AND SKILLS RELATED TO ALGEBRA

Skill 16.1   Recognizing the characteristics of patterns, identifying correct extensions of patterns, and recognizing relationships among patterns

The following table represents the number of problems Mr. Rodgers is assigning his math students for homework each day, starting with the first day of class.

Day	1	2	3	4	5	6	7	8	9	10	11
Number of Problems	1	1	2	3	5	8	13				

If Mr. Rodgers continues this pattern, how many problems will he assign on the eleventh day?

If we look for a pattern, it appears that the number of problems assigned each day is equal to the sum of the problems assigned for the previous two days. We test this as follows:

Day 2 = 1 + 0 = 1
Day 3 = 1 + 1 = 2
Day 4 = 2 + 1 = 3
Day 5 = 3 + 2 = 5
Day 6 = 5 + 3 = 8
Day 7 = 8 + 5 = 13

Therefore, Day 8 would have 21 problems; Day 9, 34 problems; Day 10, 55 problems; and Day 11, 89 problems.

A sequence is a pattern of numbers arranged in a particular order. When a list of numbers is in a sequence, a pattern may be expressed in terms of variables. Suppose we have the sequence 8, 12, 16…. If we assign the variable a to the initial term, 8, and assign the variable d to the difference between the first two terms, we can formulate a pattern of $a, a + d, a + 2d … a + (n-1)d$. With this formula, we can determine any number in the sequence. For example, let's say we want to know what the 400th term would be. Using the formula,

$$a + (n - 1)d =$$
$$8 + (400 - 1)4 =$$
$$8 + 399(4) =$$
$$8 + 1596 = 1604$$

we determine that the 400th term would be 1604.

Suppose we have an equation, $y = 2x + 1$. We construct a table of values in order to graph the equation to see if we can find a pattern.

x	y
-2	-3
-1	-1
0	1
1	3
2	5

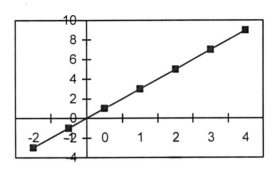

The pattern formed by the points is that they all lie on a line. Therefore, we can determine any solution of y by picking an x-coordinate and finding the corresponding point on the line. For example, if we want to know the solution of y when x is equal to 4, we find the corresponding point and see that y is equal to 9.

Skill 16.2   Applying knowledge of the concepts of variable, function, and equation to the expression of algebraic relationships

A **variable** is a letter that is used to represent one or more numbers. An algebraic expression is a collection of numbers, variables, operations, and grouping symbols.

Example:

16 times a, divided by b may be expressed algebraically as $\dfrac{16a}{b}$

An **equation** is formed when an equal sign is placed between two expressions.

Example:
$3x + y = 24$.

A **function** is a special type of relationship between two values, in which each input value corresponds to exactly one output value. Another way of defining a function is as a relation in which no two ordered pairs have the same x value.

Example:
$\{(a,1),(b,4),(c,4)\}$

Skill 16.3 Identifying relationships among variables based on mathematical expressions, tables, graphs, and rules

A relationship between two quantities can be shown using a table, graph, or rule. In this example, the rule y= 9x describes the relationship between the total amount earned, y, and the total amount of $9 sunglasses sold, x.

A table using this data would appear as:

number of sunglasses sold	1	5	10	15
total dollars earned	9	45	90	135

Each *(x,y)* relationship between a pair of values is called the **coordinate pair** that can be plotted on a graph. The coordinate pairs (1,9), (5,45), (10,90), and (15,135) are plotted on the graph below.

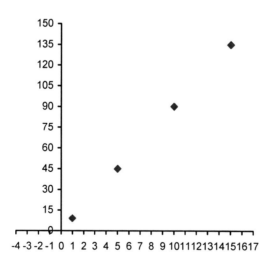

The graph above shows a linear relationship. A linear relationship is one in which two quantities are proportional to each other. Doubling x also doubles y. On a graph, a straight line depicts a linear relationship.

The function or relationship between two quantities may be analyzed to determine how one quantity depends on the other.

For example, the function above shows a relationship between *y* and *x*: y=2x+1.

The relationship between two or more variables can be analyzed using a table, graph, written description, or symbolic rule. The function, $y=2x+1$, is written as a symbolic rule. The same relationship is also shown in the table below:

x	0	2	3	6	9
y	1	5	7	13	19

This relationship could be written in words by saying that the value of y is equal to two times the value of x, plus one. This relationship could be shown on a graph by plotting given points such as the ones shown in the table above.

Another way to describe a function is as a process in which one or more numbers are input into an imaginary machine that produces another number as the output. If 5 is input, (x), into a machine with a process of $x +1$, the output, (y), will equal 6.

In real situations, relationships can be described mathematically. The function, $y=x+1$, can be used to describe the idea that people age one year on their birthday. To describe the relationship in which a person's monthly medical costs are 6 times a person's age, we could write $y=6x$. The monthly cost of medical care could be predicted using this function. A 20 year-old person would spend $120 per month ($120=20*6$). An 80 year-old person would spend $480 per month ($480=80*6$). Therefore, one could analyze the relationship to say: as you get older, medical costs increase $6.00 each year.

Skill 16.4   Applying the methods of algebra to solve equations and inequalities

Procedure for Solving Algebraic Equations

<u>Example</u>:

$3(x+3) = {}^-2x+4$ Solve for x.

1)   Expand to eliminate all parentheses.

$3x+9 = {}^-2x+4$

2)   Multiply each term by the LCD to eliminate all denominators.

3)   Combine like terms on each side when possible.

4)   Use the properties to put all variables on one side and all constants on the other side.

$\rightarrow 3x+9-9 = {}^-2x+4-9$ (subtract nine from both sides)

$\rightarrow 3x = {}^-2x-5$

$\rightarrow 3x+2x = {}^-2x+2x-5$ (add 2x to both sides)

$\rightarrow 5x = {}^-5$

$\rightarrow \dfrac{5x}{5} = \dfrac{{}^-5}{5}$ (divide both sides by 5)

$\rightarrow x = {}^-1$

Example:

Solve: $3(2x + 5) - 4x = 5(x + 9)$

$$6x + 15 - 4x = 5x + 45$$

$$2x + 15 = 5x + 45$$

$$^-3x + 15 = 45$$

$$^-3x = 30$$

$$x = {}^-10$$

Example:

Mark and Mike are twins. 3 times Mark's age, plus 4, equals 4 times Mike's age minus 14. How old are the boys?

Since the boys are twins, their ages are the same. "Translate" the English into Algebra. Let x = their age.

$3x + 4 = 4x - 14$

$18 = x$

The boys are each 18 years old.

Procedure for Solving Algebraic Inequalities

We use the same procedure used above for solving linear equations, but the answer is either represented in graphical form on the number line or in interval form.

<u>Example:</u>
Solve the inequality, show its solution using interval form, and graph the solution on the number line.

$$\frac{5x}{8} + 3 \geq 2x - 5$$

$$8\left(\frac{5x}{8}\right) + 8(3) \geq 8(2x) - 5(8) \quad \text{Multiply by LCD = 8.}$$

$$5x + 24 \geq 16x - 40$$

$$5x + 24 - 24 - 16x \geq 16x - 16x - 40 - 24$$

Subtract 16x and 24 from both sides of the equation.

$$^-11x \geq ^- 64$$

$$\frac{^-11x}{^-11} \leq \frac{^-64}{^-11}$$

$$x \leq \frac{64}{11} \quad ; \quad x \leq 5\frac{9}{11}$$

Solution in interval form: $\left(^-\infty, 5\frac{9}{11}\right]$

Note: "] " means $5\frac{9}{11}$ is included in the solution.

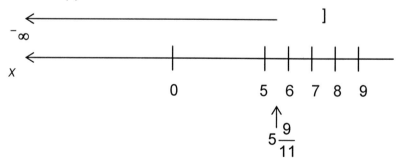

<u>Example:</u>
Solve the following inequality and express your answer in both interval and graphical form.

$3x - 8 < 2(3x - 1)$

$3x - 8 < 6x - 2$ Distributive property.

$3x - 6x - 8 + 8 < 6x - 6x - 2 + 8$

Add 8 and subtract 6x from both sides of the equation.

$^-3x < 6$

$\dfrac{^-3x}{^-3} > \dfrac{6}{^-3}$ Note the change in direction of the equality.

$x >^- 2$

Graphical form:

or

Interval form: $(^-2, \infty)$

Recall:
    a) Using a parentheses or an open circle implies the point is not included in the answer.

    b) Using a bracket or a closed circle implies the point is included in the answer.

Example:

Solve: $6x + 21 < 8x + 31$

$$^-2x + 21 < 31$$

$$^-2x < 10$$

$$x > {}^-5$$

Note that the inequality sign has changed.

The solution set of linear equations is all the ordered pairs of real numbers that satisfy both equations, thus the intersection of the lines. There are two methods for solving linear equations: *linear combinations* and *substitution*.

In the **substitution** method, an equation is solved for either variable. That solution is then substituted in the other equation to find the remaining variable.

Example:

(1) $2x + 8y = 4$
(2) $x - 3y = 5$

(2a) $x = 3y + 5$ Solve equation (2) for x.

(1a) $2(3y + 5) + 8y = 4$ Substitute x in equation (1)
         $6y + 10 + 8y = 4$ Solve.
         $14y = -6$
         $y = \frac{-3}{7}$ Solution

(2) $x - 3y = 5$
         $x - 3(\frac{-3}{7}) = 5$ Substitute the value of y.
         $x = \frac{26}{7} = 3\frac{5}{7}$ Solution

Thus, the solution set of the system of equations is $(3\frac{5}{7}, \frac{-3}{7})$.

In the **linear combinations** method, one or both of the equations are replaced with an equivalent equation so that the two equations can be combined (added or subtracted) to eliminate one variable.

Example:

(1)	$4x + 3y = -2$
(2)	$5x - y = 7$

(1)	$4x + 3y = -2$	
(2a)	$15x - 3y = 21$	Multiply equation (2) by 3

$19x = 19$	Combining (1) and (2a)
$x = 1$	Solve.

To find y, substitute the value of x in equation 1 (or 2).

(1) $4x + 3y = -2$
$4(1) + 3y = -2$
$4 + 3y = -2$
$3y = -2$
$y = -2$

Thus the solution is $x = 1$ and $y = -2$ or the order pair (1, -2).

Some word problems can be solved using a system (group) of equations or inequalities. Watch for words like greater than, less than, at least, or no more than, which indicate the need for inequalities.

Example:
Farmer Greenjeans bought 4 cows and 6 sheep for $1700. Mr. Ziffel bought 3 cows and 12 sheep for $2400. If all the cows were the same price and all the sheep were another fixed price, find the price charged for a cow or for a sheep.

Let x = price of a cow
Let y = price of a sheep

Then Farmer Greenjeans' equation would be: $4x + 6y = 1700$
Mr. Ziffel's equation would be: $3x + 12y = 2400$

To solve by **addition-subtraction**:
Multiply the first equation by $^-2$: $^-2(4x + 6y = 1700)$
Keep the other equation the same: $(3x + 12y = 2400)$

By doing this, the equations can be added to each other to eliminate one variable and solve for the other variable.

$$^-8x - 12y = {}^-3400$$
$$\underline{3x + 12y = 2400} \quad \text{Add these equations.}$$
$$^-5x \quad\quad = {}^-1000$$

$x = 200 \leftarrow$ the price of a cow was \$200.
Solving for y, $y = 150 \leftarrow$ the price of a sheep was \$150.

To solve this same equation by **substitution**:

Solve one of the equations for a variable. (Try to make an equation without fractions if possible.) Substitute this expression into the equation that you have not yet used. Solve the resulting equation for the value of the remaining variable.

$$4x + 6y = 1700$$
$$3x + 12y = 2400 \leftarrow \text{Solve this equation for } x.$$

It becomes $x = 800 - 4y$. Now substitute $800 - 4y$ in place of x in the OTHER equation. $4x + 6y = 1700$ now becomes:

$$4(800 - 4y) + 6y = 1700$$
$$3200 - 16y + 6y = 1700$$
$$3200 - 10y = 1700$$
$$^-10y = {}^-1500$$
$$y = 150 \text{, or } \$150 \text{ for a sheep.}$$

Substituting 150 back into an equation for y, find x.
$$4x + 6(150) = 1700$$
$$4x + 900 = 1700$$
$$4x = 800 \text{ so } x = 200 \text{, or } \$200 \text{ for a cow.}$$

<u>Example</u>:
Sharon's Bike Shoppe can assemble a 3 speed bike in 30 minutes or a 10 speed bike in 60 minutes. The profit on each bike sold is $60 for a 3 speed or $75 for a 10 speed bike. How many of each type of bike should they assemble during an 8 hour day (480 minutes) to make the maximum profit? Total daily profit must be at least $300.

Let x = number of 3 speed bikes.
y = number of 10 speed bikes.

Since there are only 480 minutes to use each day,
$30x + 60y \leq 480$ is the first inequality.

Since the total daily profit must be at least $300,
$60x + 75y \geq 300$ is the second inequality.

$32x + 65y \leq 480$ solves to $y \leq 8 - 1/2\,x$
$60x + 75y \geq 300$ solves to $y \geq 4 - 4/5\,x$

Graph these 2 inequalities:

$$y \leq 8 - 1/2\,x$$
$$y \geq 4 - 4/5\,x$$

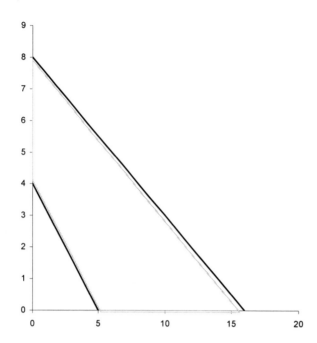

Realize that $x \geq 0$ and $y \geq 0$, since the number of bikes assembled can not be a negative number. Graph these as additional constraints on the problem. The number of bikes assembled must always be an integer value, so points within the shaded area of the graph must have integer values. The maximum profit will occur at or near a corner of the shaded portion of this graph. Those points occur at (0,4), (0,8), (16,0), or (5,0).

Since profits are \$60/3-speed or \$75/10-speed, the profit would be :

$$(0,4) \quad 60(0) + 75(4) = 300$$
$$(0,8) \quad 60(0) + 75(8) = 600$$
$$(16,0) \quad 60(16) + 75(0) = 960 \leftarrow \text{Maximum profit}$$
$$(5,0) \quad 60(5) + 75(0) = 300$$

The maximum profit would occur if 16 3-speed bikes are made daily.

Example:

The YMCA wants to sell raffle tickets to raise at least $32,000. If they must pay $7,250 in expenses and prizes out of the money collected from the tickets, how many tickets worth $25 each must they sell?

Since they want to raise <u>at least $32,000</u>, that means they would be happy to get 32,000 <u>or more</u>. This requires an inequality.

Let x = number of tickets sold
Then $25x$ = total money collected for x tickets

Total money minus expenses is greater than $32,000.

$$25x - 7250 \geq 32000$$
$$25x \geq 39250$$
$$x \geq 1570$$

If they sell 1,570 tickets or more, they will raise at least $32,000.

Example:

The Simpsons went out for dinner. All 4 of them ordered the aardvark steak dinner. Bert paid for the 4 meals and included a tip of $12 for a total of $84.60. How much was one aardvark steak dinner?

Let x = the price of one aardvark dinner.
So $4x$ = the price of 4 aardvark dinners.

$$4x + 12 = 84.60$$
$$4x = 72.60$$
$$x = \$18.50 \text{ for each dinner.}$$

Skill 16.5 **Analyzing how algebraic functions are used to plot points, describe graphs, and determine slope**

Graphically

A first degree equation has an equation of the form $ax + by = c$. To find the slope of a line, solve the equation for y. This gets the equation into **slope intercept form**, $y = mx + b$. In this equation, m is the line's slope.

The y intercept is the coordinate of the point where a line crosses the y axis. To find the y intercept, substitute 0 for x and solve for y. This is the y intercept. In slope intercept form, $y = mx + b$, b is the y intercept.

To find the x intercept, substitute 0 for y and solve for x. This is the x intercept. If the equation solves to **x = any number**, then the graph is a vertical line, because it only has an x intercept. Its slope is **undefined**.

If the equation solves to **y = any number**, then the graph is a horizontal line, because it only has a y intercept. Its slope is 0 (zero).

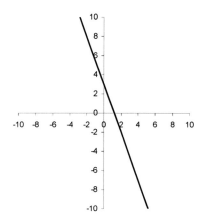

$$5x + 2y = 6$$
$$y = {}^{-}5/2\,x + 3$$

The equation of a line from its graph can be found by finding its slope and its y intercept. The slope formula looks like this:

$$m = \frac{y_2 - y_1}{x_2 - x_1}$$

The y intercept can be found using this equation:
$$Y - y_a = m(X - x_a)$$

(x_a, y_a) can be (x_1, y_1) or (x_2, y_2) If **m**, the value of the slope, is distributed through the parentheses, the equation can be rewritten into other forms of the equation of a line.

Example:

Find the equation of a line through $(9, {}^-6)$ and $({}^-1, 2)$.

$$\text{slope} = \frac{y_2 - y_1}{x_2 - x_1} = \frac{2 - {}^-6}{{}^-1 - 9} = \frac{8}{{}^-10} = \frac{{}^-4}{5}$$

$$Y - y_a = m(X - x_a) \rightarrow Y - 2 = {}^-4/5(X - {}^-1) \rightarrow$$

$$Y - 2 = {}^-4/5(X + 1) \rightarrow Y - 2 = {}^-4/5\,X - 4/5 \rightarrow$$

$$Y = {}^-4/5\,X + 6/5 \quad \text{This is the slope-intercept form.}$$

Multiplying by 5 to eliminate fractions, it is:

$$5Y = {}^-4X + 6 \rightarrow 4X + 5Y = 6 \quad \text{Standard form.}$$

Example:

Find the slope and intercepts of $3x + 2y = 14$.

$$3x + 2y = 14$$
$$2y = {}^-3x + 14$$
$$y = {}^-3/2\,x + 7$$

The slope of the line is $^-3/2$. The y intercept of the line is 7.

The intercepts can also be found by substituting 0 in place of the other variables in the equation.

To find the y intercept:

let $x = 0$; $3(0) + 2y = 14$

$0 + 2y = 14$

$2y = 14$

$y = 7$

$(0,7)$ is the y intercept.

To find the x intercept:

let $y = 0$; $3x + 2(0) = 14$

$3x + 0 = 14$

$3x = 14$

$x = 14/3$

$(14/3, 0)$ is the x intercept.

<u>Example</u>:
Sketch the graph of the line represented by $2x + 3y = 6$.

Let $x = 0 \rightarrow 2(0) + 3y = 6$
$\rightarrow 3y = 6$
$\rightarrow y = 2$
$\rightarrow (0,2)$ is the y intercept.

Let $y = 0 \rightarrow 2x + 3(0) = 6$
$\rightarrow 2x = 6$
$\rightarrow x = 3$
$\rightarrow (3,0)$ is the x intercept.

Let $x = 1 \rightarrow 2(1) + 3y = 6$
$\rightarrow 2 + 3y = 6$
$\rightarrow 3y = 4$
$\rightarrow y = \dfrac{4}{3}$
$\rightarrow \left(1, \dfrac{4}{3}\right)$ is the third point.

Plotting the three points on the coordinate system, we get the following:

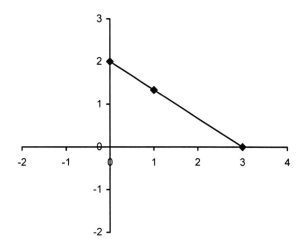

To graph an inequality, solve the inequality for y. This gets the inequality in slope intercept form, (for example: $y < mx + b$). The point $(0,b)$ is the y intercept, and m is the line's slope.

If the inequality solves to $x \geq$ **any number**, then the graph includes a vertical line.

If the inequality solves to $y \leq$ **any number**, then the graph includes a horizontal line.

When graphing a linear inequality, the line will be dotted if the inequality sign is $<$ or $>$. If the inequality signs are either $\geq$ or $\leq$, the line on the graph will be a solid line. Shade above the line when the inequality sign is $\geq$ or $>$. Shade below the line when the inequality sign is $<$ or $\leq$. For inequalities of the forms $x >$ number, $x \leq$ number, $x <$ number, or $x \geq$ number, draw a vertical line (solid or dotted). Shade to the right for $>$ or $\geq$. Shade to the left for $<$ or $\leq$.

Remember: **Dividing or multiplying by a negative number will reverse the direction of the inequality sign.**

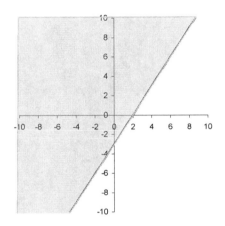

$$3x - 2y \geq 6$$
$$y \leq 3/2\, x - 3$$

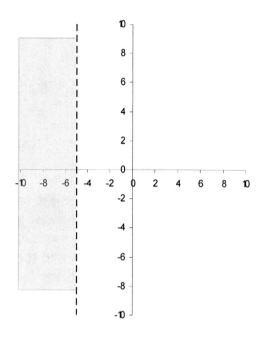

$$3x + 12 < -3$$

$$x < {}^-5$$

Example:
Solve by graphing:

$$x + y \leq 6$$
$$x - 2y \leq 6$$

Solving the inequalities for y, they become:

$y \leq {}^{-}x + 6$ (y intercept of 6 and slope = ${}^{-}1$)

$y \geq 1/2 x - 3$ (y intercept of ${}^{-}3$ and slope = $1/2$)

A graph with shading is shown below:

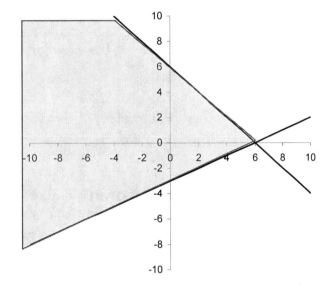

Skill 16.6   Demonstrating knowledge of applications of algebra in representing relationships and patterns in everyday life

Johannes Kepler discovered a relationship between the average distance of a planet from the sun and the time it takes the planet to orbit the sun.

The following table shows the data for the six planets closest to the sun:

	Mercury	Venus	Earth	Mars	Jupiter	Saturn
Average distance, x	0.387	0.723	1	1.523	5.203	9.541
x^3	0.058	.378	1	3.533	140.852	868.524
Time, y	0.241	0.615	1	1.881	11.861	29.457
y^2	0.058	0.378	1	3.538	140.683	867.715

Looking at the data in the table, we see that $x^3 \approx y^2$. We can conjecture the following function for Kepler's relationship: $y = \sqrt{x^3}$.

A **linear function** is a function defined by the equation $f(x) = mx + b$. This equation can be used to represent patterns in animals, people, and technology.

Example:
A model for the distance traveled by a migrating monarch butterfly looks like $f(t) = 80t$, where t represents time in days. We interpret this to mean that the average speed of the butterfly is 80 miles per day and distance traveled may be computed by substituting the number of days traveled for t. In a linear function, there is a *constant* rate of change.

COMPETENCY 17.0 UNDERSTAND CONCEPTS AND SKILLS RELATED TO DATA ANALYSIS

Skill 17.1   Applying knowledge of methods for organizing and interpreting data in a variety of formats (e.g., tables, frequency distributions, line graphs, circle graphs)

To make a **bar graph** or a **pictograph**, determine the scale to be used for the graph. Then determine the length of each bar on the graph, or determine the number of pictures needed to represent each item of information. Be sure to include an explanation of the scale in the legend.

Example:
A class had the following grades: 4 As, 9 Bs, 8 Cs, 1 D, and 3 Fs. Graph these on a bar graph and a pictograph.

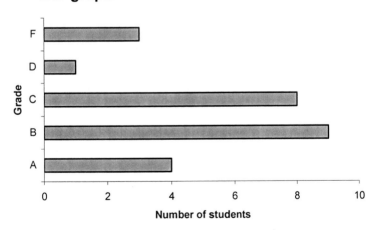

To make a **line graph**, determine appropriate scales for both the vertical and horizontal axes (based on the information to be graphed). Describe what each axis represents and mark the scale periodically on each axis. Graph the individual points of the graph and connect the points on the graph from left to right.

Example:
Graph the following information using a line graph.

The number of National Merit finalists/school year

	90-91	91-92	92-93	93-94	94-95	95-96
Central	3	5	1	4	6	8
Wilson	4	2	3	2	3	2

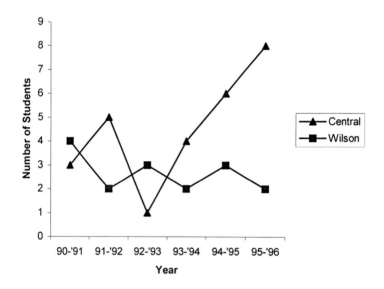

To make a **circle graph**, total all the information that is to be included on the graph. Determine the central angle to be used for each sector of the graph using the following formula:

$$\frac{\text{information}}{\text{total information}} \times 360° = \text{degrees in central} \measuredangle$$

Lay out the central angles to these sizes, label each section, and include each section's percent.

Example:
Graph this information on a circle graph: Monthly expenses:

Rent, $400
Food, $150
Utilities, $75
Clothes, $75
Church, $100
Misc., $200

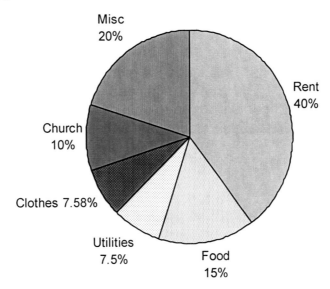

To read a bar graph or a pictograph, read the explanation of the scale that was used in the legend. Compare the length of each bar with the dimensions on the axes and calculate the value each bar represents. On a pictograph, count the number of pictures used in the chart and calculate the value of all the pictures.

To read a circle graph, find the total of the amounts represented on the entire circle graph. To determine the actual amount that each sector of the graph represents, multiply the percent in a sector times the total amount number.

To read a chart, be sure to look at the row and column headings on the table. Use this information to evaluate the given information in the chart.

Histograms are used to summarize information from large sets of data that can be naturally grouped into intervals. The vertical axis indicates **frequency** (the number of times any particular data value occurs), and the horizontal axis indicates data values or ranges of data values. The number of data values in any interval is the **frequency of the interval**.

Skill 17.2   Identifying trends and patterns in data

Random sampling supplies every combination of items from a frame, or stratum, with a known probability of occurring. However, the term "random" is somewhat misleading, as sampling is typically a very structured and scientific process. A large body of statistical theory quantifies the risk, thus enabling statisticians to determine the appropriate sample size to make it valid.

Systematic sampling selects items in a frame according to the kth sample. The first item is chosen to be the rth, where r is a random integer in the range $1,...,k-1$.

There are three stages to **cluster** or **area sampling**: the target population is divided into many regional clusters (groups), a few clusters are randomly selected for study, and a few subjects are randomly chosen from within a cluster.

Convenience sampling is the method of choosing items arbitrarily and in an unstructured manner from the frame.

Correlation is a measure of association between two variables. It varies from -1 to 1, with 0 being a random relationship, 1 being a perfect positive linear relationship, and -1 being a perfect negative linear relationship.

The **correlation coefficient** (r) is used to describe the strength of the association between the variables as well as the direction of the association.

Example:

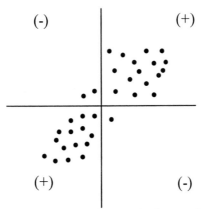

Horizontal and vertical lines are drawn through the **point of averages**, which is the point on the respective averages of the *x* and *y* values. Doing this divides the scatter plot into four quadrants. If a point is in the lower left quadrant, the product of two negatives is positive; in the upper right, the product of two positives is positive. The positive quadrants are depicted with the positive sign (+). In the two remaining quadrants (upper left and lower right), the product of a negative and a positive is negative. The negative quadrants are depicted with the negative sign (-). If r is positive, then there are more points in the positive quadrants; if r is negative, then there are more points in the two negative quadrants.

Regression is a form of statistical analysis used to predict a dependent variable (*y*) from values of an independent variable (*x*). A **regression equation** is derived from a known set of data.

The simplest regression analysis models the relationship between two variables using the following equation: $y = a + bx$, where *y* is the dependent variable and *x* is the independent variable. This simple equation denotes a linear relationship between *x* and *y*. This form would be appropriate if, when you plotted a graph of *x* and *y*, you saw the points roughly form along a straight line.

Example:

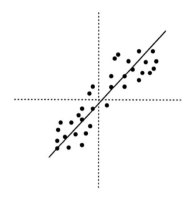

The line can then be used to make predictions.

If all of the data points fell on the line, there would be a perfect correlation ($r = 1.0$) between the x and y data points. These cases represent the best scenarios for prediction. A positive or negative r value represents how y varies with x. When r is positive, y increases as x increases. When r is negative, y decreases as x increases.

A **linear regression** equation is of the form: $Y = a + bX$.

Example:
A teacher wanted to determine how a practice test influenced a student's performance on the actual test. The practice test grade and the subsequent actual test grade for each student are given in the table below:

Practice Test (x)	Actual Test (y)
94	98
95	94
92	95
87	89
82	85
80	78
75	73
65	67
50	45
20	40

We determine the equation for the linear regression line to be $y = 14.650 + 0.834x$.

A new student comes into the class and scores 78 on the practice test. Based on the equation obtained above, what would the teacher predict this student would get on the actual test?

$$y = 14.650 + 0.834(78)$$
$$y = 14.650 + 65.052$$
$$y = 80$$
$$= 79.7$$

It is predicted that the student will get an 80.

Skill 17.3　Demonstrating knowledge of standard measures (e.g., mean, median, mode, and range) used to describe data

Mean, median, and mode are three measures of central tendency. The **mean** is the average of the data items. The **median** is found by putting the data items in order from smallest to largest and selecting the item in the middle (or the average of the two items in the middle). The **mode** is the most frequently occurring item.

Range is a measure of variability. It is found by subtracting the smallest value from the largest value.

Example:
Find the mean, median, mode, and range of the test score listed below:

85	77	65
92	90	54
88	85	70
75	80	69
85	88	60
72	74	95

Mean (X) = sum of all scores ÷ number of scores
　　= 78

Median = put numbers in order from smallest to largest. Pick middle number.
　　54, 60, 65, 69, 70, 72, 74, 75, 77, 80, 85, 85, 85, 88, 88, 90, 92, 95
　　　　　　　　　　　　　-- --
　　　　　　　　　　　both in middle
Therefore, the median is the average of two numbers in the middle, 78.5.

Mode = most frequent number
　　= 85

Range = largest number minus the smallest number
　　= 95 – 54
　　= 41

Different situations require different information. For example, examine the circumstances under which each of the following three scenarios use the numbers provided.

1) Over a 7-day period, the store owner collected data on the ice cream flavors sold. He found the mean number of scoops sold was 174 per day. The most frequently sold flavor was vanilla. This information was useful in determining how much ice cream to order overall as well as the amounts of each flavor.

   In the case of the ice cream store, the median and range had little business value for the owner.

2) Consider the set of test scores from a math class: 0, 16, 19, 65, 65, 65, 68, 69, 70, 72, 73, 73, 75, 78, 80, 85, 88, and 92. The mean is 64.06 and the median is 71. Since there are only three scores less than the mean out of the entire class, the median (71) would be a more descriptive score.

3) Retail storeowners may be most concerned with the most common dress size so they may order more of that size than any other.

An understanding of the definitions is important in determining the validity and uses of statistical data. All definitions and applications in this section apply to ungrouped data.

Data item: each piece of data is represented by the letter X.

Mean: the average of all data, with is represented by the symbol $\overline{X}$.

Range: the difference between the highest and lowest value of data items.

Sum of the squares: the sum of the squares of the differences between each item and the mean.

$$Sx^2 = (X - \overline{X})^2$$

Variance: the sum of the squares quantity divided by the number of items. The lower case Greek letter sigma squared (σ^2) represents variance.

$$\frac{Sx^2}{N} = \sigma^2$$

The larger the value of the variance, the larger the spread.

small variation   larger variation

Standard deviation: the square root of the variance. The lower case Greek letter sigma (σ) is used to represent standard deviation.

$$\sigma = \sqrt{\sigma^2}$$

Most statistical calculators have standard deviation keys on them; they should be used when asked to calculate statistical functions. It is important to become familiar with the calculator and the location of the keys needed.

Example:
Given the ungrouped data below, calculate the mean, range, standard deviation, and the variance.

> 15   22   28   25   34   38
> 18   25   30   33   19   23
>
> Mean ($\overline{X}$) = 25.8333333
> Range: $38 - 15 = 23$
> Standard deviation (σ) = 6.6936952
> Variance (σ^2) = 44.805556

Using graphing calculators or computer software has many advantages. The technology is better able to handle large data sets (such as the results of a science experiment), and it is much easier to edit and sort the data and to change the style of the graph to find its best representation. Furthermore, graphing calculators also provide a tool to plot statistics.

Skill 17.4   Drawing valid conclusions based on data

Both averages and graphs can be misleading if the data are not presented appropriately. The three types of averages used in statistics are mean, median, and mode. If a data set contains one very high or very low value, the mean will not be representative: for example, including the teacher's height in the mean height of a classroom. If the data are clustered around two numbers with a large gap between them, the median will not be representative: for example, expressing the median height in a family of two parents and two small children. Modes are best used with categorical data. In other words, do not mix apples with oranges; a mode of the sale of men's shoe sizes would be helpful to a store for reordering stock of men's shoes. However, finding the mode of men and women's shoe sizes combined would not be a good indicator of the stock that needed to be reordered.

Pictographs can also be misleading, especially if they are drawn to represent three-dimensional objects. If two or more dimensions are changed in reflecting ratio, the overall visual effect can be misinterpreted. Bar and line graphs can be misleading if the scales are changed; for example, using relatively small scale increments for large numbers will make the comparison differences seem much greater than if larger scale increments are used. Circle graphs, or pie charts, are excellent for comparing relative amounts. However, they cannot be used to represent absolute amounts, and if interpreted as such, they are misleading.

Skill 17.5   Demonstrating knowledge of applications of data analysis in everyday life

Counting Procedures

So far, in all the problems we dealt with, the **sample space** (the set of all possible outcomes for an experiment or trial) was given or can be easily obtained. In many real life situations, the sample space and the events within it are very large and difficult to find.

There are three techniques that help to find the number of elements in an event or sample space. These are: counting principle, permutations, and combinations.

The **counting principle**: In a sequence of two distinct events, in which the first one has n number of outcomes or possibilities and the second one has m number of outcomes or possibilities, the total number or possibilities of the sequence will be $n \times m$.

Example:
A car dealership has 3 Mazda models, and each model comes in a choice of 4 colors. How many Mazda cars are available at the dealership?

Number of available Mazda cars = (3)(4) = 12

Example:
If a license plate consists of 3 digits followed by 3 letters, find the possible number of licenses if:
a) repetitions of letters and digits are <u>not</u> allowed.
b) repetitions of letters and digits are allowed.

a) Since we have 26 letters and 10 digits, using the counting principle, we get:

possible # of licenses = (26)(25)(24)(10)(9)(8)
= 11,232,000

b) Since repetitions are allowed, we get

possible # of licenses = (26)(26)(26)(10)(10)(10)
$$= 17,576,000$$

The **addition principle of counting** states:

If A and B are events, $n(AorB) = n(A) + n(B) - n(A \cap B)$.

Example:
In how many ways can you select a black card or a Jack from an ordinary deck of playing cards?

Let B denote the set of black cards, and let J denote the set of Jacks. Then, $n(B) = 26, n(J) = 4, n(B \cap J) = 2$ and

$$n(BorJ) = n(B) + n(J) - n(B \cap A)$$
$$= 26 + 4 - 2$$
$$= 28.$$

The addition principle of counting for mutually exclusive events states:

If A and B are mutually exclusive events, $n(AorB) = n(A) + n(B)$.

Example:
A travel agency offers 40 possible trips: 14 to Asia, 16 to Europe, and 10 to South America. In how many ways can you select a trip to Asia or Europe through this agency?

Let A denote trips to Asia and let E denote trips to Europe. Then, $A \cap E = \varnothing$ and $n(AorE) = 14 + 16 = 30$.

Therefore, the number of ways you can select a trip to Asia or Europe is 30.

The multiplication principle of counting for dependent events states:

Let A be a set of outcomes of Stage 1, and B a set of outcomes of Stage 2. The number of ways, $n(AandB)$, that A and B can occur in a two-stage experiment is given by: $n(AandB) = n(A)n(B|A)$, where $n(B|A)$ denotes the number of ways B can occur, given that A has already occurred.

Example:
How many ways from an ordinary deck of 52 cards can 2 Jacks be drawn in succession if the first card is drawn but not replaced in the deck, and then the second card is drawn?

This is a two-stage experiment where we must compute $n(A \text{ and } B)$, where A is the set of outcomes for which a Jack is obtained on the first draw, and B is the set of outcomes for which a Jack is obtained on the second draw.

If the first card drawn is a Jack, then there are only 3 remaining Jacks left to choose from on the second draw. Thus, drawing two cards without replacement means the events A and B are dependent.

$$n(A \text{ and } B) = n(A)n(B|A) = 4 \cdot 3 = 12$$

The multiplication principle of counting for independent events states:

Let A be a set of outcomes of Stage 1, and B a set of outcomes of Stage 2. If A and B are independent events, then the number of ways, $n(A \text{ and } B)$, that A and B can occur in a two-stage experiment is given by: $n(A \text{ and } B) = n(A)n(B)$.

Example:
How many 6-letter code "words" can be formed if repetition of letters is not allowed?

Since these are code words, a word does not have to look like a word; for example, abcdef could be a code word. We must choose a first letter *and* a second letter *and* a third letter *and* a fourth letter *and* a fifth letter *and* a sixth letter, so this experiment has six stages.

Because repetition is not allowed, there are 26 choices for the first letter; 25 for the second; 24 for the third; 23 for the fourth; 22 for the fifth; and 21 for the sixth. Therefore, we have:

n(six-letter code words without repetition of letters)

$= 26 \cdot 25 \cdot 24 \cdot 23 \cdot 22 \cdot 21$

$= 165,765,600$

Permutations

In order to understand **permutations**, the concept of factorials must be addressed.

n factorial, written n!, is represented by n! = n(n-1)(n-2) . . . . . (2)(1)

5! = (5)(4)(3)(2)(1) = 120

3! = 3(2)(1) = 6

By definition: 0! = 1
1! = 1

$\dfrac{6!}{6!} = 1$ but $\dfrac{6!}{2!} \neq 3!$

$\dfrac{6!}{2!} = \dfrac{6 \cdot 5 \cdot 4 \cdot 3 \cdot 2!}{2!} = 6 \cdot 5 \cdot 4 \cdot 3 = 360$

The number of permutations represents the number of ways r items can be selected from n items and arranged in a specific order. It is written as $_nP_r$ and is calculated using the following relationship.

$$_nP_r = \frac{n!}{(n-r)!}$$

When calculating permutations, order counts. For example, 2, 3, 4 and 4, 3, 2 are counted as two different permutations. Calculating the number of permutations is not valid with experiments where replacement is allowed.

Example:
How many different ways can a president and a vice president be selected from a math class if 7 students are available?

We know we are looking for the number of permutations, since the positions of president and vice president are not equal.

$$_7P_2 = \frac{7!}{(7\text{-}2)!} = \frac{7!}{5!} = \frac{7 \cdot 6 \cdot 5!}{5!} = 7 \cdot 6 = 42$$

It is important to recognize that the number of permutations is a special case of the counting principle. Unless specifically asked to use the permutation relationship, use the counting principle to solve problems dealing with the number of permutations. For instance, in this example, we have seven available students to choose a president from. After a president is chosen, we have six available students to choose a vice president.

Hence, by using the counting principle, the ways a president and a vice president can be chosen = 7 x 6 = 42.

Combinations

When dealing with the number of **combinations**, the order in which elements are selected is not important. For instance,

2, 3, 4 and 4, 2, 3 are considered one combination.

The numbers of combinations represents the number of ways that r elements are selected from n elements (in no particular order). The number of combinations is represented by $_nC_r$ and can be calculated using the following relationship.

$$_nC_r = \frac{n!}{(n-r)r!}$$

Example:
In how many ways can 2 students be selected from a class of 7 students to represent the class?

Since both representatives have the same position, the order is not important, and we are dealing with the number of combinations.

$$_nC_r = \frac{7!}{(7-2)!2!} = \frac{7 \cdot 6 \cdot 5!}{5!2 \cdot 1} = 21$$

Example:
In a club, there are 6 women and 4 men. A committee of 2 women and 1 man is to be selected. How many different committees can be selected?

This problem has a sequence of two events. The first event involves selecting 2 women out of 6 women and the second event involves selecting 1 man out of 4 men. We use the combination relationship to find the number of ways in events 1 and 2, and the counting principle to find the number of ways the sequence can happen.

$$\text{# of Committees} = _6C_2 \cdot _4C_1$$
$$\frac{6!}{(6-2)!2!} \times \frac{4!}{(4-1)!1!}$$
$$= \frac{6 \cdot 5 \cdot 4!}{4! \cdot 2 \cdot 1} \times \frac{4 \cdot 3!}{3! \cdot 1}$$
$$= (15) \times (4) = 60$$

Using Tables

Example:
The results of a survey of 47 students are summarized in the table below.

	Black Hair	Blonde Hair	Red Hair	Total
Male	10	8	6	24
Female	6	12	5	23
Total	16	20	11	47

Use the table to answer questions a - c.

a) If 1 student is selected at random, find the probability of selecting a male student.

$$\frac{\text{Number of male students}}{\text{Number of students}} = \frac{24}{47}$$

b) If 1 student is selected at random, find the probability of selecting a female with red hair.

$$\frac{\text{Number of red hair females}}{\text{Number of students}} = \frac{5}{47}$$

c) If 1 student is selected at random, find the probability of selecting a student that does not have red hair.

$$\frac{\text{Red hair students}}{\text{Number of students}} = \frac{11}{47}$$

$$1 - \frac{11}{47} = \frac{36}{47}$$

DOMAIN IV.   SCIENCE

COMPETENCY 18.0 UNDERSTAND THE CHARACTERISTICS AND PROCESSES OF SCIENCE

Skill 18.1   Demonstrating knowledge of the nature of scientific knowledge and the values of science (e.g., importance of curiosity, honesty, openness, and skepticism; reliance on verifiable evidence)

Learning can be broadly divided into two kinds: active and passive. Active learning involves, as the name indicates, a learning atmosphere full of action. In passive learning, students are taught in a non-stimulating and inactive atmosphere. Active learning involves and draws students into it, thereby interesting them to the point of participating and purposely engaging in learning.

It is crucial that students are actively engaged, not entertained. They should be taught the answers for "How" and "Why" questions and encouraged to be inquisitive and interested.

Active learning is conceptualized as follows:

A Model of Active Learning

Experience of	Dialogue with
Doing	Self
Observing	Others

This model suggests that all learning activities involve some kind of experience or some kind of dialogue. The two main kinds of dialogue are "Dialogue with self" and "Dialogue with others." The two main kinds of experience are "Observing" and "Doing."

Dialogue with self: This is what happens when learners think reflectively about a topic. They ask themselves a number of things about the topic.

Dialogue with others: When the students are listening to a book being read by another student or when the teacher is teaching, a partial dialogue takes place because the dialogue is only one-sided. When they are listening to an another and when there is an exchange of ideas back and forth, it is said to be a dialogue with others.

Observing: This is a very important skill in science. This occurs when a learner carefully watches or observes someone else doing an activity or experiment. This is a good experience, although it is not quite like doing something for oneself.

Doing: This refers to any activity where a learner actually does something, giving the learner a firsthand experience that is very valuable.

The scientific attitude is to be curious, open to new ideas, and skeptical. In science, there are always new discoveries, new research, and new theories proposed. Sometimes, old theories are disproved. To view these changes rationally, one must have openness, curiosity, and skepticism. (Skepticism is a Greek word, meaning a method of obtaining knowledge through systematic doubt and continual testing. A scientific skeptic is one who refuses to accept certain types of claims without subjecting them to a systematic investigation.)

The students may not have these attitudes inherently, but it is the responsibility of the teacher to encourage, nurture, and practice these attitudes so that students will have a good role model.

Skill 18.2 Demonstrating knowledge of the principles of scientific inquiry and the design of scientific investigations

Processes by which Hypotheses are Generated and Tested

Science can be defined as a body of knowledge that is systematically derived from study, observations, and experimentation. Its goal is to identify and establish principles and theories that may be applied to solve problems. **Pseudoscience**, on the other hand, is a belief that is not warranted. There is no scientific methodology or application. Some of the more classic examples of pseudoscience include witchcraft, alien encounters, or any topic that is explained by hearsay.

Scientific theory and experimentation must be repeatable, meaning that the findings of one experiment are able to be duplicated during any number of repetitions. They are also capable of change and possible to be disproved. Science depends on communication, agreements, and disagreements among scientists. It is composed of theories, laws, and hypotheses.

Theory - the formation of principles or relationships that have been verified and accepted.

Law - an explanation of events that occur with uniformity under the same conditions (e.g., laws of nature, law of gravitation).

Hypothesis - an unproved theory or educated guess followed by research to best explain a phenomena. A theory is a proven hypothesis.

Science is limited by the available technology. An example of this would be the relationship of the discovery of the cell and the invention of the microscope. As our technology improves, more hypotheses will become theories and possibly laws.

Science is also limited by the data that are able to be collected. Data may be interpreted differently on different occasions. Science limitations cause explanations to be changeable as new technologies emerge.

The first step in scientific inquiry is posing a question to be answered. Next, a hypothesis is formed to provide a plausible explanation. An experiment is then proposed and performed to test this hypothesis. A comparison between the predicted and observed results is the next step. Conclusions are then formed, and it is determined whether the hypothesis is correct or incorrect. If incorrect, the next step is to form a new hypothesis and the process is repeated.

Methods or Procedures for Collecting Data

The procedure used to obtain data is important to the outcome. Experiments consist of **controls** and **variables**. A control is the experiment run under normal conditions. The variable includes a factor that is changed. In biology, the variable may be light, temperature, pH, or time. The differences in tested variables may be used to make a prediction or to form a hypothesis. Only one variable should be tested at a time; for example, one would not alter both the temperature and pH of the experimental subject.

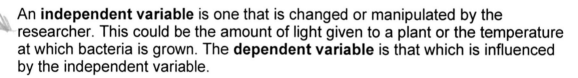

An **independent variable** is one that is changed or manipulated by the researcher. This could be the amount of light given to a plant or the temperature at which bacteria is grown. The **dependent variable** is that which is influenced by the independent variable.

Skill 18.3   Recognizing and applying the unifying concepts of science (e.g., systems, models, scale)

Unifying Concepts and Processes among the Sciences

The following are the concepts and processes generally recognized as those common to all scientific disciplines:

1. Systems, order, and organization
2. Constancy, change, and measurement
3. Evolution and equilibrium
4. Form and function
5. Evidence, models, and explanation
6. ~~Systems, order, and organization~~   *repeat*

Because the natural world is so complex, the study of science involves the **organization** of items into smaller groups based on interaction or interdependence. These groups are called **systems**. Examples of organization include the periodic table of elements and the five-kingdom classification scheme for living organisms. Examples of systems include the solar system, the cardiovascular system, Newton's laws of force and motion, and the laws of conservation.

Order refers to the behavior and measurability of organisms and events in nature. The arrangement of planets in the solar system and the life cycle of bacterial cells are examples of order.

Constancy, Change, and Measurement

Constancy and **change** describe the observable properties of natural organisms and events. Scientists use different systems of **measurement** to observe change and constancy. For example, the freezing and melting points of given substances as well as the speed of sound are constant under constant conditions. Growth, decay, and erosion are all examples of natural change.

Evolution and Equilibrium

Evolution is the process of change over a long period of time. While biological evolution is the most common example, one can also classify technological advancements, changes in the universe, and changes in the environment as evolution.

Equilibrium is the state of balance between opposing forces of change. Homeostasis and ecological balance are examples of equilibrium.

Form and Function

Form and **function** are properties of organisms and systems that are closely related. The function of an object usually dictates its form, and the form of an object usually facilitates its function. For example, the form of the heart (e.g., muscle and valves) allows it to perform its function of circulating blood through the body.

Evidence, Models, and Explanations

Scientists use **evidence** and **models** to form **explanations** of natural events. Models are miniaturized representations of a larger event or system. Evidence is anything that furnishes proof.

Some things happen at too fast or too slow a rate, or are too small or too large for use to see. In these cases, we have to rely on indirect evidence to develop models of what is intangible. Once data has been collected and analyzed, it is useful to generalize the information by creating a model. A model is a conceptual representation of a phenomenon. Models are useful in that they clarify relationships, helping us to understand the phenomenon and make predictions about future outcomes. The natural sciences and social sciences employ modeling for this purpose.

Many scientific models are mathematical in nature and contain a set of variables linked by logical and quantitative relationships. These mathematical models may include functions, tables, formulas, and graphs. Typically, such mathematical models include assumptions that restrict them to very specific situations. Oftentimes, this means they can only provide an *approximate* description of what occurs in the natural world. These assumptions, however, prevent the model from becoming overly complicated. For a mathematical model to fully explain a natural or social phenomenon, it has to contain many variables and may become too cumbersome to use. Accordingly, it is critical that assumptions be carefully chosen and thoroughly defined.

Certain models are abstract and contain sets of logical principles rather than relying on mathematics. These types of models are generally vaguer and are more useful for discovering and understanding new ideas. Abstract models can also include actual physical models built to make concepts more tangible. Abstract models, to an even greater extent than mathematical models, make assumptions and simplify actual phenomena.

Proper scientific models must be able to be tested and verified using experimental data. Often these experimental results are necessary to demonstrate the superiority of a model when two or more conflicting models seek to explain the same phenomenon. Computer simulations are increasingly used in both testing and developing mathematical and even abstract models. These types of simulations are especially useful in situations, such as ecology or manufacturing, where experiments are not feasible or variables are not fully under control.

Skill 18.4   Applying knowledge of strategies for observing, collecting, analyzing, and communicating scientific data (e.g., using graphs, charts, and tables)

The scientific method is the basic process behind science. It involves several steps beginning with hypothesis formulation and working through to the conclusion.

Pose a question: Although many discoveries happen by chance, the standard thought process of a scientist begins with forming a question to research. The more limited the question, the easier it is to set up an experiment to answer it.

Form a hypothesis: Once the question is formulated, scientists take an educated guess about the answer to the problem or question. This "best guess" is the hypothesis.

Conducting the test: To make a test fair, data from an experiment must have a variable or any condition that can be changed, such as temperature or mass. A good test will try to manipulate as few variables as possible so as to see which variable is responsible for the result. This requires a second example of a control. A control is an extra setup in which all the conditions are the same except for the variable being tested.

Observe and record the data: Reporting data should state specifics of how the measurements were calculated. For example, a graduated cylinder needs to be read with proper procedures. As beginning students, technique must be part of the instructional process so as to give validity to the data.

Drawing a conclusion: After recording data, compare it with that of other groups. A conclusion is the judgment derived from the data results.

Graphing Data

Graphing is an important skill to visually display collected data for analysis. It utilizes numbers to demonstrate patterns. The patterns offer a visual representation, making it easier to draw conclusions.

The two types of graphs most commonly used are the **line graph** and the **bar graph** (histogram). Line graphs are set up to show two variables represented by one point on the graph. The X axis is the horizontal axis; it represents the dependent variable. Dependent variables are those that would be present independently of the experiment. A common example of a dependent variable is time. Time proceeds regardless of anything else occurring. The Y axis is the vertical axis; it represents the independent variable. Independent variables are manipulated by the experiment, such as the amount of light or the height of a plant.

Graphs should be calibrated at equal intervals. If one space represents one day, the next space may not represent ten days. A "best fit" line can be drawn to join the points, and it does not always include all the points in the data. Axes must always be labeled for the graph to be meaningful. A good title will describe both the dependent and the independent variable.

Bar graphs are set up similarly in regards to axes, but points are not plotted. Instead, the dependent variable is set up as a bar where the X axis intersects with the Y axis. Each bar is a separate item of data and is not joined by a continuous line.

Apply Knowledge of Designing and Performing Investigations

Normally, knowledge is integrated in the form of a lab report. A report has many sections. It should include a specific **title** that tells exactly what is being studied. The **abstract** is a summary of the report; it is written at the beginning of the paper. The **purpose** should always be defined as it will state the problem. The purpose should include the **hypothesis** (educated guess) of what is expected from the outcome of the experiment. The entire experiment should relate to this problem.

It is important to describe exactly what was done to prove or disprove a hypothesis. A **control** is necessary to prove that the results occurred from the changed conditions and would not have happened normally. Only one variable should be manipulated at a time. **Observations** and **results** of the experiment should be recorded, including all results from data. Drawings, graphs, and illustrations should be included to support information. Observations are objective, whereas analysis and interpretation is subjective. A **conclusion** should explain why the results of the experiment either proved or disproved the hypothesis.

A scientific theory is an explanation of a set of related observations based on a proven hypothesis. A scientific law usually lasts longer than a scientific theory and has more experimental data to support it.

Science uses the metric system, as it is accepted worldwide and allows easier comparison among experiments done by scientists around the world. It is important to learn the following basic units and prefixes:

meter - measure of length
liter - measure of volume
gram - measure of mass

deca-(meter, liter, gram)= 10X the base unit   *deci*= 1/10 the base unit
hecto-(meter, liter, gram)= 100X the base unit   *centi*= 1/100 the base unit
kilo-(meter, liter, gram)= 1000X the base unit   *milli*= 1/1000 the base unit

Skill 18.5   Recognizing appropriate tools, instruments, methods, process skills, and safety procedures associated with given scientific investigations

Procedures and Tools

Knowledge of appropriate use of laboratory materials:
Light microscopes are commonly used in high school laboratory experiments. Total magnification is determined by multiplying the ocular (usually 10X) and the objective (usually 10X on low, 40X on high) lenses. Several procedures should be followed to properly care for this equipment.

- Clean all lenses with lens paper only.
- Carry microscopes with two hands; one on the arm and one on the base.
- Always begin focusing on low power, then switch to high power.
- Store microscopes with the low power objective down.
- Always use a coverslip when viewing wet mount slides.
- Bring the objective down to its lowest position, then focus, moving up to avoid breaking the slide or scratching the lens.

Wet mount slides should be made by placing a drop of water on the specimen and then putting a glass coverslip on top of the drop of water. Dropping the coverslip at a forty-five degree angle will help to avoide air bubbles.

Chromatography uses the principles of capillarity to separate substances such as plant pigments. Molecules of a larger size will move slowly up the paper, whereas smaller molecules will move more quickly, producing lines of pigment.

An **indicator** is any substance used to assist in the classification of another substance. An example of an indicator is **litmus paper**. Litmus paper is a way to measure whether a substance is acidic or basic. Blue litmus turns pink when an acid is placed on it, and pink litmus turns blue when a base is placed on it. A more accurate measure of pH is pH paper; the paper turns different colors depending on the pH value.

Spectrophotometry measures the percent of light at different wavelengths absorbed and transmitted by a pigment solution.

Centrifugation involves spinning substances at a high speed. The more dense part of a solution will settle to the bottom of the test tube, whereas the lighter material will stay on top. Centrifugation is used to separate blood into blood cells and plasma, with the heavier blood cells settling to the bottom.

Electrophoresis uses electrical charges of molecules to separate them according to their size. The molecules, such as DNA or proteins, are pulled through a gel towards either the positive end of the gel box (if the material has a negative charge) or the negative end of the gel box (if the material has a positive charge). DNA is negatively charged and moves towards the positive charge.

Storing, Identifying, and Disposing of Chemicals and Biological Materials

All laboratory solutions should be prepared as directed in the lab manual. Care should be taken to avoid contamination. All glassware should be rinsed thoroughly with distilled water before using, and cleaned well after use. In case of an accident, safety goggles should be worn while working with glassware. All solutions should be made with distilled water, as tap water contains dissolved particles that may affect the results of an experiment. Chemical storage should be located in a secured, dry area. Chemicals should be stored in accordance with reactability. Acids are to be locked in a separate area. Used solutions should be disposed of according to local disposal procedures. Any questions regarding safe disposal or chemical safety may be directed to the local fire department.

The "Right to Know Law" covers science teachers who work with potentially hazardous chemicals. Briefly, the law states that employees must be informed of potentially toxic chemicals. An inventory must be made available if requested. The inventory must contain information about the hazards and properties of the chemicals. This inventory is to be checked against the "substance list." Training must be provided on the safe handling and interpretation of the Material Safety Data Sheet.

The following chemicals are potential carcinogens and are not allowed in school facilities: acrylonitrile, arsenic compounds, asbestos, benzidine, benzene, cadmium compounds, chloroform, chromium compounds, ethylene oxide, ortho-toluidine, nickel powder, and mercury.

Chemicals should not be stored on bench tops or heat sources. They should be stored in groups based on their reactivity with one another and in protective storage cabinets. All containers within the lab must be labeled. Suspect and known carcinogens must be labeled as such and segregated within trays to contain leaks and spills.

Chemical waste should be disposed of in properly labeled containers. Waste should be separated based on its reactivity with other chemicals.

Biological material should never be stored near food or water used for human consumption. All biological materials should be appropriately labeled. All blood and bodily fluids should be put into well-contained containers with secure lids to prevent leaking. All biological waste should be disposed of in biological hazardous waste bags.

Material Safety Data Sheets are available for every chemical and biological substance. These are available directly from the company of acquisition or the internet. The manuals for equipment used in the lab should be read and understood before using them.

Dissection and Alternatives to Dissection

Dissections - Animals that are not obtained from recognized sources should never be used. Decaying animals or those of unknown origin may harbor pathogens and/or parasites. Specimens should be rinsed before handling. Latex gloves are desirable. If gloves are not available, students with sores or scratches should be excused from the activity. Formaldehyde is a carcinogen and should be avoided or disposed of according to district regulations.

Students objecting to dissections for moral reasons should be given an alternative assignment. Interactive dissections are available online or from software companies for those students who object to performing dissections. There should be no penalty for those students who refuse to physically perform a dissection.

Live specimens - No dissections may be performed on living mammalian vertebrates or birds. Lower order life and invertebrates may be used. Biological experiments may be done with all animals except mammalian vertebrates or birds. No physiological harm may result to the animal. All animals housed and cared for in the school must be handled in a safe and humane manner. Animals are not to remain on school premises during extended vacations unless adequate care is provided. Many state laws stipulate that any instructor who intentionally refuses to comply with the laws may be suspended or dismissed.

Microbiology - Pathogenic organisms must never be used for experimentation. Students should adhere to the following rules at all times when working with microorganisms to avoid accidental contamination:

1. Treat all microorganisms as if they were pathogenic.
2. Maintain sterile conditions at all times

If taking a national level exam, it is important to check with the Department of Education for specific state safety procedures. Teachers should know what their state expects not only for the test, but also for performance in the classroom and for the welfare of students. It is the responsibility of the teacher to provide a safe environment for the students. Proper supervision greatly reduces the risk of injury, and a teacher should never leave a class for any reason without providing alternate supervision.

After an accident, two factors are considered; *foreseeability* and *negligence*. **Foreseeability** is the anticipation that an event may occur under certain circumstances. **Negligence** is the failure to exercise ordinary or reasonable care. Safety procedures should be a part of the science curriculum, and a well-managed classroom is important to avoid potential lawsuits.

All science labs should contain the following items of safety equipment. The following are requirements by law:

- Fire blanket that is visible and accessible
- Ground Fault Circuit Interrupters (GFCI) within two feet of water supplies
- Emergency shower capable of providing a continuous flow of water
- Signs designating room exits
- Emergency eye wash station that can be activated by the foot or forearm
- Eye protection for every student as well as a means of sanitizing equipment
- Emergency exhaust fans providing ventilation to the outside of the building
- Master cut-off switches for gas, electric, and compressed air. Switches must have permanently attached handles. Cut-off switches must be clearly labeled.
- An ABC fire extinguisher
- Storage cabinets for flammable materials

Also recommended, but not required by law:
- Chemical spill control kit
- Fume hood with a motor that is spark proof
- Protective laboratory aprons made of flame retardant material
- Signs that will alert people to potential hazardous conditions
- Containers for broken glassware, flammables, corrosives, and waste
- Containers should be labeled

Skill 18.6 Demonstrating knowledge of the connections among science, mathematics, technology, society, and everyday life

Biological science is closely connected to technology and the other sciences; it greatly impacts society and everyday life. Scientific discoveries often lead to technological advances and, conversely, technology is often necessary for scientific investigation. Biology and the other scientific disciplines share several unifying concepts and processes that help to unify the study of science. Because biology is the science of living systems, biology directly impacts society and everyday life.

Science and technology, while distinct concepts, are closely related. Science attempts to investigate and explain the natural world, while technology attempts to solve human adaptation problems. Technology often results from the application of scientific discoveries, and advances in technology can increase the impact of scientific discoveries. For example, Watson and Crick used science to discover the structure of DNA; their discovery led to many biotechnological advances in the manipulation of DNA. These technological advances greatly influenced the medical and pharmaceutical fields. The success of Watson and Crick's experiments, however, was dependent on the technology available. Without the necessary technology, the experiments would have failed.

Biologists use a variety of tools and technologies to perform tests, to collect and display data, and to analyze relationships. Examples of commonly used tools include computer-linked probes, spreadsheets, and graphing calculators.

Biologists use **computer-linked probes** to measure various environmental factors including temperature, dissolved oxygen, pH, ionic concentration, and pressure. The advantage of computer-linked probes, as compared to more traditional observational tools, is that the probes automatically gather data and present it in an accessible format. This property of computer-linked probes eliminates the need for constant human observation and manipulation.

Biologists use **spreadsheets** to organize, analyze, and display data. For example, conservation ecologists use spreadsheets to model population growth and development, to apply sampling techniques, and to create statistical distributions to analyze relationships. Spreadsheet use simplifies data collection and manipulation, and it also allows the presentation of data to be done in a logical and understandable format.

Graphing calculators are another technology with many applications to biology. For example, biologists use algebraic functions to analyze growth, development, and other natural processes. Graphing calculators can manipulate algebraic data and create graphs for analysis and observation. In addition, biologists use the matrix function of graphing calculators to model problems in genetics. The use of graphing calculators simplifies the creation of graphical displays, including histograms, scatter plots, and line graphs. Biologists can transfer data and displays to computers for further analysis. Finally, biologists also connect computer-linked probes, used to collect data, to graphing calculators to ease the collection, transmission, and analysis of data.

The combination of biology and technology has improved the human standard of living in many ways. However, the negative impact of increasing human life expectancy and population on the environment is problematic. In addition, advances in biotechnology (e.g. genetic engineering, cloning) produce ethical dilemmas that society must consider.

COMPETENCY 19.0 UNDERSTAND CONCEPTS AND PRINCIPLES OF EARTH SCIENCE

Skill 19.1 **Comparing characteristics of objects in the solar system and universe (e.g., stars, planets) and analyzing the effects (e.g., seasons, phases of the moon) of the relative positions and motions of the earth, moon, and sun**

There are eight established planets in our solar system: Mercury, Venus, Earth, Mars, Jupiter, Saturn, Uranus, and Neptune. Pluto was an established planet in our solar system, but as of the summer of 2006, its status is being reconsidered. The planets are divided into two groups based on distance from the sun. The inner planets include Mercury, Venus, Earth, and Mars. The outer planets include Jupiter, Saturn, Uranus, and Neptune.

Planets

Mercury is the closest planet to the sun. Its surface has craters and rocks. The atmosphere is composed of hydrogen, helium, and sodium. Mercury was named after the Roman messenger god.

Venus has a slow rotation when compared to Earth. Venus and Uranus rotate in opposite directions from the other planets (this opposite rotation is called **retrograde rotation**). The surface of Venus is not visible due to the extensive cloud cover. The atmosphere is composed mostly of carbon dioxide, and sulfuric acid droplets in the dense cloud cover give Venus a yellow appearance. It has a greater greenhouse effect than observed on Earth; the dense clouds combined with carbon dioxide trap heat. Venus was named after the Roman goddess of love.

Earth is considered a water planet, with 70 percent of its surface covered by water. Gravity holds the masses of water in place. The different temperatures observed on Earth allow for the different states (solid, liquid, and gas) of water to exist. The atmosphere is composed mainly of oxygen and nitrogen. Earth is the only planet that is known to support life.

Mars has a surface that contains numerous craters, active and extinct volcanoes, ridges, and valleys with extremely deep fractures. Iron oxide found in the dusty soil makes the surface seem rust-colored and the skies seem pink in color. The atmosphere is composed of carbon dioxide, nitrogen, argon, oxygen, and water vapor. Mars has Polar Regions with icecaps composed of water. Mars has two satellites. Mars was named after the Roman war god.

Jupiter is the largest planet in the solar system. It has sixteen moons. The atmosphere is composed of hydrogen, helium, methane, and ammonia. There are white-colored bands of clouds indicating rising gases, and dark-colored bands of clouds indicating descending gases. The gas movement is caused by heat resulting from the energy of Jupiter's core. Jupiter has a Great Red Spot that is thought to be a hurricane-like cloud. Jupiter has a strong magnetic field.

Saturn is the second largest planet in the solar system. Saturn has rings of ice, rock, and dust particles circling it. Saturn's atmosphere is composed of hydrogen, helium, methane, and ammonia, and it has twenty or more satellites. Saturn was named after the Roman god of agriculture.

Uranus is the second largest planet in the solar system with retrograde revolution. Uranus is a gaseous planet. It has ten dark rings and fifteen satellites. Its atmosphere is composed of hydrogen, helium, and methane. Uranus was named after the Greek god of the heavens.

Neptune is another gaseous planet with an atmosphere consisting of hydrogen, helium, and methane. Neptune has three rings and two satellites. Neptune was named after the Roman sea god because its atmosphere is the same color as the seas.

Pluto was once considered the smallest planet in the solar system; its status as a planet is being reconsidered. Pluto's atmosphere probably contains methane, ammonia, and frozen water. Pluto has one satellite. It revolves around the sun every 250 years. Pluto was named after the Roman god of the underworld.

Comets, Asteroids, and Meteors

Astronomers believe that rocky fragments may be the remains of the birth of the solar system that never formed into a planet. **Asteroids** are found in the region between Mars and Jupiter.

Comets are masses of frozen gases, cosmic dust, and small rocky particles. Astronomers think that most comets originate in a dense comet cloud beyond Pluto. Comets consist of a nucleus, a coma, and a tail. A comet's tail always points away from the sun. The most famous comet, **Halley's Comet**, is named after the person who first discovered it in 240 BCE. It returns to the skies near the earth every seventy-five to seventy-six years.

Meteoroids are composed of particles of rock and metal of various sizes. When a meteoroid travels through the earth's atmosphere, friction causes its surface to heat up and it begins to burn. The burning meteoroid falling through the earth's atmosphere is called a **meteor** (also known as a "shooting star").

Meteorites are meteors that strike the earth's surface. A physical example of a meteorite's impact can be seen in Arizona; the *Barringer Crater* is a huge crater left by a meteor strike. There are many other meteor craters throughout the world.

Sun

Parts of the sun include:
1) The **core,** the inner portion of the sun where fusion takes place.
2) The **photosphere,** or the surface of the sun that produces **sunspots** (cool, dark areas that can be seen on its surface).
3) The **chromosphere**, which includes hydrogen gases that cause this portion to be red in color; **solar flares** (sudden brightness of the chromosphere); and **solar prominences** (gases that shoot outward from the chromosphere).
4) The **corona**, which is the transparent area of the sun visible only during a total eclipse.

Solar radiation is energy traveling from the sun into space. **Solar flares** produce excited protons and electrons that shoot outward from the chromosphere at great speeds reaching Earth. These particles disturb radio reception and also affect the magnetic field on Earth.

Earth's orbit around the sun and the earth's axis of rotation determine the seasons of the year. When the northern and southern hemispheres of Earth are pointed towards the sun, it is summer, and when it is pointed away from the sun, it is winter. Because of the axis of rotation, both hemispheres cannot be in the same season simultaneously. The two hemispheres have opposite seasons at all times.

Moon

The *moon* is a sphere that is always half illuminated by the sun. The moon phase we see is dependent of the position of the moon to the earth. During each lunar orbit (a lunar month), we see the moon's appearance change from not visibly illuminated to partially illuminated to fully illuminated, then back through partially illuminated to not illuminated again. Although this cycle is a continuous process, there are eight distinct, traditionally recognized stages, called **phases**. The phases designate both the degree to which the moon is illuminated and the geometric appearance of the illuminated part.

New Moon: This occurs when the moon's non-illuminated side is facing the earth. The moon is not visible (except during a solar eclipse).

Waxing Crescent: This is when the moon appears to be less than one-half illuminated by direct sunlight. The fraction of the moon's disk that is illuminated is increasing.

First Quarter: One-half of the moon appears to be illuminated by direct sunlight during this time. The fraction of the moon's disk that is illuminated is increasing.

Waxing Gibbous: In this phase, the moon appears to be more than one-half but not fully illuminated by direct sunlight. The fraction of the Moon's disk that is illuminated is increasing.

Full Moon: This occurs when the moon's illuminated side is facing the earth. The moon appears to be completely illuminated by direct sunlight.

Waning Gibbous: This is when the moon appears to be more than one-half but not fully illuminated by direct sunlight. The fraction of the moon's disk that is illuminated is decreasing.

Last Quarter: One-half of the moon is illuminated by direct sunlight in this phase. The fraction of the moon's disk that is illuminated is decreasing.

Waning Crescent: During this time, the moon is less than one-half illuminated by direct sunlight. The fraction of the moon's disk that is illuminated is decreasing.

The moon, the earth, and the sun affect ocean tides. Along the west coast of the United States, we experience four different tides per day: two highs and two lows. When the moon, the earth, and the sun are in a line, **spring tides** occur. During these tides, one may observe higher and lower than normal tides. In other words, there will be very high tides and very low tides. When the moon, the earth, and sun are at right angles to each other, **neap tides** are formed. During these tides, one is not able to observe a great deal of difference in the heights of the high and low tides.

Skill 19.2 Demonstrating knowledge of the composition, structure, and processes of the earth's lithosphere (e.g., rocks, minerals), hydrosphere, and atmosphere and the interactions among these systems (e.g., water cycle, weather patterns)

Earth's Atmosphere

El Niño refers to a sequence of changes in the ocean and atmospheric circulation across the Pacific Ocean. It causes the water around the equator to be unusually hot every two to seven years. Trade winds normally blow east to west across the equatorial latitudes, piling warm water into the western Pacific. A huge mass of heavy thunderstorms usually forms in the area and produces vast currents of rising air that displace heat pole-ward. This helps to create the strong mid-latitude jet streams. When it occurs, the world's climate patterns are disrupted by a change in location of thunderstorm activity.

Air masses moving toward or away from the earth's surface are called **air currents**. Air moving parallel to the earth's surface is called **wind**. Weather conditions are generated by winds and air currents carrying large amounts of heat and moisture from one part of the atmosphere to another. Wind speeds are measured by instruments called **anemometers**.

The wind belts in each hemisphere consist of convection cells that encircle Earth like belts. There are three major wind belts on Earth: 1) trade winds, 2) prevailing westerlies, and 3) polar easterlies. Wind belt formation depends on the differences in air pressures that develop in the doldrums, the horse latitudes, and the polar regions. The **doldrums** surround the equator. Within this belt, heated air usually rises straight up into Earth's atmosphere. The **horse latitudes** are regions of high barometric pressure with calm and light winds, and the **polar regions** contain cold dense air that sinks to Earth's surface.

Winds caused by local temperature changes include sea breezes and land breezes. **Sea breezes** are caused by the unequal heating of the land and a large, adjacent body of water. Land heats up faster than water. The movement of cool ocean air toward the land is called a sea breeze. Sea breezes usually begin blowing about mid-morning; ending about sunset. A breeze that blows from the land to the ocean or a large lake is called a **land breeze**.

Monsoons are huge wind systems that cover large geographic areas and that reverse direction seasonally. The monsoons of India and Asia are examples of these seasonal winds. They alternate wet and dry seasons. As denser, cooler air over the ocean moves inland, a steady seasonal wind called a summer or wet monsoon is produced.

Cloud types

- *Cirrus clouds* - white and feathery; high in the sky
- *Cumulus* - thick, white, and fluffy
- *Stratus* - layers of clouds that cover most of the sky
- *Nimbus* - heavy, dark clouds that represent thunderstorm clouds

Variations on the clouds mentioned above:

- *Cumulo-nimbus*
- *Strato-nimbus*

The air temperature at which water vapor begins to condense is called the **dew point**.

Relative humidity is the actual amount of water vapor in a certain volume of air compared to the maximum amount of water vapor this air could hold at a given temperature.

Types of Storms

A **thunderstorm** is a brief, local storm produced by the rapid upward movement of warm, moist air within a cumulo-nimbus cloud. Thunderstorms produce lightning and thunder, and are accompanied by strong wind gusts and heavy rain or hail.

A severe storm with swirling winds that may reach speeds of hundreds of km per hour is called a **tornado**. Such a storm is also referred to as a "twister." When it occurs, the sky is covered by large cumulo-nimbus clouds and violent thunderstorms. A funnel-shaped swirling cloud may extend downward from a cumulo-nimbus cloud and reach the ground. Tornadoes are storms that leave a narrow path of destruction on the ground. A swirling, funnel-shaped cloud that extends downward and touches a body of water is called a **waterspout**.

Hurricanes are storms that develop when warm, moist air carried by trade winds rotate around a low-pressure "eye." A large, rotating, low-pressure system accompanied by heavy precipitation and strong winds is called a tropical cyclone (better known as a hurricane). In the Pacific region, a hurricane is called a typhoon.

Storms that occur only in the winter are known as blizzards or ice storms. A **blizzard** is a storm with strong winds, blowing snow and frigid temperatures. An **ice storm** consists of falling rain that freezes when it strikes the ground, covering everything with a layer of ice.

Hydrologic Cycle

Water that falls to Earth in the form of rain and snow is called **precipitation**. Precipitation is part of a continuous process in which water at Earth's surface evaporates, condenses into clouds, and returns. This process is termed the **water cycle**. The water located below the land surface is called **groundwater**.

The impacts of altitude upon climatic conditions are primarily related to temperature and precipitation. As altitude increases, climatic conditions become increasingly drier and colder; solar radiation becomes more severe, while the effects of convection forces are minimized.

Climatic changes as a function of latitude follow a similar pattern (as a reference, latitude moves either north or south from the equator). The climate becomes colder and drier as the distance from the equator increases. Proximity to land or water masses produce climatic conditions based upon the available moisture. Dry and arid climates prevail where moisture is scarce; lush tropical climates can prevail where moisture is abundant. Climate, as described above, depends upon the specific combination of conditions making up an area's environment. Man impacts all environments by producing pollutants in earth, air, and water. It follows then, that man is a major player in world climatic conditions.

Lithosphere

Plates are rigid blocks of the earth's crust and upper mantle. These rigid solid blocks make up the lithosphere. The earth's lithosphere is broken into nine large sections and several small ones. These moving slabs are called plates. The major plates are named after the continents they are "transporting."

The plates float on and move with a layer of hot, plastic-like rock in the upper mantle. Geologists believe that the heat currents circulating within the mantle cause this plastic zone of rock to slowly flow, carrying along the overlying crustal plates.

Earth/Water Interactions

Erosion is the inclusion and transportation of surface materials by another moveable material (usually water, wind, or ice). The most important cause of erosion is running water. Streams, rivers, and tides are constantly at work removing weathered fragments of bedrock and carrying them away from their original location.

A stream erodes bedrock through the grinding action of the sand, pebbles, and other rock fragments. This grinding is called **abrasion**. Streams also erode rocks by dissolving or absorbing their minerals. Limestone and marble are readily dissolved by streams.

The breaking down of rocks at or near to the earth's surface is known as **weathering**. Weathering breaks down these rocks into smaller and smaller pieces. There are two types of weathering: physical weathering and chemical weathering.

Physical weathering is the process by which rocks are broken down into smaller fragments without undergoing any change in chemical composition. Physical weathering is mainly caused by the freezing of water, the expansion of rock, and the activities of plants and animals.

Some examples of physical weathering include frost wedging and exfoliation. **Frost wedging** is the cycle of daytime thawing and refreezing at night. This cycle causes large rock masses, especially the rocks exposed on mountain tops, to be broken into smaller pieces. The peeling away of the outer layers from a rock is called **exfoliation**. Rounded mountain tops are called exfoliation domes because they have been formed in this way.

Chemical weathering is the breakdown of rocks through changes in their chemical composition. An example would be the change of feldspar in granite to clay. Water, oxygen, and carbon dioxide are the main agents of chemical weathering. When water and carbon dioxide combine chemically, they produce a weak acid that breaks down rocks.
Soils are composed of particles of sand, clay, various minerals, tiny living organisms, and humus, plus the decayed remains of plants and animals.

Soils are divided into three classes according to their texture. These classes are sandy soils, clay soils, and loamy soils. Sandy soils are gritty and their particles do not bind together firmly. Sandy soils are porous; water passes through them rapidly. Therefore, sandy soils do not hold much water and have poor **absorption**. Clay soils are smooth and greasy; their particles bind together firmly. Clay soils are moist and usually do not allow water to pass through easily. This type of soil has the lowest potential for **run off**. Loamy soils feel somewhat like velvet and their particles clump together. Loamy soils are made up of sand, clay, and silt. Loamy soils hold water but some water can pass through. **Percolation** is best in this type of soil.

Sinkholes

Large features formed by dissolved limestone (calcium carbonate), include sinkholes, caves, and caverns. **Sinkholes** are funnel-shaped depressions created by dissolved limestone. Many sinkholes started life as limestone caverns. Erosion weakens the cavern roof causing it to collapse, forming a sinkhole.

Groundwater usually contains large amounts of dissolved minerals, especially if the water flows through limestone. As groundwater drips through the roof of a cave, gases dissolved in the water can escape into the air. A deposit of calcium carbonate is left behind. **Stalactites** are icicle-like structures of calcium carbonate that hang from the roofs of caves. Water that falls on a constant spot on the cave floor and evaporates, leaving a deposit of calcium carbonate, builds a **stalagmite**.

Skill 19.3   Applying knowledge of strategies and tools for observing, measuring, predicting, and communicating weather data

Every day, each person on Earth is affected by weather. It may be in the form of a typical thunderstorm, bringing moist air and cumulo-nimbus clouds, or a severe storm with pounding winds that can cause either hurricanes or tornadoes. These terms we are all typically familiar with.

The daily newscast relates terms such as dew point, barometric pressure, and relative humidity. Suddenly, all too common terms become clouded with those more frequently used by a meteorologist (someone who forecasts weather). Yet it is important to understand the terms in order to understand the weather.

The **dew point** is the air temperature at which water vapor begins to condense.

Weather instruments that forecast weather include the aneroid barometer and the mercury barometer, both of which measure air pressure (**barometric pressure**). The aneroid barometer works because air exerts varying pressures on a metal diaphragm that will then read air pressure. The mercury barometer operates when atmospheric pressure pushes on a pool of (mercury) in a glass tube. The higher the pressure, the higher up the tube mercury will rise.

Relative humidity is measured by two kinds of weather instruments, the **psychrometer** and the **hair hygrometer**. Relative humidity simply indicates the amount of moisture in the air. Relative humidity is defined as a ration of existing amounts of water vapor and moisture in the air when compared to the maximum amount of moisture that the air can hold at the same given pressure and temperature. Relative humidity is stated as a percentage; for example, if you were to analyze relative humidity from data, a parcel of air may be saturated (meaning it now holds all the moisture it can hold at a given temperature), placing the relative humidity at 100 percent.

Lesson Plans for teachers to analyze data and predict weather can be found at: http://www.srh.weather.gov/srh/jetstream/synoptic/ll_analyze.htm. ←

Analyzing Weather Maps

Once you can read a station plot, you can begin to perform map analyses. Meteorologists use the station plots to draw lines of constant pressure (isobars), temperature (isotherms), and the dew point (isodrosotherms) to achieve an understanding of the current state of the atmosphere. This knowledge ultimately leads to better weather forecasts and warnings.

Decoding these plots is easier than it may seem. The values are located in a form similar to a tic-tac-toe pattern.

In the upper left, the temperature is plotted in Fahrenheit. In our example, the temperature is 77°F.

Along the center, the cloud types are indicated. The top symbol is the high-level cloud type followed by the mid-level cloud type. The lowest symbol represents the low-level cloud, over a number which tells the height of the base of that cloud (in hundreds of feet). In this example, the high level cloud is Cirrus, the mid-level cloud is Alto-cumulus, and the low-level cloud is a cumulo-nimbus with a base height of 2000 feet.

At the upper right is the atmospheric pressure reduced to mean sea level in milli-bars (mb) to the nearest tenth with the leading 9 or 10 omitted. In this case, the pressure would be 999.8 mb. If the pressure was plotted as 024 it would be 1002.4 mb. When trying to determine whether to add a 9 or 10, use the number that will give you a value closest to 1000 mb.

On the second row, the far left number is the visibility in miles. In this example, the visibility is 5 miles.

Next to the visibility is the present weather symbol. There are ninety-five symbols that represent the weather (whether it is presently occurring or if it has ended within the previous hour). In this example, a light rain shower was occurring at the time of the observation.

The circle symbol in the center represents the amount of total cloud cover reported in eighths. This cloud cover includes all low, middle, and high level clouds. In this example, 7/8th of the sky was covered with clouds.

This number and symbol tell how much the pressure has changed (in tenths of milli-bars) in the past three hours as well as the trend in the change of the pressure during that same period. In this example, the pressure was steady then fell (lowered) becoming 0.3 milli-bars LOWER than it was three hours ago.

Lines indicate wind direction and speed rounded to the nearest 5 knots. The longest line, extending from the sky cover plot, points in the direction that the wind is blowing from. Thus, in this case, the wind is blowing from the southwest. The shorter lines, called **barbs**, indicate the wind speed in knots (kt). The speed of the wind is calculated by the barbs. Each long barb represents 10 kt, with short barbs representing 5 kt. In this example, the station plot contains two long barbs so the wind speed is 20 kt, or about 24 mph.

The 71 at the lower left is the dew point temperature. The dew point temperature is the temperature the air would have to cool to become saturated, or in other words, to reach a relative humidity of 100 percent.

The lower right area is reserved for the past weather, which is the most significant weather that has occurred within the past six hours (excluding the most recent hour).

Analyze a Map on Your Own

The following are a few sources of current weather maps. Sometimes a site may be down or experiencing data losses. In such a case, try another site listed. This is not meant to be an exhaustive list. These are provided for your convenience.

1. NCAR, pick your regional plot: http://www.rap.ucar.edu/weather/surface/
2. UNISYS: http://weather.unisys.com/surface/sfc_map.html
3. College of DuPage: http://weather.cod.edu/analysis/analysis.sfcplots.html
4. NOAA http://www.nws.noaa.gov/
5. Ohio State University: http://asp1.sbs.ohio-state.edu/ (Click on "Current Weather" and choose your map)

Weather Map Symbols

Surface Station Model

Temp (F) Weather Dewpoint (F)		Pressure (mb) Sky Cover Wind (kts)	**Data at Surface Station** Temp 45 °F, dewpoint 29 °F, overcast, wind from SE at 15 knots, weather light rain, pressure 1004.5 mb

Upper Air Station Model

Temp (C) Dewpoint (C)		Height (m) Wind (kts)	**Data at Pressure Level - 850 mb** Temp -5 °C, dewpoint -12 °C, wind from S at 75 knots, height of level 1564 m

Forecast Station Model

Temp (F) Weather Dewpoint (F)		PoP (%) Sky Cover Wind (kts)	**Forecast at Valid Time** Temp 78 °F, dewpoint 64 °F, scattered clouds, wind from E at 10 knots, probability of precipitation 70% with rain showers

Map Symbols

Sky Cover	Wind
clear	Calm
1/8	1-2 knots (1-2 mph)
scattered	3-7 knots (3-8 mph)
3/8	8-12 knots (9-14 mph)
4/8	13-17 knots (15-20 mph)
5/8	18-22 knots (21-25 mph)
broken	23-27 knots (26-31 mph)
7/8	48-52 knots (55-60 mph)
overcast	73-77 knots (84-89 mph)
obscured	103-107 knots (119-123 mph)
missing	Shaft in direction wind is coming from

Skill 19.4 **Recognizing the natural and human-caused constructive and destructive processes that shape the earth's surface**

Orogeny is the term given to natural mountain building.

A mountain is terrain that has been raised high above the surrounding landscape by volcanic action or some form of tectonic plate collision. The plate collisions could be either intercontinental or an ocean floor collision with a continental crust (**subduction**). The physical composition of mountains includes igneous, metamorphic, and sedimentary rocks; some may have rock layers that are tilted or distorted by plate collision forces.

There are many different types of mountains. The physical attributes of a mountain range depends upon the angle at which plate movement thrust layers of rock to the surface. Many mountains (Adirondacks, Southern Rockies) were formed along high angle faults.

Folded mountains (Alps, Himalayas) are produced by the folding of rock layers during their formation. The Himalayas are the highest mountains in the world and contain Mount Everest, which rises almost 9 km above sea level. The Himalayas were formed when India collided with Asia. The movement which created this collision is still in process at the rate of a few centimeters per year.

Fault-block mountains (Utah, Arizona, and New Mexico) are created when plate movement produces tension forces instead of compression forces. The area under tension produces normal faults; rock along these faults is displaced upward.

Dome mountains are formed as magma tries to push up through the crust but fails to break the surface. Dome mountains resemble huge blisters on the earth's surface.

Upwarped mountains (Black Hills of South Dakota) are created in association with a broad arching of the crust. They can also be formed by rock thrust upward along high angle faults.

Volcanism is the term given to the movement of magma through the crust as well as its emergence as lava onto the earth's surface. Volcanic mountains are built up by successive deposits of volcanic materials.

An **active volcano** is one that is presently erupting or building to an eruption. A **dormant volcano** is one that is between eruptions but still shows signs of internal activity that might lead to an eruption in the future. An **extinct volcano** is said to be no longer capable of erupting. Most of the world's active volcanoes are found along the rim of the Pacific Ocean, which is also a major earthquake zone. This curving belt of active faults and volcanoes is often called the Ring of Fire. The world's best known volcanic mountains include Mount Etna in Italy and Mount Kilimanjaro in Africa. The Hawaiian Islands are actually the tops of a chain of volcanic mountains that rise from the ocean floor.

There are three types of volcanic mountains: shield volcanoes, cinder cones, and composite volcanoes.

Shield Volcanoes are associated with quiet eruptions. Lava emerges from the vent or opening in the crater and flows freely out over the earth's surface until it cools and hardens into a layer of igneous rock. A repeated lava flow builds this type of volcano into the largest volcanic mountain. Mauna Loa in Hawaii is the largest shield volcano on Earth.

Cinder Cone Volcanoes are associated with explosive eruptions as lava is hurled high into the air in a spray of droplets of various sizes. These droplets cool and harden into cinders and particles of ash before falling to the ground. The ash and cinder pile up around the vent to form a steep, cone-shaped hill called the cinder cone. Cinder cone volcanoes are relatively small but may form quite rapidly.

Composite Volcanoes are described as being built by both lava flows and layers of ash and cinders. Mount Fuji in Japan, Mount St. Helens in Washington, USA, and Mount Vesuvius in Italy are all famous composite volcanoes.

Mechanisms of Producing Mountains

Mountains are produced by different types of mountain-building processes. Most major mountain ranges are formed by the processes of folding and faulting.

Folded mountains are produced by the folding of rock layers. Crustal movements may press horizontal layers of sedimentary rock together from the sides, squeezing them into wavelike folds. Up-folded sections of rock are called **anticlines**; down-folded sections of rock are called **synclines**. The Appalachian Mountains are an example of folded mountains, with long ridges and valleys in a series of anticlines and synclines formed by folded rock layers.

Faults are fractures in the earth's crust that have been created by either tension or compression forces transmitted through the crust. These forces are produced by the movement of separate blocks of crust.

Fault lines are categorized on the basis of the relative movement between the blocks on both sides of the fault plane. The movement can be horizontal, vertical, or oblique.

A **dip-slip fault** occurs when the movement of the plates is vertical and opposite. The displacement is in the direction of the inclination, or dip, of the fault. Dip-slip faults are classified as normal faults wherein the rock above the fault plane moves down relative to the rock below.

Reverse faults are created when the rock above the fault plane moves up relative to the rock below. Reverse faults with a very low angle to the horizontal are also referred to as **thrust faults**.

Faults in which the dominant displacement is horizontal movement along the trend or strike (length) of the fault are called **strike-slip faults**. When a large strike-slip fault is associated with plate boundaries, it is called a **transform fault**. The San Andreas Fault in California is a well-known transform fault.

Faults that have both vertical and horizontal movement are called **oblique-slip faults**.

When lava cools, igneous rock is formed. This formation can occur either above ground or below ground.

Intrusive rock includes any igneous rock that was formed below the earth's surface. **Batholiths** are the largest structures of intrusive type rock; they are composed of near-granite materials and are the core of the Sierra Nevada Mountains.

Extrusive rock includes any igneous rock that was formed at the earth's surface.

Dikes are old lava tubes formed when magma entered a vertical fracture and hardened. Sometimes, magma squeezes between two rock layers and hardens into a thin horizontal sheet called a **sill**. A **laccolith** is formed in much the same way as a sill, but the magma that creates a laccolith is very thick and does not flow easily. It pools and forces the overlying strata into creating an obvious surface dome.

A **caldera** is normally formed by the collapse of the top of a volcano. This collapse can be caused by a massive explosion that destroys the cone and empties most if not all of the magma chamber below the volcano. The cone collapses into the empty magma chamber, forming a caldera.

An inactive volcano may have magma solidified in its pipe. This structure, called a volcanic neck, is resistant to erosion; today, it may be the only visible evidence of the past presence of an active volcano.

When lava cools, igneous rock is formed. This formation can occur either above ground or below ground.

Glaciation

About 12,000 years ago, a vast sheet of ice covered a large part of the northern United States. This huge, frozen mass had moved southward from the northern regions of Canada as several large bodies of slow-moving ice, or **glaciers.** A time period in which glaciers advance over a large portion of a continent is called an **ice age**. A glacier is a large mass of ice that moves or flows over the land in response to gravity. Glaciers form among high mountains and in other cold regions.

There are two main types of glaciers: valley glaciers and continental glaciers. Erosion by valley glaciers is characteristic of U-shaped erosion. They produce sharp-peaked mountains such as the Matterhorn in Switzerland. Continental glaciers ride over mountains in their paths, leaving smoothed, rounded mountains and ridges.

Evidence of the North American glacial coverage during the most recent ice age remains as large boulders from northern environments dropped in southerly locations; abrasive grooves; glacial troughs created by the rounding out of steep valleys through glacial scouring; and the remains of glacial sources, called cirques, that were created by frost wedging the rock at the bottom of the glacier. Remains of plants and animals typically found in warm climates that have been discovered in the moraines and outwash plains help to support the theory of periods of warmth during the past ice ages.

The Ice Age began about 2 -3 million years ago. This age saw the advancement and retreat of glacial ice over millions of years. Theories relating to the origin of glacial activity include **plate tectonics**, in which it is demonstrated that some continental masses, now in temperate climates, were at one time blanketed by ice and snow. Another theory involves changes in the earth's orbit around the sun, changes in the angle of the earth's axis, and the wobbling of the earth's axis. Support for the validity of this theory has come from deep ocean research that indicates a correlation between climatic sensitive microorganisms and the changes in the earth's orbital status.

Movement of Tectonic Plates

Data obtained from many sources led scientists to develop the theory of plate tectonics. This theory is the most current model to explain not only the movement of the continents, but also the changes in the earth's crust caused by internal forces.

Plates are rigid blocks of the earth's crust and upper mantle. Movement of these crustal plates creates areas where the plates diverge as well as areas where the plates converge. A major area of divergence is located in the Mid-Atlantic. Currents. Here, hot mantle rock rises and separates at the point of divergence, creating new oceanic crust at the rate of 2 to 10 centimeters per year. Convergence occurs when the oceanic crust collides with either another oceanic plate or a continental plate. The oceanic crust sinks, forming an enormous trench and generating volcanic activity. Convergence also includes continent-to-continent plate collisions. When two plates slide past one another, a transform fault is created.

These movements produce many major features of the earth's surface, including mountain ranges, volcanoes, and earthquake zones. Most of these features are located at plate boundaries, where the plates interact by spreading apart, pressing together, or sliding past each other. These movements are very slow, averaging only a few centimeters a year.

Boundaries form between spreading plates where the crust is forced apart in a process called **rifting**. Rifting generally occurs at mid-ocean ridges. Rifting can also take place within a continent, splitting the continent into smaller landmasses that drift away from each other, thereby forming an ocean basin between them. The Red Sea is a product of rifting. As the seafloor spreading takes place, new material is added to the inner edges of the separating plates. In this way, the plates grow larger and the ocean basin widens. This is the process that broke up the super continent Pangaea and created the Atlantic Ocean.

Boundaries between colliding plates are zones of intense crustal activity. When a plate of ocean crust collides with a plate of continental crust, the more dense oceanic plate slides under the lighter continental plate and plunges into the mantle. This process is called **subduction**, and the site where it takes place is called a **subduction zone**. A subduction zone is usually visible on the sea-floor as a deep depression called a **trench**.

The crustal movement identified by plates sliding sideways past each other produces a plate boundary that is characterized by major faults. These faults are capable of unleashing powerful earthquakes. The San Andreas Fault forms such a boundary between the Pacific Plate and the North American Plate.

Natural Disasters

An important topic in science is the effect of natural disasters and events on society, as well as the effect human activity has on inducing such events. Naturally occurring geological, climatic, and environmental events can greatly affect the lives of humans. At the same time, the activities of humans can induce such events that would not normally occur.

Nature-induced hazards include floods, landslides, avalanches, volcanic eruptions, wildfires, earthquakes, hurricanes, tornadoes, droughts, and disease. Such events often occur naturally due to changing weather patterns or geological conditions. Property damage, resource destruction, and the loss of human life are the possible outcomes of natural hazards. Thus, natural hazards are often extremely costly on both an economic and personal level.
While many nature-induced hazards occur naturally, human activity can often stimulate such events. For example, destructive land use practices such as mining can induce landslides or avalanches if not properly planned and monitored. In addition, human activities can cause other hazards, including global warming and waste contamination. Global warming is an increase in the earth's average temperature resulting, at least in part, from the burning of fuels by humans. Global warming is hazardous because it disrupts the earth's environmental balance and can negatively affect weather patterns. Ecological and weather pattern changes can promote the natural disasters listed above.

Improper hazardous waste disposal by humans can contaminate the environment, resulting in a variety of changes. One devastating effect of hazardous waste contamination is the stimulation of disease in human populations. Thus, hazardous waste contamination negatively affects both the environment and the people that live in it.

Skill 19.5 Demonstrating knowledge of how fossils are formed and how they provide evidence of organisms that lived long ago

A **fossil** is the remains or trace of an ancient organism that has been preserved naturally in the earth's crust. Sedimentary rocks usually are rich sources of fossil remains. Those fossils found in layers of sediment were embedded in the slowly forming sedimentary rock strata. The oldest fossils known are the traces of 3.5 billion-year-old bacteria found in sedimentary rocks. Few fossils are found in metamorphic rock, and virtually none are found in igneous rocks. The magma is so hot that any organism trapped in the magma is destroyed.

Although the fairly well-preserved remains of a woolly mammoth embedded in ice were found in Russia in May of 2007, the best-preserved animal remains are typically discovered in natural tar pits. When an animal accidentally falls into the tar, it becomes trapped, sinking to the bottom. Preserved bones of the saber-toothed cat have been found in tar pits.

Prehistoric insects have been found trapped in ancient amber or fossil resin that was excreted by some extinct species of pine trees. Fossil molds are the hollow spaces in a rock previously occupied by bones or shells. A fossil cast is a fossil mold that fills with sediments or minerals that later hardens to form a cast.

Fossil tracks are the imprints in hardened mud left behind by birds or animals.

COMPETENCY 20.0 UNDERSTAND CONCEPTS AND PRINCIPLES OF PHYSICAL SCIENCE

Skill 20.1   Demonstrating knowledge of the structure and properties of matter (e.g., atoms, elements, molecules, density, boiling and freezing points)

An **atom** is the smallest particle of an element that retains the properties of that element. All of the atoms of a particular element are the same. The atoms of each element are different from the atoms of other elements.

An **element** is a substance that can not be broken down into other substances. To date, scientists have identified 109 elements; eighty-nine are found in nature and twenty are synthetic. Elements are assigned an identifying symbol of one or two letters. For example, the symbol for oxygen is O, which stands for one atom of oxygen. However, because oxygen atoms in nature are joined together in pairs, the symbol O_2 represents oxygen as we know it.

This pair of oxygen atoms is a molecule. A **molecule** is the smallest particle of substance that can exist independently and has all of the properties of that substance. A molecule of most elements is made up of one atom. However, oxygen, hydrogen, nitrogen, and chlorine molecules are made of two atoms each.

A **compound** is made of two or more elements that have been chemically combined. Each element's atoms join together when they bind chemically; the result is that the elements lose their individual identities. The compound that they become has different properties.

We use a formula to show the elements of a chemical compound. A **chemical formula** is a shorthand way of showing what is in a compound by using symbols and subscripts. The letter symbols let us know which elements are involved, and the number subscript tells how many atoms of each element are involved. No subscript is used if there is only one atom involved. For example, carbon dioxide is made up of one atom of carbon (C) and two atoms of oxygen (O_2), so the formula would be represented as CO_2.

Substances can combine without a chemical change. A **mixture** is any combination of two or more substances in which the substances keep their own properties. A fruit salad is a mixture. So is an ice cream sundae, although you might not recognize each part if it is stirred together. Colognes and perfumes are other examples. You may not readily recognize the individual elements; however, they can be separated.

Compounds and mixtures are similar in that they are made up of two or more substances. However, they have the following opposite characteristics:

Compounds:
1. Made up of one kind of particle
2. Formed during a chemical change
3. Broken down only by chemical changes
4. Properties are different from its parts
5. Has a specific amount of each ingredient.

Mixtures:
1. Made up of two or more particles
2. Not formed by a chemical change
3. Can be separated by physical changes
4. Properties are the same as its parts
5. Does not have a definite amount of each ingredient

Common compounds are acids, bases, salts, and oxides. They are classified according to their characteristics.

An **acid** contains one element of hydrogen (H). Although it is never wise to taste a substance to identify it, acids have a sour taste. Vinegar and lemon juice are both acids, and acids occur in many foods in a weak state. Strong acids can burn skin and destroy materials. Common acids include:

Sulfuric acid (H_2SO_4)-   Used in medicines, alcohol, dyes, and car batteries

Nitric acid (HNO_3)-   Used in fertilizers, explosives, and cleaning materials

Carbonic acid (H_2CO_3)-   Used in soft drinks

Acetic acid ($HC_2H_3O_2$)-   Used in making plastics, rubber, photographic film, and as a solvent.

Bases have a bitter taste, and the stronger ones feel slippery. Like acids, strong bases can be dangerous and should be handled carefully. All bases contain the elements oxygen and hydrogen (OH). Many household cleaning products contain bases. Common bases include:

Sodium hydroxide (NaOH)-   Used in making soap, paper, vegetable oils, and refining petroleum.

Ammonium hydroxide (NH_4OH)-   Used for making deodorants, bleaching compounds, and cleaning compounds

Potassium hydroxide (KOH)-   Used for making soaps, drugs, dyes, alkaline batteries, and purifying industrial gases

Calcium ($Ca(OH)_2$)-   Used in making cement and plaster hydroxide

An **indicator** is a substance that changes color when it comes in contact with an acid or a base. Litmus paper is an indicator. Blue litmus paper turns red in an acid. Red litmus paper turns blue in a base.

A substance that is neither acid nor base is **neutral**. Neutral substances do not change the color of litmus paper.

Salt is formed when an acid and a base combine chemically. Water is also formed. The process is called neutralization. Table salt (NaCl) is an example of this process. Salts are also used in toothpaste, epsom salts, and cream of tartar. Calcium chloride ($CaCl_2$) is used on frozen streets and walkways to melt the ice.

Oxides are compounds that are formed when oxygen combines with another element. Rust is an oxide formed when oxygen combines with iron.

Melting point refers to the temperature at which a solid becomes a liquid. Melting takes place when there is sufficient energy available to break the intermolecular forces that hold molecules together in a solid.

Boiling point refers to the temperature at which a liquid becomes a gas. Boiling occurs when there is enough energy available to break the intermolecular forces holding molecules together as a liquid.

Density is the mass of a substance contained per unit of volume. It is stated in grams per cubic centimeter (g / cm^3).

Skill 20.2   Distinguishing between physical and chemical changes

Everything in the world is made up of **matter**, whether it is a rock, a building, an animal, or a person. Matter is defined by its characteristics: It takes up space and it has mass.

Mass is a measure of the amount of matter in an object. Two objects of equal mass will balance each other on a simple balance scale no matter where the scale is located. For instance, two rocks with the same amount of mass that are in balance on the earth will also be in balance on the moon. They will feel **heavier** on earth than on the moon because of the gravitational pull of the earth. So, although the two rocks have the same mass, they will have different weight.

Weight is the measure of the earth's pull of gravity on an object. It can also be defined as the pull of gravity between other bodies. The units of weight measure commonly used are the pound in English measure and the **kilogram** in metric measure.

In addition to mass, matter also has the property of volume. **Volume** is the amount of cubic space that an object occupies. Volume and mass together give a more exact description of the object. Two objects may have the same volume, but different mass, the same mass but different volumes, etc. For instance, consider two cubes that are each one cubic centimeter, one made from plastic, one from lead. They have the same volume, but the lead cube has more mass. The measure that we use to describe the cubes takes into consideration both the mass and the volume. **Density** is the mass of a substance contained per unit of volume. If the density of an object is less than the density of a liquid, the object will float in the liquid. If the object is denser than the liquid, the object will sink.

Density is stated in grams per cubic centimeter (g / cm^3), where the gram is the standard unit of mass. To find an object's density, one must measure its mass and its volume, then divide the mass by the volume ($D = m / V$).

To find an object's density, first use a balance to find its mass. Then calculate its volume. If the object is a regular shape, one can find the volume by multiplying the length, width, and height together. However, if it is an irregular shape, one can find the volume by seeing how much water it displaces. Measure the water in the container before and after the object is submerged. The difference will be the volume of the object.

Specific gravity is the ratio of the density of a substance to the density of water. For instance, the specific density of one liter of turpentine is calculated by comparing its mass (0.81 kg) to the mass of one liter of water (1 kg):

$$\frac{\text{mass of 1 L alcohol}}{\text{mass of 1 L water}} = \frac{0.81 \text{ kg}}{1.00 \text{ kg}} = 0.81$$

Physical properties and chemical properties of matter describe the appearance or behavior of a substance. A **physical property** can be observed without changing the identity of a substance. For instance, one can describe the color, mass, shape, and volume of a book. **Chemical properties** describe the ability of a substance to be changed into new substances. Baking powder goes through a chemical change as it changes into carbon dioxide gas during the baking process.

Matter constantly changes. A **physical change** is a change that does not produce a new substance. The freezing and melting of water is an example of physical change. A **chemical change** (or **chemical reaction**) changes the inherent properties of a substance. This includes things such as burning materials that turn into smoke or a seltzer tablet that fizzes into gas bubbles when submerged in water.

The **phase of matter** (solid, liquid, or gas) is identified by its shape and volume. A **solid** has a definite shape and volume. A **liquid** has a definite volume, but no shape. A **gas** has no shape or volume because it will spread out to occupy the entire space of whatever container it is in.

Energy is the ability to cause change in matter. Applying heat to a frozen liquid changes it from solid back to liquid. Continue heating it, and it will boil and give off steam, a gas.

Evaporation is the change in phase from liquid to gas. **Condensation** is the change in phase from gas to liquid.

Skill 20.3   Demonstrating knowledge of the concepts of conservation of matter and conservation of energy as they are applied to physical systems

The **law of conservation of energy** states that energy is neither created nor destroyed. Thus, energy changes form whenever energy transactions occur in nature. Because the total energy in the universe is constant, energy continually transitions between forms. For example, an engine burns gasoline, converting the chemical energy of the gasoline into mechanical energy. A plant converts radiant energy of the sun into chemical energy found in glucose. A battery converts chemical energy into electrical energy.

Chemical reactions are the interactions of substances that result in chemical changes and changes in energy. Chemical reactions involve changes in electron motion as well as the breaking up and formation of chemical bonds. **Reactants** are the original substances that interact to form distinct products. **Endothermic** chemical reactions consume energy, while **exothermic** chemical reactions release energy with product formation. Chemical reactions occur continually in nature and are also induced by man for many purposes.

Nuclear reactions, or **atomic reactions**, are reactions that change the composition, energy, or structure of atomic nuclei. Nuclear reactions change the number of protons and neutrons in the nucleus. The two main types of nuclear reactions are **fission** (splitting of nuclei) and **fusion** (joining of nuclei). Fusion reactions are exothermic, releasing heat energy. Fission reactions are endothermic, absorbing heat energy. Fission of large nuclei (e.g. uranium) releases energy because the products of fission undergo further fusion reactions. Fission and fusion reactions can occur naturally, but are most recognized as man-made events. Particle acceleration and bombardment with neutrons are two methods of inducing nuclear reactions.

The law of conservation can also be applied to physical and biological processes. For example, when a rock is weathered, it does not just lose pieces; instead, it is broken down into its composite minerals, many of which enter the soil. Biology takes advantage of decomposers to recycle decaying material. Since energy is neither created nor destroyed, we know that it must change form. An animal may die, but its body will either be consumed by other animals or decay into the ecosystem. Either way, it enters another form and the matter still exists in some form or another.

Skill 20.4 Recognizing forms of energy (e.g., heat, light), processes of energy transfer, and the interactions of energy and matter

The relationship between heat, forms of energy, and work (mechanical, electrical, etc.) are the **laws of thermodynamics**. These laws deal strictly with systems in thermal equilibrium and not those within the process of rapid change or in a state of transition. Systems that are nearly always in a state of equilibrium are called **reversible systems**.

The **first law of thermodynamics** is a restatement of the conservation of energy. The change in heat energy supplied to a system (Q) is equal to the sum of the change in the internal energy (U) and the change in the work done by the system against internal forces.

$$\Box Q = \Box U + \Box W$$

The **second law of thermodynamics** is stated in two parts:

1. No machine is 100 percent efficient. It is impossible to construct a machine that only absorbs heat from a heat source and performs an equal amount of work because some heat will always be lost to the environment.
2. Heat cannot spontaneously pass from a colder to a hotter object. An ice cube sitting on a hot sidewalk will melt into a little puddle, but it will never spontaneously cool and form the same ice cube. Certain events have a preferred direction called the **arrow of time**.

Entropy is the measure of how much energy or heat is available for work. Work occurs only when heat is transferred from hot to cooler objects. Once this is done, no more work can be extracted. The energy is still being conserved, but it is not available for work when the objects are the same temperature. Theory has it that, eventually, all things in the universe will reach the same temperature. If this happens, energy will no longer be usable.

Remember that the law of conservation of energy states that energy is neither created nor destroyed. Thus, energy changes form when energy transactions occur in nature. The following are the major forms energy can take:

Thermal energy is the total internal energy of objects created by the vibration and movement of atoms and molecules. Heat is the transfer of thermal energy.

Acoustical energy, or sound energy, is the movement of energy through an object in waves. Energy that forces an object to vibrate creates sound.

Radiant energy is the energy of electromagnetic waves. Light—visible and otherwise—is an example of radiant energy.

Electrical energy is the movement of electrical charges in an electromagnetic field. Examples of electrical energy are electricity and lightning.

Chemical energy is the energy stored in the chemical bonds of molecules. For example, the energy derived from gasoline is chemical energy.

Mechanical energy is the potential and kinetic energy of a mechanical system. Rolling balls, car engines, and body parts in motion exemplify mechanical energy.

Nuclear energy is the energy present in the nucleus of atoms. The division, combination, or collision of nuclei release nuclear energy.

Skill 20.5   Demonstrating knowledge of types of forces (e.g., gravity, friction) and their effects on the position, motion, and behavior of objects

Forces

Dynamics is the study of the relationship between motion and the forces affecting motion. **Force** causes motion.

Mass and weight are not the same quantities. An object's **mass** gives it a reluctance to change its current state of motion. It is also the measure of an object's resistance to acceleration. The force that the earth's gravity exerts on an object with a specific mass is called the object's weight on earth. Weight is a force that is measured in newtons. Weight (W) = mass times acceleration due to gravity ($W = mg$).

Newton's Laws of Motion

Newton's first law of motion is also called the law of inertia. It states that an object at rest will remain at rest and an object in motion will remain in motion at a constant velocity unless acted upon by an external force.

Newton's second law of motion states that if a net force acts on an object, it will cause the acceleration of the object. The relationship between force and motion is: force equals mass times acceleration ($F = ma$).

Newton's third law states that for every action there is an equal and opposite reaction. Therefore, if an object exerts a force on another object, that second object exerts an equal and opposite force on the first.

Surfaces that touch each other have a certain resistance to motion. This resistance is **friction**.

1. The materials that make up the surfaces will determine the magnitude of the frictional force.
2. The frictional force is independent of the area of contact between the two surfaces.
3. The direction of the frictional force is opposite to the direction of motion.
4. The frictional force is proportional to the normal force between the two surfaces in contact.

Static friction describes the force of friction of two surfaces that are in contact but do not have any motion relative to each other, such as a block sitting on an inclined plane. **Kinetic friction** describes the force of friction of two surfaces in contact with each other when there is relative motion between the surfaces.

When an object moves in a circular path, a force must be directed toward the center of the circle in order to keep the motion going. This constraining force is called **centripetal force**. Gravity is the centripetal force that keeps a satellite circling the earth.

Push and pull - Pushing a volleyball or pulling a bowstring applies muscular force as the muscles expand and contract. Elastic force occurs when any object returns to its original shape (for example, when the bow is released).

Rubbing - Friction opposes the motion of one surface past another. Friction is common when slowing down a car or sledding down a hill.

Pull of gravity - The pull of gravity is a force of attraction between two objects. Gravity questions can be raised not only on Earth but also between planets and even black hole discussions.

Inertia and circular motion - The centripetal force is provided by the high banking of a curved road and by friction between the wheels and the road. This inward force that keeps an object moving in a circle is another example of a centripetal force.

Skill 20.6   Identifying types and characteristics of simple machines (e.g., lever, pulley)

Forces on objects at rest - The formula F= m/a is shorthand for force equals mass over acceleration. An object will not move unless the force is strong enough to move the mass. Also, there can be opposing forces holding the object in place. For instance, a boat may want to be forced by the currents to drift away, but an equal and opposite force is a rope holding it to a dock.

Forces on a moving object - Overcoming inertia is the tendency of any object to oppose a change in motion. An object at rest tends to stay at rest. An object that is moving tends to keep moving.

Work is done on an object when an applied force moves through a distance.

Power is the work done divided by the amount of time that it took to do it.
(Power = Work / time)

Simple machines include the following:
1. Inclined plane
2. Lever
3. Wheel and axle
4. Pulley

Compound machines are two or more simple machines working together. A wheelbarrow is an example of a complex machine. It uses a lever and a wheel and axle. Machines of all types ease workload by changing the size or direction of an applied force. The amount of effort saved when using simple or complex machines is called mechanical advantage, or MA.

Skill 20.7   Recognizing characteristics of light, sound, electricity, and magnetism

Shadows illustrate one of the basic properties of light. Light travels in a straight line. If you put your hand between a light source and a wall, you will interrupt the light and produce a shadow.

When light hits a surface, it is **reflected**. The angle of the incoming light (angle of incidence) is the same as the angle of the reflected light (angle of reflection). It is this reflected light that allows you to see objects. You see the objects when the reflected light reaches your eyes.

Different surfaces reflect light differently. Rough surfaces scatter light in many different directions. A smooth surface reflects the light in one direction. If it is smooth and shiny (like a mirror) you see your image in the surface.

When light enters a different medium, it bends. This bending, or change of speed, is called **refraction**.

Light can be **diffracted**, or bent around the edges of an object. Diffraction occurs when light goes through a narrow slit. As light passes through it, the light bends slightly around the edges. You can demonstrate this by pressing your thumb and forefinger together, making a very thin slit between them. Hold them about 8 cm from your eye and look at a distant source of light. The pattern you observe is caused by the diffraction of light.

Wave **interference** occurs when two waves meet while traveling along the same medium. The medium takes on a shape that results from the net effect of the individual waves upon the particles of the medium. There are two types of interference: constructive and destructive.

Constructive interference occurs when two crests or two troughs of the same shape meet. The medium will take on the shape of a crest or a trough with twice the amplitude of the two interfering crests or troughs. If a trough and a crest of the different shapes meet, the two pulses will cancel each other out, and the medium will assume the equilibrium position. This is called **destructive** interference.

Destructive interference in sound waves will reduce the loudness of the sound. This is a disadvantage in rooms such as auditoriums, where sound needs to be at its optimum. However, it can be used as an advantage in noise reduction systems. When two sound waves differing slightly in frequency are superimposed, beats are created by the alternation of constructive and destructive interference. The frequency of the beats is equal to the difference between the frequencies of the interfering sound waves.

Wave interference occurs with light waves in much the same manner that it does with sound waves. If two light waves of the same color, frequency, and amplitude are combined, the interference shows up as fringes of alternating light and dark bands. In order for this to happen, the light waves must come from the same source.

Wave-particle duality is the exhibition of both wavelike and particle-like properties by a single entity. Wave-particle duality is usually a quantum phenomenon relating to photons, electrons, and protons. Quantum mechanics shows that such objects sometimes behave like particles, sometimes like waves, and sometimes both. All objects exhibit wave-particle duality to some extent, but the larger the object, the harder it is to observe. Individual molecules are often too large to show their quantum mechanical behavior.

An everyday example of wave-particle duality is sunlight. When standing in the sun, the shadow your body makes suggests that the light travels straight from the sun and is blocked by your body. Here the light is behaving like a collection of particles sent from the sun. However, if you take two pieces of glass with a little water between them and hold them in the sun, you will see fringes; these are formed by the interference of waves.

When a piano tuners tune a piano, they only use one tuning fork, even though there are many strings on the piano. They adjust the first string to be the same as that of the tuning fork. Then they listen to the beats that occur when both the tuned and un-tuned strings are struck. They adjust the un-tuned string until they can hear the correct number of beats per second. This process of striking the un-tuned and tuned strings together and timing the beats is repeated until all the piano strings are tuned.

Pleasant sounds have a regular wave pattern that is repeated over and over. Sounds that do not happen with regularity are typically unpleasant and are called *noise*. Change in experienced frequency due to relative motion of the source of the sound is called the **Doppler Effect**. When a siren approaches, the pitch is high. When it passes, the pitch drops. As a moving sound source approaches a listener, the sound waves are closer together, causing an increase in frequency in the sound that is heard. As the source passes the listener, the waves spread out and the sound experienced by the listener is lower.

A **converging lens** produces a real image whenever the object is far enough from the lens so that the rays of light from the object can hit the lens and be focused into a real image on the other side of the lens.

Electrostatics is the study of stationary electric charges. A plastic rod that is rubbed with fur or a glass rod that is rubbed with silk will become electrically charged and will attract small pieces of paper. The charge on the plastic rod rubbed with fur is negative, and the charge on glass rod rubbed with silk is positive.

Electrically charged objects share these characteristics:

1.   Like charges repel one another.
2.   Opposite charges attract each other.
3.   Charge is conserved. A neutral object has no net change.

Imagine if the plastic rod and fur are initially neutral. When the rod becomes charged by the fur, a negative charge is transferred from the fur to the rod. The net negative charge on the rod is equal to the net positive charge on the fur.

Materials through which electric charges can easily flow are called **conductors**. Conversely, an **insulator** is a material through which electric charges do not move easily, if at all. A simple device used to indicate the existence of a positive or negative charge is called an **electroscope**. An electroscope is made up of a conducting knob and attached very lightweight conducting leaves—usually made of gold foil or aluminum foil. When a charged object touches the knob, the leaves push away from each other because like charges repel. It is not possible to tell whether or not the charge is positive or negative.

If one touches the electroscope knob with a finger while a charged rod is nearby, the electrons will be repulsed and flow out of the electroscope through the hand. If the hand is removed while the charged rod remains close, the electroscope will retain the charge.

When an object is rubbed with a charged rod, the object will take on the same charge as the rod. However, *charging by induction* gives the object the opposite charge as that of the charged rod.

Charge can be removed from an object by connecting it to the earth through a conductor. The removal of static electricity by conduction is called **grounding**.

Magnets have a north pole and a south pole. Like poles repel and different poles attract. A **magnetic field** is the space around a magnet where its force will affect objects. The closer you are to a magnet, the stronger the force. As you move away, the force becomes weaker.

Some materials act as magnets and some do not. This is because magnetism is the result of electrons in motion. The most important motion in this case is the spinning of the individual electrons. Electrons spin in pairs in opposite directions in most atoms. Each spinning electron has the magnetic field that it creates canceled out by the electron that is spinning in the opposite direction.

In an atom of iron, there are four unpaired electrons. The magnetic fields of these are not canceled out. Their fields add up to make a tiny magnet. Their fields exert forces on each other, setting up small areas in the iron called **magnetic domains** where atomic magnetic fields line up in the same direction.

You can make a magnet out of an iron nail by stroking the nail in the same direction repeatedly with a magnet. This causes poles in the atomic magnets in the nail to be attracted to the magnet. The tiny magnetic fields in the nail line up in the direction of the magnet. The magnet causes the domains pointing in its direction in the nail to grow. Eventually, one large domain results and the nail becomes a magnet.

A bar magnet has a north pole and a south pole. If you break the magnet in half, each piece will have a north and south pole.

The earth has a magnetic field. In a compass, a tiny, lightweight magnet is suspended and will line its south pole up with the north pole magnet of the earth.

A magnet can be made out of a coil of wire by connecting the ends of the coil to a battery. When the current goes through the wire, the wire acts in the same way that a magnet does; it is called an **electromagnet**.

The poles of the electromagnet will depend upon which way the electric current runs. An electromagnet can be made more powerful in three ways:
1. Make more coils.
2. Put an iron core (nail) inside the coils.
3. Use more battery power.

COMPETENCY 21.0 UNDERSTAND CONCEPTS AND PRINCIPLES OF LIFE SCIENCE

Skill 21.1   Distinguishing between living and nonliving things

The organization of living systems builds by levels from small to increasingly larger and more complex. All aspects, whether they are cells or ecosystems, have the same requirements to sustain life. Life is organized from simple to complex in the following way:

Organelles make up **cells**, which make up **tissues**. Tissues make up **organs**, and groups of organs make up **organ systems**. Organ systems work together to provide life for the **organism**.

Several characteristics have been described to identify living versus non-living substances.

1. **Living things are made of cells.** They grow, are capable of reproduction, and respond to stimuli.

2. **Living things must adapt to environmental changes or perish**.

3. **Living things carry on metabolic processes**. They use and make energy.

All organic life has a common element: carbon. Carbon is recycled through the ecosystem through both biotic and abiotic means. It is the link between biological processes and the chemical make-up of life.

Skill 21.2   Demonstrating knowledge of different types of organisms and methods of classification

Carolus Linnaeus is termed the father of taxonomy. **Taxonomy** is the science of classification. **Classifying** is the grouping of items according to their similarities. It is important for students to realize relationships and similarity as well as differences to reach a reasonable conclusion in a lab experience. Linnaeus based his system on morphology (study of structure). Later on, evolutionary relationships (phylogeny) were also used to sort and group species. The modern classification system uses binomial nomenclature. This consists of a two-word name for every species. The genus is the first part of the name and the species is the second part. Notice in the levels explained below that Homo sapiens is the scientific name for humans. Starting with the kingdom, the groups get smaller and more alike as one moves down the levels in human classification:

Kingdom: Animalia
Phylum: Chordata
Subphylum: Vertebrata
Class: Mammalia
Order: Primate
Family: Hominidae
Genus: Homo
Species: sapiens

Species are defined by the ability to successfully reproduce with members of their own kind.

Members of the five different kingdoms of the classification system of living organisms often differ in their basic life functions. Here we compare and analyze how members of the five kingdoms obtain nutrients, excrete waste, and reproduce.

Bacteria are prokaryotic, single-celled organisms that lack cell nuclei. The different types of bacteria obtain nutrients in a variety of ways. Most bacteria absorb nutrients from the environment through small channels in their cell walls and membranes (chemotrophs), while some perform photosynthesis (phototrophs). Chemoorganotrophs use organic compounds as energy sources while chemolithotrophs can use inorganic chemicals as energy sources. Depending on the type of metabolism and energy source, bacteria release a variety of waste products (e.g., alcohols, acids, carbon dioxide) to the environment through diffusion.

All bacteria reproduce through binary fission (asexual reproduction), producing two identical cells. Bacteria reproduce very rapidly, dividing or doubling every twenty minutes in optimal conditions. Asexual reproduction does not allow for genetic variation, but bacteria achieve genetic variety by absorbing DNA from ruptured cells and conjugating or swapping chromosomal or plasmid DNA with other cells.

Animals are multi-cellular, eukaryotic organisms. All animals obtain nutrients by eating food (ingestion). Different types of animals derive nutrients from eating plants, other animals, or both. Animal cells perform respiration, which converts food molecules—mainly carbohydrates and fats—into energy. The excretory systems of animals, like animals themselves, vary in complexity. Simple invertebrates eliminate waste through a single tube, while complex vertebrates have a specialized system of organs that process and excrete waste.

Most animals, unlike bacteria, exist in two distinct sexes. Members of the female sex give birth or lay eggs. Some less developed animals can reproduce asexually. For example, flatworms can divide into two, and some unfertilized insect eggs can develop into viable organisms. Most animals reproduce sexually through various mechanisms. For example, aquatic animals reproduce by external fertilization of eggs, while mammals reproduce by internal fertilization. More developed animals possess specialized reproductive systems and cycles that facilitate reproduction and promote genetic variation.

Plants, like animals, are multi-cellular, eukaryotic organisms. Plants obtain nutrients from the soil through their root systems and convert sunlight into energy through photosynthesis. Many plants store waste products in vacuoles or organs (e.g., leaves, bark) that are discarded. Some plants also excrete waste through their roots.

More than half of the plant species reproduce by producing seeds from which new plants grow. Depending on the type of plant, flowers or cones produce seeds. Other plants reproduce by spores, tubers, bulbs, buds, and grafts. The flowers of flowering plants contain the reproductive organs. *Pollination* is the joining of male and female gametes; it is often facilitated through the movement of wind or animals.

Fungi are eukaryotic, mostly multi-cellular organisms. All fungi are heterotrophs, obtaining nutrients from other organisms. More specifically, most fungi obtain nutrients by digesting and absorbing nutrients from dead organisms. Fungi secrete enzymes outside of their body to digest organic material and then absorb the nutrients through their cell walls.

Most fungi can reproduce asexually and sexually. Different types of fungi reproduce asexually by mitosis, budding, sporification, or fragmentation. Sexual reproduction of fungi is different from sexual reproduction of animals. The two mating types of fungi are plus and minus, not male and female. The fusion of hyphae, the specialized reproductive structure in fungi, between plus and minus types produces and scatters diverse spores.

Protists are eukaryotic, single-celled organisms. Most protists are heterotrophic, obtaining nutrients by ingesting small molecules and cells and digesting them in vacuoles. All protists reproduce asexually by either binary or multiple fission. Like bacteria, protists achieve genetic variation by exchange of DNA through conjugation.

Behavioral Responses to External and Internal Stimuli

Response to stimuli is one of the key characteristics of any living thing. Any detectable change in the internal or external environment (the stimulus) may trigger a response in an organism. Just like physical characteristics, organisms' responses to stimuli are adaptations that allow them to better survive. While these responses may be more noticeable in animals that can move quickly, all organisms are actually capable of responding to changes.

Single-Celled Organisms
These organisms are able to respond to basic stimuli such as the presence of light, heat, or food. Changes in the environment are typically sensed via cell surface receptors. These organisms may respond to such stimuli by making changes in internal biochemical pathways or by initiating reproduction or phagocytosis. Those capable of simple motility, using flagella for instance, may respond by moving toward food or away from heat.

Plants
Plants typically do not possess sensory organs; thus, individual cells recognize stimuli through a variety of pathways. When many cells respond to stimuli together, a response becomes apparent. Logically then, the responses of plants occur on a rather longer timescale that those of animals. Plants are capable of responding to a few basic stimuli including light, water, and gravity. Some common examples include the way plants turn and grow toward the sun, the sprouting of seeds when exposed to warmth and moisture, and the growth of roots in the direction of gravity.

Animals
Lower members of the animal kingdom have responses similar to those seen in single-celled organisms. However, higher animals have developed complex systems to detect and respond to stimuli. The nervous system, sensory organs (eyes, ears, skin, etc), and muscle tissue all allow animals to sense and quickly respond to changes in their environment. As in other organisms, many responses to stimuli in animals are involuntary. For example, pupils dilate in response to the reduction of light. Such reactions are typically called reflexes. However, many animals are also capable of voluntary response. In many animal species, voluntary reactions are instinctual. For instance, a zebra's response to a lion is a voluntary one, but, instinctually, it will flee quickly as soon as the lion's presence is sensed. Complex responses, which may or may not be instinctual, are typically termed **behavior**. An example is the annual migration of birds when seasons change.

Skill 21.3 Demonstrating knowledge of the basic needs, characteristics, structures, and life processes of organisms

Ecology is the study of organisms, where they live, and their interactions with the environment. A **population** is a group of the same species in a specific area. A **community** is a group of populations residing in the same area. Communities that are ecologically similar in regards to temperature, rainfall, and the species that live there are called **biomes**. Specific biomes include:

Marine: It covers 75 percent of the earth. This biome is organized by the depth of water. The *intertidal* zone is located from the tide line to the edge of the water. The *littoral* zone is found from the water's edge to the open sea. It includes coral reef habitats; it is the most densely populated area of the marine biome. The open sea zone is divided into the *epipelagic* zone and the *pelagic* zone. The epipelagic zone receives more sunlight and has a larger number of species. The ocean floor is called the *benthic* zone. It is populated with bottom feeders.

Tropical Rain Forest: Here, temperature is fairly constant (25 degrees C) and rainfall exceeds 200 cm per year. Located around the equator, rain forests have abundant, diverse species of plants and animals.

Savanna: The temperatures range from 0-25 degrees C depending on the location. Rainfall is from 90 to 150 cm per year. Plants include shrubs and grasses. The savanna is a transitional biome between the rain forest and the desert.

Desert: Temperatures range from 10-38 degrees C in the desert. Rainfall is under 25 cm per year. Plant species include xerophytes and succulents. Lizards, snakes, and small mammals are common animals

Temperate Deciduous Forest: In this biome, temperatures range from -24 to 38 degrees C. Rainfall is 65 to 150 cm per year. Deciduous trees are common, as well as deer, bear, and squirrels.

Taiga: Here, temperatures range from -24 to 22 degrees C. Rainfall is 35 to 40 cm per year. Taiga is located north and south of the equator, close to the poles. Plant life includes conifers and plants that can withstand harsh winters. Animals include weasels, mink, and moose.

Tundra: Temperatures range from -28 to 15 degrees C in the tundra. Rainfall is limited, ranging from 10 to 15 cm per year. The tundra is located even further north and south of the taiga. Common plants include lichens and mosses. Animals include polar bears and musk ox.

Polar or Permafrost: This is where temperatures range from -40 to 0 degrees C. It rarely gets above freezing. Rainfall is below 10 cm per year. Most water is bound up as ice. Life is limited.

Succession is an orderly process of replacing a community that has been damaged or has begun where no life previously existed. **Primary succession** occurs after a community has been totally wiped out by a natural disaster or where life never existed before, as in a flooded area. **Secondary succession** takes place in communities that were once flourishing but disturbed by some force, either human or natural, but not totally stripped. A **climax community** is a community that is established and flourishing.

Definitions of Feeding Relationships

See Skill 21.7 for a more comprehensive overview of the feeding relationships.

Parasitism is when two species occupy a similar place, but the parasite benefits from the relationship while the host is harmed.

Commensalism occurs when two species occupy a similar place, and neither species is harmed by or benefits from the relationship.

Mutualism is when two species occupy a similar place and both species benefit from the relationship.

Competition occurs when two species that occupy the same habitat and eat the same food are said to be in competition with each other.

Predation is when animals eat other animals. The animals they feed on are called prey. Population growth depends upon competition for food, water, shelter, and space. The amount of predators determines the amount of prey, which in turn affects the number of predators.

Carrying Capacity is the total amount of life a habitat can support. Once the habitat runs out of food, water, shelter or space, the carrying capacity decreases, and then stabilizes.

Biotic factors are living things in an ecosystem: plants, animals, bacteria, fungi, etc.

Abiotic factors are non-living aspects of an ecosystem: soil quality, rainfall, temperature, etc.

Biogeochemical cycles

Essential elements are recycled through an ecosystem. At times, the element needs to be "fixed" in a useable form. Some cycles are dependent on plants, algae, and bacteria to fix nutrients for use by animals.

Water cycle: Two percent of all the available water is fixed and unavailable in ice or the bodies of organisms. Available water includes surface water (lakes, ocean, rivers) and ground water (aquifers, wells). Ninety-six percent of all available water is from ground water. Water is recycled through the processes of evaporation and precipitation. The water present on the earth now is the water that has been here since our atmosphere formed.

Carbon cycle: Ten percent of all available carbon in the air (from carbon dioxide gas) is fixed by photosynthesis. Plants fix carbon in the form of glucose, and animals then eat the plants and are able to obtain their source of carbon. When animals release carbon dioxide through respiration, the plants have a source of carbon to fix once more.

Nitrogen cycle: Eighty percent of the atmosphere is nitrogen gas. Nitrogen must be in non-gaseous form to be incorporated into an organism. Only a few genera of bacteria have the correct enzymes to break the triple bond between nitrogen atoms. These bacteria live within the roots of legumes (peas, beans, alfalfa) and add bacteria to the soil so that it may be taken up by plants. Nitrogen is necessary to make amino acids and the nitrogenous bases of DNA.

Phosphorus cycle: Phosphorus is a mineral; it is not found in the atmosphere. Fungi and plant roots have a structure called mycorrhizae that are able to fix insoluble phosphates into useable phosphorus. Urine and decayed matter return phosphorus to the earth where it can be incorporated in the plant. Phosphorus is needed for the backbone of DNA and for ATP manufacture.

Ecological Problems

Non-renewable resources are fragile and must be conserved for use in the future. Man's impact on the environment and knowledge of conservation will determine the future.

Biological magnification: Chemicals and pesticides accumulate in the food chain. Tertiary consumers have more accumulated toxins than animals at the bottom of the food chain.

Simplification of the food web: Three major crops feed the world (rice, corn, and wheat). Planting these crops wipes out other habitats and pushes animals into smaller areas, causing overpopulation or extinction.

Fuel sources: Strip mining and the overuse of oil reserves have depleted these resources. At the current rate of consumption, conservation or alternate fuel sources will be key to our future.

Pollution: Although technology gives us many advances, pollution is a side effect of production. Waste disposal and the burning of fossil fuels have polluted our land, water, and air. Global warming and acid rain are two results of the burning of hydrocarbons and sulfur.

Global warming: Rain forest depletion, fossil fuels, and aerosols have caused an increase in carbon dioxide production. This leads to a decrease in the amount of oxygen, which is directly proportional to the amount of ozone. As the ozone layer depletes, more heat enters our atmosphere and is trapped. This causes an overall warming effect that may eventually melt the polar ice caps, causing a rise in water levels and changes in climate. This will, in turn, affect weather systems.

Endangered species: Construction to house our overpopulated world has caused a destruction of habitats for other animals, often leading to their extinction.

Overpopulation: The human race is still growing at an exponential rate. Carrying capacity has not been met due to our ability to use technology to produce more food.

Skill 21.4 Applying knowledge of the basic principles of heredity and life cycles

Gregor Mendel is recognized as the father of genetics. His work in the late 1800s is the basis of our knowledge of genetics. Although unaware of the presence of DNA or genes, Mendel realized there were factors (now known as **genes**) that were transferred from parents to their offspring. Mendel worked with pea plants, fertilizing them himself and keeping track of subsequent generations. His findings led to the Mendelian laws of genetics. Mendel found that two "factors" governed each trait, one from each parent. Traits or characteristics came in several forms, known as **alleles**. For example, the trait for flower color had both white alleles and purple alleles.

Mendel formed three laws:

Law of dominance - In a pair of alleles, one trait may cover up the allele of the other trait. Example: brown eyes are dominant to blue eyes.

Law of segregation - Only one of the two possible alleles from each parent is passed on to the offspring from each parent. (During meiosis, the haploid number insures that half the sex cells get one allele, half get the other.)

Law of independent assortment - Alleles sort independently of each other. (Many combinations are possible depending on which sperm ends up with which egg. Compare this to the many combinations of hands possible when dealing a deck of cards).

Punnet squares are used to show the possible ways that genes combine and indicate the probability of the occurrence of a certain genotype or phenotype. One parent's genes are put at the top of the box and the other parent at the side of the box. Genes combine on the square just like numbers that are added in addition tables learned in elementary school. Below is an example of a **monohybrid cross**, which is a cross using only one trait—in this case, a trait labeled "g."

	G	g
G	GG	Gg
g	Gg	gg

In a **dihybrid cross**, sixteen gene combinations are possible, as each cross has two traits.

Definitions to know:

Dominant - the stronger of the two traits. If a dominant gene is present, it is expressed as a capital letter.

Recessive - the weaker of the two traits. In order for the recessive gene to be expressed, there must be two recessive genes present. It is expressed as a lower case letter.

Homozygous - (purebred) having two of the same genes present. An organism may be homozygous dominant, with two dominant genes, or homozygous recessive, with two recessive genes.

Heterozygous - (hybrid) having one dominant gene and one recessive gene. The dominant gene is the one that is expressed.

Genotype - the genes the organism has. Genes are represented with letters. AA, Bb, and tt are examples of genotypes.

Phenotype - how the trait is expressed in an organism. Blue eyes, brown hair, and red flowers are examples of phenotypes.

Incomplete dominance - neither gene masks the other so that a new phenotype is formed. For example, red flowers and white flowers may have equal strength. A heterozygote (Rr) would have pink flowers. If a problem occurs with a third phenotype, incomplete dominance is occurring.

Co-dominance - genes may form new phenotypes. The ABO blood grouping is an example of co-dominance. A and B are of equal strength and O is recessive. Therefore, type A blood may have the genotypes of AA or AO, type B blood may have the genotypes of BB or BO, type AB blood has the genotype A and B, and type O blood has two recessive O genes.

Linkage - genes that are found on the same chromosome usually appear together unless crossing over has occurred in meiosis (for example, blue eyes and blonde hair often show up together).

Lethal alleles - usually recessive due to the early death of the offspring. If a 2:1 ratio of alleles is found in offspring, a lethal gene combination is usually the reason. Some examples of lethal alleles include sickle cell anemia, Tay-Sachs disease, and cystic fibrosis. In these cases, the coding for an important protein is usually affected.

Inborn errors of metabolism – the affected protein is an enzyme. Examples include PKU (phenylketonuria) and albinism.

Polygenic characters - many alleles code for a phenotype. There may be as many as twenty genes that code for skin color. This is why there is such a variety of skin tones. Another example is height. A couple of medium height may have very tall offspring.

Sex linked traits - the Y chromosome found only in males (XY) carries very little genetic information, whereas the X chromosome found in females (XX) carries very important information. Since men have no second X chromosome to cover up a recessive gene, the recessive trait is expressed more often in men. Women need the recessive gene on both X chromosomes to show the trait. Examples of sex linked traits include hemophilia and color-blindness.

Sex influenced traits - traits that are influenced by the sex hormones. Male pattern baldness is an example of a sex influenced trait. Testosterone influences the expression of the gene. Mostly men lose their hair due to this trait.

Common Life Cycles

Bacteria are commonly used in laboratories for research. Bacteria reproduce by binary fission. This asexual process is simply a division of the bacterium in half. All new organisms are exact clones of the parent. The obvious advantage of asexual reproduction is that it does not require a partner. This is a huge advantage for organisms that do not move around; not having to move around to reproduce allows organisms to conserve energy. Asexual reproduction also tends to be faster. However, as asexual reproduction produces only exact copies of the parent organism, it does not allow for genetic variation, which means that mutations, or weaker qualities, will always be passed on.

Butterflies actually go through four different stages of life, but they only look like butterflies in the final stage. In the first stage, the adult butterfly lays an egg. In the second stage, the egg hatches into a caterpillar or larva. The third stage is when the caterpillar forms the chrysalis or pupa. Finally, the chrysalis matures and the adult butterfly emerges.

Frogs also have multiple stages in their life cycle. Initially, an adult frog lays its eggs in the water (all amphibians require water for reproduction). In the second stage, tadpoles hatch from the eggs. The tadpoles swim in the water and use gills for breathing. Tadpoles have a tail that is used for locomotion, but they will grow legs as well. Somewhere between two and four months old, the tadpole is known as a froglet. You can recognize a froglet because the rim around its tail, which appears fish-like, has disappeared, its tail is shorter, and its four legs have grown to the extent that its rear legs are bent underneath it. The final stage of a frog's life is spent as an adult. Its tail has been entirely reabsorbed, it has a chubby frog-like appearance instead of the tadpole's fish-like appearance, and as a mature frog it can lay eggs.

Skill 21.5   Demonstrating knowledge of the interactions of organisms with one another and their environment and the flow of energy and matter within an ecosystem

Trophic levels are based on the feeding relationships that determine energy flow and chemical cycling.

Autotrophs are the primary **producers** of the ecosystem. They consist mainly of plants.

Primary consumers are the next trophic level. The primary consumers are the herbivores that eat plants or algae.

Secondary consumers are the carnivores that eat the primary consumers.

Tertiary consumers eat the secondary consumer. These trophic levels may go higher depending on the ecosystem.
Decomposers are consumers that feed off animal waste and dead organisms.

This pathway of food transfer is known as a food chain. Most food chains are more elaborate, becoming food webs.

Energy is lost as the trophic levels progress from producer to tertiary consumer. The amount of energy that is transferred between trophic levels is called the **ecological efficiency**. The visual of this energy flow is represented in a **pyramid of productivity**, seen below:

Tertiary
Consumers

Secondary Consumers

P r i m a r y C o n s u m e r s

P   r   o   d   u   c   e   r   s

The **biomass pyramid** represents the total dry weight of organisms in each trophic level. A **pyramid of numbers** is a representation of the population size of each trophic level. The producers, being the most populous, are on the bottom of this pyramid with the tertiary consumers on the top with the fewest numbers.

Skill 21.6   Analyzing the effects of humans on the environment

For centuries, humans have been increasingly altering the environments in which they live. Everything from driving cars to logging has had a toll on the environment.

Pollutants are impurities in the air and water that may be harmful to life. Oil is a major pollutant that can cause severe destruction of the oceans, beaches, and animal life when there is a spill.

Global warming is an enormous environmental issue today; it is caused by the "greenhouse effect." In it, atmospheric greenhouse gases such as water vapor, carbon dioxide, and other gases trap some of the outgoing energy, retaining heat somewhat like the glass panels of a greenhouse. This occurs naturally; without it, the temperature on the earth would be too low to sustain life. The problem occurs when these gases enter the atmosphere in large amounts; their heat-trapping ability results in global warming.

Over the past 100 years, the earth's surface temperature has risen 1 degree Fahrenheit, with accelerated warming occurring in the past two decades. The increase of gases in the atmosphere is caused by the burning of fossil fuels and emissions of carbon dioxide from cars and factories.

All acids contain hydrogen. Substances from factory and car exhaust dissolve in rain water, forming **acid rain**. When this rain falls onto stone, the acids can react with metallic compounds and gradually wear the stone away.

Since radioactive material has become readily available, it has been a major concern as a threat of **nuclear disaster**. Radioactivity ionizes the air it travels through. It is strong enough to kill cancer cells or dangerous enough to cause illness or even death. Gamma rays can penetrate the body and damage its cells. In a nuclear disaster, damage to the land and all living organisms is inevitable.

Logging also has a negative impact on the environment. Clear-cutting forests leaves the soil unprotected and can cause disasters such as mudslides. Also, the quality of soil in that area diminishes the chances of successful re-growth for living organisms.

There are some benefits of human activities in the environment. The populations of many animal species that were endangered have risen because of protection laws and the study of the animals and their habitats.

With the development of new technology, other benefits accrue to the environment. The recycling process has prevented the unnecessary waste of plastics, glass, and paper.

Skill 21.7   Demonstrating knowledge of factors that affect the survival or extinction of organisms

There are many interactions that may occur between different species living together. Predation, parasitism, competition, commensalisms, and mutualism are the different types of relationships populations have between each other.

Predation and **parasitism** result in a benefit for one species and a detriment for the other. Predation occurs when a predator eats its prey. The common conception of predation is of a carnivore consuming other animals. This is one form of predation. Although not always resulting in the death of the plant, herbivory is a form of predation. Some animals eat enough of a plant to cause death. However, many plants and animals have defenses against predators. Some plants have poisonous chemicals that will harm the predator if ingested, and some animals are camouflaged so they are harder to detect.

Parasitism involves a predator that lives on or in its host, causing detrimental effects to the host but not the parasite. Insects and viruses living off of and reproducing in their hosts is an example of parasitism.

Competition occurs when two or more species in a community use the same resources. Competition is usually detrimental to both populations. It is often difficult to find in nature, because competition between two populations is not continuous. Either the weaker population will no longer exist, or one population will evolve to utilize other available resources.

Symbiosis is when two species live close together. Parasitism, described above, is one example of symbiosis. Another example of symbiosis is commensalism. **Commensalism** occurs when one species benefits from the other without harmful effects. **Mutualism** is when both species benefit from the other. Species involved in mutualistic relationships must co-evolve to survive; as one species evolves, the other must as well. For example, grouper and a species of shrimp live in a mutualistic relationship. The shrimp feed off parasites living on the grouper; thus the shrimp are fed and the grouper stays healthy and parasite-free. Many microorganisms are in mutualistic relationships.

The Concepts of Niche and Carrying Capacity

The term **niche** describes the relational position of a species or population in an ecosystem. Niche includes how a population responds to the abundance of its resources and its enemies (e.g., growing when resources are abundant and predators, parasites, and pathogens are scarce).

Niche also indicates the life history of an organism, its habitat, and its place in the food chain. According to the competitive exclusion principle, no two species can occupy the same niche in the same environment for a long time.

The full range of environmental conditions (biological and physical) under which an organism can exist describes its **fundamental niche**. Because of the pressure from superior competitors, organisms that survive over the long term are driven to occupy a niche that is narrower than their previous one. This is known as the **realized niche**.

Examples of niches include:
Oak trees

- live in forests
- absorb sunlight by photosynthesis
- provide shelter for many animals
- act as support for creeping plants
- serve as a source of food for animals
- cover their ground with dead leaves in the autumn

If the oak trees were cut down or destroyed by fire or storms, they would no longer be doing theses jobs. In turn, this would have a disastrous effect on all the other organisms living in the same habitat.

Hedgehogs

- eat a variety of insects and other invertebrates that live underneath the dead leaves and twigs in the garden
- have spines that are a superb environment for fleas and ticks
- put the nitrogen back into the soil when they urinate
- eat slugs and protect plants from them

If the hedgehog population was drastically reduced, the number of slugs would explode and the nutrients in the dead leaves and twigs would not recycle.

A **population** is a group of individuals of one species that live in the same general area. Many factors can affect the population size and its growth rate. For example, population size depends on the total amount of life a habitat can support. This is called the **carrying capacity** of the environment.

Limiting factors can also affect population growth. As a population increases, the competition for resources is more intense, and the growth rate declines. This is a **density-dependent** growth factor. The carrying capacity can be determined by the density-dependent factor.

Density-independent factors affect individuals regardless of population size. The weather and climate are good examples. Too hot or too cold of temperatures may kill many individuals from a population even if it has not reached its carrying capacity.

Human population increased slowly until 1650. Since 1650, the human population has grown almost exponentially, reaching its current population of over 6 billion. Factors that have led to this increased growth rate include improved nutrition, sanitation, and health care. In addition, advances in technology, agriculture, and scientific knowledge have made the use of resources more efficient and readily available.

While the earth's ultimate carrying capacity for humans is uncertain, some factors that may limit growth are the availability of food, water, space, and fossil fuels. There is a finite amount of land on Earth available for food production. In addition, providing clean, potable water for a growing human population is a real concern. Fossil fuels, important energy sources for human technology, are scarce. The inevitable shortage of energy in the earth's future will require the development of alternative energy sources to maintain or increase human population growth.

<u>DOMAIN V.</u>   **HEALTH, PHYSICAL EDUCATION, AND THE ARTS**

COMPETENCY 22.0 UNDERSTAND BASIC PRINCIPLES AND PRACTICES RELATED TO HEALTH AND SAFETY

Skill 22.1   Demonstrating knowledge of the primary functions of the human body systems, the processes of human growth and development, and the basic principles of human nutrition

The major systems of the human body consist of organs working together to perform important physiological tasks. To understand how all of these systems work together, it is important to have a grasp of several major body systems, including the musculoskeletal system, the cardiovascular system, the respiratory/excretory system, the nervous system, the endocrine system, the reproductive system, and the immune system. In addition, it is valuable to know how these systems adapt to physical activity, produce movement, and contribute to fitness.

Structures, Locations, and Functions of the Three Types of Muscular Tissue

The main function of the muscular system is movement. There are three types of muscle tissue: skeletal, cardiac, and smooth.

Skeletal muscle is voluntary. These muscles are attached to bones and are responsible for their movement. Skeletal muscle consists of long fibers and is striated due to the repeating patterns of the myofilaments (made of the proteins actin and myosin) that make up the fibers.

Cardiac muscle is found in the heart. Cardiac muscle is striated like skeletal muscle, but differs in that the plasma membrane of the cardiac muscle causes the muscle to beat even when away from the heart. The action potentials of cardiac and skeletal muscles also differ.

Smooth muscle is involuntary. It is found in organs and enables functions such as digestion and respiration. Unlike skeletal and cardiac muscle, smooth muscle is not striated. Smooth muscle has less myosin and does not generate as much tension as skeletal muscle.

Mechanism of Skeletal Muscle Contraction

To begin, a nerve impulse strikes a muscle fiber. This causes calcium ions to flood the sarcomere (the muscle's filaments). These calcium ions allow adenosine triphosphate (ATP), which is basically the "gasoline" of the human body, to expend energy. The myosin fibers then creep along the actin, causing the muscle to contract. Once the nerve impulse has passed, calcium is pumped out and the contraction ends.

Phosphorous needed

Movement of Body Joints

The axial skeleton consists of the bones of the skull and vertebrae. The appendicular skeleton consists of the bones of the legs, arms and tail, and shoulder girdle.

Bone is a connective tissue. Parts of the bone include compact bone, which gives strength; spongy bone, which contains red marrow to make blood cells and yellow marrow in the center of long bones to store fat cells; and the periosteum, which is the protective covering on the outside of the bone.

A **joint** is a place where two bones meet; they enable movement. Within the joint, ligaments attach bone to bone, and tendons attach bone to muscle. All of these parts work together to allow the joint to move. There are three types of joints:

1. **Ball and socket** – allows for rotational movement. An example is the joint between the shoulder and the humerus. Ball and socket joints allow humans to move their arms and legs in many different ways.

2. **Hinge** – movement is restricted to a single plane. An example is the joint between the humerus and the ulna.

3. **Pivot** – allows for the rotation of the forearm at the elbow and the hands at the wrist.

Human Nervous and Endocrine Systems

The **central nervous system** (CNS) consists of the *brain* and *spinal cord*. The CNS is responsible for the body's response to environmental stimuli. The **spinal cord** is located inside the spine. It sends out motor commands for movement in response to stimuli. The **brain** is where responses to more complex stimuli occur.

The meninges are the connective tissues that protect the CNS. The CNS also contains fluid filled spaces called ventricles. These ventricles are filled with cerebrospinal fluid, which is formed in the brain. This fluid cushions the brain and circulates nutrients, white blood cells, and hormones.

The CNS's response to stimuli is a reflex. A reflex is an unconscious, automatic response.

The **peripheral nervous system** (PNS) consists of the nerves that connect the CNS to the rest of the body. The **sensory division** of the PNS brings information to the CNS from sensory receptors, and the motor division sends signals from the CNS to effector cells. The **motor division** consists of the somatic nervous system and the autonomic nervous system. The body consciously controls the somatic nervous system in response to external stimuli. The hypothalamus in the brain unconsciously controls the autonomic nervous system to regulate the internal environment. This system is responsible for the movement of smooth muscles, cardiac muscles, and the muscles of other organ systems.

Role of Nerve Impulses and Neurons

The **neuron** is the basic unit of the nervous system. It consists of an **axon**, which carries impulses away from the cell body to the tip of the neuron; the **dendrite**, which carries impulses toward the cell body; and the **cell body**, which contains the nucleus. Synapses are the spaces between neurons. Chemicals called neurotransmitters are found close to the synapses. The myelin sheath, composed of Schwann cells, covers the neurons and provides insulation.

Nerve action depends on depolarization and an imbalance of electrical charges across the neuron. A polarized nerve has a positive charge outside the neuron. A depolarized nerve has a negative charge outside the neuron.

Neurotransmitters turn off the sodium pump, which results in depolarization of the membrane. This wave of depolarization (as it moves from neuron to neuron) carries an electrical impulse. This is actually a wave of opening and closing gates that allows for the flow of ions across the synapse.

All nerves have an action potential. There is a threshold of the level of chemicals that must be met or exceeded in order for muscles to respond. This is the "all or nothing" response.

Major Endocrine Glands and the Function of their Hormones

The function of the **endocrine system** is to manufacture proteins called hormones. **Hormones** circulate in the bloodstream and stimulate actions when they interact with target tissue. There are two classes of hormones: steroid and peptide. Steroid hormones come from cholesterol and include the sex hormones. Amino acids are the source of peptide hormones.

Hormones are specific; they fit receptors on the target tissue cell surface. The receptor activates an enzyme that converts ATP to cyclic AMP. Cyclic AMP (cAMP) is a second messenger from the cell membrane to the nucleus. The genes found in the nucleus turn on or off to cause a specific response.

Endocrine cells, which make up endocrine glands, secrete hormones. The major endocrine glands and their hormones include:

Hypothalamus – located in the lower brain, it signals the pituitary gland.

Pituitary gland – located at the base of the hypothalamus, it releases growth hormones and antidiuretic hormone (retention of water in kidneys).

Thyroid gland – located on the trachea, it lowers blood calcium levels (calcitonin) and maintains metabolic processes (thyroxine).

Gonads – located in the testes of the male and the ovaries of the female, the testes release androgens to support sperm formation, and ovaries release estrogens to stimulate uterine lining growth and progesterone to promote uterine lining growth.

Pancreas – secretes insulin in order to lower blood glucose levels and glucagon to raise blood glucose levels.

Structure and Function of The Skin

The skin consists of two distinct layers: the **epidermis** and the **dermis**. The epidermis is the thinner outer layer, and the dermis is the thicker inner layer. Layers of tightly packed epithelial cells make up the epidermis. The tight packaging of the epithelial cells supports the skin's function as a protective barrier against infection.

The top layer of the epidermis consists of dead skin cells and contains keratin, a waterproofing protein. The dermis layer consists of connective tissue. It contains blood vessels, hair follicles, sweat glands, and sebaceous glands. The body releases an oily secretion called sebum, produced by the sebaceous gland, to the outer epidermis through the hair follicles. Sebum maintains the pH of the skin between 3 and 5, which inhibits most microorganism growth.

The skin also plays a role in thermoregulation. Increased body temperature causes skin blood vessels to dilate, which then causes heat to radiate from the skin's surface. Increased temperature also activates sweat glands, increasing evaporative cooling. Decreased body temperature causes skin blood vessels to constrict. This results in blood from the skin diverting to deeper tissues, thereby reducing heat loss from the surface of the skin.

Human Respiratory and Excretory Systems

Surface area, Volume, and Function of the Respiratory and Excretory Systems

The **lungs** are the respiratory surface of the human respiratory system. A dense net of capillaries contained just beneath the epithelium form the respiratory surface. The surface area of the epithelium is about $100m^2$ in humans.

Based on the surface area, the volume of air inhaled and exhaled is known as the tidal volume. This is normally about 500mL in adults. Vital capacity is the maximum volume the lungs can inhale and exhale. This is usually around 3400mL.

The **kidneys** are the primary organ in the excretory system. Each of the two kidneys in humans is about 10cm long. Despite their small size, they receive about 20 percent of the blood pumped with each heartbeat. The function of the excretory system is to rid the body of nitrogenous wastes in the form of urea.

Knowledge of the Process of Breathing and Gas Exchange

The respiratory system functions in the gas exchange of oxygen and carbon dioxide waste. It delivers oxygen to the bloodstream and picks up carbon dioxide for release from the body. Air enters the mouth and nose, where it is warmed, moistened, and filtered of dust and particles. Cilia in the trachea trap and expel unwanted material in mucus. The trachea splits into two bronchial tubes, and the bronchial tubes divide into smaller and smaller bronchioles in the lungs. The internal surface of the lung is composed of alveoli, which are thin walled air sacs. These allow for a large surface area for gas exchange. Capillaries line the alveoli.

Oxygen diffuses into the bloodstream and carbon dioxide diffuses out of the capillaries. It is then exhaled from the lungs due to partial pressure. Hemoglobin, a protein containing iron, carries the oxygenated blood to the heart and all parts of the body.

The thoracic cavity holds the lungs. The diaphragm muscle below the lungs is an adaptation that makes inhalation possible. As the volume of the thoracic cavity increases, the diaphragm muscle flattens out and inhalation occurs. When the diaphragm relaxes, exhalation occurs.

Human Circulatory and Immune Systems

Structure, Function, and Regulation of the Heart

The function of the closed circulatory system (**cardiovascular system**) is to carry oxygenated blood and nutrients to all cells of the body and to return carbon dioxide waste to the lungs for expulsion. The heart, blood vessels, and blood make up the cardiovascular system. The following diagram shows the structure of the heart:

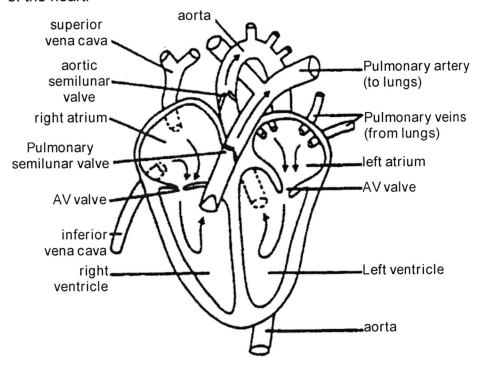

The atria are the chambers that receive blood returning to the heart, and the ventricles are the chambers that pump blood out of the heart. There are four valves, two atrioventricular (AV) valves and two semilunar valves. The AV valves are located between each atrium and ventricle. The contraction of the ventricles closes the AV valve to keep blood from flowing back into the atria. The semilunar valves are located where the aorta leaves the left ventricle and the pulmonary artery leaves the right ventricle. Ventricular contraction opens the semilunar valves, pumping blood out into the arteries, and ventricular relaxation closes the valves.

Cardiac output is the volume of blood per minute that the left ventricle pumps. This output depends on the heart rate and stroke volume. The **heart rate** is the number of times the heart beats per minute, and the **stroke volume** is the amount of blood pumped by the left ventricle each time it contracts. Humans have an average cardiac output of about 5.25 L/min. Heavy exercise can increase cardiac output up to five times. Epinephrine and increased body temperature can also increase heart rate and, thus, the cardiac output.

Cardiac muscle can contract without any signal from the nervous system. The sinoatrial node is the pacemaker of the heart. It is located on the wall of the right atrium; it generates electrical impulses that make the cardiac muscle cells contract in unison. The atrioventricular node briefly delays the electrical impulse to ensure the atria empty before the ventricles contract.

Structure, Function, and Regulation of the Immune System

The immune system is responsible for defending the body against foreign invaders. There are two defense mechanisms: non-specific and specific.

The **non-specific** immune mechanism has two lines of defense. The first line of defense is the physical barriers of the body. These include the skin and mucous membranes. The skin prevents the penetration of bacteria and viruses as long as there are no abrasions on the skin. Mucous membranes form a protective barrier around the digestive, respiratory, and genitourinary tracts. In addition, the pH of the skin and mucous membranes inhibit the growth of many microbes. Mucous secretions (tears and saliva) wash away many microbes; they also contain lysozyme, which kills microbes.

The second line of defense includes white blood cells and the inflammatory response. **Phagocytosis** is the ingestion of foreign particles. Neutrophils make up about 70 percent of all white blood cells. Monocytes mature to become macrophages, which are the largest phagocytic cells. Eosinophils are also phagocytic. Natural killer cells destroy the body's own infected cells instead of invading the microbe directly.

The other second line of defense is the inflammatory response. When this occurs, the blood supply to the injured area increases, causing redness and heat. Swelling also typically occurs with inflammation. Basophils and mast cells release histamine in response to cell injury. This triggers the inflammatory response.

The **specific** immune mechanism recognizes specific foreign material and responds by destroying the invader. These mechanisms are specific and diverse. They are able to recognize individual pathogens. An **antigen** is any foreign particle that elicits an immune response. The body manufactures **antibodies** that recognize and latch onto antigens, hopefully destroying them. They also discriminate between foreign materials versus self material. Memory of the invaders provides immunity upon further exposure.

Immunity is the body's ability to recognize and destroy an antigen before it causes harm. Active immunity develops after recovery from an infectious disease (e.g., chickenpox) or after a vaccination (e.g., mumps, measles, and rubella). Passive immunity may be passed from one individual to another and is not permanent. A good example of passive immunities are those passed from mother to nursing child. A baby's immune system is not well-developed, so the passive immunity they receive through nursing keeps them healthier.
There are two main responses made by the body after exposure to an antigen:

1. **Humoral response**: Free antigens activate this response. During it, B-cells (lymphocytes from bone marrow) give rise to plasma cells that secrete antibodies as well as memory cells that will recognize future exposures to the same antigen. The antibodies defend against extracellular pathogens by binding to the antigen and making them an easy target for phagocytes to engulf and destroy. Antibodies are in a class of proteins called **immunoglobulins**. There are five major classes of immunoglobulins (Ig) involved in the humoral response: IgM, IgG, IgA, IgD, and IgE.

2. **Cell mediated response**: Infected cells activate T-cells (lymphocytes from the thymus) in this response. These activated T-cells defend against pathogens in the body cells or cancer cells by binding to the infected cells and destroying them along with the antigen. T-cell receptors on the T helper cells recognize antigens bound to the body's own cells. T helper cells release IL-2, which stimulates other lymphocytes (cytotoxic T-cells and B-cells). Cytotoxic T-cells kill infected host cells by recognizing specific antigens.

Vaccines are antigens given in very small amounts. They stimulate both humoral and cell mediated responses. After vaccination, memory cells recognize future exposure to the antigen so that the body can produce antibodies much faster.

Human Digestive System

Roles of Basic Nutrients Found in Foods

The function of the digestive system is to break food down into nutrients, to absorb them into the blood stream, and to deliver them to all cells of the body for use in cellular respiration.

Essential nutrients are those nutrients that the body needs but cannot make. There are four groups of essential nutrients: essential amino acids, essential fatty acids, vitamins, and minerals.

There are about eight essential amino acids humans need. A lack of these amino acids results in protein deficiency. There are only a few essential fatty acids.

Vitamins are organic molecules essential for a nutritionally adequate diet. Scientists have identified thirteen vitamins essential to humans. There are two groups of vitamins: water-soluble (includes the vitamin B complex and vitamin C) and water insoluble (vitamins A, D, and K). Vitamin deficiencies can cause severe health problems.

Unlike vitamins, minerals are inorganic molecules. Calcium is important in bone construction and maintenance. Iron is important in cellular respiration and is a major component of hemoglobin.
Carbohydrates, fats, and proteins are fuel for the generation of ATP. Water is necessary to keep the body hydrated.

Essential Amino Acids	Essential Vitamins
• Arginine	• Vitamin A
• Histidine	• Vitamin B complex (8 vitamins)
• Isoleucine	• Vitamin C
• Leucine	• Vitamin D
• Lysine	• Vitamin E
• Methionine	• Vitamin K
• Phenylalanine	
• Threonine	
• Tryptophan	
• Valine	

Mechanical and Chemical Digestion

The teeth and saliva begin digestion by breaking food down into smaller pieces and lubricating it to allow swallowing. The lips, cheeks, and tongue form a bolus, or ball of food. The process of **peristalsis** (wave-like contractions) carries the food down the pharynx, where it enters the stomach through the sphincter. Once through, the sphincter closes to keep food from going back up.

In the stomach, pepsinogen and hydrochloric acid form pepsin, the enzyme that hydrolyzes proteins. This chemical action breaks the food down further and churns it into a semifluid mass called acid chyme.

The pyloric sphincter muscle opens to allow the food to enter the small intestine. Most nutrient absorption occurs in the small intestine. Its large surface area, resulting from its length and protrusions called villi and microvilli, allow for a great absorptive surface into the bloodstream.

Neutralization of the chyme after arrival from the acidic stomach allows the local enzymes to function. Accessory organs function in the production of necessary enzymes and bile. The pancreas makes many enzymes necessary to break down food in the small intestine. The liver makes bile, which breaks down and emulsifies fatty acids. Any food left after the trip through the small intestine enters the large intestine. The large intestine functions to reabsorb water and produce vitamin K. The feces, or remaining waste, passes out through the anus.

Human Reproductive System

The Function of Male and Female Reproductive Systems

Hormones regulate sexual maturation in humans. Humans cannot reproduce until puberty, about the age of eight to fourteen, depending on the individual. Prior to puberty, the hypothalamus begins secreting hormones that help to mature the reproductive system and to develop the secondary sex characteristics. Reproductive maturity in girls occurs with the first menstruation; it occurs in boys with the first ejaculation of viable sperm.

Hormones also regulate reproduction. In males, the primary sex hormones are the androgens, testosterone being the most important. The testes produce androgens that dictate the primary and secondary sex characteristics of the male.

Female hormone patterns are cyclic and complex. Most women have a reproductive cycle length of about twenty-eight days. The menstrual cycle is specific to the changes in the uterus. The ovarian cycle results in ovulation; it occurs in parallel with the menstrual cycle. Hormones regulate this parallelism. Five hormones participate in this regulation, most notably estrogen and progesterone. Estrogen and progesterone play an important role in sending signals to the uterus and in developing and maintaining the endometrium. Estrogen also dictates the secondary sex characteristics of females.

Gametogenesis, Fertilization, and Birth control

Gametogenesis is the production of the sperm (spermatogenesis) and egg cells (oogenesis). **Spermatogenesis** begins at puberty in the male. One spermatogonia, the diploid precursor of sperm, produces four sperm. The sperm mature in the seminiferous tubules, which are located in the testes. **Oogenesis**, the production of egg cells (ova), is usually complete by the birth of a female. Females do not release egg cells until menstruation begins at puberty. Meiosis forms one ovum with all the cytoplasm, and three polar bodies that the body reabsorbs. The ovaries store the ovum and release them each month from puberty to menopause.

Seminiferous tubules in the testes house sperm, where they mature. The epididymis, located on top of the testes, contains mature sperm. After ejaculation, the sperm travel up the vas deferens where they mix with semen made in the prostate and seminal vesicles; they then travel out the urethra.

Ovulation releases the egg into the fallopian tubes, where cilia move the egg along the length of the tubes. Fertilization of the egg by the sperm normally occurs in the fallopian tube. If pregnancy does not occur, the egg passes through the uterus and is expelled through the vagina during menstruation. Levels of progesterone and estrogen stimulate menstruation. Implantation of a fertilized egg down-regulates the levels, stopping menstruation.

There are many methods of contraception (birth control) that affect different stages of fertilization. Chemical contraception (birth control pills) prevent ovulation by synthetic estrogen and progesterone. Several physical barrier methods of contraception are also available. Male and female condoms block semen from contacting the egg. Sterilization is another method of birth control. Tubal ligation in women prevents eggs from entering the uterus. A vasectomy in men involves the cutting of the vas deferens. This prevents the sperm from entering the urethra. The most effective method of birth control is abstinence. Programs exist worldwide that promote abstinence, especially amongst teenagers.

Stages and Characteristics of Physical, Cognitive, Social, and Emotional Growth and Development

Physical development – Small children (ages three to five) have a propensity for engaging in periods of a great deal of physical activity, punctuated by a need for a lot of rest. Children at this stage lack fine motor skills and cannot focus on small objects for very long. Their bones are still developing. At this age, girls tend to be better coordinated, and boys tend to be stronger.

The lag in fine motor skills continues during the early elementary school years (ages six to eight).

Pre-adolescent children (ages nine to eleven) become stronger, leaner, and taller. Their motor skills improve, and they are able to sit still and focus for longer periods. Growth during this period is constant. This is also the time when gender-related physical predispositions will begin to show. Pre-adolescents are at risk of obesity without proper nutrition or adequate activity.

Young adolescents (ages twelve to fourteen) experience drastic physical growth (girls earlier than boys), and are highly preoccupied with their physical appearance.

As children proceed to the later stages of adolescence (ages fifteen to seventeen), girls will reach their full height, while boys will still have some growth remaining. The increase in hormone levels will cause acne, which coincides with a slight decrease of preoccupation with physical appearance. At this age, children may begin to initiate sexual activity (boys generally more motivated by hormones, and girls more by peer pressure). There is a risk of teen pregnancy and sexually transmitted diseases.

Cognitive development – Language development is the most important aspect of cognitive development in small children (ages three to five). Acknowledging successes, rewarding mature behavior, and allowing the child to explore can improve confidence and self-esteem at this age.

Early elementary school children (ages six to eight) are eager to learn and love to talk. Children at this age have a very literal understanding of rules and verbal instructions, and must develop strong listening skills.

Pre-adolescent children (ages nine to eleven) display increased logical thought, but their knowledge or beliefs may be unusual or surprising. Differences in cognitive styles develop at this age (e.g., field dependant or independent preferences).

In early adolescence (ages twelve to fourteen), boys tend to score higher on mechanical/spatial reasoning, and girls on spelling and language tasks. Boys are better with mental imagery, and girls have better access and retrieval of information from memory. Self-efficacy (the ability to self-evaluate) becomes very important at this stage.

In later adolescence (ages fifteen to seventeen), children are capable of formal thought, but don't always apply it. Conflicts between teenagers' and parents' opinions and worldviews will arise. Children at this age may become interested in advanced political thinking.

Social development – Small children (ages three to five) are socially flexible. Different children will prefer solitary play, parallel play, or cooperative play. Frequent minor quarrels will occur between children, and boys will tend to be more aggressive (children at these ages are already aware of gender roles).

Early elementary school children (ages six to eight) are increasingly selective of friends (usually of the same sex). Children at this age enjoy playing games, but are excessively preoccupied by the rules. Verbal aggression becomes more common than physical aggression, and adults should encourage children of this age to solve their own conflicts.

Pre-adolescent children (ages nine to eleven) place great importance on the (perceived) opinions of their peers and on their social stature, and will go to great lengths to "fit in." Friendships at this age are very selective, and usually of the same sex.

Young adolescents (ages twelve to fourteen) develop a greater understanding of the emotions of others, which results in increased emotional sensitivity and impacts peer relationships. Children at this age develop an increased need to perform.

In the later stages of adolescence (ages fifteen to seventeen), peers are still the primary influence on day-to-day decisions, but parents will have increasing influence on long-term goals. Girls' friendships tend to be close and intimate, whereas boys' friendships are based on competition and similar interests. Many children this age will work part-time, and educators should be alert to signs of potential school dropouts.

Emotional development – Small children (ages three to five) express emotion freely and have a limited ability to learn how emotions influence behavior. Jealousy at this age is common.

Early elementary school children (ages six to eight) have easily bruised feelings and are just beginning to recognize the feelings of others. Children this age will want to please teachers and other adults.

Pre-adolescent children (ages nine to eleven) develop a global and stable self-image (self-concept and self-esteem). Comparisons to their peers and the opinions of their peers are important. An unstable home environment at this age contributes to an increased risk of delinquency.

Young adolescence (ages twelve to fourteen) can be a stormy and stressful time for children, but, in reality, this is only the case for roughly 20 percent of teens. Boys may have trouble controlling their anger and display impulsive behavior. Girls may suffer depression. Young adolescents are very egocentric and concerned with appearance; they often feel very strongly that "adults don't understand."

In later stages of adolescence (ages fifteen to seventeen), educators should be alert to signs of surfacing mental health problems (e.g., eating disorders, substance abuse, schizophrenia, depression, and suicide).

Nutrition and Weight Control

Identifying the Components of Nutrition

The components of nutrition are carbohydrates, proteins, fats, vitamins, minerals, and water.

Carbohydrates are the main source of energy (glucose) in the human diet. The two types of carbohydrates are simple and complex. Complex carbohydrates have greater nutritional value because they take longer to digest, contain dietary fiber, and do not excessively elevate blood sugar levels. Common sources of carbohydrates are fruits, vegetables, grains, dairy products, and legumes.

Proteins are necessary for growth, development, and cellular function. The body breaks down consumed protein into component amino acids for future use. Major sources of protein are meat, poultry, fish, legumes, eggs, dairy products, grains, and legumes.

Fats are a concentrated energy source and important component of the human body. The different types of fats are saturated, monounsaturated, and polyunsaturated. Polyunsaturated fats are the healthiest because they may lower cholesterol levels, while saturated fats increase cholesterol levels. Common sources of saturated fats include dairy products, meat, coconut oil, and palm oil. Common sources of unsaturated fats include nuts, most vegetable oils, and fish.

Vitamins and minerals are organic substances that the body requires in small quantities for proper functioning. People acquire vitamins and minerals in their diets and in supplements. Important vitamins include A, B, C, D, E, and K. Important minerals include calcium, phosphorus, magnesium, potassium, sodium, chlorine, and sulfur.

Water makes up 55 to 75 percent of the human body. It is essential for most bodily functions and obtained through foods and liquids.

Determining the Adequacy of Diets in Meeting the Nutritional Needs of Students

Nutritional requirements vary from person-to-person. General guidelines for meeting adequate nutritional needs are no more than 30 percent total caloric intake from fats (preferably 10 percent from saturated fats, 10% percent from monounsaturated fats, and 10 percent from polyunsaturated fats); no more than 15 percent total caloric intake from proteins (complete); and at least 55 percent of caloric intake from carbohydrates (mainly complex carbohydrates).

Exercise and diet help to maintain proper body weight by equalizing caloric intake and caloric output.

Choosing a Healthy Diet

A healthy diet is essential for achieving and maintaining optimum mental and physical health. Making the decision to eat well is a powerful investment. Selecting foods that encompass a variety of healthy nutrients will help to reduce the risk of developing common medical conditions; it will also boost one's immune system while increasing energy level.

Experts agree that the key to healthy eating is balance, variety, and moderation. Other tips include:

- Enjoy plenty of whole grains, fruits, and vegetables
- Maintain a healthy weight
- Eat moderate portions
- Eat regular meals
- Reduce but don't eliminate certain foods
- Balance your food choices over time
- Know your diet pitfalls
- Make changes gradually—remember, foods are not good or bad.
- Select foods based on your total eating patterns, not whether any individual food is "good" or "bad."

Food Guide Pyramid and Dietary Guidelines

The Food Guide Pyramid illustrates the different components of a healthy diet and number of servings of each food group people should consume. Specifically, people should consume the greatest number of servings of carbohydrate-based products like cereals, breads, and pasta; a large number of vitamin- and mineral-rich carbohydrates like fruits and vegetables; a number of protein-rich foods; and very few foods with higher fat content.

The Dietary Guidelines for Americans is a document published by the United States Department of Health and Human Services and the United States Department of Agriculture. It is a primary source of dietary health information for policymakers, nutrition educators, and health providers so they can help direct the individuals that they represent, teach, and care for to make informed and healthy decisions regarding their diets.

Regulations related to food labels and packaging ensure that consumers receive accurate information about the products they buy. Food labels include the breakdown of ingredients, nonfood components, nutritional values, and accuracy of claims relating to the food product.

Skill 22.2 **Recognizing the differences between communicable and non-communicable diseases and strategies for preventing or treating them (e.g., vaccinations, hand washing, regular exercise, antibiotics)**

Types of Diseases: Causes, Characteristics, and Methods for Detecting and Preventing Them

Pathogens that enter the body through direct or indirect contact cause communicable, or infectious, diseases. A **pathogen** is a disease-causing organism. Familiar communicable diseases include influenza, the common cold, chickenpox, pneumonia, measles, mumps, and mononucleosis. To minimize the circulation of pathogens that cause these illnesses, people must follow simple precautions. Individuals who are ill with these diseases should stay away from others during the contagious period of the infection. All people should avoid sharing items such as towels, toothbrushes, and silverware. At home, thorough clothes washing, dishwashing, and frequent hand washing can decrease pathogen transmission. Keeping immunizations up-to-date is also important in reducing the spread of communicable diseases.

Sexual activity is the source of transmission for many other communicable diseases. The commonly used term for these types of diseases is **sexually transmitted disease** (STD) or **sexually transmitted infection** (STI). Common STIs include chlamydia, gonorrhea, syphilis, genital herpes, genital warts, bacterial vaginosis, human papillomavirus (HPV), pediculosis pubis (pubic lice), hepatitis B, and HIV. Certain STIs can result in infertility. HPV can result in a deadly form of cervical cancer. HIV may result in acquired immunodeficiency syndrome (AIDS), which can be fatal. Some of these diseases, such as genital herpes, last a lifetime.

A **chronic disease** is a disease that is long-lasting; it typically continues for more than three months. Examples of chronic conditions include diseases such as heart disease, cancer, and diabetes. These diseases are currently the leading causes of death and disability in the United States. Many forms of these widespread and expensive diseases are preventable. Choosing nutritious foods, participating in physical activity, and avoiding tobacco use can prevent or control these illnesses.

A **degenerative disease** is a condition in which diseased tissues or organs steadily deteriorate. The deterioration may be due to ordinary wear and tear, or lifestyle choices such as lack of exercise or poor nutrition. In addition, many degenerative diseases are of questionable origin, and may be linked to heredity and environmental factors. Some examples of degenerative diseases include: osteoporosis, Alzheimer's disease, ALS (Lou Gehrig's disease), osteoarthritis, inflammatory bowel disease (IBD), and Parkinson's disease.

Preventing Health Problems

Primary Prevention activities are the most cost-effective in health care, as they help to avoid the suffering, cost, and burden associated with a particular disease or condition. These precautions promote health by targeting specific health care concerns.

Examples of primary prevention include both active and passive immunization against disease. **Passive immunization** is treatment that provides immunity through the transfer of antibodies obtained from an immune individual. **Active immunization** is treatment that provides immunity by challenging an individual's own immune system to produce an antibody against a particular organism. Recently developed vaccines include the ones for hepatitis A and chicken pox.

Education to promote health protection is also a primary prevention strategy. Advising automobile drivers and passengers to use seat belts while in transit illustrates an action of primary prevention, as does advocating the use of helmets while riding a bicycle or motorcycle.

Secondary Prevention is early detection using accepted screening technologies. The intent is to identify patients with an increased risk, since many conditions do not show symptoms until the disease is well established, significantly reducing chances of recovery. Finding problems early in the development of diseases such as hyperlipidemia, hypertension, and breast and prostate cancer can frequently curb or eliminate the damage and reduce pain and suffering (U.S. Preventative Services Task Force (1996) Guide to Clinical Preventative Services (2d edition) Baltimore: Williams & Wilkins).

Children who are disruptive, inattentive, hyperactive, impulsive, or aggressive may be at heightened risk for the development of antisocial behavior, substance abuse, and school dropout in later years (Barkley, Fischer, Edelbrock, & Smallish, 1990). Secondary prevention in these cases includes skill-building interventions such as teaching children problem-solving strategies and educating parents to use these techniques at home. Instructors can create environments that allow children to work together with their peers, their parents, and school personnel to channel their energy into positive outcomes (Weissberg, Caplan, & Sivo, 1989).

Natural Defense Mechanisms

The body fights disease through **immunity**, through which special proteins called antibodies destroy infection. Lymphocytes, or white blood cells, and cells of the reticuloendothelial system are responsible for establishing active acquired immunity in the body. This is one of the body's defense mechanisms against disease.

Another defense mechanism that the body uses to prevent the spread of infection is **inflammation**, which occurs in damaged tissues. Fluids surrounding the infection clot, preventing any flow from the damaged tissues to other areas.

Relationship Between Diet and the Prevention of Disease

Diet plays an important role in the prevention of disease. Consuming a healthy diet that is rich in polyunsaturated fats, whole grains, fish, fruits, vegetables, and lean protein, and low in saturated fat and sugar, reduces the risk of many chronic diseases. Proper nutrition can help to prevent heart disease, strokes, osteoporosis, and many types of cancers. In addition, good nutrition helps to boost the body's immune system, lowering the risk of infectious disease.

Issues Related to Ideal Weight and Body Composition

Nutrition and exercise are closely related concepts that are important to student health. A primary responsibility of health instructors is to teach students about proper nutrition and exercise, as well as how they relate to each other.

The two key components of a healthy lifestyle are the consumption of a balanced diet and regular physical activity. Exercise and diet maintain proper body weight by equalizing caloric intake to caloric output. Nutrition can affect physical performance. Proper nutrition produces high energy levels and allows for peak performance. Inadequate or improper nutrition can impair physical performance and lead to short-term and long-term health problems (e.g., depressed immune system and heart disease, respectively). Regular exercise improves overall health. The benefits of regular exercise include a stronger immune system, weight management, a reduced risk of premature death, a reduced risk of heart disease, improved psychological well-being, and stronger muscles, bones, and joints.

Body Composition Management

It is vital to analyze procedures, activities, resources, and benefits involved in developing and maintaining healthy levels of body composition. Maintaining a healthy body composition allows an individual to move freely and to obtain a certain pattern necessary for activity. Furthermore, maintaining a healthy body composition is positively related with long-term health and resistance to disease and sickness.

The total weight of an individual is a combination of bones, ligaments, tendons, organs, fluids, muscles, and fat. Because muscle weighs three times more than fat per unit of volume, a person who exercises often gains muscle. This could cause an individual to be smaller physically, but weigh more than he or she appears to weigh.

The only proven method for maintaining a healthy body composition is following a healthy diet and engaging in regular exercise. A healthy program of nutrition and exercise helps to balance caloric intake and output, thus preventing excessive body fat production.

Skill 22.3   **Recognizing characteristics of interpersonal relationships (e.g., within families, among peers) and strategies for maintaining healthy interpersonal relationships (e.g., using conflict resolution and positive character development skills)**

Families and Family Structures

Today's family is often quite different from the traditional mom, dad, and biological children. Divorce, stepfamilies, and adoption have changed the typical American family. Studies show that children suffer the most with divorce, remarriage, and stepfamily situations. They are particularly at risk if their biological parents are in conflict. Divorce takes a long time, and unhappy parents, who are focused on severing ties with the ex-spouse and starting over, often overlook their children. Relationships with the absent parent change as well (*Family Relations* (Vol. 52, No. 4, pages 352–362) by Emery of UVA and Joan B. Kelly, PhD).

The adjustment of children of divorce is more dependent on the child's resiliency than anything else. Contributing factors include the child's age during the divorce, the amount of time elapsed, parenting style, financial security, and parental conflict. For example, 50 percent of adjustment problems for children of divorce are due to economic problems faced by divorced households.

Adoptions of international children and those of ethnicities that are different from the parents are creating multicultural families and communities. Attachment disorder is often a problem in these types of adoptions—often due to lack of nurturing early in a child's life. More same-sex couples and single parents adopt, and grandparents often adopt their grandchildren following parental abuse or neglect. The twenty-first century American family is very different from what was common thirty years ago (Adam Pertman, "Adoption Nation: How the Adoption Revolution is Transforming America", Basic Books, 2001).

The demographics of stepfamilies are complex, with nearly 25 percent of the parents unmarried. Both heterosexual parents and gay, lesbian, or bisexual partners may head families. Stepfamilies are a blend of parents, their respective children, the nonresidential parents of those children, grandparents, and other members of the extended family, as well as children born to remarried ex-spouses.

The blended family's challenges include parenting, disciplining, developing new relationships between the stepparent and other spouse's children, strengthening the marital relationship, and working to include nonresidential family (divorced spouses and children not living with the stepfamily).

One in three Americans is part of a stepfamily, each with its own character. The stepchildren rarely see a new stepparent as a "real parent," and years may pass before they gain acceptance. It is also difficult for parents in second marriages to treat their stepchildren the same as their biological children. Children are often given too much power in the new family, and may try to create conflict between their biological parent and the stepparent in an attempt to make the stepparent leave.

Creating family stability requires the same steps, whether the situation is a first-marriage, stepfamily, or a single-parent family. What really matters is that parents maintain a routine that fosters security. How families resolve conflicts is also important. Children need an anchor when it seems that everything in their lives is changing. This could be a special friend, neighbor, or relative outside the immediate family. Consistency in school settings helps to predict positive adjustment in children, especially when their home lives are chaotic.

Strategies recommended for parents of second marriages include:

- Discussing and deciding on finances before getting married.
- Building a strong marital bond that will benefit everybody.
- Developing a parenting plan, which likely will involve having the stepparent play a secondary, non-disciplinary role for the first year or two. Letting the children adjust slowly prepares for a successful transition.
- Taking the time to process each change.
- Making sure that big changes are communicated adult-to-adult, not via the children.
- Working with therapists who are specially trained in stepfamily dynamics.

Key factors that contribute to healthy adjustments post-divorce include appropriate parenting, access to the non-residential parent, custody arrangements, and low parental conflict. Appropriate parenting includes providing emotional support, monitoring children's activities, disciplining authoritatively, and maintaining age-appropriate expectations. Finally, the research demonstrates that the best predictor of child's adjustment following divorce is the parents' psychological health and the quality of the parent-child relationship.

Maintaining Healthy Relationships

Mutual respect, shared values and interests, and a mutually felt ability to trust and depend on each other all characterize a responsible friendship. Genuine respect for one's friends is vital for the creation of a positive and responsible friendship. It is much easier to dismiss commitments towards and the needs of those we do not respect. Shared values are the foundation for mutual respect, and shared interests are necessary for the exploration and development of a friendship. Trust and dependability are the cement that holds responsible friendships together.

Individuals can develop positive interpersonal relationships by devoting time to character-building activities that strengthen the traits listed above. They can work to become people who espouse the values that they would like to see in their friends, and they can make efforts toward becoming trustworthy and dependable. Specific techniques that can be applied to develop positive interpersonal relationships with others include active listening and considerate respect for the things others value.

Active listening is the process of repeating back what was said in the form of a question (e.g., if someone tells you, "I'm thinking of taking a vacation, maybe to Florida", you might repeat back, "You're saying that you want to take a vacation to Florida"). These exercises should not be performed mechanically (i.e., parroting); they should be done as a personal reminder to listen to the concerns and interests of others.

Considerate respect for others can be developed by actively asking ourselves what about the current scenario that we are facing would others see as significant. It is an exercise aimed at placing value and emphasis on the priorities of others.

Social support systems are the networks that students develop with their peers that provide support when students experience challenges and difficulties. The support offered by these systems is often emotional and sometimes logistical. Financial support in these relationships is generally inappropriate. Social support systems are vital to students (and individuals in general), especially students who don't have other support mechanisms in place.

The benefits of maintaining healthy peer relationships include having a social support system to assist in difficult times as well as having knowledge of the existence of that system. This means that students can feel confident to take greater risks (within reason) and achieve more because they know the support system is there if they need it.

Conflict Management

Interpersonal conflict is a major source of stress and worry. Common sources of interpersonal conflict include problems with family relationships, competition, and disagreement over values or decisions. Teaching students to manage conflict will help them to reduce stress levels throughout their lives, thereby limiting the adverse health effects of stress. The following is a list of conflict resolution principles and techniques.

1. Think before reacting – In a conflict situation, it is important to resist the temptation to react immediately. You should step back, consider the situation, and plan an appropriate response. Do not react to petty situations with anger.

2. Listen – Be sure to listen carefully to the opposing party. Try to understand the other person's point of view.

3. Find common ground – Try to find some common ground as soon as possible. Early compromise can help to ease the tension.

4. Accept responsibility – In every conflict there is plenty of blame to go around. Admitting when you are wrong shows you are committed to resolving the conflict.

5. Attack the problem, not the person – Personal attacks are never beneficial and usually lead to greater conflicts and hard feelings.

6. Focus on the future – Instead of trying to assign blame for past events, focus on what needs to be done differently to avoid future conflict.

Skill 22.4   **Identifying strategies for maintaining personal emotional and physical health (e.g., stress management, sleep, proper diet)**

Physical activity and inactivity greatly affect many aspects of a person's life, including physical fitness abilities, general health, physical resilience, physical self-confidence, psychological well-being, and cognitive function. Regular physical activity can improve or increase these elements, while inactivity can damage or decrease these elements.

The most obvious and direct benefit of physical activity is the physical dimension, which includes fitness and general health. Regular physical activity leads to improved physical fitness, improved strength and endurance of the muscular and cardio-respiratory systems, and improved function of the circulatory system. Improved function of all these systems means that the body expends far less energy is on day-to-day activities, significantly increasing overall energy levels. Conversely, a lifestyle of physical inactivity will gradually lead to a deterioration of the muscular, cardio-respiratory, and circulatory systems, which leads to decreased energy levels.

Regular physical activity also contributes to increased physical resilience. When coupled with sufficient rest and a healthy diet, physical activity strengthens the musculoskeletal system, which makes the individual less susceptible to injury. Physical activity also tends to improve reflexes and balance, reducing the likelihood of injury. Conversely and as previously mentioned, a lifestyle of physical inactivity leads to a deterioration of the same physical systems that regular exercise strengthens; it also contributes to a gradual "de-sharpening" of reflexes and balance. In sum, these changes increase the likelihood and susceptibility of the individual to injury.

The bridge between physical and psychological benefits is the physical self-confidence derived from regular physical activity. The individual's increased ability to perform physical tasks leads to the growth of their sense of ability to perform any physical activity (for example, you don't have to actually climb ten flights of stairs to know that you could if you wanted to—this is very liberating, as it creates options). Conversely, a lifestyle of physical inactivity, which implies a decreased fitness level, will often eat away at an individual's physical self-confidence.

Regarding psychological well-being, physical activity causes the brain to release **endorphins**, which function to reduce stress levels (prolonged physical endurance activities can produce levels of endorphins that induce a pleasant and healthy "runner's high"). Most physical activities also mix a degree of repetitive motion and action that require directed attention. In combination, this can function as a sort of meditative activity. For all of these reasons, regular physical activity contributes to psychological balance and well-being as well as reduced stress levels. Conversely, a lifestyle of physical inactivity allows physical confidence to deteriorate and removes alternatives of stress-relief, which can contribute negatively to the individual's psychological well-being.

Finally, regular physical activity benefits the circulatory system, which improves blood flow to the brain. This, in turn, leads to increased cognitive function and mental acuity. Those who are physically inactive do not experience these benefits.

Benefits Of Sleep

Sleep gives the body a break from the normal tasks of daily living. During sleep, the body performs many important cleansing and restorative tasks. The immune and excretory systems clear waste and repair cellular damage that accumulates in the body each day. Similarly, the body requires adequate rest and sleep to build and repair muscles. Without adequate rest, even the most strenuous exercise program will not produce muscular development. A lack of rest and sleep leaves the body vulnerable to infection and disease.

Stress management and good nutrition are among the cornerstones of healthy living. Physical education instructors can introduce students to these important concepts through the development of individualized fitness and wellness plans. Fitness and wellness plans should include a concrete exercise plan and a detailed nutritional plan.

Skill 22.5 **Recognizing the effects of substance abuse, factors contributing to substance abuse (e.g., media advertising, peer pressure), and strategies for resisting pressure to use alcohol, tobacco products, and other drugs**

Contributing Factors to Substance Abuse

Factors that contribute to the misuse and abuse of tobacco, alcohol, and other drugs include mental health problems, stress, difficult life circumstances, and peer pressure. Identifying alternatives to substance abuse is an important preventative and coping strategy.

Alternatives to substance use and abuse include regular participation in stress-relieving activities like meditation, exercise, and therapy, all of which can have a relaxing effect. More importantly, the acquisition of longer-term coping strategies (for example, self-empowerment through the practice of problem-solving techniques) is key to maintaining a commitment to alternatives to substance use and abuse.

Aspects of substance abuse treatment that must be considered include the processes of physical and psychological withdrawal from the addictive substance, acquisition of coping strategies and replacement techniques to fill the void left by the addictive substance, limiting access to the addictive substance, and acquiring self-control strategies.

Withdrawal from an addictive substance has both psychological and physical symptoms. The psychological symptoms include depression, anxiety, and strong cravings for the substance. Physical withdrawal symptoms stem from the body, which is adapted to a steady intake of the addictive substance. When removed, the body must adapt to accommodate the no-longer-available substance. Depending on the substance, medical intervention may be necessary.

Coping strategies and replacement techniques, as discussed earlier, center around providing the individual with an effective alternative to the addictive substance as a solution to the situations that they feel would necessitate the substance.

Limiting access to the addictive substance (opportunities for use) is important, because the symptoms of withdrawal and the experiences associated with the substance can provide a strong impetus to return to using it. Recovering addicts should learn strategies of self-control and self-discipline to help them stay off the addictive substance.

Implications of Substance Abuse

Disease and substance abuse issues have significant implications for both individuals and for society as a whole. Specific implications, though, will depend greatly on the perception of the disease or substance abuse problem (defined by the Surgeon General as a disease) in the society. Education that gives the individuals in a society a clear understanding of the nature of diseases—what they are and are not linked to, how they can and cannot be transmitted, and what effects they will and will not exert on the afflicted individuals—will positively impact both the afflicted individual and society as a whole.

This same education is often the deciding factor that dictates the willingness of the community to allocate resources to programs for treatment and prevention. It is this willingness to "get involved" on a societal level that plays a central role in the likelihood of improved resources for substance abuse issues.

On the individual level, one very important implication of disease and substance abuse problems relate to responsible behavior. This is not a simple matter, as both disease and substance abuse problems will often lead to highly impaired judgment, making the choice to act responsibly and seek out help on an individual level much harder to do. Individuals in a society must act responsibly to help those around them who are diseased or in the throes of a substance abuse problem to seek appropriate treatment.

Skill 22.6   Identifying safety practices to avoid accidents and injuries

Basic healthy behaviors reduce the risk of injuries, illness, disease, and other health problems.

Injuries are usually a result of unforeseen accidents. Falls are the leading cause of death among home accidents. Falls occur most frequently among the elderly and young children. The most common location of falls is in bathtubs and showers. Examples of precautions that can help to decrease the risk of falls include using rubber mats in bathtubs and showers, using safety gates to block young children from stairs, wearing appropriate safety equipment during physical activity, and promptly removing ice and snow from steps and sidewalks.

At a more cognitive level, rules, discipline, cooperation, etiquette, and safety practices play a vital role in staying safe during personal performance and other movement-based activities. These activities, by their very nature, will often challenge individuals to push their limitations, both in terms of their current physical and psychological limitations, and in terms of what they might consider to be behaviorally acceptable in competitive situations. Rules and discipline are critical in competitive situations where there is a strong drive to "achieve at any cost" (at least in terms of personal sacrifice and dedication).

Rules and self-discipline are the lines that divide healthy athletes from those who engage in unsportsmanlike behavior and training practices that do not fit into a balanced lifestyle. Similarly, cooperation is the element that allows athletes in a hard-training situation, who are both physically and mentally exhausted, to rely on each other for support. This is a critical factor to healthy training practices. Etiquette is the formalization of these cooperative practices. In situations where individuals might try to push their personal limits beyond what they know they are capable of, safety practices are critical to prevent injuries and accidents.

General Safety Concerns

Safety education related to outdoor pursuits and recreation should emphasize the importance of planning and research. Students should consider in advance what the potential dangers of an activity might be; they should prepare accordingly (for example, students and instructors should examine weather forecasts). Of course, educator supervision is required; first-aid equipment and properly trained educators must be present for all outdoor education activities. Students should use proper safety gear when appropriate (e.g., helmets, harnesses, etc.). Parental consent is also generally required for these types of scenarios.

Actions that Promote Safety and Injury Prevention

The following is a list of practices that promote safety in all types of physical education and athletic activities.

1. Having an instructor who is properly trained and qualified.

2. Organizing the class by size, activity, and conditions of the class.

3. Inspecting buildings and other facilities regularly, and immediately giving notice of any hazards.

4. Avoiding overcrowding.

5. Using adequate lighting.

6. Ensuring that students dress in appropriate clothing and shoes.

7. Presenting organized activities.

8. Inspecting all equipment regularly.

9. Adhering to building codes and fire regulations.

10. Using protective equipment.

11. Using spotters.

12. Eliminating hazards.

13. Teaching students correct ways of performing skills and activities.

14. Teaching students how to use the equipment properly and safely.

Strategies For Injury Prevention

- Participant screenings – evaluate injury history, anticipate and prevent potential injuries, watch for hidden injuries and the reoccurrence of an injury, and maintain communication.

- Standards and discipline – ensure that athletes obey rules of sportsmanship, supervision, and biomechanics.

- Education and knowledge – stay current in knowledge of first aid, sports medicine, sport technique, and injury prevention through clinics, workshops, and communication with staff and trainers.

- Conditioning – programs should be year-long and participants should have access to conditioning facilities in and out of season to produce more fit and knowledgeable athletes who are less prone to injury.

- Equipment – perform regular inspections; ensure proper fit and proper use.

- Facilities – maintain standards and use safe equipment.

- Field care – establish emergency procedures for serious injury.

- Rehabilitation – use objective measures such as power output on an isokinetic dynamometer.

Prevention Of Common Athletic Injuries

- Foot – start with good footwear, foot exercises.

- Ankle – use high top shoes and tape support; strengthen plantar (calf), dorsiflexor (shin), and ankle eversion (ankle outward).

- Shin splints – strengthen ankle dorsiflexors.

- Achilles tendon – stretch dorsiflexion and strengthen plantar flexion (heel raises).

- Knee – increase strength and flexibility of calf and thigh muscles.

- Back – use proper body mechanics.

- Tennis elbow – avoid lateral epicondylitis caused by bent elbow, hitting late, not stepping into the ball, heavy rackets, and rackets with strings that are too tight.

- Head and neck injuries – avoid dangerous techniques (e.g., grabbing a facemask) and carefully supervise dangerous activities like the trampoline.

COMPETENCY 23.0 UNDERSTAND BASIC PHYSICAL EDUCATION PRINCIPLES, PRACTICES, AND ACTIVITIES

Skill 23.1 **Identifying the components of health-related fitness (e.g., cardiovascular endurance, muscular strength, flexibility) and appropriate activities for promoting each of the different components**

There are five health-related components of physical fitness: cardio-respiratory or cardiovascular endurance, muscle strength, muscle endurance, flexibility, and body composition.

Cardiovascular endurance – the ability of the body to sustain aerobic activities (activities requiring oxygen utilization) for extended periods.

Muscle strength – the ability of muscle groups to contract and support a given amount of weight.

Muscle endurance – the ability of muscle groups to contract continually over a period of time and to support a given amount of weight.

Flexibility – the ability of muscle groups to stretch and bend.

Body composition – an essential measure of health and fitness. The most important aspects of body composition are body fat percentage and ratio of body fat to muscle.

Physical activity improves each of the components of physical fitness. Aerobic training improves cardiovascular endurance. Weight training, body support activities, and calisthenics increase muscular strength and endurance. Stretching improves flexibility. All types of physical activity improve body composition by increasing muscle and decreasing body fat.

Activities for Various Objectives, Situations, and Developmental Levels

The following is a list of physical activities that may reduce specific health risks, improve overall health, and develop skill-related components of physical activity. Some of these activities, such as walking and calisthenics, are more suitable to students at beginning developmental levels, while others, such as circuit training and rowing, are best suited for students at more advanced levels of development.

1. Aerobic Dance:
Health-related components of fitness = *cardio-respiratory, body composition.*
Skill-related components of fitness = *agility, coordination.*

2. Bicycling:
Health-related components of fitness = *cardio-respiratory, muscle strength, muscle endurance, body composition.*
Skill-related components of fitness = *balance.*

3. Calisthenics:
Health-related components of fitness = *cardio-respiratory, muscle strength, muscle endurance, flexibility, body composition.*
Skill-related components of fitness = *agility.*

4. Circuit Training:
Health-related components of fitness = *cardio-respiratory, muscle strength, muscle endurance, body composition.*
Skill-related components of fitness = *power.*

5. Cross Country Skiing:
Health-related component of fitness = *cardio-respiratory, muscle strength, muscle endurance, body composition.*
Skill-related components of fitness = *agility, coordination, power.*

6. Jogging/Running:
Health-related components of fitness = *cardio-respiratory, body composition.*

7. Rope Jumping:
Health-related components of fitness = *cardio-respiratory, body composition.*
Skill-related components of fitness = *agility, coordination, reaction time, speed.*

8. Rowing:
Health-related components of fitness = *cardio-respiratory, muscle strength, muscle endurance, body composition.*
Skill-related components of fitness = *agility, coordination, power.*

9. Skating:
Health-related components of fitness = *cardio-respiratory, body composition.*
Skill-related components of fitness = *agility, balance, coordination, speed.*

10. Swimming/Water Exercises::
Health-related components of fitness = *cardio-respiratory, muscle strength, muscle endurance, flexibility, body composition.*
Skill-related components of fitness = *agility, coordination.*

11. Walking (brisk):
Health-related components of fitness = *cardio-respiratory, body composition.*

Cardiovascular Activities

Walking is a good generic cardio-respiratory activity for promoting basic fitness. Instructors can incorporate it into a variety of class settings (not only physical education instructors—for example, a Biology class might include a field trip to a natural setting that would involve a great deal of walking). Walking is appropriate for practically all age groups, but can only serve as noteworthy exercise for students who lead a fairly sedentary lifestyle (athletic students who train regularly or participate in some sport will not benefit greatly from walking).

Jogging or **Running** is a classic cardio-respiratory activity in which instructors can adjust the difficulty level by modifying the running speed or the incline of the track. It is important to stress proper footwear and the gradual increase of intensity to prevent overuse injuries (e.g., stress fractures or shin splints).

Bicycling is another good cardio-respiratory activity that is appropriate for most age groups. Obviously, knowing how to ride a bicycle is a prerequisite, and it is important to follow safety procedures (e.g., ensuring that students wear helmets). An additional benefit of bicycle riding is that it places less strain on the knee joints than walking or running.

Swimming is an excellent cardio-respiratory activity that has the added benefit of working more of the body's muscles more evenly than most other exercises, without excessive resistance to any one part of the body that could result in an overuse injury. To use swimming as an educational cardio-respiratory activity, there must be qualified lifeguards present, and all students must have passed basic tests of swimming ability.

There are many alternatives for cardio-respiratory activities, like **inline skating** and **cross-country skiing**. More importantly, instructors should modify the above exercises to match the developmental needs of the students—for example, younger students should receive most of their exercise in the form of games. An instructor could incorporate running in the form of a game of tag, soccer, or a relay race.

Flexibility Training

Flexibility is the range of motion around a joint or muscle. Flexibility has two major components: static and dynamic. **Static flexibility** is the range of motion without a consideration for speed of movement. **Dynamic flexibility** is the use of the desired range of motion at a desired velocity. These movements are useful for most athletes. **Static active flexibility** refers to the ability to stretch an antagonist muscle using only the tension in the antagonist muscle. **Static-passive flexibility** is the ability to hold a stretch using body weight or some other external force.

Good flexibility can help to prevent injuries during all stages of life and can keep an athlete safe. To improve flexibility, you can lengthen muscles through activities such as swimming, a basic stretching program, or Pilates. These activities all improve the muscles' range of motion. While joints also consist of ligaments and tendons, muscles are the main target of flexibility training. Muscles are the most elastic component of joints, while ligaments and tendons are less elastic and resist elongation. Overstretching tendons and ligaments can weaken joint stability and lead to injury.

Coaches, athletes, and sports medicine personnel should always use stretching methods as part of their training routine for athletes. They help the body to relax and to warm-up for more intense fitness activities.

The following is an example of a flexibility program design:

- **mode:** stretching

- **frequency:** 3 to 7 days/week

- **intensity:** just below individual's threshold of pain

- **time:** 3 sets with 3 reps holding stretches 15 to 30 seconds, with a 60 rest interval between sets

Dynamic stretching is generally very safe and very effective for warming up muscle groups and moderately improving flexibility. When performing dynamic stretches, participants must be careful to avoid sudden, jerky movements.

Static stretching is also safe, if the participant warms up the muscles prior to stretching. Because cold muscles are less elastic, static stretching without adequate warm-up time can lead to injury. Static stretching is very effective in increasing muscle flexibility.

Isometric, PNF, and ballistic stretching are more advanced techniques that require extreme caution and supervision. Most physical trainers believe ballistic stretching (bouncing into stretches) is ineffective and dangerous. Most trainers do not recommend ballistic stretching. PNF and isometric stretching are effective in certain situations such as rehabilitation and advanced training, but require close supervision.

Muscular Strength and Endurance Activities

Possessing the strength and ability to overcome any resistance in one single effort or in repeated efforts over a period of time is known as muscular strength and endurance. They represent the ability to complete a heavy task in a single effort. Muscular strength and endurance not only help in keeping body ailments in check, but also in enabling better performance in any sporting event. Most fitness experts regard calisthenics as the best form of exercise to increase muscular development and strength. Although calisthenics are good beginning exercises, participants should complement them with progressive resistance training later on so that there will be an increase in bone mass and connective tissue strength. Such a combination also helps in minimizing any damages or injuries that are apt to occur at the beginning or initial training stages.

Besides calisthenics and progressive resistance training, aerobics can also help in maintaining muscular strength and endurance.

Muscular strength is the maximum amount of force that one can generate in an isolated movement. **Muscular endurance** is the ability of the muscles to perform a sub-maximal task repeatedly or to maintain a sub-maximal muscle contraction for extended periods. Body-support activities (e.g., push-ups and sit-ups) and callisthenic activities (e.g., rope jumping) are good exercises for young students or beginners of all ages. Such exercises use multiple muscle groups and have minimal risk of injury. At more advanced levels of development, and for those students interested in developing higher levels of strength and muscle mass, weight lifting is the optimal activity.

To improve muscular strength and endurance a student can:

- Train with free weights
- Perform exercises that use an individual's body weight for resistance (e.g., push-ups, sit-ups, dips, etc.)
- Do strength training exercises that incorporate all major muscle groups two times per week

Skill 23.2   Demonstrating knowledge of activities that promote the development of locomotor, nonlocomotor, manipulative, and perceptual awareness skills in children

Motor-development learning theories that pertain to a general skill, activity, or age level are important and necessary background details for effective lesson planning. Motor-skill learning is unique to each individual but does follow a general sequential skill pattern, starting with general gross motor movements and ending with specific or fine motor skills. Teachers must begin instruction at a level where all children are successful and proceed through the activity only to the point where frustration for the majority is hindering performance.

Students must learn the fundamentals of a skill, or subsequent learning of more advanced skills becomes extremely difficult. Instructors must spend enough time on beginning skills to enable them to become second nature. Teaching in small groups with enough equipment for everyone is essential. Practice sessions that are too long or too demanding can cause physical and/or mental burnout. Teaching skills over a longer period of time, but with slightly different approaches, helps to keep students attentive and involved as they internalize the skill. The instructor can then teach more difficult skills while continuing to review the basics. If the skill is challenging for most students, allow plenty of practice time so they retain it before having to use it in a game situation.

Visualizing and breaking the skill down mentally are other ways to enhance the learning of motor movements. Instructors can teach students to "picture" the steps involved and to see themselves executing the skill. An example is teaching dribbling in basketball. Start teaching the skill with a demonstration of the steps involved in dribbling. Starting with the first skill, introduce key language terms, and have students visualize themselves performing the skill. A sample-progression lesson plan to teach dribbling could begin with students practicing while standing still. Next, add movement while dribbling. Finally, introduce how to control dribbling while being guarded by another student.

Knowledge of Activities for Body Management Skill Development

Sequential Development and Activities for Locomotor Skills Acquisition

Sequential Development = crawl, creep, walk, run, jump, hop, gallop, slide, leap, skip, step-hop.

- **Activities to develop walking skills** include walking slower and faster in place; walking forward, backward, and sideways with slower and faster paces in straight, curving, and zigzag pathways with various lengths of steps; pausing between steps; and changing the height of the body.

- **Activities to develop running skills** include having students pretend they are playing basketball, trying to score a touchdown, trying to catch a bus, finishing a lengthy race, or running on a hot surface.

- **Activities to develop jumping skills** include alternating jumping with feet together and feet apart, taking off and landing on the balls of the feet, clicking the heels together while airborne, and landing with a foot forward and a foot backward.

- **Activities to develop galloping skills** include having students play a game of Fox and Hound, with the lead foot representing the fox and the back foot the hound trying to catch the fox (alternate the lead foot).

- **Activities to develop sliding skills** include having students hold hands in a circle and sliding in one direction, then sliding in the other direction.

- **Activities to develop hopping skills** include having students hop all the way around a hoop and hopping in and out of a hoop, reversing direction. Students can also place ropes in straight lines and hop side-to-side over the rope from one end to the other and change (reverse) the direction.

- **Activities to develop skipping skills** include having students combine walking and hopping activities leading up to skipping.

- **Activities to develop step-hopping skills** include having students practice stepping and hopping activities while clapping hands to an uneven beat.

Sequential Development and Activities for Nonlocomotor Skill Acquisition

Sequential Development = stretch, bend, sit, shake, turn, rock and sway, swing, twist, dodge, and fall.

- **Activities to develop stretching** include lying on the back and stomach and stretching as far as possible; stretching as though one is reaching for a star, picking fruit off of a tree, climbing a ladder, shooting a basketball, placing an item on a high self, and yawning.

- **Activities to develop bending** include touching knees and toes then straightening the entire body and straightening the body halfway, bending as though picking up a coin, tying shoes, picking flowers/vegetables, and petting animals of different sizes.

- **Activities to develop sitting** include practicing sitting up from standing, kneeling, and lying positions without the use of hands.

- **Activities to develop falling skills** include first collapsing in one's own space and then pretending to fall like bowling pins, raindrops, snowflakes, a rag doll, or Humpty Dumpty.

Manipulative Skill Development

Sequential Development = striking, throwing, kicking, ball rolling, volleying, bouncing, catching, and trapping.

- **Activities to develop striking** begin with the striking of stationary objects by a participant in a stationary position. Next, the person remains still while trying to strike a moving object. Then, both the object and the participant are in motion as the participant attempts to strike the moving object.

- **Activities to develop throwing** include throwing yarn/foam balls against a wall, then at a big target, and finally at targets decreasing in size.

- **Activities to develop kicking** include alternating feet to kick balloons/beach balls, then kicking them under and over ropes. Change the type of ball as proficiency develops.

- **Activities to develop ball rolling** include rolling different size balls to a wall, then to targets decreasing in size.

- **Activities to develop volleying** include using a large balloon and hitting it with both hands, then hitting it with one hand (alternating hands), and then hitting it using different parts of the body. Change the object as students progress (balloon, beach ball, foam ball, etc.)

- **Activities to develop bouncing** include starting with large balls and using both hands to bounce, then using one hand (alternate hands).

- **Activities to develop catching** include using various objects (balloons, beanbags, balls, etc.) to catch, first catching the object the participant has thrown him/herself, then catching objects someone else threw, and finally increasing the distance between the catcher and the thrower.

- **Activities to develop trapping** include trapping slow and fast rolling balls; trapping balls (or other objects such as beanbags) that are lightly thrown at waist, chest, and stomach levels; and trapping different size balls.

Rhythmic Skill Development

Dancing is an excellent activity for the development of rhythmic skills. In addition, any activity that involves moving the body to music can promote rhythmic skill development.

Skill 23.3   Applying knowledge of basic rules and strategies for developmentally appropriate physical activities, cooperative and competitive games, and sports

Rules for Individual and Dual Sports

Archery:
- Arrows that bounce off the target or go through the target count as 7 points.
- Arrows landing on lines between two rings receive the higher score of the two rings.
- Arrows hitting the petticoat receive no score.

Badminton:
- Intentionally balking the opponent or making preliminary feints results in a fault (side in = loss of serve; side out = point awarded to side in).
- When a shuttlecock falls on a line, it is in play (i.e., a fair play).
- If the striking team hits a shuttlecock before it crosses net, it is a fault.
- Touching the net when the shuttlecock is in play is a fault.
- The same player hitting the shuttlecock twice is a fault.
- The shuttlecock going through the net is a fault.

Bowling:
- There is no score for a pin knocked down by a pinsetter (human or mechanical).
- There is no score for the pins knocked down when any part of the foot, hand, or arm extends or crosses over the foul line (even after the ball leaves the hand) or if any part of the body contacts the division boards, walls, or uprights that are beyond the foul line.
- There is no count for pins displaced or knocked down by a ball leaving the lane before it reaches the pins.
- There is no count when balls rebound from the rear cushion.

Racquetball/Handball:
- A server stepping outside the service area when serving faults.
- The server is out (relinquishes serve) if he or she steps outside of the serving zone twice in succession while serving.
- A server is out if he or she fails to hit the ball rebounding off the floor during the serve.
- The opponent must have a chance to take a position or the referee must call for play before the server can serve the ball.
- The server re-serves the ball if the receiver is not behind the short line at the time of the serve.

- A served ball that hits the front line and does not land back of the short line is "short"; therefore, it is a fault. The ball is also short when it hits the front wall and two sidewalls before it lands on the floor back of the short line.
- A serve is a fault when the ball touches the ceiling from rebounding off the front wall.
- A fault occurs when any part of the foot steps over the outer edges of the service or the short line while serving.
- A hinder (dead ball) is called when a returned ball hits an opponent on its way to the front wall—even if the ball continues to the front wall.
- A hinder is any intentional or unintentional interference of an opponent's opportunity to return the ball.

Tennis:
A player loses a point when:
- The ball bounces twice on his or her side of the net.
- The player returns the ball to any place outside of designated areas.
- The player stops or touches the ball in the air before it lands out-of-bounds.
- The player intentionally strikes the ball twice with the racket.
- The ball strikes any part of a player or racket after the initial attempt to hit the ball.
- A player reaches over the net to hit the ball.
- A player throws his or her racket at the ball.
- The ball strikes any permanent fixture that is out-of-bounds (other than the net).
- A ball touching the net and landing inside the boundary lines is in play (except on the serve, where a ball contacting the net results in a "let" or replay of the point).
- A player fails, on two consecutive attempts, to serve the ball into the designated area (i.e., a double fault).

Appropriate Behavior in Physical Education Activities

Appropriate Student Etiquette/Behaviors: following the rules and accepting the consequences of unfair action, good sportsmanship, respecting the rights of other students, reporting accidents and mishaps, not engaging in inappropriate behavior under peer pressure encouragement, cooperation, paying attention to instructions and demonstrations, moving to assigned places and remaining in the designated space, complying with directions, practicing as instructed to do so, properly using equipment, and not interfering with the practice of others.

Appropriate Content Etiquette/Behaviors: the teacher describing the performance of tasks and students engaging in the task, the teacher assisting students with task performance, and the teacher modifying and developing tasks.

Appropriate Management Etiquette/Behaviors: the teacher directing the management of equipment, students, and space prior to practicing tasks; students getting equipment and partners; the teacher requesting that students stop "fooling around."

Rules of Team Sports

Basketball:
- A player touching the floor on or outside the boundary line is out-of-bounds.
- The ball is out of bounds if it touches anything (a player, the floor, an object, or any person) that is on or outside the boundary line.
- An offensive player remaining in the three-second zone of the free-throw lane for more than three seconds is a violation.
- A ball firmly held by two opposing players results in a jump ball.
- A throw-in is awarded to the opposing team of the last player touching a ball that goes out-of-bounds.

Soccer:
The following are direct free-kick offenses:
- There is hand or arm contact with the ball.
- A player uses his or her hands to hold an opponent.
- A player pushes an opponent.
- The player engages in striking/kicking/tripping or attempting to strike/kick/trip an opponent.
- The goalie uses the ball to intentionally strike an opponent.
- A player jumps at or charges an opponent.
- The player knees an opponent.
- There are any contact fouls.

The following are indirect free-kick offenses:
- The same player plays the ball twice at the kickoff, on a throw-in, on a goal kick, on a free kick, or on a corner kick.
- The goalie delays the game by holding the ball or carrying the ball more than four steps.
- There is a failure to notify the referee of substitutions/re-substitutions, and that player then handles the ball in the penalty area.
- Any person who is not a player enters the playing field without a referee's permission.
- There are unsportsmanlike actions or words following a referee's decision.
- A player dangerously lowers his or her head or raises his or her foot too high to make a play.
- A player resumes play after being ordered off the field.
- Offsides occurs (offensive players must have at least one defender between themselves and the goal when a teammate passes the ball).

- Players attempt to kick the ball when the goalkeeper has possession or they interfere with the goalkeeper to hinder the release of the ball.
- Illegal charging occurs.
- Players leave the playing field without the referee's permission while the ball is in play.

Softball:
- Each team plays nine players in the field (sometimes ten for slow pitch).
- Field positions are one pitcher, one catcher, four infielders, and three outfielders (four outfielders in ten player formats).
- The four bases are 60 feet apart.
- Any ball hit outside of the first or third base line is a foul ball (i.e., runners cannot advance and the pitch counts as a strike against the batter).
- If a batter receives three strikes (i.e., failed attempts at hitting the ball) in a single at bat, he or she strikes out.
- The pitcher must start with both feet on the pitcher's rubber and can only take one step forward when delivering the underhand pitch.
- A team must maintain the same batting order throughout the game.
- Runners cannot lead off.
- Runners may overrun first base, but they can be tagged out if they run off any other base.

A base runner is out if:
- The opposition tags the runner with the ball before he or she reaches a base.
- The ball reaches first base before the runner does.
- The runner runs outside of the base path to avoid a tag.
- A batted ball strikes him or her in fair territory.

Volleyball:
The following infractions by the receiving team result in a point awarded to the serving side, and an infraction by the serving team results in a side-out:
- Illegal serves or serving out of turn occurs.
- Illegal returns, catching, or holding the ball occurs.
- Dribbling occurs or a player touches the ball twice in succession.
- There is contact with the net (two opposing players making contact with the net at the same time results in a replay of the point).
- The ball is touched after it has been played three times without passing over the net.
- A player's foot completely touches the floor over the centerline.
- A player reaches under the net and touches another player or the ball while the ball is in play.
- The players change positions prior to the serve.

Applying Appropriate Strategies to Game and Sport Situations

Basketball Strategies:
Use a zone defense
- To prevent drive-ins for easy lay-up shots.
- When the playing area is small.
- When the team is in foul trouble.
- To keep an excellent rebounder near the opponent's basket.
- When the opponents' outside shooting is weak.
- When opponents have an advantage in height.
- When opponents have an exceptional offensive player, or when the best defenders cannot handle one-on-one defense.

Offensive strategies against zone defense
- Use quick, sharp passing to penetrate the zone, forcing the opposing player out of assigned position.
- Use overloading and mismatching.

Offensive strategies for one-on-one defense
- Use the "pick-and-roll" and the "give-and-go" to screen defensive players to open up offensive players for shot attempts.
- Teams may use free-lancing (spontaneous one-one-one offense), but more commonly they use "sets" of plays.

Soccer Strategies:
- Heading – use the head to pass, to shoot, or to clear the ball.
- Tackling – the objective is to take possession of the ball from an opponent.
- Successful play requires knowledgeable utilization of space.

Badminton Strategies:
Strategies for return of service
- Return serves with shots that are straight ahead.
- Return service so that opponent must move out of his or her starting position.
- Return long serves with an overhead clear or drop shot to the near corner.
- Return short serves with an underhand clear or a net drop to the near corner.

Strategies for serving
- Serve long to the backcourt near the centerline.
- Serve short when the opponent is standing too deep in his or her receiving court to return the serve
- Use a short serve to eliminate a smash return if the opponent has a powerful smash from the backcourt.

Handball or Racquetball Strategies:

- Identify the opponent's strengths and weaknesses.
- Make the opponent use his or her less dominant hand or backhand shots if they are weaker.
- Frequently alternate fastballs and lobs to change the pace (changing the pace is particularly effective for serving).
- Maintain a position near the middle of the court (the well), close enough to play low balls and corner shots.
- Place shots that keep the opponent's position at a disadvantage to return cross-court and angle shots.
- Use high lob shots that go overhead but do not hit the back wall with enough force to rebound and drive an opponent out of position when he or she persistently plays close to the front wall.

Tennis Strategies:

- Lobbing – use a high, lob shot for defense, giving one more time to get back into position.
- Identify the opponent's weaknesses, attack them, and recognize and protect one's own weaknesses.
- Outrun and out-think the opponent.
- Use a change of pace, lobs, spins, approaching the net, and deception at the correct time.
- Hit cross-court (from corner to corner of the court) for maximum safety and an opportunity to regain position.
- Direct the ball where the opponent is not.

Volleyball Strategies:

- Use forearm passes (bumps, digs, or passes) to play balls below the waist, to play hard driven balls, to pass the serve, and to contact balls distant from a player.

Skill 23.4 Recognizing the role that participation in physical activities can play in promoting positive personal and social behaviors

For most people, the development of social roles and appropriate social behaviors occurs during childhood. Physical play between parents and children, as well as between siblings and peers, serves as a strong regulator in the developmental process. Chasing games, roughhousing, wrestling, or practicing sport skills such as jumping, throwing, catching, and striking, are some examples of childhood play. These activities may be competitive or non-competitive; they are important for promoting the social and moral development of both boys and girls. Unfortunately, fathers often engage in this sort of activity more with their sons than their daughters. Regardless of the sex of the child, both boys and girls enjoy these types of activities.

Physical play during infancy and early childhood is central to the development of social and emotional competence. Research shows that children who engage in play that is more physical with their parents, particularly with parents who are sensitive and responsive to the child, exhibited greater enjoyment during the play sessions and were more popular with their peers. Likewise, these early interactions with parents, siblings, and peers are important in helping children to become more aware of their emotions and to learn to monitor and regulate their own emotional responses. Children learn quickly through watching the responses of their parents which behaviors make their parents smile and laugh as well as which behaviors cause their parents to frown and disengage from the activity.

If children want the fun to continue, they engage in the behaviors that please others. As children near adolescence, they learn through rough-and-tumble play that there are limits to how far they can go before hurting someone (physically or emotionally), which results in a termination of the activity or later rejection of the child by peers. These early interactions with parents and siblings are important in helping children learn appropriate behavior in the social situations of sports and physical activities.

Children learn to assess their social competence (e.g., their ability to get along with peers as well as acceptance by peers, family members, teachers, and coaches) in sports through the feedback received from parents and coaches. Initially, authority figures teach children, "You can't do that because I said so." As children approach school age, parents begin the process of explaining why a behavior is right or wrong because children continuously ask, "Why?"

Similarly, when children engage in sports, they learn about taking turns with their teammates, sharing playing time, and valuing rules. They understand that rules are important for everyone, and that without these regulations, the game would become unfair. Learning social competence is continuous as we expand our social arena and learn about different cultures. A constant in the learning process is the role of feedback as we assess the responses of others to our behaviors and comments.

In addition to the development of social competence, sports participation can help youth to develop other forms of self-competence. Most important among these self-competencies is self-esteem. Self-esteem is how we judge our worth; it indicates the extent to which an individual believes he or she is capable, significant, successful, and worthy. Educators have suggested that one of the biggest barriers to success in the classroom today is low self-esteem.

Children develop self-esteem by evaluating abilities and by evaluating the responses of others. Children actively observe parents' and coaches' responses to their performances, looking for signs of approval or disapproval of their behavior. Children often interpret feedback and criticism as either a negative or a positive response to the behavior. In sports, research shows that the coach is a critical source of information that influences the self-esteem of children.

Little League baseball players whose coaches use a "positive approach" to coaching (e.g., more frequent encouragement, positive reinforcement for efforts, and corrective, instructional feedback) had significantly higher self-esteem ratings over the course of a season than children whose coaches used these techniques less frequently. The most compelling evidence supporting the importance of coaches' feedback was found for those children who started with the lowest self-esteem ratings and considerably increased their self-assessment and self-worth throughout the season. In addition to evaluating themselves more positively, low self-esteem children evaluated their coaches more positively than did children with higher self-esteem who played for coaches who used the "positive approach." Moreover, studies show that 95 percent of children who played for coaches trained to use the positive approach signed up to play baseball the next year, compared with 75 percent of the youth who played for untrained adult coaches.

We cannot overlook the importance of enhanced self-esteem on future participation. A major part of the development of high self-esteem is the pride and joy that children experience as their physical skills improve. Children will feel good about themselves as long as their skills are improving. If children feel that their performance during a game or practice is not as good as that of others, or as good as they think mom and dad would want, they often experience shame and disappointment.

Some children will view mistakes made during a game as a failure and will look for ways to avoid participating in the task if they receive no encouragement to continue. At this point, it is critical that adults (e.g., parents and coaches) intervene to help children to interpret the mistake or "failure." We must teach children that a mistake is not synonymous with failure. Rather, a mistake shows us that we need a new strategy, more practice, and/or greater effort to succeed at the task.

Fairness is another trait that physical activities, especially rules-based sports, can foster and strengthen. Children are by nature very rules-oriented, and have a keen sense of what they believe is and isn't fair. Fair play, teamwork, and sportsmanship are all values that stem from proper practice of the spirit of physical education classes. Of course, a pleasurable physical education experience goes a long way towards promoting an understanding of the innate value of physical activity throughout the life cycle.

Social Development

Physical education activities can promote positive social behaviors and traits in a number of different ways. Instructors can foster improved relations with adults and peers by making students active partners in the learning process and delegating responsibilities within the class environment to students. Giving students leadership positions (e.g., team captain) can give them a heightened understanding of the responsibilities and challenges facing educators.

Team-based physical activities like team sports promote collaboration and cooperation. In such activities, students learn to work together, both pooling their talents and minimizing the weaknesses of different team members in order to achieve a common goal. The experience of functioning as a team can be very productive for the development of loyalty between children, and seeing their peers in stressful situations that they can relate to can promote a more compassionate and considerate attitude among students. Similarly, the need to maximize the strengths of each student on a team (who can complement each other and compensate for weaknesses) is a powerful lesson about valuing and respecting diversity and individual differences. Varying students between leading and following positions in a team hierarchy are good ways to help students gain comfort levels being both followers and leaders.

Physical fitness activities incorporate group processes, group dynamics, and a wide range of cooperation and competition issues. Ranging from team sports (which are both competitive and cooperative in nature) to individual competitive sports (like racing), to cooperative team activities without a winner and loser (like a gymnastics team working together to create a human pyramid), there is a great deal of room for the development of mutual respect and support among the students, safe cooperative participation, and analytical, problem-solving, teamwork, and leadership skills.

Teamwork situations are beneficial to students because they create opportunities for them to see classmates with whom they might not generally socialize, and with whom they may not even get along, in a new light. It also creates opportunities for students to develop reliance on each other and to practice interdependence. Cooperation and competition can also offer opportunities for children to practice group work. These situations provide good opportunities to practice analytical thinking and problem-solving in a practical setting.

The social skills and values gained from participation in physical activities include:

- The ability to make adjustments to both self and others by an integration of the individual to society and the environment.

- The ability to make judgments in a group situation.

- Learning to communicate with others and to be cooperative.

- The development of the social phases of personality, attitudes, and values in order to become a functioning member of society (such as being considerate).

- The development of a sense of belonging and acceptance by society.

- The development of positive personality traits.

- Learning for constructive use of leisure time.

- A development of attitude that reflects good moral character.

- Respect of school rules and property.

The above list represents a sample of the socio-cultural benefits of participating in physical activity with others. Physical activity serves as a very important part of the socialization process. Physical activity during the socialization process creates an opportunity for children to define personal comfort levels with different types of physical interaction, as well as to establish guidelines for what is (and is not) acceptable physical behavior as related to their relationship with other individuals.

Participating in physical activity with others is also a step away from the trend of "playground to PlayStation," where students are less and less physically active, and spend less and less time engaging in outdoor physical activity. Physical activity on a socio-cultural level is an important aspect of the struggle against rising obesity levels in the United States, as well as related problems (like heart disease).

COMPETENCY 24.0 UNDERSTAND BASIC ELEMENTS, CONCEPTS, AND TECHNIQUES ASSOCIATED WITH THE ARTS

Skill 24.1 **Identifying the basic elements, concepts, and terms associated with dance, music, drama, and the visual arts (e.g., pathways, rhythm, plot, perspective)**

Elements of Music

Accent - Stress of one tone over others, making it stand out; often it is the first beat of a measure.

Accompaniment - Music that goes along with a more important part; often it is harmony or rhythmic patterns accompanying a melody.

Adagio - Slow, leisurely

Allegro - Lively, brisk, rapid

Cadence - A closing of a phrase or section of music.

Chord - Three or more tones combined and sounded simultaneously.

Crescendo - Gradually growing louder

Dissonance - A simultaneous sounding of tones that produce a feeling of tension or unrest and a feeling that further resolution is needed.

Harmony - The sound resulting from the simultaneous sounding of two or more tones consonant with each other.

Interval - The distance between two tones.

Melody - An arrangement of single tones in a meaningful sequence.

Phrase - A small section of a composition comprising a musical thought.

Rhythm - The regular occurrence of accented beats that shape the character of music or dance.

Scale - A graduated series of tones arranged in a specified order.

Staccato - Separate; sounded in a short, detached manner

Syncopation - The rhythmic result produced when a regularly accented beat is displaced onto an unaccented beat.

Tempo - The rate of speed at which a musical composition is performed.

Theme - A short musical passage that states an idea. It often provides the basis for variations, development, etc.

Timbre - The quality of a musical tone that distinguishes voices.

Elements of Theatre

It is vital that teachers be trained in critical areas that focus on important principles of theatre education. The basic course of study should include state-mandated topics in arts education, instructional materials, products in arts, both affective and cognitive processes of art, world and traditional cultures, and the most recent teaching tools: media and technology.

Areas that should be included:

Acting - Acting requires the student to demonstrate the ability to effectively communicate using skillful speaking, movement, rhythm, and sensory awareness.

Directing - Direction requires management skills to produce and perform an onstage activity. This requires guiding and inspiring students as well as script and stage supervision.

Designing - Designing involves creating and initiating the onsite management of the art of acting.

Scriptwriting - Scriptwriting demands that a leader be able to produce original material and staging for an entire production. It includes writing and designing a story that has performance value.

Each of the above mentioned skills should be incorporated into daily activities with young children. It is important that children are exposed to character development through stories, role-play, and modeling through various teacher guided experiences. Some of these experiences that are age appropriate for early childhood level include puppet theatre, paper dolls, character sketches, storytelling, and re-telling of stories in a student's own words.

Elements of Dance

Dance is an artistic form of self expression that uses the various elements of physical movement such as use of space, time, levels, and force—all of which form a composition.

The primary grades have a gross understanding of their motor movements, whereas older children are apt to have a more refined concept of their bodies. Individual movements should be developed by the instructor with attention to various aspects such as:

1. The **range** of movement or gestures through space.
2. The **direction** of the action or imaginary lines that the body flows through space.
3. The timing of when movements form the dramatic effects.
4. Students being made aware of the **planes** formed by any two areas, such as height and width or width and depth.
5. The introduction of **levels** so that the composition incorporates sitting, standing, and kneeling, etc.
6. Using **elevation**—the degree of lift, as in leaping, and movements that are done under that allusion of suspension.
7. The force and energy of dance can be a reflection of the music, such as adagio (slow music) or allegro (quickening steps).

The various *styles* of dance can be explained as follows:
- Creative dance
- Modern dance
- Social dance
- Dance of other cultures
- Structured dance
- Ritual dance
- Ballet

Creative dance is the type of dance that is most natural to a young child. Creative dance depicts feelings through movement. It is the initial reaction to sound and movement. Older elementary students will often incorporate mood and expressiveness. Stories can be told to release the dancer into imagination.

Isadora Duncan is credited with being the mother of modern dance. **Modern dance** today refers to a concept of dance where the expressions of opposites are developed—for example, concepts of fast-slow, contract-release, varying heights, and levels to fall and recover. Modern dance is based on four principles: substance, dynamism, metakinesis, and form.

Social dance requires a steadier capability that the previous levels. Social dances refer to a cooperative form of dance with respect for sharing the dance floor with others and for one's partner. The social aspect of dance, rather than romantic aspect, represents a variety of customs and pastimes. Changing partners frequently within the dance is something that is subtly important to maintain. Social dance may be in the form of marches, the waltz, or the two-step.

Upper level elementary students can learn dance in connection with historical **cultures** (such as the minuet). The minuet was introduced to the court in Paris in 1650, and it dominated the ballroom until the end of the eighteenth century. The waltz was introduced around 1775; it was an occasion of fashion and courtship. The pomp and ceremony of it all makes for fun classroom experiences. Dance is central to many cultures, and the interrelatedness of teaching history and dance (such as a Native American dance, the Mexican hat dance, or Japanese theater) can be highly beneficial to the students.

Structured dances are recognized by particular patterns, such as the tango. They were made popular in dance studios and gym classes alike.

Ritual dances are often of a religious nature; they may celebrate a significant life event such as a harvest season, the rain season, the gods, or ask for favors in hunting, birth, and death. Many of these themes are carried out in movies and theaters today, but they have their roots in Africa.

Dancing at weddings today is a prime example of ritual dance. The father dances with the bride, then the husband dances with the bride. The two families then dance with one other.

Basic **ballet** uses a barre to practice the five basic positions used in ballet. Alignment is the way in which various parts of the dancer's body are in line with one another while the dancer is moving. It is a very precise dance that is executed with grace and form. The mood and expressions of the music are very important to ballet, as they form the canvas upon which the dance is performed.

Skill 24.2   Recognizing the basic techniques, processes, tools, and materials for creating, performing, and producing works in the various arts

The components and strands of visual art encompass many areas. Students are expected to fine tune observation skills and be able to identify and recreate the experiences that teachers provide for them as learning tools. For example, students may walk as a group on a nature hike, taking in the surrounding elements, and then begin to discuss the repetition found in the leaves of trees, the bricks of the sidewalk, or the size and shapes of the buildings. They may also use such an experience to describe lines, colors, shapes, forms, and textures. Beginning elements of perspective are noticed at an early age. The questions of why buildings look smaller when they are at a far distance and bigger when they are closer are sure to spark the imagination of early childhood students.

Students can also take their inquiries to a higher level of learning with some hands-on activities, such as building three-dimensional buildings using paper and geometric shapes. Eventually, students should acquire higher level thinking skills, such as analysis, in which they will begin to question artists and art work and analyze many different aspects of visual art.

It is vital that students learn to identify the characteristics of visual arts that include materials, techniques, and those processes necessary to establish a connection between art and daily life. Early ages should begin to experience art in a variety of forms. Students should be introduced to the recognition of simple patterns found in the art environment. They must also identify art materials such as clay, paint, and crayons. Each of these types of materials should be introduced and explained for use in daily lessons with young children. Young students may need to be introduced to items that are developmentally appropriate for their age and for their fine motor skills.

Many pre-kindergarten and kindergarten students use oversized pencils and crayons for their first semester. Typically, after this first semester, development occurs enough to enable children to start using smaller sized materials. Students should begin to explore artistic expression at this age using colors and mixing. The color wheel is a vital lesson for young children, as they can begin to learn the uses of primary colors and secondary colors. By the middle of the school year, students should be able to explain the process of mixing. For example, a student may need orange paint but only has a few colors. He or she should be able to determine that by mixing red and yellow, orange is then created.

Teachers should also use variation in lines, shapes, textures, and many different principles of design. By using common environmental figures such as people, animals, and buildings, teachers can base many art lessons on characteristics of readily available examples.

Students should be introduced to as many techniques as possible to ensure that all strands of the visual arts and materials are experienced at a variety of levels. By using original works of art, students should be able to identify visual and actual textures of art and to base their judgments of objects found in everyday scenes. Other examples that can be included as subjects are landscapes, portraits, and still life. The major areas that young students should experience should consist of the following:

- Painting, using tempera or watercolors
- Sculpture, typically using clay or play-dough
- Architecture, performing building or structuring design with 3D materials such as cardboard or poster-board
- Ceramics, using a hollow clay sculpture and pots made from clay and fired in a kiln
- Metalworking (another term for engraving or cutting design or letters into metal), using a sharp tool
- Printmaking or Lithography, drawing a design on a surface and lifting the print from the surface

An excellent opportunity for teachers is to create an "art sample book" with the students. These books can include a different variety of textured materials, including sandpaper and cotton balls. Samples of pieces of construction paper designed into various shapes can be used to represent shapes. String samples can represent the element of lines. The sampling of art should also focus clearly on basic colors. Color can be introduced more in-depth when discussing intensity, the strength, and the lightness or darkness of the colors.

Skill 24.3 Applying knowledge of diverse strategies for promoting critical analysis, cultural perspectives, and aesthetic understandings of the arts

Although the elements of design have remained consistent throughout history, the emphasis on specific aesthetic principles has periodically shifted. Aesthetic standards or principles vary from time period to time period and from society to society.

East and West

An obvious difference in aesthetic principles occurs between works created by eastern and western cultures. Eastern works of art are more often based on spiritual considerations, while much Western art is secular in nature. In attempting to convey reality, Eastern artists generally prefer to use line, local color, and a simplistic view. Western artists tend toward a literal use of line, shape, color, and texture to convey a concise, detailed, complicated view. Eastern artists portray the human figure with symbolic meanings and little regard for muscle structure, resulting in a mystical view of the human experience. Western artists use the "principle of ponderation," which requires the knowledge of both human anatomy and an expression of the human spirit.
In attempts to convey the illusion of depth or visual space in a work of art, Eastern and Western artists use different techniques. Eastern artists generally prefer a diagonal projection of eye movement into the picture plane, and they often leave large areas of the surface untouched by detail. The result is the illusion of vast space, an infinite view that coincides with the spiritual philosophies of the Orient. Western artists rely on several techniques, such as overlapping planes, variation of object size, object position on the picture plane, linear and aerial perspective, color change, and various points of perspective to convey the illusion of depth. The result is space that is limited and closed.

In the application of color, Eastern artists use arbitrary choices of color. Western artists generally rely on literal color usage or emotional choices of color. The end result is that Eastern art tends to be more universal in nature, while Western art is more individualized.

Renaissance and Baroque

An interesting change in aesthetic principles occurred between the Renaissance period (1400-1630 CE) and the Baroque period (1630-1700 CE) in Europe.

The Renaissance period was concerned with the rediscovery of the works of classical Greece and Rome. The art, literature, and architecture were inspired by classical orders, which tended to be formal, simple, and concerned with the ideal human proportions. This means that the paintings, sculptures, and architecture were of a closed nature, composed of forms that were restrained and compact. For example, consider the visual masterpieces of the period: Raphael's painting *The School of Athens*, with its precise use of space; Michelangelo's sculpture *David*, with its compact mass; and the facade of the *Palazzo Strozzi*, with its defined use of the rectangle, arches, and rustication of the masonry.

Compare the Renaissance characteristics to those of the Baroque period. The word "baroque" means "grotesque," which was the contemporary criticism of the new style. In comparison to the styles of the Renaissance, the Baroque was concerned with the imaginative flights of human fancy. The paintings, sculptures, and architecture were of an open nature, composed of forms that were whimsical and free-flowing. Consider again the masterpieces of the period: Ruben's painting *The Elevation of the Cross*, with its turbulent forms of light and dark tumbling diagonally through space; Puget's sculpture *Milo of Crotona*, with its use of open space and twisted forms; and Borromini's *Chapel of St. Ivo*, with a facade that plays convex forms against concave ones.

In the 1920s and 30s, the German art historian, Professor Wolfflin, outlined these shifts in aesthetic principles in his influential book *Principles of Art History*. He arranged these changes into five categories of "visual analysis," sometimes referred to as the "categories of stylistic development." Wolfflin was careful to point out that no style is inherently superior to any other, they are simply indicators of the phase of development of that particular time or society. However, Wolfflin goes on to state, correctly or not, that once the evolution occurs, it is impossible to regress. These modes of perception apply to drawing, painting, sculpture, and architecture. They are as follows:

From a linear mode to a painterly mode
This shift refers to stylistic changes that occur when perception or expression evolves from a linear form that is concerned with the contours and boundaries of objects to a perception or expression that stresses the masses and volumes of objects. To move from viewing objects in isolation to seeing the relationships between objects is an important change in perception. Linear mode implies that objects are stationary and unchanging, while the painterly mode implies that objects and their relationships to other objects are always in a state of flux.

From plane to recession
This shift refers to the perception or expression that evolves from a planar style, wherein the artist views movement in the work in an "up and down" and "side to side" manner, to a recessional style, wherein the artist views the balance of a work in an "in and out" manner. The illusion of depth may be achieved through either style, but only the recessional style uses an angular movement forward and backward through the visual plane.

From closed to open form
This shift refers to the perception or expression that evolves from a sense of enclosure, or limited space in "closed form," to a sense of freedom in "open form." The concept is obvious in architecture, as in buildings that clearly differentiate between "outside" and "inside" space, and buildings that open up the space to allow the outside to interact with the inside.

From multiplicity to unity

This shift refers to an evolution from expressing unity through the use of balancing many individual parts to expressing unity by subordinating some individual parts to others. Multiplicity stresses the balance between existing elements, whereas unity stresses emphasis, domination, and the accent of some elements over other elements.

From absolute to relative clarity

This shift refers to an evolution from works that clearly and thoroughly express everything there is to know about the object to works that express only part of what there is to know, and leave the viewer to fill in the rest from his or her own experiences. Relative clarity, then, is a sophisticated mode, because it requires the viewer to actively participate in the "artistic dialogue." Each of the previous four categories is reflected in this, as linearity is considered to be concise, while painterliness is more subject to interpretation. Planarity is more factual, while recessional movement is an illusion, and so on.

Skill 24.5   Recognizing how the arts can be used as a form of communication, self-expression, and social expression

Music

When we listen to certain music styles, they often connect us to a memory, a time in the past, or even an entire historical period. Very often, classical pieces, such as Bach or Beethoven, create a picture in our minds of the Baroque Period. The historical perspective of music can deepen one's musical understanding.

Throughout history, different cultures have developed different styles of music. Most of the written records of music developed from Western civilization.

Music styles varied across cultures as periods in history. As in the opening discussion, classical music, although still popular and being created today, is often associated with traditional classical periods in history such as the Renaissance.

As world contact merged more and more as civilizations developed and prospered, more and more influence from various cultural styles emerged across music styles. For example, African drums emerged in some Contemporary and Hip Hop music. Also, the Bluegrass music in the United States developed from the "melting pot" contributions from Irish, Scottish, German, and African-American instrumental and vocal traditions.

In addition, the purposes for music changed throughout cultures and times. Music has been used for entertainment, but also for propaganda, worship, ceremony, and communication.

Common Musical Styles

Medieval
Classical Music (loosely encompassing Renaissance and Baroque)
Gospel Music
Jazz
Latin Music
Rhythm and Blues
Funk
Rock
Country
Folk
Bluegrass
Electronic (Techno)
Melodic
Island (Ska, Reggae, and other)
Hip Hop
Pop
African
Contemporary

Visual Art

Teachers should be able to utilize and teach various techniques when analyzing works of art. Students will learn and then begin to apply what they have learned in the arts to all subjects across the curriculum. By using problem-solving techniques and creative skills, students will begin to master the techniques necessary to derive meaning from both visual and sensory aspects of art.

Students should be asked to review, respond, and analyze various types of art. They must learn to be critical, and it is necessary that students relate art in terms of life and human aspects of life. Students should be introduced to the wide range of opportunities to explore such art. Examples may include exhibits, galleries, museums, libraries, and personal art collections. It is imperative that students learn to research and locate artistic opportunities that are common in today's society. Some opportunities for research include reproductions, art slides, films, print materials, and electronic media.

Once students are taught how to effectively research and use sources, they should be expected to graduate to higher level thinking skills. Students should be able to begin to reflect on, interpret, evaluate, and explain how works of art and various styles of art work explain social, psychological, cultural, and environmental aspects of life.

Theatre and Dance

Students are expected to be able to meet a variety of standards set forth for performing arts and dance. It is necessary for young students to master skills such as walking, running, galloping, jumping, hopping, and balance. Students must also learn to discriminate between opposites used to describe performance activities such a high/low, forward/backward, and move/freeze. Creative movements and expressions are necessary tools for dance as well. Students must be able to recall a feeling or personal experience they have had and perform accordingly. Students must learn to discern between different types of dance and dance experiences as well as learn what to expect from performances regarding staging, costume, setting, and music.

Skill 24.6 Demonstrating knowledge of the connections among the arts as well as between the arts and other areas of the curriculum and everyday life

The field of the humanities is overflowing with examples of works of art that hold in common various themes, motifs, and symbols. Themes, motifs, and symbols effortlessly cross the lines between the visual arts, literature, music, theater, and dance. Listed below are a few examples culled from the immense heritage of the arts.

Examples of Works that Share Thematic and Symbolic Motifs

A popular symbol or motif of the fifteenth, sixteenth, and seventeenth centuries was David, the heroic second king of the Hebrews. The richness of the stories pertaining to David and the opportunities for visual interpretation made him a favorite among artists, all of whom cast him in different lights. Donatello's bronze statue of *David* is a classically proportioned nude, portrayed with Goliath's head between his feet. His *David* is not gloating over his kill, but instead seems to be viewing his own, sensuous body with a Renaissance air of self-awareness. Verrocchio's bronze sculpture of *David*, also with the severed head of Goliath, represents a confident young man, proud of his accomplishment, and seemingly basking in praise. Michelangelo, always original, gives us a universal interpretation of the David theme. Weapon in hand, Michelangelo's marble *David* tenses muscles as he summons up the power to deal with his colossal enemy, symbolizing as he does so, every person or community who has had to do battle against overwhelming odds. Bernini's marble *David*, created as it was during the Baroque era, explodes with energy as it captures forever the most dramatic moment of David's action, the throwing of the stone that kills Goliath. Caravaggio's painting, *David and Goliath*, treats the theme in yet another way. Here David is shown as if in the glare of a spotlight, looking with revulsion at the bloodied, grotesque head of Goliath, leaving the viewer to speculate about the reason for disgust. Is David revolted at the ungodliness of Goliath, or is he sickened at his own murderous action?

Symbols related to the David theme include David, Goliath's head, and the stone and slingshot.

Another popular religious motif, especially during the Medieval and Renaissance periods, was the Annunciation. This event was the announcement by the archangel Gabriel to the Virgin Mary that she would bear a son and name him Jesus. It is also believed that this signified the moment of Incarnation. Anonymous medieval artists treated this theme in altarpieces, murals, and illuminated manuscripts. During the thirteenth century, both Nicola Pisano and his son, Giovanni, carved reliefs of the Annunciation theme. Both men included the Annunciation and the Nativity theme into a single panel. Martini's painted rendition of *The Annunciation* owes something to the court etiquette of the day in the use of the heraldic devises of the symbolic colorings and stilted manner of the Virgin. Della Francesca's fresco of the Annunciation borders on the abstract, with it's simplified gestures, its lack of emotion, and the ionic column providing a barrier between Gabriel and Mary. Fra Angelico's *Annunciation* is a lyrical painting, combining soft, harmonious coloring with simplicity of form and gesture.

Symbols related to the Annunciation theme are Gabriel, Mary, the dove of the Holy Spirit, the lily, an olive branch, a garden, a basket of wool, a closed book, and various inscriptions.

During the 1800s, a new viewpoint surfaced in Europe. Intellectuals from several countries became painfully aware of the consequences of social conditions and abuses of the day and set out to expose them.

The English social satirist Hogarth created a series of paintings entitled *Marriage a-la-Mode*, which honed in on the absurdity of arranged marriages. Other works by Hogarth explored conditions that led to prostitution and the poor-house.

In France, Voltaire was working on the play *Candide*, which recounted the misfortunes of a young man while providing biting commentary on the social abuses of the period.

In the field of music, Mozart's *Marriage of Figaro*, based on a play by Beaumarchais, explores the emotion of love as experienced by people from all ages and walks of life. At the same time, it portrays the follies of convention in society.

The Effect of a Particular Work Upon Another

The history of the humanities is replete with examples of artists in every field being influenced and inspired by specific works of others. Influence and inspiration continuously cross the lines between the various disciples in the humanities.

Examples of Artistic Works that Influence Another

A) Michelangelo's painting of the Sistine Chapel ceiling (1508-1512) had a profound effect on Raphael, as evidenced by his fresco *The School of Athens* (1509-1511). The influence can be seen by the treatment of the human figures, particularly in the gestures and chiaroscuro.

B) Virgil's epic, the *Aeneid* (29-19) was a source of inspiration to Dante Alighieri, the renowned Florentine writer who claimed to have memorized the lengthy piece. When Dante wrote *The Divine Comedy* (1308-1321), he included Virgil as his (Dante's) guide through hell and purgatory, a character who represents the highest pinnacle of human reason. In addition, his poetry imitates the form of the *Aeneid* in several places.

C) Dante's *The Divine Comedy* (1308-1321), in turn, served as inspiration for many devotees of the Romantic school in the 1800s. In 1822, the French painter Eugene Delacroix painted a canvas entitled *Dante and Virgil in Hell*, an emotional painting illustrating the anguish of tormented souls drowning in the river Styx, as Dante and Virgil pass over them in a capsizing bark. One of Delacroix's companions read the "Inferno" (the first book of *The Divine Comedy*) to him as he painted. Later, Delacroix claimed that the section that most electrified him was the eighth canto of the "Inferno."

Also during the mid-1800s, the French author, Victor Hugo, wrote a poem entitled *After Reading Dante*, a Romantic piece full of melancholy ruminations. This poem was later used as the basis for a piano program by the Hungarian composer, Franz Liszt (1811-1886); inspired by *The Divine Comedy* and dedicated to the Romantic notion that the arts be related, Liszt wrote the *Dante Symphony*, reflecting the pathos he found in Dante's work.

D) Homer's *Odyssey* (ca 950-ca 800 BCE) has influenced many of the classical writers, but it is surprising to discover that it also influenced the writing of *Ulysses* (1922) by James Joyce. Because the "stream-of-consciousness" technique is so confusing to readers, Joyce used the classical allusions of the *Odyssey* as a sort of map to help guide readers through his work.

Recognizing Connections Between the Arts and Other Disciplines

Whether we express ourselves creatively from the theatrical stage, visually through fine art and dance, or musically, appreciating and recognizing the interrelationships of various art forms are essential to an understanding of ourselves and our diverse society.

By studying and experiencing works of fine art and literature, and by understanding their place in cultural and intellectual history, we can develop an appreciation of the human significance of the arts and humanities through history and across cultures.

Through art projects, field trips, and theatrical productions, students can learn that all forms of art are a way for cultures to communicate with each other and the world at large. By understanding the concepts, techniques, and various materials used in the visual arts, music, dance, and written word, students can begin to appreciate the concept of using art to express oneself. Perhaps they can begin by writing a short story, which can then be transformed into a play with costumes, music, and movement to experience the relationship between different art forms.

The arts have played a significant role throughout history. The communicative power of the arts is notable. Cultures use the arts to impart specific emotions and feelings, to tell stories, to imitate nature, and to persuade others. The arts bring meaning to ceremonies, rituals, celebrations, and recreation. By creating their own art and by examining art made by others, children can learn to make sense of and communicate ideas. This can be accomplished through dance, verbal communication, music, and other visual arts.

Through the arts and humanities, students will realize that although people are different, they share common experiences and attitudes. They will also learn that the use of nonverbal communication can be a strong adjunct to verbal communication.

Skill 24.7   Recognizing the role and function of the arts in various cultures and throughout history

The greatest works in art, literature, music, theater, and dance all mirror universal themes. **Universal themes** are themes that reflect the human experience, regardless of time period, location, or socioeconomic standing. Universal themes tend to fall into broad categories, such as Man vs. Society, Man vs. Himself, Man vs. God, Man vs. Nature, and Good vs. Evil, to name the most obvious. The general themes listed below all fall into one of these broad categories.

Prehistoric Arts (ca 1,000,000-ca 8,000 BCE)
> Major themes of this vast period appear to center around religious fertility rites and sympathetic magic, consisting of the imagery of pregnant animals and faceless, pregnant women.

Mesopotamian Arts (ca 8,000-400 BCE)
> The prayer statues and cult deities of the period point to the theme of polytheism in religious worship.

Egyptian Arts (ca 3,000-100 BCE)
> The predominance of funerary art from ancient Egypt illustrates the theme of preparation for the afterlife and polytheistic worship. Another dominant theme, reflected by artistic convention, is the divinity of the pharaohs. In architecture, the themes are monumentality and adherence to ritual.

Greek Arts (800-100 BCE)
> The sculptures of ancient Greece are replete with human figures—most nude and some draped. The majority of these sculptures represent athletes and various gods and goddesses. The predominant theme is that of the ideal human, in both mind and body. In architecture, the theme is scale based on the ideal human proportions.

Roman Arts (ca 480 BCE- 476 CE)
> Judging from Roman arts, the predominant themes of the period deal with the realistic depiction of human beings and how they relate to Greek classical ideals. The emphasis is on practical realism. Another major theme is the glory in serving the Roman state. In architecture, the theme is rugged practicality mixed with Greek proportions and elements.

Middle Ages Arts (300-1400 CE)

Although the time span is expansive, the major themes remain relatively constant. Since the Roman Catholic Church was the primary patron of the time, most work is religious in nature. The purpose of much of the art is to educate. Specific themes vary from the illustration of Bible stories to interpretations of theological allegory, and the lives of the saints to consequences of good and evil. Depictions of the Holy Family are popular. Themes found in secular art and literature center on chivalric love and warfare. In architecture, the theme is the glorification of God and the education of the congregation to religious principles.

Renaissance Arts (ca 1400-1630 CE)

Renaissance themes include Christian religious depiction (see Middle Ages), but they tend to reflect a renewed interest in all things classical. Specific themes include Greek and Roman mythological and philosophic figures, ancient battles, and legends. Dominant themes mirror the philosophic beliefs of Humanism, emphasizing individuality and human reason, such as those of the High Renaissance, which center around the psychological attributes of individuals. In architecture, the theme is scale based on human proportions.

Baroque Arts (1630-1700 CE)

The predominant themes found in the arts of the Baroque period include the dramatic climaxes of well-known stories, legends, and battles and the grand spectacle of mythology. Religious themes are found frequently, but it is drama and insight that are emphasized, and not the medieval "salvation factor." Baroque artists and authors incorporated various types of characters into their works, often being careful to include minute details. Portraiture focuses on the psychology of the sitters. In architecture, the theme is large scale grandeur and splendor.

Eighteenth Century Arts (1700-1800 CE)

Rococo themes of this century focus on religion, light mythology, portraiture of aristocrats, pleasure, and escapism (and occasionally satire). In architecture, the theme is artifice and gaiety, combined with an organic quality of form. Neo-classical themes center on examples of virtue and heroism, usually in classical settings and historical stories. In architecture, classical simplicity and utility of design is regained.

Nineteenth Century Arts (1800-1900 CE)

Romantic themes include human freedom, equality, civil rights, a love for nature, and a tendency toward the melancholic and mystic. The underlying theme is that the most important discoveries are made within the self, and not in the exterior world. In architecture, the theme is fantasy and whimsy, known as "picturesque." Realistic themes include social awareness and a focus on society victimizing individuals. The themes behind Impressionism demonstrate the constant flux of the universe and the immediacy of the moment. In architecture, the themes are strength, simplicity, and upward thrust as skyscrapers entered the scene.

Twentieth Century Arts (1900-2000 CE)

Diverse artistic themes of the century reflect a parting with traditional religious values and a painful awareness of man's inhumanity to man. Themes also illustrate a growing reliance on science, while simultaneously expressing disillusionment with man's failure to adequately control science. A constant theme is the quest for originality and self-expression, while seeking to express the universal in human experience. In architecture, "form follows function."

Genres By Historical Periods

Ancient Greek Art (ca 800-323 BCE)

Dominant genres from this period are vase paintings, both black-figure and red-figure, and classical sculpture.

Roman Art (ca 480 BCE- 476 CE)

Major genres from the Romans include frescoes (murals done in fresh plaster to affix the paint), classical sculpture, funerary art, state propaganda art, and relief work on cameos.

Middle Ages Art (ca 300-1400 CE)

Significant genres during the Middle Ages include Byzantine mosaics, illuminated manuscripts, ivory relief, altarpieces, cathedral sculpture, and fresco paintings in various styles.

Renaissance Art (1400-1630 CE)

Important genres from the Renaissance include Florentine fresco painting (mostly religious), High Renaissance painting and sculpture, Northern oil painting, Flemish miniature painting, and Northern printmaking.

Baroque Art (1630-1700 CE)

Pivotal genres during the Baroque era include Mannerism, Italian Baroque painting and sculpture, Spanish Baroque, Flemish Baroque, and Dutch portraiture. Genre paintings in still-life and landscape appear prominently in this period.

Eighteenth Century Art (1700-1800 CE)

Predominant genres of the century include Rococo painting, portraiture, social satire, Romantic painting, and Neoclassic painting and sculpture.

Nineteenth Century Art (1800-1900 CE)

Important genres include Romantic painting, academic painting and sculpture, landscape painting of many varieties, realistic painting of many varieties, impressionism, and many varieties of post-impressionism.

Twentieth Century Art (1900-2000 CE)

Major genres of the twentieth century include symbolism, art nouveau, fauvism, expressionism, cubism (both analytical and synthetic), futurism, non-objective art, abstract art, surrealism, social realism, constructivism in sculpture, Pop and Op art, and conceptual art.

Pre Test

Subarea I. Child Development and Learning

1. **What developmental patterns should a professional teacher assess to meet the needs of each student?**

    A. Academic, regional, and family background

    B. Social, physical, and academic

    C. Academic, physical, and family background

    D. Physical, family, and ethnic background

2. **The various domains of development are best described as:**

    A. Integrated

    B. Independent

    C. Simultaneous

    D. Parallel

3. **Which of the following best describes how different areas of development impact each other?**

    A. Development in other areas cannot occur until cognitive development is complete.

    B. Areas of development are inter-related and impact each other.

    C. Development in each area is independent of development in other areas.

    D. Development in one area leads to a decline in other areas.

4. **A student has developed and improved in vocabulary. However, the student is not confident enough to use the improved vocabulary, and the teacher is not aware of the improvement. What is this an example of?**

    A. Latent development

    B. Dormant development

    C. Random development

    D. Delayed development

5. Which of the following has been shown to have the greatest impact on a student's academic performance?

A. The teacher's expectations

B. Strict discipline

C. The student's social skills

D. Measurable objectives

6. According to Piaget, when does the development of symbolic functioning and language first take place?

A. Concrete operations stage

B. Formal operations stage

C. Sensory-motor stage

D. Pre-operational stage

7. Playing team sports at young ages should be done for the following purpose:

A. To develop the child's motor skills

B. To prepare children for competition in high school

C. To develop the child's interests

D. Both A and C

8. The stages of play development from infancy stages to early childhood includes a move from:

A. Cooperative to solitary

B. Solitary to cooperative

C. Competitive to collaborative

D. Collaborative to competitive

9. Which of the following is NOT an economic factor that may influence the health of a child?

A. Pollution

B. Malnutrition

C. Neglect

D. Poor medical care

10. Which of the following is the main source of energy in the diet?

A. Vitamins

B. Minerals

C. Water

D. Carbohydrates

11. Which of the following would be likely to influence a student's learning and academic progress?

A. Relocation

B. Emotional abuse

C. Bullying

D. All of the above

12. Which of the following best explains why emotional upset and emotional abuse can reduce a child's classroom performance?

A. They reduce the energy that students put towards schoolwork.

B. They lead to a reduction in cognitive ability.

C. They contribute to learning disorders such as dyslexia.

D. They result in the development of behavioral problems.

13. A teacher has a class with several students from low income families in it. What would it be most important for a teacher to consider when planning homework assignments to ensure that all students have equal opportunity for academic success?

A. Access to technology

B. Ethnicity

C. Language difficulties

D. Gender

14. Family members with high levels of education often have high expectations for student success. This shows how students are influenced by their family's:

A. Attitude

B. Resources

C. Income

D. Culture

15. Why is it most important for teachers to ensure that students from different economic backgrounds have access to the resources they need to acquire the academic skills being taught?

A. All students must work together on set tasks.

B. All students must achieve the same results in performance tasks.

C. All students must have equal opportunity for academic success.

D. All students must be fully included in classroom activities.

16. A teacher attempting to create a differentiated classroom should focus on incorporating activities that:

A. Favor academically advanced students

B. Challenge special education students to achieve more

C. Are suitable for whichever group of students is the majority

D. Meet the needs of all the students in the class

17. When developing lessons, it is important that teachers provide equity in pedagogy so that:

A. Unfair labeling of students will not occur

B. Student experiences will be positive

C. Students will achieve academic success

D. All of the above

18. Which of the following is NOT a communication issue related to diversity within the classroom?

A. Learning disorders

B. Sensitive terminology

C. Body language

D. Discussing differing viewpoints and opinions

19. One common factor for students with all types of disabilities is that they are also likely to demonstrate difficulty with:

A. Social skills

B. Cognitive skills

C. Problem-solving skills

D. Decision-making skills

20. **A student does not respond to any signs of affection and responds to other children by repeating back what they have said. What condition is the student most likely to have?**

    A.   Mental retardation

    B.   Autism

    C.   Giftedness

    D.   Hyperactivity

21. **Which of the following conditions is more common for girls than boys?**

    A.   Attention deficit disorder

    B.   Aggression

    C.   Phobias

    D.   Autism

22. **In successful inclusion of students with disabilities:**

    A.   A variety of instructional arrangements are available

    B.   School personnel shift the responsibility for learning outcomes to the student

    C.   The physical facilities are used as they are

    D.   Regular classroom teachers have sole responsibility for evaluating student progress

23. **Mr. Gorman has taught a concept to his class. All of the students have grasped the concept except for Sam. Mr. Gorman should:**

    A.   Reteach the concept to the whole class in exactly the same way

    B.   Reteach the concept to Sam in exactly the same way

    C.   Reteach the concept to Sam in a different way

    D.   Reteach the concept to the whole class in a different way

24. **Mrs. Gomez has a fully integrated early childhood curriculum. This is beneficial to students because it:**

    A. Is easier to plan for and maintain

    B. Allows students to apply their unique skills

    C. Helps the students see the relationships between subjects and concepts

    D. Provides opportunities for social interaction

Subarea II. Communication, Language and Literacy Development

25. **The relationship between oral language and reading skills is best described as:**

    A. Reciprocal

    B. Inverse

    C. Opposite

    D. There is no relationship.

26. **A teacher is showing students how to construct grammatically correct sentences. What is the teacher focusing on?**

    A. Morphology

    B. Syntax

    C. Semantics

    D. Pragmatics

27. **A teacher writes the following words on the board: cot, cotton, and cottage. What is the teacher most likely teaching the students about?**

    A. Morphology

    B. Syntax

    C. Semantics

    D. Pragmatics

28. While standing in line at the grocery store, three-year-old Megan says to her mother in a regular tone of voice, "Mom, why is that woman so fat?" What does this indicate a lack of understanding of?

A. Syntax

B. Semantics

C. Morphology

D. Pragmatics

29. Which of the following is the first component of the constructivist model?

A. There are at least seven different types of learning.

B. Learning depends on the social environment.

C. Learner creates knowledge

D. Learning progresses through set stages.

30. Students are about to read a text that contains words that will need to be understood for the students to understand the text. When should the vocabulary be introduced to students?

A. Before reading

B. During reading

C. After reading

D. It should not be introduced.

31. Which of the following are examples of temporal words?

A. Beside and behind

B. Hotter and colder

C. In and on

D. Before and after

32. Which principle of Stephen Krashen's research suggests that the learning of grammatical structures is predictable?

A. The affective filter hypothesis

B. The input hypothesis

C. The natural order hypothesis

D. The monitor hypothesis

33. Above what age does learning a language become increasingly difficult?

 A. 3

 B. 5

 C. 7

 D. 10

34. Ms. Chomski is presenting a new story to her class of first graders. In the story, a family visits their grandparents where they all gather around a record player and listen to music. Many students do not understand what a record player is, especially some children for whom English is not their first language. Which of the following would Ms. Chomski be best to do?

 A. Discuss what a record player is with her students

 B. Compare a record player with a CD player

 C. Have students look up record player in a dictionary

 D. Show the students a picture of a record player

35. Jose moved to the United States last month. He speaks little to no English at this time. His teacher is teaching the class about habitats in science and has chosen to read a story about various habitats to the class. The vocabulary is difficult. What should Jose's teacher do with Jose? (Skill 5.3; Average rigor)

 A. Provide Jose with additional opportunities to learn about habitats

 B. Read the story to Jose multiple times

 C. Show Jose pictures of habitats from his native country

 D. Excuse Jose from the assignment

36. In the early childhood classroom, it is important to limit teacher talk. What is the main problem with teacher talk?

A. It is often one sided and limited.

B. The vocabulary is too difficult for children.

C. It promotes misbehavior.

D. It only creates gains in receptive language.

37. Which of the following is a convention of print that children learn during reading activities?

A. The meaning of words

B. The left to right motion

C. The purpose of print

D. The identification of letters

38. In her kindergarten class, Mrs. Thomas has been watching the students in the drama center. She has watched the children pretend to complete a variety of magic tricks. Mrs. Thomas decides to use stories about magic to share with her class. Her decision to incorporate their interests into the reading shows that Mrs. Thomas understands that:

A. Including student interests is important at all times

B. Teaching by themes is crucial for young children

C. Young children respond to literature that reflects their lives

D. Science fiction and fantasy are the most popular genres

39. Which of the following is NOT a characteristic of a fable?

A. Have animal characters that act like humans

B. Considered to be true

C. Teaches a moral

D. Reveals human foibles

40. Alphabet books are classified as:

    A. Concept books

    B. Easy-to-read books

    C. Board books

    D. Pictures books

41. The works of Paul Bunyan, John Henry, and Pecos Bill are all exaggerated accounts of individuals with superhuman strength. What type of literature are these works?

    A. Fables

    B. Fairytales

    C. Tall tales

    D. Myths

42. Which of the following is NOT a motivation behind providing reading activities, including reading aloud, to young children?

    A. Developing word consciousness skills

    B. Developing functions of print skills

    C. Developing phonics skills

    D. Developing language skills

43. Which of the following is an appropriate way for students to respond to literature?

    A. Art

    B. Drama

    C. Writing

    D. All of the above

44. John is having difficulty reading the word reach. In isolation, he pronounces each sound as /r/ /ee/ /sh/. Which of the following is a possible instructional technique which could help solve John's reading difficulty?

    A. Additional phonemic awareness instruction

    B. Additional phonics instruction

    C. Additional skill and drill practice

    D. Additional minimal pair practice

45. According to Marilyn Jager Adams, which skill would a student demonstrate by identifying that cat does not belong in the group of words containing dog, deer, and dress?

A. Recognize the odd member in a group

B. Replace sounds in words

C. Count the sounds in a word

D. Count syllables in a word

46. Which of the following is NOT true about phonological awareness?

A. It may involve print.

B. It is a prerequisite for spelling and phonics.

C. Activities can be done by the children with their eyes closed.

D. It starts before letter recognition is taught.

47. Which of the following explains a significant difference between phonics and phonemic awareness?

A. Phonics involves print, while phonemic awareness involves language.

B. Phonics is harder than phonemic awareness.

C. Phonics involves sounds, while phonemic awareness involves letters.

D. Phonics is the application of sounds to print, while phonemic awareness is oral.

48. To decode is to:

A. Construct meaning

B. Sound out a printed sequence of letters

C. Use a special code to decipher a message

D. Revise for errors in grammar

49. Ms. Walker's lesson objective is to teach her first graders the concept of morphology in order to improve their reading skills. Which group of words would be most appropriate for her to use in this lesson?

A. Far, farm, farmer

B. Far, feather, fever

C. Far, fear, fare

D. Far, fare, farce

50. Which stage of reading skill development occurs first?

A. Schema stage

B. Early semantic stage

C. Orthographic stage

D. Simultaneous stage

51. Which of the following is an important feature of vocabulary instruction according to the National Reading Panel?

A. Repetition of vocabulary items

B. Keeping a consistent task structure at all times

C. Teaching vocabulary in more than one language

D. Isolation vocabulary instruction from other subjects

52. The attitude an author takes toward his or her subject is the:

A. Style

B. Tone

C. Point of view

D. Theme

53. George has read his second graders three formats of the story "The Three Little Pigs." One is the traditional version, one is written from the wolf's point of view, and the third is written from the first pig's point of view. As George leads a discussion on the three texts with his students, he is trying to help his students develop their ability to:

A. Compare and contrast texts

B. Understand point of view

C. Recognize metaphors

D. Rewrite fictional stories

54. What is the first step in developing writing skills?

A. Early writing

B. Experimental writing

C. Role play writing

D. Conventional writing

55. Which of the following is NOT a prewriting strategy?

A. Analyzing sentences for variety

B. Keeping an idea book

C. Writing in a daily journal

D. Writing down whatever comes to mind

56. Which of the following is probably the most important step for the writer in the writing process?

A. Revision

B. Discovery

C. Conclusion

D. Organization

57. The students in Tina's classroom are working together in pairs. Each student is reading another student's paper and asking who, what, when, where, why, and who questions. What is this activity helping the students to do?

A. Draft their writing

B. Paraphrase their writing

C. Revise their writing

D. Outline their writing

58. Young children learning to write commonly grip the pencil:

A. Too far from the point

B. With the wrong hand

C. With too many fingers

D. Too tightly

59. Which of the following approaches to student writing assignments is most likely to lead to students becoming disinterested?

A. Designing assignments where students write for a variety of audiences.

B. Designing assignments where the teacher is the audience.

C. Designing assignments where students write to friends and family.

D. Designing assignments where students write to real people such as mayors, the principle, or companies.

60. As a part of prewriting, students should identify their audience. Which of the following questions will help students to identify their audience?

A. Why is the audience reading my writing?

B. What does my audience already know about my topic?

C. Both A and B

D. None of the above

61. **Which of these describes the best way to teach spelling?**

    A. At the same time that grammar and sentence structure is taught.

    B. Within the context of meaningful language experiences.

    C. Independently so that students can concentrate on spelling.

    D. In short lessons as students pick up spelling almost immediately.

62. **When editing, teachers should direct students to:**

    A. Edit for general understanding, while ignoring grammar and spelling.

    B. Edit for one specific purpose at a time.

    C. Identify all spelling, capitalization, and punctuation errors.

    D. Be critical of their work and that of others.

Subarea III. Learning in the Content Areas

63. **Kindergarten students are participating in a calendar time activity. One student adds a straw to the "ones can" to represent that day of school. What math principle is being reinforced?**

    A. Properties of a base ten number system

    B. Sorting

    C. Counting by twos

    D. Even and odd numbers

64. **First grade students are arranging four small squares of identical size to form a larger square. Each small square represents what part of the larger square?**

    A. One half

    B. One whole

    C. One fourth

    D. One fifth

65. What is the answer to this problem?

    25 ÷ 5 =

    A. 5

    B. 30

    C. 125

    D. 20

66. Third grade students are studying percents. When looking at a circle graph divided into three sections, they see that one section is worth 80% and one section is worth 5%. What will the remaining section be worth?

    A. 100%

    B. 85%

    C. 75%

    D. 15%

67. Which of the following letters does NOT have a line of symmetry?

    A. O

    B. D

    C. M

    D. J

68. Kindergarten students are doing a butterfly art project. They fold paper in half. On one half, they paint a design. Then they fold the paper closed and reopen. The resulting picture is a butterfly with matching sides. What math principle does this demonstrate?

    A. Slide

    B. Rotate

    C. Symmetry

    D. Transformation

69. What number comes next in this pattern?

    3, 8, 13, 18, ____

    A. 21

    B. 26

    C. 23

    D. 5

70. **What is the main purpose of having kindergarten students count by twos?**

   A. To hear a rhythm

   B. To recognize patterns in numbers

   C. To practice addition

   D. To become familiar with equations

71. **The term *millimeters* indicates which kind of measurement?**

   A. Volume

   B. Weight

   C. Length

   D. Temperature

72. **What type of graph would be best to use to show changes in the height of a plant over the course of a month?**

   A. Circle graph

   B. Bar graph

   C. Line graph

   D. Pictograph

73. **A teacher completes a survey of student eye color. The teacher then creates a graph so students can compare how many students have each eye color. What type of graph should be used?**

   A. Bar graph

   B. Pictograph

   C. Circle graph

   D. Line graph

74. **Which of the following skills would a student develop first?**

   A. Understanding place value

   B. Recognizing number patterns

   C. Counting objects

   D. Solving number problems

75. Maddie is a first grade teacher who understands the importance of including the family when providing instruction. She wants to take several steps to provide families with a connection to what the students are doing in her math class. Which of the following is NOT a strategy she could incorporate?

    A. Including a math portion in her regular newsletter

    B. Incorporating manipulatives into her math lessons

    C. Translating math homework into the native language of the students in her classroom

    D. Having a family math night at school

76. George has successfully mastered his basic addition facts. However, as his teacher presents more complex addition problems, it is obvious to him that George is lacking a basic understanding of the concept of addition. What would George's teacher be best to do to increase his basic understanding?

    A. Provide additional instruction with hands on materials

    B. Have George practice his addition facts more frequently

    C. Have George complete more challenging addition problems

    D. Provide George with remediation

77. Carrie approaches her teacher after class and expresses her personal frustration with math and her feeling that she will never get it. Which of the following is NOT a suitable method Carrie's teacher can utilize to improve Carrie's feelings about math?

   A. Incorporating some of Carrie's specific interests into math lessons

   B. Holding Carrie to high expectations

   C. Sharing with Carrie her own struggles and dislike for math

   D. Providing Carrie with extra positive reinforcement and encouragement

78. The principal walks into your classroom during math class. He sees your students making cake mixtures. Later, the principal questions your lesson. What would be the best explanation for your lesson?

   A. The students earned a reward time and it was free choice.

   B. You were teaching the students how math is used in real-life situations.

   C. You had paperwork to complete and needed the time to complete it.

   D. It kept the students interested in math and prevented boredom.

79. What is a large, rotating, low-pressure system accompanied by heavy precipitation and strong winds known as?

   A. A hurricane

   B. A tornado

   C. A thunderstorm

   D. A tsunami

80. **What does a primary consumer most commonly refer to?**

    A. Herbivore

    B. Autotroph

    C. Carnivore

    D. Decomposer

81. **Airplanes generate pressure and remain balanced by:**

    A. Fast air movement over wings and slow movement under wings

    B. Slow air movement over wings and fast movement under wings

    C. Air movement that is equal above and below wings

    D. Air movement that only occurs over the wings

82. **The breakdown of rock due to acid rain is an example of:**

    A. Physical weathering

    B. Frost wedging

    C. Chemical weathering

    D. Deposition

83. **What is the last step in the scientific method?**

    A. Pose a question

    B. Draw a conclusion

    C. Conduct a test

    D. Record data

84. **Which term best describes Newton's universal gravitation?**

    A. Theory

    B. Hypothesis

    C. Inference

    D. Law

85. **When teaching science, which of the following is a method of focusing on students' intrinsic motivation?**

    A. Adapting the lessons to students' interests

    B. Providing regular feedback

    C. Supplying rewards for the highest achievers

    D. Having regular science tests

86. **What does geography include the study of?**

    A. Location

    B. Distribution of living things

    C. Distribution of the earth's features

    D. All of the above

87. **Economics is the study of how a society allocates its scarce resources to satisfy:**

    A. Unlimited and competing wants

    B. Limited and competing wants

    C. Unlimited and cooperative wants

    D. Limited and cooperative wants

88. **The two elements of a market economy are:**

    A. Inflation and deflation

    B. Supply and demand

    C. Cost and price

    D. Wants and needs

89. **Who has the power to veto a bill that has passed the House of Representatives and the Senate?**

    A. The President

    B. The Vice President

    C. The Speaker of the House

    D. Any member of Congress

90. Which part of a map shows the relationship between a unit of measurement on the map versus the real world measure on the Earth?

A. Scale

B. Title

C. Legend

D. Grid

91. What is the most important focus in developing social studies skills during the early years?

A. Recalling facts

B. Understanding statistics

C. Discussing ideas

D. Memorizing rights and responsibilities

92. What is one of the ten essential themes identified by the National Council for Social Studies?

A. Culture

B. Lifestyle

C. Population

D. Democracy

93. Which subject would a color wheel most likely be used for?

A. Visual arts

B. Music

C. Movement

D. Drama

94. A student art sample book would include cotton balls and sand paper to represent:

A. Color

B. Lines

C. Texture

D. Shape

95. Which terms refers to the arrangement of one or more items so that they appear symmetrical or asymmetrical?

A. Balance

B. Contrast

C. Emphasis

D. Unity

96. The four principles of modern dance are substance, form, metakinesis, and:

    A. Dynamism

    B. Function

    C. Space

    D. Performance

97. What should the arts curriculum for early childhood avoid?

    A. Judgment

    B. Open expression

    C. Experimentation

    D. Discovery

98. What would the viewing of a dance company performance be most likely to promote?

    A. Critical-thinking skills

    B. Appreciation of the arts

    C. Improvisation skills

    D. Music vocabulary

99. In which subject is it most important for students to work with costumes and props?

    A. Visual arts

    B. Music

    C. Movement

    D. Drama

100. According to Charles Fowler, why is it important for arts to be incorporated into the teaching of other subject areas?

    A. It reduces loss of interest in the subject.

    B. It enhances the likelihood that students will retain the information.

    C. It provides a three dimensional view of the subject.

    D. It encourages the development of personal connections with the subject.

Answer Key: Pre Test

1.	B	35.	A	69.	C
2.	A	36.	A	70.	B
3.	B	37.	B	71.	C
4.	A	38.	C	72.	C
5.	A	39.	B	73.	A
6.	D	40.	A	74.	C
7.	D	41.	C	75.	B
8.	B	42.	C	76.	A
9.	A	43.	D	77.	C
10.	D	44.	A	78.	B
11.	D	45.	A	79.	A
12.	A	46.	A	80.	A
13.	A	47.	D	81.	A
14.	A	48.	B	82.	C
15.	C	49.	A	83.	B
16.	D	50.	A	84.	D
17.	D	51.	A	85.	A
18.	A	52.	B	86.	D
19.	A	53.	A	87.	A
20.	B	54.	C	88.	B
21.	C	55.	A	89.	A
22.	A	56.	A	90.	A
23.	C	57.	C	91.	C
24.	C	58.	D	92.	A
25.	A	59.	B	93.	A
26.	B	60.	C	94.	C
27.	A	61.	B	95.	A
28.	D	62.	B	96.	A
29.	C	63.	A	97.	A
30.	A	64.	C	98.	B
31.	D	65.	A	99.	D
32.	C	66.	D	100.	C
33.	C	67.	D		
34.	D	68.	C		

Rationales with Sample Questions: Pre Test

Subarea I. Child Development and Learning

1. **What developmental patterns should a professional teacher assess to meet the needs of each student? (**

   A. Academic, regional, and family background
   B. Social, physical, and academic
   C. Academic, physical, and   family background
   D. Physical, family, and ethnic background

Answer B: Social, physical, and academic

The effective teacher applies knowledge of physical, social, and academic developmental patterns and of individual differences, to meet the instructional needs of all students in the classroom.

2. **The various domains of development are best described as:**

   A. Integrated
   B. Independent
   C. Simultaneous
   D. Parallel

Answer A: Integrated

The most important premise of child development is that all domains of development (physical, social, and academic) are integrated.

3. **Which of the following best describes how different areas of development impact each other?**

    A. Development in other areas cannot occur until cognitive development is complete.
    B. Areas of development are inter-related and impact each other.
    C. Development in each area is independent of development in other areas.
    D. Development in one area leads to a decline in other areas.

Answer B: Areas of development are inter-related and impact each other.

Child development does not occur in a vacuum. Each element of development impacts other elements of development. For example, as cognitive development progresses, social development often follows. The reason for this is that all areas of development are fairly inter-related.

4. **A student has developed and improved in vocabulary. However, the student is not confident enough to use the improved vocabulary, and the teacher is not aware of the improvement. What is this an example of?**

    A. Latent development
    B. Dormant development
    C. Random development
    D. Delayed development

Answer A: Latent development

Latent development refers to the way that development in students may not always be observable. A student that has developed and improved in the area of vocabulary, but lacks the confidence to use the vocabulary would not show any outward signs of the development, and so the change may remain hidden. Teachers should be aware of this in order to identify a child's future or near-future capabilities.

5. Which of the following has been shown to have the greatest impact on a student's academic performance?

    A.   The teacher's expectations
    B.   Strict discipline
    C.   The student's social skills
    D.   Measurable objectives

Answer A: The teacher's expectations

Considerable research has been done, over several decades, regarding student performance. Time and again, a direct correlation has been demonstrated between the teacher's expectations for a particular student and that student's academic performance. This may be unintended and subtle, but the effects are manifest and measurable.

6. According to Piaget, when does the development of symbolic functioning and language first take place?

    A.   Concrete operations stage
    B.   Formal operations stage
    C.   Sensory-motor stage
    D.   Pre-operational stage

Answer D: Pre-operational stage

The pre-operational stage is where children begin to understand symbols. For example, as they learn language, they begin to realize that words are symbols of thoughts, actions, items, and other elements in the world. This stage lasts into early elementary school.

7. Playing team sports at young ages should be done for the following purpose:

    A.   To develop the child's motor skills
    B.   To prepare children for competition in high school
    C.   To develop the child's interests
    D.   Both A and C

Answer D: Both A and C

Sports, for both boys and girls, can be very valuable. Parents and teachers, though, need to remember that sports at young ages should only be for the purpose of development of interests and motor skills—not competition. Many children will learn that they do not enjoy sports, and parents and teachers should be respectful of these decisions.

8. **The stages of play development from infancy stages to early childhood includes a move from:**

    A. Cooperative to solitary
    B. Solitary to cooperative
    C. Competitive to collaborative
    D. Collaborative to competitive

Answer B: Solitary to cooperative

The stages of play development move from mainly solitary in the infancy stages to cooperative in early childhood. However, even in early childhood, children should be able to play on their own and entertain themselves from time to time.

9. **Which of the following is NOT an economic factor that may influence the health of a child?**

    A. Pollution
    B. Malnutrition
    C. Neglect
    D. Poor medical care

Answer A: Pollution

Malnutrition, neglect, and poor medical care are economic factors that may influence the health of a child. Pollution could influence the health of a child, but it is not an economic factor.

10. **Which of the following is the main source of energy in the diet?**

    A. Vitamins
    B. Minerals
    C. Water
    D. Carbohydrates

Answer D: Carbohydrates

The components of nutrition are carbohydrates, proteins, fats, vitamins, minerals, and water. Carbohydrates are the main source of energy (glucose) in the human diet. Common sources of carbohydrates are fruits, vegetables, grains, dairy products, and legumes.

11. **Which of the following would be likely to influence a student's learning and academic progress?**

    A. Relocation
    B. Emotional abuse
    C. Bullying
    D. All of the above

Answer D: All of the above

Children can be influenced by social and emotional factors. Relocation, emotional, abuse, and bullying can all have a negative impact on a student's learning and academic progress.

12. **Which of the following best explains why emotional upset and emotional abuse can reduce a child's classroom performance?**

    A. They reduce the energy that students put towards schoolwork.
    B. They lead to a reduction in cognitive ability.
    C. They contribute to learning disorders such as dyslexia.
    D. They result in the development of behavioral problems.

Answer A: They reduce the energy that students put towards schoolwork.

Although cognitive ability is not lost due to abuse, neglect, emotional upset, or lack of verbal interaction, the child will most likely not be able to provide as much intellectual energy as the child would if none of these things were present. This explains why classroom performance is often negatively impacted.

13. **A teacher has a class containing several students from low income families. What would be the most important factor for a teacher to consider when planning homework assignments to ensure that all students have equal opportunity for academic success?**

    A. Access to technology
    B. Ethnicity
    C. Language difficulties
    D. Gender

Answer A: Access to technology

Families with higher incomes are able to provide increased opportunities for students. Students from lower income families will need to depend on the resources available from the school system and the community. To ensure that all students have equal opportunity for academic success, teachers should plan assessments so that not having access to technology does not disadvantage students from low income families.

14. **Family members with high levels of education often have high expectations for student success. This shows how students are influenced by their family's:**

    A. Attitude
    B. Resources
    C. Income
    D. Culture

Answer A: Attitude

Parental/family influences on students include the influence of attitude. Family members with high levels of education often have high expectations for student success and this can have a positive impact on the student. The opposite can occur for some students from families with low levels of education. However, some families have high expectations for student success based on aspirations for their children regardless of their own status.

15. **Why is it most important for teachers to ensure that students from different economic backgrounds have access to the resources they need to acquire the academic skills being taught?**

    A. All students must work together on set tasks.
    B. All students must achieve the same results in performance tasks.
    C. All students must have equal opportunity for academic success.
    D. All students must be fully included in classroom activities.

Answer C: All students must have equal opportunity for academic success.

The economic backgrounds of students can impact the resources they have. Regardless of the positive or negative impacts on the students' education from outside sources, it is the teacher's responsibility to ensure that all students in the classroom have an equal opportunity for academic success. This includes ensuring that all students have equal access to the resources needed to acquire the skills being taught.

16. **A teacher attempting to create a differentiated classroom should focus on incorporating activities that:**

    A. Favor academically advanced students
    B. Challenge special education students to achieve more
    C. Are suitable for whichever group of students is the majority
    D. Meet the needs of all the students in the class

Answer D: Meet the needs of all the students in the class

A differentiated classroom is one that meets the needs of special education students, the regular mainstream students, and those that are academically advanced. The purpose of the differentiated classroom is to provide appropriate activities for students at all levels.

17. **When developing lessons, it is important that teachers provide equity in pedagogy so that:**

    A.   Unfair labeling of students will not occur
    B.   Student experiences will be positive
    C.   Students will achieve academic success
    D.   All of the above

Answer D: All of the above

When there is equity pedagogy, teachers can use a variety of instructional styles to facilitate diversity in cooperative learning and individualized instruction that will provide more opportunities for positive student experiences and academic success. Empowering the school culture and climate by establishing an anti-bias learning environment and promoting multicultural learning inclusion will also discourage unfair labeling of certain students.

18. **Which of the following is NOT a communication issue related to diversity within the classroom?**

    A.   Learning disorders
    B.   Sensitive terminology
    C.   Body language
    D.   Discussing differing viewpoints and opinions

Answer A: Learning disorders

There are several communication issues that the teacher in a diverse classroom should be aware of. These include being sensitive to terminology, being aware of body language, and emphasizing the discussion of differing viewpoints and opinions.

19. **One common factor for students with all types of disabilities is that they are also likely to demonstrate difficulty with:**

    A. Social skills
    B. Cognitive skills
    C. Problem-solving skills
    D. Decision-making skills

Answer A: Social skills

Students with disabilities (in all areas) may demonstrate difficulty in social skills. For a student with a hearing impairment, social skills may be difficult because of not hearing social language. However, the emotionally disturbed student may have difficulty because of a special type of psychological disturbance. An autistic student, as a third example, would be unaware of the social cues given with voice, facial expression, and body language. Each of these students would need social skill instruction but in a different way.

20. **A student does not respond to any signs of affection and responds to other children by repeating back what they have said. What condition is the student most likely to have?**

    A. Mental retardation
    B. Autism
    C. Giftedness
    D. Hyperactivity

Answer B: Autism

There are six common features of autism. They are:

Apparent sensory deficit – lack of reaction to or overreaction to a stimulus.

Severe affect isolation – lack of response to affection, such as smiles and hugs.

Self-stimulation – repeated or ritualistic actions that make no sense to others.

Tantrums and self-injurious behavior (SIB) – throwing tantrums, injuring oneself, or aggression.

Echolalia (also known as "parrot talk") – repetition of sounds or responding to others by repeating what was said to him.

Severe deficits in behavior and self-care skills – behaving like children much younger than themselves.

21. **Which of the following conditions is more common for girls than boys?**

   A. Attention deficit disorder
   B. Aggression
   C. Phobias
   D. Autism

Answer C: Phobias

Many more boys than girls are identified as having emotional and behavioral problems, especially hyperactivity and attention deficit disorder, autism, childhood psychosis, and problems with undercontrol such as aggression and socialized aggression. Girls have more problems with overcontrol, such as withdrawal and phobias.

22. **In successful inclusion of students with disabilities:**

   A. A variety of instructional arrangements are available
   B. School personnel shift the responsibility for learning outcomes to the student
   C. The physical facilities are used as they are
   D. Regular classroom teachers have sole responsibility for evaluating student progress

Answer A: A variety of instructional arrangements are available

All students have the right to an education, but there cannot be a singular path to that education. A teacher must acknowledge the variety of learning styles and abilities among students within a class apply multiple instructional and assessment processes to ensure that every child has appropriate opportunities to master the subject matter, demonstrate such mastery, and improve and enhance learning skills with each lesson.

23. **Mr. Gorman has taught a concept to his class. All of the students have grasped the concept except for Sam. Mr. Gorman should:**

A. Reteach the concept to the whole class in exactly the same way
B. Reteach the concept to Sam in exactly the same way
C. Reteach the concept to Sam in a different way
D. Reteach the concept to the whole class in a different way

Answer C: Reteach the concept to Sam in a different way

There is always more than one way to approach a problem, an example, a process, fact or event, or any learning situation. Varying approaches for instruction helps to maintain the students' interest in the material and enables the teacher to address the diverse needs of individuals to comprehend the material.

24. **Mrs. Gomez has a fully integrated early childhood curriculum. This is beneficial to students because it:**

A. Is easier to plan for and maintain
B. Allows students to apply their unique skills
C. Helps the students see the relationships between subjects and concepts
D. Provides opportunities for social interaction

Answer C: Helps the students see the relationships between subjects and concepts

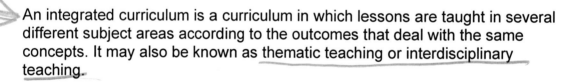

An integrated curriculum is a curriculum in which lessons are taught in several different subject areas according to the outcomes that deal with the same concepts. It may also be known as thematic teaching or interdisciplinary teaching.

Subarea II. Communication, Language and Literacy Development

25. **The relationship between oral language and reading skills is best described as:**

    A. Reciprocal
    B. Inverse
    C. Opposite
    D. There is no relationship.

Answer A: Reciprocal

A highly developed oral language vocabulary helps to build reading skills comprehension. The inverse is true as well, with highly developed reading and comprehension skills helping to develop oral language skills.

26. **A teacher is showing students how to construct grammatically correct sentences. What is the teacher focusing on?**

    A. Morphology
    B. Syntax
    C. Semantics
    D. Pragmatics

Answer B: Syntax

Syntax refers to the rules or patterned relationships that correctly create phrases and sentences from words. When readers develop an understanding of syntax, they begin to understand the structure of how sentences are built, and eventually the beginning of grammar.

27. A teacher writes the following words on the board: cot, cotton, and cottage. What is the teacher most likely teaching the students about?

   A.   Morphology
   B.   Syntax
   C.   Semantics
   D.   Pragmatics

Answer A: Morphology

Morphology is the study of word structure. When readers develop morphemic skills, they are developing an understanding of patterns they see in words. For example, English speakers realize that cat, cats, and caterpillar share some similarities in structure. This understanding helps readers to recognize words at a faster and easier rate, since each word doesn't need individual decoding.

28. While standing in line at the grocery store, three-year-old Megan says to her mother in a regular tone of voice, "Mom, why is that woman so fat?" What does this indicate a lack of understanding of?

   A.   Syntax
   B.   Semantics
   C.   Morphology
   D.   Pragmatics

Answer D: Pragmatics

Pragmatics is the development and understanding of social relevance to conversations and topics. It develops as children age. In this situation, Megan simply does not understand to the same level of an adult how that question could be viewed as offensive to certain members of society.

29. Which of the following is the first component of the constructivist model?

    A.   There are at least seven different types of learning.
    B.   Learning depends on the social environment.
    C.   Learner creates knowledge
    D.   Learning progresses through set stages.

Answer C: Learner creates knowledge

Researchers have shown that the constructivist model is comprised of the four components:

1. Learner creates knowledge

2. Learner constructs and makes meaningful new knowledge from existing knowledge

3. Learner shapes and constructs knowledge by life experiences and social interactions

4. In constructivist learning communities, the student, teacher and classmates establish knowledge cooperatively on a daily basis.

30. Students are about to read a text that contains words that will need to be understood for the students to understand the text. When should the vocabulary be introduced to students?

    A.   Before reading
    B.   During reading
    C.   After reading
    D.   It should not be introduced.

Answer A: Before reading

Vocabulary should be introduced before reading if there are words within the text that are definitely keys necessary for reading comprehension.

31. Which of the following are examples of temporal words?

    A. Beside and behind
    B. Hotter and colder
    C. In and on
    D. Before and after

Answer D: Before and after

Temporal words are words that indicate time. Before and after are two examples of temporal words.

32. Which principle of Stephen Krashen's research suggests that the learning of grammatical structures is predictable?

    A. The affective filter hypothesis
    B. The input hypothesis
    C. The natural order hypothesis
    D. The monitor hypothesis

Answer C: The natural order hypothesis

Stephen Krashen's natural order hypothesis suggests that the learning of grammatical structures is predictable and follows a natural order.

33. Above what age does learning a language become increasingly difficult?

    A. 3
    B. 5
    C. 7
    D. 10

Answer C: 7

The most important concept to remember regarding the difference between learning a first language and a second one is that if the learner is approximately age seven or older, learning a second language will occur very differently in the learner's brain than it would had the learner been younger. The reason for this is that there is a language-learning function that exists in young children that appears to go away as they mature. Learning a language prior to age seven is almost guaranteed, with relatively little effort.

34. Ms. Chomski is presenting a new story to her class of first graders. In the story, a family visits their grandparents where they all gather around a record player and listen to music. Many students do not understand what a record player is, especially some children for whom English is not their first language. Which of the following would Ms. Chomski be best to do?

    A.   Discuss what a record player is with her students
    B.   Compare a record player with a CD player
    C.   Have students look up record player in a dictionary
    D.   Show the students a picture of a record player

Answer D: Show the students a picture of a record player

The most effective method for ensuring adequate comprehension is through direct experience. Sometimes this cannot be completed and therefore it is necessary to utilize pictures or other visual aids to provide the students with experience in another mode besides oral language.

35. Jose moved to the United States last month. He speaks little or no English at this time. His teacher is teaching the class about habitats in science and has chosen to read a story about various habitats to the class. The vocabulary is difficult. What should Jose's teacher do with Jose?

    A.   Provide Jose with additional opportunities to learn about habitats
    B.   Read the story to Jose multiple times
    C.   Show Jose pictures of habitats from his native country
    D.   Excuse Jose from the assignment

Answer A: Provide Jose with additional opportunities to learn about habitats

Students who are learning English should be exposed to a variety of opportunities to learn the same concepts as native speakers. Content should not be changed, but the manner in which it is presented and reinforced should be changed.

36. **In the early childhood classroom, it is important to limit teacher talk. What is the main problem with teacher talk?**

    A.   It is often one sided and limited.
    B.   The vocabulary is too difficult for children.
    C.   It promotes misbehavior.
    D.   It only creates gains in receptive language.

Answer A: It is often one sided and limited.

While it is important to expose children to numerous opportunities throughout the day to read and interact with print, it is equally important for students to have the opportunity to express themselves and communicate with each other. Teacher-talk, is often one sided and limited. Instead, teachers should provide opportunities for students to develop and expand their vocabularies.

37. **Which of the following is a convention of print that children learn during reading activities?**

    A.   The meaning of words
    B.   The left to right motion
    C.   The purpose of print
    D.   The identification of letters

Answer B: The left to right motion

During reading activities, children learn conventions of print. Children learn the way to hold a book, where to begin to read, the left to right motion, and how to continue from one line to another.

38. In her kindergarten class, Mrs. Thomas has been watching the students in the drama center. She has watched the children pretend to complete a variety of magic tricks. Mrs. Thomas decides to use stories about magic to share with her class. Her decision to incorporate their interests into the reading shows that Mrs. Thomas understands that:

    A. Including student interests is important at all times
    B. Teaching by themes is crucial for young children
    C. Young children respond to literature that reflects their lives
    D. Science fiction and fantasy are the most popular genres

Answer C: Young children respond to literature that reflects their lives

Children's literature is intended to instruct students through entertaining stories, while also promoting an interest in the very act of reading, itself. Young readers respond best to themes that reflect their lives.

39. Which of the following is NOT a characteristic of a fable?

    A. Have animal characters that act like humans
    B. Considered to be true
    C. Teaches a moral
    D. Reveals human foibles

Answer B: Considered to be true

The common characteristics of fables are animals that act like humans, a focus on revealing human foibles, and teaching a moral or lesson. Fables are not considered to be true.

40. Alphabet books are classified as:

    A. Concept books
    B. Easy-to-read books
    C. Board books
    D. Pictures books

Answer A: Concept books

Concept books are books that combine language and pictures to show concrete examples of concepts. One category of concept books is alphabet books, which are popular with children from preschool through to grade 2.

41. The stories of Paul Bunyan, John Henry, and Pecos Bill are all exaggerated accounts of individuals with superhuman strength. What type of literature are these works?

    A. Fables
    B. Fairytales
    C. Tall tales
    D. Myths

Answer C: Tall tales

Tall tales are purposely exaggerated accounts of individuals with superhuman strength. The stories of Paul Bunyan, John Henry, and Pecos Bill are all examples of tall tales. Fables are usually stories about animals with human features that often teach a lesson. Fairytales usually focus on good versus evil, reward and punishment. Myths are stories about events from the earliest times.

42. Which of the following is NOT a motivation behind providing reading activities, including reading aloud, to young children?

    A. Developing word consciousness skills
    B. Developing functions of print skills
    C. Developing phonics skills
    D. Developing language skills

Answer C: Developing phonics skills

There are almost unlimited positive reasons for encouraging adults to provide reading activities for young children. While it can be true that reading aloud may improve the phonics skills for some students, it is not a motivation for providing such activities to students.

43. **Which of the following is an appropriate way for students to respond to literature?**

    A. Art
    B. Drama
    C. Writing
    D. All of the above

Answer D: All of the above

Responding to literature through art, writing, and drama helps children to reflect on the books they have read and make them a part of their lives.

44. **John is having difficulty reading the word reach. In isolation, he pronounces each sound as /r/ /ee/ /sh/. Which of the following is a possible instructional technique which could help solve John's reading difficulty?**

    A. Additional phonemic awareness instruction
    B. Additional phonics instruction
    C. Additional skill and drill practice
    D. Additional minimal pair practice

Answer A: Additional phonemic awareness instruction

John is having difficulty with the sound symbol relationship between the /ch/ and /sh/. While it may appear at first that this is a phonics problem, in fact, it is important to begin with the earlier skill of phonemic awareness to ensure the student has a solid foundational understanding of the oral portions before moving totally into the sound symbol arena. If John is able to distinguish between the two sounds orally, it is obvious more phonics instruction is needed. However, proceeding directly to phonics instruction may be pointless and frustrating for John if he is unable to hear the distinctions.

45. According to Marilyn Jager Adams, which skill would a student demonstrate by identifying that cat does not belong in the group of words containing dog, deer, and dress?

    A. Recognize the odd member in a group
    B. Replace sounds in words
    C. Count the sounds in a word
    D. Count syllables in a word

Answer A: Recognize the odd member in a group

One of Marilyn Jager Adams' basic types of phonemic awareness tasks involves the ability to do oddity tasks, which involves recognizing the member of a set that is different among the group. In this example, the word cat is the odd member because it starts with a different sound.

46. Which of the following is NOT true about phonological awareness? (Skill 7.2; Average rigor)

    A. It may involve print.
    B. It is a prerequisite for spelling and phonics.
    C. Activities can be done by the children with their eyes closed.
    D. It starts before letter recognition is taught.

Answer A: It may involve print.

All of the options are correct aspects of phonological awareness except the first one, because phonological awareness does not involve print.

47. Which of the following explains a significant difference between phonics and phonemic awareness?

    A. Phonics involves print, while phonemic awareness involves language.
    B. Phonics is harder than phonemic awareness.
    C. Phonics involves sounds, while phonemic awareness involves letters.
    D. Phonics is the application of sounds to print, while phonemic awareness is oral.

Answer D: Phonics is the application of sounds to print, while phonemic awareness is oral.

Both phonics and phonemic awareness activities involve sounds, but it is with phonics that the application of these sounds is applied to print. Phonemic awareness is an oral activity.

48. To decode is to:

    A. Construct meaning
    B. Sound out a printed sequence of letters
    C. Use a special code to decipher a message
    D. Revise for errors in grammar

Answer B: Sound out a printed sequence of letters

Decoding is the process students use to figure out unknown words when reading.

49. **Ms. Walker's lesson objective is to teach her first graders the concept of morphology in order to improve their reading skills. Which group of words would be most appropriate for her to use in this lesson?**

    A. Far, farm, farmer
    B. Far, feather, fever
    C. Far, fear, fare
    D. Far, fare, farce

Answer A: Far, farm, farmer

The concept of morphology is to understand how words relate to each other and can be built upon to increase reading skills. In the correct answer, the student can utilize the information they learned from learning to read far to help them decode the other words.

50. **Which stage of reading skill development occurs first?**

    A. Schema stage
    B. Early semantic stage
    C. Orthographic stage
    D. Simultaneous stage

What are the stages in order?

Answer A: Schema stage

Reading develops in sequential skills levels. The first stage is the schema stage. This stage is a pre-reading level involving page turning and telling story from memory.

51. **Which of the following is an important feature of vocabulary instruction according to the National Reading Panel?**

   A.   Repetition of vocabulary items
   B.   Keeping a consistent task structure at all times
   C.   Teaching vocabulary in more than one language
   D.   Isolation vocabulary instruction from other subjects

Answer A: Repetition of vocabulary items

According to the National Reading Panel, repetition and multiple exposures to vocabulary items are important. Students should be given items that will be likely to appear in many contexts.

52. **The attitude an author takes toward his or her subject is the:**

   A.   Style
   B.   Tone
   C.   Point of view
   D.   Theme

Answer B: Tone

Tone is the attitude an author takes toward his or her subject. That tone is exemplified in the language of the text.

53. **George has read his second graders three formats of the story "The Three Little Pigs." One is the traditional version, one is written from the wolf's point of view, and the third is written from the first pig's point of view. As George leads a discussion on the three texts with his students, he is trying to help his students develop their ability to:**

   A.   Compare and contrast texts
   B.   Understand point of view
   C.   Recognize metaphors
   D.   Rewrite fictional stories

Answer A: Compare and contrast texts

George understands the importance of developing critical thinking skills in young children. He has read three different formats of the same story in order to help his students develop their ability to compare texts.

54. What is the first step in developing writing skills?

   A.   Early writing
   B.   Experimental writing
   C   Role play writing
   D.   Conventional writing

Answer C: Role play writing

Children develop writing skills through a series of steps. These steps are: role play writing, experimental writing, early writing, and then conventional writing. In the role play writing stage, the child writes in scribbles and assigns a message to the symbols. Even though an adult would not be able to read the writing, the child can read what is written although it may not be the same each time the child reads it. S/he will be able to read back the writing because of prior knowledge that print carries a meaning.

55. Which of the following is NOT a prewriting strategy?

   A.   Analyzing sentences for variety
   B.   Keeping an idea book
   C.   Writing in a daily journal
   D.   Writing down whatever comes to mind

Answer A: Analyzing sentences for variety

Prewriting strategies assist students in a variety of ways. Common prewriting strategies include keeping an idea book for jotting down ideas, writing in a daily journal, and writing down whatever comes to mind, which is also called "free writing." Analyzing sentences for variety is a revising strategy.

56. Which of the following is probably the most important step for the writer in the writing process?

    A.   Revision
    B.   Discovery
    C.   Conclusion
    D.   Organization

Answer A: Revision

Revision is probably the most important step for the writer in the writing process. Here, students examine their work and make changes in wording, details, and ideas. So many times, students write a draft and then feel they're done. Students must be encouraged to develop, change, and enhance their writing as they go, as well as once they've completed a draft.

57. The students in Tina's classroom are working together in pairs. Each student is reading another student's paper and asking who, what, when, where, why, and who questions. What is this activity helping the students to do?

    A.   Draft their writing
    B.   Paraphrase their writing
    C.   Revise their writing
    D.   Outline their writing

Answer C: Revise their writing

Students need to be trained to become effective at proofreading, revising and editing strategies. One way to do this is to have the students read their partners' papers and ask at least three who, what, when, why, how questions. The students answer the questions and use them as a place to begin discussing the piece.

58. **Young children learning to write commonly grip the pencil:**

    A.   Too far from the point
    B.   With the wrong hand
    C.   With too many fingers
    D.   Too tightly

Answer D: Too tightly

A common problem for all young children learning to write is gripping the pencil too tightly, which makes writing tiresome. Usually the student learns to relax their grip as writing skill develops, but teachers can remind students to hold the instrument gently.

59. **Which of the following approaches to student writing assignments is most likely to lead to students becoming disinterested?**

    A.   Designing assignments where students write for a variety of audiences.
    B.   Designing assignments where the teacher is the audience.
    C.   Designing assignments where students write to friends and family.
    D.   Designing assignments where students write to real people such as mayors, the principle, or companies.

Answer B: Designing assignments where the teacher is the audience

In the past, teachers have assigned reports, paragraphs and essays that focused on the teacher as the audience with the purpose of explaining information. However, for students to be meaningfully engaged in their writing, they must write for a variety of reasons. Writing for different audiences and aims allows students to be more involved in their writing. If they write for the same audience and purpose, they will continue to see writing as just another assignment

60. **As a part of prewriting, students should identify their audience. Which of the following questions will help students to identify their audience?**

    A.   Why is the audience reading my writing?
    B.   What does my audience already know about my topic?
    C.   Both A and B
    D.   None of the above

Answer C: Both A and B

As part of prewriting, students should identify the audience. Make sure students consider the following when analyzing the needs of their audience: why the audience is reading the writing; what the audience already knows about the topic; what the audience needs or wants to know; what will interest the reader; and what type of language will suit the reader.

61. **Which of these describes the best way to teach spelling?**

    A.   At the same time that grammar and sentence structure is taught.
    B.   Within the context of meaningful language experiences.
    C.   Independently so that students can concentrate on spelling.
    D.   In short lessons as students pick up spelling almost immediately.

Answer B: Within the context of meaningful language experiences.

Spelling should be taught within the context of meaningful language experiences. Giving a child a list of words to learn to spell and then testing the child on the words every Friday will not aid in the development of spelling. The child must be able to use the words in context and they must have some meaning for the child. The assessment of how well a child can spell or where there are problems also has to be done within a meaningful environment.

62. **When editing, teachers should direct students to:**

    A.   Edit for general understanding, while ignoring grammar and spelling.
    B.   Edit for one specific purpose at a time.
    C.   Identify all spelling, capitalization, and punctuation errors.
    D.   Be critical of their work and that of others.

Answer B: Edit for one specific purpose at a time.

Editing is a time-consuming task and it would be unreasonable to expect students to pick up on all the mistakes in a piece of writing. Therefore, teachers should ask students to edit for specific purposes at one time, such as correct spelling, capitalization or punctuation.

Subarea III. Learning in the Content Areas

63. **Kindergarten students are participating in a calendar time activity. One student adds a straw to the "ones can" to represent that day of school. What math principle is being reinforced?**

    A.   Properties of a base ten number system
    B.   Sorting
    C.   Counting by twos
    D.   Even and odd numbers

Answer A: Properties of a base ten number system

As the students group craft sticks into groups of tens to represent the days of school, they are learning the properties of our base ten number system.

64. **First grade students are arranging four small squares of identical size to form a larger square. Each small square represents what part of the larger square?**

    A.   One half
    B.   One whole
    C.   One fourth
    D.   One fifth

Answer C: One fourth

Four of the small squares make up the area of the large square. Each small square is one fourth of the larger square.

65. **What is the answer to this problem?**

   25 ÷ 5 =

   A.   5
   B.   30
   C.   125
   D.   20

Answer A: 5

Twenty-five can be divided into five equal groups of five.

66. **Third grade students are studying percents. When looking at a circle graph divided into three sections, they see that one section is worth 80% and one section is worth 5%. What will the remaining section be worth?**

   A.   100%
   B.   85%
   C.   75%
   D.   15%

Answer D: 15%

Percentages use the base ten number system. Percentages of a total amount will always add up to 100%. Since the two sections add to 85%, the third section must be 15%.

67. **Which of the following letters does NOT have a line of symmetry?**

   A.   O
   B.   D
   C.   M
   D.   J

Answer D: J

For an object to show symmetry, it must be able to be divided into identical halves. The letter O has an unlimited number of lines of symmetry. The letter D has a horizontal line of symmetry. The letter M has a vertical line of symmetry. The letter J does not have a line of symmetry.

68. **Kindergarten students are doing a butterfly art project. They fold paper in half. On one half, they paint a design. Then they fold the paper closed and reopen. The resulting picture is a butterfly with matching sides. What math principle does this demonstrate?**

    A.   Slide
    B.   Rotate
    C.   Symmetry
    D.   Transformation

Answer C: Symmetry

By folding the painted paper in half, the design is mirrored on the other side, creating symmetry and reflection. The butterfly design is symmetrical about the center.

69. **What number comes next in this pattern?**

    3, 8, 13, 18, _____

    A.   21
    B.   26
    C.   23
    D.   5

Answer C: 23

This pattern is made by adding five to the preceding number. The next number is found by adding 5 to 18, which gives the answer 23.

70. **What is the main purpose of having kindergarten students count by twos?**

    A.   To hear a rhythm
    B.   To recognize patterns
            in numbers
    C.   To practice addition
    D.   To become familiar with equations

Answer B: To recognize patterns in numbers

Recognizing patterns in numbers is an early skill for multiplication. It will also help children recognize patterns in word families such as *bit, hit, fit.*

71. The term *millimeters* indicates which kind of measurement?

    A. Volume
    B. Weight
    C. Length
    D. Temperature

Answer C: Length

The term *millimeters* is a reference to length in the metric system.

72. What type of graph would be best to use to show changes in the height of a plant over the course of a month?

    A. Circle graph
    B. Bar graph
    C. Line graph
    D. Pictograph

Answer C: Line graph

A line graph shows trends over time. A line graph would show how the plant's height changed over time.

73. A teacher completes a survey of student eye color. The teacher then creates a graph so students can compare how many students have each eye color. What type of graph should be used?

    A. Bar graph
    B. Pictograph
    C. Circle graph
    D. Line Graph

Answer A: Bar graph

Bar graphs are used to compare various quantities. In this case, the bar graph would show the number of students with each eye color. By looking at the graph, students would be able to compare how many students have each eye color. While a pictograph is also possible, if there are many different eye colors in the class, it would take up a lot of space to graph it this way.

74. **Which of the following skills would a student develop first?**

    A. Understanding place value
    B. Recognizing number patterns
    C. Counting objects
    D. Solving number problems

Answer C: Counting objects

As with the phonemic awareness skills in reading, number sense is the foundation upon which all future math topics will be built. While in this beginning stage, children will be able to identify how many objects are in a group.

75. **Maddie is a first grade teacher who understands the importance of including the family when providing instruction. She wants to take several steps to provide families with a connection to what the students are doing in her math class. Which of the following is NOT a strategy she could incorporate?**

    A. Including a math portion in her regular newsletter
    B. Incorporating manipulatives into her math lessons
    C. Translating math homework into the native language of the students in her classroom
    D. Having a family math night at school

Answer B: Incorporating manipulatives into her math lessons

While incorporating manipulatives into her curriculum is an excellent strategy, which should take place in every math classroom, it does not promote the inclusion of family into the curriculum.

76. **George has successfully mastered his basic addition facts. However, as his teacher presents more complex addition problems, it is obvious to him that George is lacking a basic understanding of the concept of addition. What would George's teacher be best to do to increase his basic understanding?**

   A. Provide additional instruction with hands on materials
   B. Have George practice his addition facts more frequently
   C. Have George complete more challenging addition problems
   D. Provide George with remediation

Answer A: Provide additional instruction with hands on materials

When students have the time to explore and build their own constructs using concrete objects, they are able to make more generalizations. Students may be able to memorize pieces of rote information, but without the foundational exposure to hands on materials they may not be able to demonstrate these generalizations. It is the role of the teacher to take the time to provide these opportunities.

77. **Carrie approaches her teacher after class and expresses her personal frustration with math and her feeling that she will never get it. Which of the following is NOT a suitable method Carrie's teacher can utilize to improve Carrie's feelings about math?**

   A. Incorporating some of Carrie's specific interests into math lessons
   B. Holding Carrie to high expectations
   C. Sharing with Carrie her own struggles and dislike for math
   D. Providing Carrie with extra positive reinforcement and encouragement

Answer C: Sharing with Carrie her own struggles and dislike for math

While it may seem to be a bonding experience to share your own personal struggles and dislike for the subject with a student who feels the same way, it is important for the teacher to maintain excitement and enthusiasm for the subject. Carrie's teacher would be better to share positive aspects about how math as affected her life, than to share any negative feelings. Building a positive excitement and interest in the subject is an important part of teaching.

78. **The principal walks into your classroom during math class. He sees your students making cake mixtures. Later, the principal questions your lesson. What would be the best explanation for your lesson?**

    A. The students earned a reward time and it was free choice.
    B. You were teaching the students how math is used in real-life situations.
    C. You had paperwork to complete and needed the time to complete it.
    D. It kept the students interested in math and prevented boredom.

Answer B: You were teaching the students how math is used in real-life situations.

Providing the students with the opportunity to explore how math is around them and how it is utilized in everyday experiences is important. As students identify and realize the importance of the skills being learned to their lives at home, they will become more involved in the learning, as it has new and better value for them.

79. **What is a large, rotating, low-pressure system accompanied by heavy precipitation and strong winds known as?**

    A. A hurricane
    B. A tornado
    C. A thunderstorm
    D. A tsunami

Answer A: A hurricane

Hurricanes are storms that develop when warm, moist air carried by trade winds rotates around a low-pressure "eye". These form a large, rotating, low-pressure system and are accompanied by heavy precipitation and strong winds. They are also known as tropical cyclones or typhoons.

80. **What does a primary consumer most commonly refer to?**

    A. Herbivore
    B. Autotroph
    C. Carnivore
    D. Decomposer

Answer A: Herbivore

Autotrophs are the primary producers of the ecosystem. Producers mainly consist of plants. Primary consumers are the next trophic level. The primary consumers are the herbivores that eat plants or algae. Secondary consumers are the carnivores that eat the primary consumers. Tertiary consumers eat the secondary consumer. These trophic levels may go higher depending on the ecosystem.

81. **Airplanes generate pressure and remain balanced by:**

    A. Fast air movement over wings and slow movement under wings
    B. Slow air movement over wings and fast movement under wings
    C. Air movement that is equal above and below wings
    D. Air movement that only occurs over the wings

Answer A: Fast air movement over wings and slow movement under wings

Airplanes or fixed-wing aircraft are heavier than aircraft that utilize the laws of physics to achieve flight. As the aircraft is propelled forward by thrust from the engines, air moves faster over the top of the wings and slower under the bottom. The slower airflow beneath the wing generates more pressure, while the faster airflow above generates less. This difference in pressure results in upward lift.

82. **The breakdown of rock due to acid rain is an example of:**

   A. Physical weathering
   B. Frost wedging
   C. Chemical weathering
   D. Deposition

Answer C: Chemical weathering

The breaking down of rocks at or near to the Earth's surface is known as weathering. Chemical weathering is the breaking down of rocks through changes in their chemical composition. The breakdown of rock due to acid rain is an example of chemical weathering.

83. **What is the last step in the scientific method?**

   A. Pose a question
   B. Draw a conclusion
   C. Conduct a test
   D. Record data

Answer B: Draw a conclusion

The steps in the scientific method, in order, are: pose a question, form a hypothesis, conduct a test, observe and record data, and draw a conclusion.

84. Which term best describes Newton's universal gravitation?

A. Theory
B. Hypothesis
C. Inference
D. Law

Answer D: Law

A hypothesis is an unproved theory or educated guess followed by research to best explain a phenomenon. A theory is the formation of principles or relationships, which have been verified and accepted. It is a proven hypothesis. A law is an explanation of events that occur with uniformity under the same conditions, such as laws of nature or laws of gravitation.

85. When teaching science, which of the following is a method of focusing on students' intrinsic motivation?

A. Adapting the lessons to students' interests
B. Providing regular feedback
C. Supplying rewards for the highest achievers
D. Having regular science tests

Answer A: Adapting the lessons to students' interests

Teachers can focus on students' intrinsic motivation through adapting the tasks to students' interests, providing opportunities for active response, including a variety of tasks, providing rapid feedback, incorporating games into the lesson, and allowing students the opportunity to make choices, create, and interact with peers.

86. What does geography include the study of?

A. Location
B. Distribution of living things
C. Distribution of the earth's features
D. All of the above

Answer D: All of the above

Geography involves studying location and how living things and earth's features are distributed throughout the earth. It includes where animals, people, and plants live and the effects of their relationship with earth's physical features.

87. **Economics is the study of how a society allocates its scarce resources to satisfy:**

    A. Unlimited and competing wants
    B. Limited and competing wants
    C. Unlimited and cooperative wants
    D. Limited and cooperative wants

Answer A: Unlimited and competing wants

Economics is the study of how a society allocates its scarce resources to satisfy what are basically unlimited and competing wants. A fundamental fact of economics is that resources are scarce and that wants are infinite.

88. **The two elements of a market economy are:**

    A. Inflation and deflation
    B. Supply and demand
    C. Cost and price
    D. Wants and needs

Answer B: Supply and demand

A market economy is based on supply and demand. Demand is based on consumer preferences and satisfaction and refers to the quantities of a good or service that buyers are willing and able to buy at different prices during a given period of time. Supply is based on costs of production and refers to the quantities that sellers are willing and able to sell at different prices during a given period of time.

89. **Who has the power to veto a bill that has passed the House of Representatives and the Senate?**

    A. The President
    B. The Vice President
    C. The Speaker of the House
    D. Any member of Congress

Answer A: The President

Once a bill receives final approval by a conference committee, it is signed by the Speaker of the House and the Vice President, who is also the President of the Senate, and sent to the President for consideration. The President may either sign the bill or veto it. If he vetoes the bill, his veto may be overruled if two-thirds of both the Senate and the House vote to do so. Once the President signs it the bill becomes a law.

90. Which part of a map shows the relationship between a unit of measurement on the map versus the real world measure on the Earth?

    A. Scale
    B. Title
    C. Legend
    D. Grid

Answer A: Scale

The scale of a map is used to show the relationship between a unit of measurement on the map versus the real world measure on the Earth.

91. What is the most important focus in developing social studies skills during the early years?

    A. Recalling facts
    B. Understanding statistics
    C. Discussing ideas
    D. Memorizing rights and responsibilities

Answer C: Discussing ideas

The early years of childhood education is important in shaping the values of a democracy and preparing students for citizenship in later life. Social studies begin the exploration of the processes, rights and freedoms of a democracy. Early in a child's education they begin to learn cooperation, tolerance, and sharing. During the early years, the recalling of factual information is not as important as encouraging discussion and exploration of different perspectives.

92. What is one of the ten essential themes identified by the National Council for Social Studies?

    A. Culture
    B. Lifestyle
    C. Population
    D. Democracy

Answer A: Culture

The National Council for Social Studies identifies 10 themes essential to social science instruction. These are:
1. Culture
2. Time, Continuity and Change
3. People, Places and Environments
4. Individual development and identity
5. Individuals, Groups and Institutions
6. Power, Authority and Governance
7. Production, Distribution and Consumption
8. Science, Technology and Society
9. Global Connections
10. Civic Ideals and Practices

93. Which subject would a color wheel most likely be used for?

    A. Visual arts
    B. Music
    C. Movement
    D. Drama

Answer A: Visual arts

A color wheel is an important tool in teaching students visual arts. It is used to teach students about primary colors and secondary colors. It is also used to help students learn about mixing colors.

94. A student art sample book would include cotton balls and sand paper to represent:

A. Color
B. Lines
C. Texture
D. Shape

Answer C: Texture

Texture refers to the way something feels because of the tactile quality of its surface. An art sample book can include materials such as cotton balls and sand paper as examples of different textures.

95. Which terms refers to the arrangement of one or more items so that they appear symmetrical or asymmetrical?

A. Balance
B. Contrast
C. Emphasis
D. Unity

Answer A: Balance

The principles of visual are that students should be introduced to include abstract, background, balance, contrast, emphasis, sketch, texture, and unity. Balance refers to the arrangement of one or more elements in a work of art so that they appear symmetrical or asymmetrical in design and proportion.

96. The four principles of modern dance are substance, form, metakinesis, and:

A. Dynamism
B. Function
C. Space
D. Performance

Answer A: Dynamism

Modern dance is a type of dance where the focus is on expressing opposites, such as fast-slow or contract-release. Modern dance is based on four principles. These are substance, form, metakinesis, and dynamism.

97. **What should the arts curriculum for early childhood avoid?**

   A.   Judgment
   B.   Open expression
   C.   Experimentation
   D.   Discovery

Answer A: Judgment

The arts curriculum for early childhood should focus on the experimental and discovery aspects of the arts. The emphasis should be on creative processes with little judgment and criticism should be minimal.

98. **What would the viewing of a dance company performance be most likely to promote?**

   A.   Critical-thinking skills
   B.   Appreciation of the arts
   C.   Improvisation skills
   D.   Music vocabulary

Answer B: Appreciation of the arts

Live performances are an important part of learning arts and help to develop aesthetic appreciation of the arts. A dance company performance is one example of a live performance that students could attend.

99. **In which subject is it most important for students to work with costumes and props?**

   A.   Visual arts
   B.   Music
   C.   Movement
   D.   Drama

Answer D: Drama

When studying drama, students should experience working with props and performing in costume. These can both help students act out experiences and tend to increase creativity.

100. **According to Charles Fowler, why is it important for arts to be incorporated into the teaching of other subject areas?**

    A. It reduces loss of interest in the subject.
    B. It enhances the likelihood that students will retain the information.
    C. It provides a three dimensional view of the subject.
    D. It encourages the development of personal connections with the subject.

Answer C: It provides a three dimensional view of the subject.

Charles Fowler has argued that the best schools also have the best arts programs. According to Fowler, integrating arts with other subject areas gives a more complete view of the subject. Students then gain a more three dimensional understanding of the subject.

Sample Test

Reading, Language & Literature

1. Which of the following is not a strategy of teaching reading comprehension?
   (Rigorous) (Skill 1.1)

   A. Asking questions

   B. Utilizing graphic organizers

   C. Focusing on mental images

   D. Manipulating sounds

2. All of the following are true about phonological awareness EXCEPT:
   (Average Rigor) (Skill 1.3)

   A. It may involve print.

   B. It is a prerequisite for spelling and phonics.

   C. Activities can be done by the children with their eyes closed.

   D. It starts before letter recognition is taught.

3. Oral language development includes which of the following:
   (Average Rigor) (Skill 2.1)

   A. Listening comprehension

   B. Storytelling

   C. Developing vocabulary

   D. All of the above

4. How do children make the transition from letter forms to invented spelling?
   (Average Rigor) (Skill 2.1)

   A. Write strings of letters

   B. Organize group of letters

   C. Leave spaces

   D. All of the above

5. Which aspect of language is innate?
(Rigorous) (Skill 2.1)

A. Biological capability to articulate sounds understood by other humans

B. Cognitive ability to create syntactical structures

C. Capacity for using semantics to convey meaning in a social environment

D. Ability to vary inflections and accents

6. To decode is to:
(Easy) (Skill 2.2)

A. Construct meaning

B. Sound out a printed sequence of letters

C. Use a special code to decipher a message

D. None of the above

7. To encode means that you:
(Easy) (Skill 2.2)

A. Decode a second time

B. Construct meaning from a code

C. Tell someone a message

D. None of the above

8. The arrangement and relationship of words in sentences or sentence structure best describes:
(Average Rigor) (Skill 2.4)

A. Style

B. Discourse

C. Thesis

D. Syntax

9. Effective reading comprehension requires:
(Rigorous) (Skill 2.5)

A. Encoding

B. Decoding

C. Both A and B

D. Neither A nor B

10. Contextual redefinition is a strategy that encourages children to use the context more effectively by presenting them with sufficient vocabulary _____ the reading of a text. *(Rigorous) (3.3)*

A. After

B. Before

C. During

D. None of the above

11. **What is the best place for students to find appropriate synonyms, antonyms, and other related words to enhance their writing?**
(Average Rigor) (Skill 3.4)

A. Dictionary

B. Spell check

C. Encyclopedia

D. Thesaurus

12. **Which is an untrue statement about a theme in literature?**
(Rigorous) (Skill 5.2)

A. The theme is always stated directly somewhere in the text.

B. The theme is the central idea in a literary work.

C. All parts of the work (plot, setting, mood) should contribute to the theme in some way.

D. By analyzing the various elements of the work, the reader should be able to arrive at an indirectly stated theme.

13. **If a student has a poor vocabulary, the teacher should recommend that:**
(Average Rigor) (Skill 4.1)

A. The student read newspapers, magazines, and books on a regular basis.

B. The student enroll in a Latin class.

C. The student write the words repetitively after looking them up in the dictionary.

D. The student use a thesaurus to locate synonyms and incorporate them into his/her vocabulary.

14. **Which of the following indicates that a student is a fluent reader?**
(Easy) (Skill 4.1)

A. Reads texts with expression or prosody

B. Reads word-to-word and haltingly

C. Must intentionally decode a majority of the words

D. In a writing assignment, sentences are poorly-organized structurally

15. All of the following are examples of ongoing informal assessment techniques used to observe student progress EXCEPT:
(Rigorous) (Skill 4.1)

A. Analysis of student work product

B. Collection of data from assessment tests

C. Effective questioning

D. Observation of students

16. Which of the following is a formal reading level assessment?
(Easy) (4.1)

A. A standardized reading test

B. A teacher-made reading test

C. An interview

D. A reading diary

17. Which of the following is an opinion? *(Easy) (Skill 4.4)*

A. Subjective evaluation based upon personal bias

B. A statement that is readily provable by objective empirical data

C. The sky is blue.

D. Airplanes flew into the World Trade Center on September 11, 2001.

18. Which of the following is a fact? *(Easy) (Skill 4.4)*

A. It's going to rain.

B. John is a liar.

C. Joe said he believes John is a liar.

D. The world is going to the dogs.

19. Exposition occurs within a story:
(Rigorous) (Skill 5.2)

A. After the rising action

B. After the denouement

C. Before the rising action

D. Before the setting

20. **Which of the following are important reasons for teaching literature?**
(Easy) (Skill 5.3)

A. Active involvement with the literature

B. Appreciate written text

C. Make sense of meaning

D. All of the above

21. **Which of the following is not a characteristic of a fable?**
(Easy) (Skill 5.3)

A. Animals that feel and talk like humans

B. Happy solutions to human dilemmas.

C. Teaches a moral or standard for behavior.

D. Illustrates specific people or groups without directly naming them

22. **Which of the following is an example of alliteration?**
(Average Rigor) (Skill 5.4)

A. "The City's voice itself is soft like Solitude."

B. "Both in one faith unanimous; though sad"

C. "By all their country's wishes blest!"

D. "In earliest Greece to thee with partial choice"

23. **Which of the following is a ballad?**
(Average Rigor) (Skill 5.4)

A. "The Knight's Tale"

B. *Julius Caesar*

C. *Paradise Lost*

D. "The Rime of the Ancient Mariner"

24. **Which of the following is an epic?**
(Average Rigor) (Skill 5.4)

A. *On the Choice of Books*

B. *The Faerie Queene*

C. *Northanger Abbey*

D. *A Doll's House*

25. The children's literature genre came into its own in the:
(Average Rigor)) (Skill 5.4)

A. Seventeenth century

B. Eighteenth century

C. Nineteenth century

D. Twentieth century

26. A sixth-grade science teacher has given her class a paper to read on the relationship between food and weight gain. The writing contains signal words such as "because," "consequently," "this is how," and "due to." This paper has which text structure?

(Average Rigor) (Skill 5.5)

A. Cause & effect

B. Compare & contrast

C. Description

D. Sequencing

27. A teacher has taught his students several strategies to monitor their reading comprehension. These strategies include identifying where in the passage they are having difficulty, identifying what the difficulty is, and restating the difficult sentence or passage in their own words. These strategies are examples of:
(Average Rigor) (Skill 5.6)

A. Graphic and semantic organizers

B. Metacognition

C. Recognizing story structure

D. Summarizing

28. A student has written a paper with the following characteristics: written in first person; characters, setting, and plot; some dialogue; events organized in chronological sequence with some flashbacks. In what genre has the student written?
(Easy) (Skill 6.2)

A. Expository writing

B. Narrative writing

C. Persuasive writing

D. Technical writing

29. Which of the following should not be included in the opening paragraph of an informative essay?
(Rigorous) (Skill 6.2)

A. Thesis sentence

B. Details and examples supporting the main idea

C. A broad general introduction to the topic

D. A style and tone that grabs the reader's attention

30. Our borders must be protected from illegal immigrants. Which of the following does NOT support this thesis?
(Rigorous) (Skill 6.2)

A. Terrorists can get across the border undetected.

B. Illegal drugs flow across the unprotected borders.

C. Illegal aliens are a drain on the American economy.

D. Illegal aliens make good citizens.

31. Which of the following are good choices for supporting a thesis?
(Rigorous) (Skill 6.2)

A. Reasons

B. Examples

C. Answer to the question why

D. All of the above

32. Which of the following is a good definition of the *purpose* for an essay?
(Easy) (Skill 6.2)

A. To get a good grade

B. To fulfill an assignment

C. To change the minds of the readers

D. The point of the writing

33. Which of the following is not an approach to keep students ever conscious of the need to write for audience appeal?
(Average Rigor) (Skill 6.2)

A. Pairing students during the writing process

B. Reading all rough drafts before the students write the final copies

C. Having students compose stories or articles

D. Writing letters to friends or relatives

34. **Which of the following is not a technique of prewriting?**
(Average Rigor) (Skill 6.3)

   A. Clustering

   B. Listing

   C. Brainstorming

   D. Proofreading

35. **Which is not a true statement concerning an author's literary tone?**
(Rigorous) (Skill 6.3)

   A. Tone is partly revealed through the selection of details.

   B. Tone is the expression of the author's attitude toward his/her subject.

   C. Tone in literature is usually satiric or angry.

   D. Tone in literature corresponds to the tone of voice a speaker uses.

36. **Which of the following contains an error in possessive inflection?**
(Rigorous) (Skill 7.2)

   A. Doris's shawl

   B. Mother's-in-law frown

   C. Children's lunches

   D. Ambassador's briefcase

37. **Which of the following sentences contains an error in agreement?**
(Rigorous) (Skill 7.4)

   A. Jennifer is one of the women who writes for the magazine.

   B. Each one of their sons plays a different sport.

   C. This band has performed at the Odeum many times.

   D. The data are available online at the listed website.

38. **Which of the following is a valid conclusion?**
(Rigorous) (Skill 8.1)

   A. Based on the evidence, I believe John Jones stole the car.

   B. I suspect that John Jones stole the car.

   C. John Jones looks guilty, so he must have stolen the car.

   D. Of the two suspects, John Jones' cynical expression makes me think he's guilty.

History & Social Science

39. **Which of the following were results of the Age of Exploration?**
    (Easy) (Skill 9.1)

    A. More complete and accurate maps and charts

    B. New and more accurate navigational instruments

    C. Proof that the earth is round

    D. All of the above

40. **What was the long-term importance of the Mayflower Compact?**
    (Rigorous) Skill 9.1)

    A. It established the foundation of all later agreements with the Native Peoples

    B. It established freedom of religion in the original English colonies

    C. It ended the war in Europe between Spain, France and England

    D. It established a model of small, town-based government that was adopted throughout the New England colonies

41. **The end of the feudal manorial system was caused by:**
    (Easy) (Skill 9.2)

    A. The Civil War

    B. The Black Plague

    C. The Christian Riots

    D. Westward Expansion

42. **What intellectual movement during the period of North American colonization contributed to the development of public education and the founding of the first colleges and universities?**
    (Average Rigor) (Skill 9.2)

    A. Enlightenment

    B. Great Awakening

    C. Libertarianism

    D. The Scientific Revolution

43. In 1957, the formation of the Southern Christian Leadership Conference was started by:
(Rigorous) (Skill 9.2)

   o Martin Luther King, Jr

   o Rev. T. J. Jemison

   o Ella Baker

   D. All of the above

44. In the early 1730s, James Oglethorpe, a British Member of Parliament engaged in a campaign to bring _____ to the America.
(Average Rigor) (Skill 9.2)

   A. Soldiers

   B. Farmers

   C. Prisoners

   D. Parliament

45. Which of the following contributed to the severity of the Great Depression?
(Average Rigor) (Skill 9.2)

   A. An influx of Chinese immigrants

   B. The dust bowl drove people out of the cities

   C. An influx of Mexican immigrants

   D. An influx of Oakies

46. The first real party organization developed soon after the inauguration of Washington as President. It included which of the following:
(Rigorous) (Skill 9.4)

   A. Democrats

   B. Republicans

   C. Nationalists

   D. All of the above

47. What was the name of the cultural revival after the Civil War?
(Rigorous) (Skill 9.4)

   A. The Revolutionary War

   B. The Second Great Awakening

   C. The Harlem Renaissance

   D. The Gilded Age

48. **Which one of the following is not a reason why Europeans came to the New World?** *(Average Rigor) (Skill 9.4)*

A. To find resources in order to increase wealth

B. To establish trade

C. To increase a ruler's power and importance

D. To spread Christianity

49. **The Westward expansion occurred for a number of reasons, however, the most important reason was:** *(Average Rigor) (Skill 9.4)*

A. Colonization

B. Slavery

C. Independence

D. Economics

50. **The year 1619 was memorable for the colony of Virginia. Three important events occurred, resulting in lasting effects on U.S. history. Which one of the following is not one of the events?** *(Rigorous) (Skill 9.4)*

A. Twenty African slaves arrived.

B. The London Company granted the colony a charter making it independent.

C. The colonists were given the right by the London Company to govern themselves through representative government in the Virginia House of Burgesses

D. The London Company sent to the colony 60 women who were quickly married, establishing families and stability in the colony.

51. **The "divine right" of kings was the key political characteristic of:** *(Rigorous) (Skill 9.4)*

A. The Age of Absolutism

B. The Age of Reason

C. The Age of Feudalism

D. The Age of Despotism

52. During the 1920s, the United States almost completely stopped all immigration. One of the reasons was:
(Rigorous) (Skill 9.4)

A. Plentiful cheap unskilled labor was no longer needed by industrialists

B. War debts from World War I made it difficult to render financial assistance

C. European nations were reluctant to allow people to leave since there was a need to rebuild populations and economic stability

D. The United States did not become a member of the League of Nations

53. Which one of the following would not be considered a result of World War II?
(Average Rigor) (Skill 9.4)

A. Economic depressions and slow resumption of trade and financial aid

B. Western Europe was no longer the center of world power

C. The beginnings of new power struggles not only in Europe but in Asia as well

D. Territorial and boundary changes for many nations, especially in Europe

54. The belief that the United States should control all of North America was called:
(Easy) (Skill 9.4)

A. Westward Expansion

B. Pan Americanism

C. Manifest Destiny

D. Nationalism

55. Capitalism and communism are alike in that they are both:
(Easy) (Skill 9.4)

A. Organic systems

B. Political systems

C. Centrally planned systems

D. Economic systems

56. An economist might engage in which of the following activities?
(Easy) (Skill 9.4)

A. An observation of the historical effects of a nation's banking practices

B. The application of a statistical test to a series of data

C. Introduction of an experimental factor into a specified population to measure the effect of the factor

D. An economist might engage in all of these

57. The advancement of understanding in dealing with human beings has led to a number of interdisciplinary areas. Which of the following interdisciplinary studies would NOT be considered under the social sciences?
(Average Rigor) (Skill 9.4)

A. Molecular biophysics

B. Peace studies

C. African-American studies

D. Cartographic information systems

58. For the historian studying ancient Egypt, which of the following would be least useful?
(Average Rigor) (Skill 9.5)

A. The record of an ancient Greek historian on Greek-Egyptian interaction

B. Letters from an Egyptian ruler to his/her regional governors

C. Inscriptions on stele of the Fourteenth Egyptian Dynasty

D. Letters from a nineteenth century Egyptologist to his wife

Mathematics

59. $\left(\dfrac{^-4}{9}\right)+\left(\dfrac{^-7}{10}\right)=$

(Easy) (Skill 13.1)

A. $\dfrac{23}{90}$

B. $\dfrac{^-23}{90}$

C. $\dfrac{103}{90}$

D. $\dfrac{^-103}{90}$

60. $(5.6)\times(^-0.11)=$

(Average Rigor) (Skill 13.1)

A. $^-0.616$

B. 0.616

C. $^-6.110$

D. 6.110

61. An item that sells for $375 is put on sale at $120. What is the percent of decrease?
(Average Rigor) (Skill 13.2)

A. 25%

B. 28%

C. 68%

D. 34%

62. Two mathematics classes have a total of 410 students. The 8:00 am class has 40 more than the 10:00 am class. How many students are in the 10:00 am class?
(Average Rigor) (Skill 13.2)

A. 123.3

B. 370

C. 185

D. 330

63. What measure could be used to report the distance traveled in walking around a track?
(Easy) (Skill 13.3)

A. Degrees

B. Square meters

C. Kilometers

D. Cubic feet

64. What is the area of a square whose side is 13 feet?
(Rigorous) (Skill 13.3)

A. 169 feet

B. 169 square feet

C. 52 feet

D. 52 square feet

65. What is the greatest common factor of 16, 28, and 36?

(Easy) (Skill 13.4)

A. 2

B. 4

C. 8

D. 16

66. If $4x - (3 - x) = 7(x - 3) + 10$, then

(Average Rigor) (Skill 13.5)

A. $x = 8$ $32 - ^-5 = 35 + 10$

B. $x = -8$

C. $x = 4$ $16 - ^-1 = 17$

D. $x = -4$

67. Given the formula $d = rt$, (where d = distance, r = rate, and t = time), calculate the time required for a vehicle to travel 585 miles at a rate of 65 miles per hour.

$t \times 65 = 585$

$$65 \overline{\smash{\big)}\,585.00} = 9$$
$$585$$

(Average Rigor) (Skill 13.6)

A. 8.5 hours

B. 6.5 hours

C. 9.5 hours

D. 9 hours

68. The following chart shows the yearly average number of international tourists visiting Palm Beach for 1990-1994. How may more international tourists visited Palm Beach in 1994 than in 1991?
(Rigorous) (Skill 14.1)

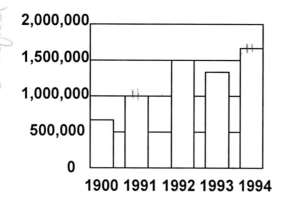

A. 100,000

B. 600,000

C. 1,600,000

D. 8,000,000

69. What is the probability of drawing 2 consecutive aces from a standard deck of cards?
(Rigorous) (Skill 14.1)

A. $\dfrac{3}{51}$

B. $\dfrac{1}{221}$

C. $\dfrac{2}{104}$

D. $\dfrac{2}{52}$

70. Which of the following is an irrational number?
(Rigorous) (Skill 14.1)

A. .362626262...

B. $4\frac{1}{3}$

C. $\sqrt{5}$

D. $-\sqrt{16}$

71. Corporate salaries are listed for several employees. Which would be the best measure of central tendency?
(Average Rigor) (Skill 14.2)

$24,000 $24,000 $26,000
$28,000 $30,000 $120,000

A. Mean

B. Median

C. Mode

D. No difference

72. Which statement is true about George's budget? *(Easy) (Skill 14.2)*

A. George spends the greatest portion of his income on food.

B. George spends twice as much on utilities as he does on his mortgage.

C. George spends twice as much on utilities as he does on food.

D. George spends the same amount on food and utilities as he does on mortgage.

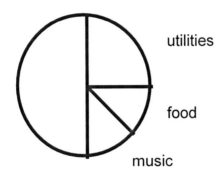

mortgage · utilities · food · music

73. Given a drawer with 5 black socks, 3 blue socks, and 2 red socks, what is the probability that you will draw two black socks in two draws in a dark room?
(Rigorous) (Skill 14.2)

A. 2/9
B. 1/4
C. 17/18
D. 1/18

74. Solve for x: $|2x + 3| > 4$

(Rigorous) (Skill 14.3)

A. $-\frac{7}{2} > x > \frac{1}{2}$

B. $-\frac{1}{2} > x > \frac{7}{2}$

C. $x < \frac{7}{2}$ or $x < -\frac{1}{2}$

D. $x < -\frac{7}{2}$ or $x > \frac{1}{2}$

75. Graph the solution:
$|x| + 7 < 13$
(Rigorous) (Skill 14.3)

A.

B.

C.

D.

76. A boat travels 30 miles upstream in three hours. It makes the return trip in one and a half hours. What is the speed of the boat in still water?
(Average Rigor) (Skill 14.3)

A. 10 mph
B. 15 mph
C. 20 mph
D. 30 mph

77. Given segment AC with B as its midpoint, find the coordinates of C if A = (5,7) and B = (3, 6.5).
(Rigorous) (Skill 14.4)

   A. (4, 6.5)
   B. (1, 6)
   C. (2, 0.5)
   D. (16, 1)

78. 3 km is equivalent to
(Easy) (Skill 14.4)

   A. 300 cm
   B. 300 m
   C. 3000 cm
   D. 3000 m

79. The mass of a cookie is closest to:
(Easy) (Skill 14.4)

   A. 0.5 kg
   B. 0.5 grams
   C. 15 grams
   D. 1.5 grams

80. If the radius of a right circular cylinder is doubled, how does its volume change?
(Rigorous) (14.5)

   A. No change
   B. Also is doubled
   C. Four times the original
   D. Pi times the original

81. In similar polygons, if the perimeters are in a ratio of x:y, the sides are in a ratio of
(Average Rigor) (Skill 14.5)

   A. x : y
   B. $x^2 : y^2$
   C. 2x : y
   D. 1/2 x : y

82. Find the midpoint of (2,5) and (7,-4).
(Average Rigor) (Skill 14.6)

   A. (9,-1)
   B. (5,9)
   C. (9/2 , -1/2)
   D. (9/2, 1/2)

83. 3x + 2y = 12
12x + 8y = 15
Solve for x and y.
(Average Rigor) (Skill 14.6)

   A. All real numbers
   B. x = 4, y = 4
   C. x = 2, y = -1
   D. ∅

Science

84. Carbon bonds with hydrogen by _____ *(Average Rigor) (Skill 20.1)*

A. Ionic bonding.
B. Non-polar covalent bonding.
C. Polar covalent bonding.
D. Strong nuclear force

85. Which of the following is a misconception about the task of teaching science in elementary school? *(Average Rigor) (Skill 20.1)*

A. Teach facts as a priority over teaching how to solve problems.
B. Involve as many senses as possible in the learning experience.
C. Accommodate individual differences in pupils' learning styles.
D. Consider the effect of technology on people rather than on material things.

86. The Doppler Effect is associated most closely with which property of waves? *(Average Rigor) (Skill 20.2)*

A. Amplitude.
B. Wavelength.
C. Frequency.
D. Intensity.

87. Accepted procedures for preparing solutions should be made with ____. *(Easy) (Skill 20.2)*

A. alcohol.
B. hydrochloric acid.
C. distilled water.
D. tap water.

88. Enzymes speed up reactions by _____. *(Rigorous) (Skill 20.2)*

A. utilizing ATP.
B. lowering pH, allowing reaction speed to increase.
C. increasing volume of substrate.
D. lowering energy of activation.

89. The transfer of heat by electromagnetic waves is called _____. *(Easy) (Skill 20.3)*

A. conduction.
B. convection.
C. phase change.
D. radiation.

90. Which of the following is *not* considered ethical behavior for a scientist? *(Easy) (Skill 20.4)*

   A. Using unpublished data and citing the source.
   B. Publishing data before other scientists have had a chance to replicate results.
   C. Collaborating with other scientists from different laboratories.
   D. Publishing work with an incomplete list of citations.

91. Sound waves are produced by _____ . *(Easy) (Skill 20.5)*

   A. pitch.
   B. noise.
   C. vibrations.
   D. sonar.

92. In an experiment measuring the growth of bacteria at different temperatures, what is the independent variable? *(Rigorous) (Skill 20.5)*

   A. Number of bacteria.
   B. Growth rate of bacteria.
   C. Temperature.
   D. Size of bacteria.

93. Which is the correct order of methodology? *(Average Rigor) (Skill 20.6)*

   1. collecting data
   2. planning a controlled experiment
   3. drawing a conclusion
   4. hypothesizing a result
   5. re-visiting a hypothesis to answer a question

   A. 1,2,3,4,5
   B. 4,2,1,3,5
   C. 4,5,1,3,2
   D. 1,3,4,5,2

94. What cell organelle contains the cell's stored food? *(Rigorous) (Skill 20.6)*

   A. Vacuoles
   B. Golgi Apparatus
   C. Ribosomes
   D. Lysosomes

95. Identify the correct sequence of organization of living things from lower to higher order: *(Rigorous) (Skill 20.6)*

   A. Cell, Organelle, Organ, Tissue, System, Organism
   B. Cell, Tissue, Organ, Organelle, System, Organism
   C. Organelle, Cell, Tissue, Organ, System, Organism
   D. Organelle, Tissue, Cell, Organ, System, Organism

96. **Which of the following is a correct explanation for scientific 'evolution'?**
    (Rigorous) (Skill 21.2)

    A. Giraffes need to reach higher for leaves to eat, so their necks stretch. The giraffe babies are then born with longer necks. Eventually, there are more long-necked giraffes in the population.
    B. Giraffes with longer necks are able to reach more leaves, so they eat more and have more babies than other giraffes. Eventually, there are more long-necked giraffes in the population.
    C. Giraffes want to reach higher for leaves to eat, so they release enzymes into their bloodstream, which in turn causes fetal development of longer-necked giraffes. Eventually, there are more long-necked giraffes in the population.
    D. Giraffes with long necks are more attractive to other giraffes, so they get the best mating partners and have more babies. Eventually, there are more long-necked giraffes in the population.

97. **Which of the following is the most accurate definition of a nonrenewable resource?**
    (Average Rigor) (Skill 21.2)

    A. A nonrenewable resource is never replaced once used.
    B. A nonrenewable resource is replaced on a timescale that is very long relative to human life spans.
    C. A nonrenewable resource is a resource that can only be manufactured by humans.
    D. A nonrenewable resource is a species that has already become extinct.

98. **Which kingdom is comprised of organisms made of one cell with no nuclear membrane?**
    (Average Rigor) (Skill 21.3)

    A. Monera.
    B. Protista.
    C. Fungi.
    D. Algae.

99. **What are the most significant and prevalent elements in the biosphere?** *(Rigorous) (Skill 21.4)*

A. Carbon, Hydrogen, Oxygen, Nitrogen, Phosphorus
B. Carbon, Hydrogen, Sodium, Iron, Calcium
C. Carbon, Oxygen, Sulfur, Manganese, Iron
D. Carbon, Hydrogen, Oxygen, Nickel, Sodium, Nitrogen

100. **Which of the following types of rock are made from magma?**

(Rigorous) (21.5)

A. Fossils
B. Sedimentary
C. Metamorphic
D. Igneous

101. **What is the most accurate description of the Water Cycle?**

(Average Rigor) (Skill 21.6)

A. Rain comes from clouds, filling the ocean. The water then evaporates and becomes clouds again.
B. Water circulates from rivers into groundwater and back, while water vapor circulates in the atmosphere.
C. Water is conserved except for chemical or nuclear reactions, and any drop of water could circulate through clouds, rain, ground water, and surface-water.
D. Weather systems cause chemical reactions to break water into its atoms.

102. **The theory of 'sea floor spreading' explains** _____

(Average Rigor) (Skill 21.6)

A. the shapes of the continents.
B. how continents collide.
C. how continents move apart.
D. how continents sink to become part of the ocean floor.

103. Which of the following is the best definition for 'meteorite'?
(*Rigorous*) (*Skill 21.6*)

   A. A meteorite is a mineral composed of mica and feldspar.
   B. A meteorite is material from outer space that has struck the earth's surface.
   C. A meteorite is an element that has properties of both metals and nonmetals.
   D. A meteorite is a very small unit of length measurement.

Physical Education & Health

104. Which of the following is not a type of muscle tissue?
(*Easy*) (*Skill 22.1*)

   A. Skeletal
   B. Cardiac
   C. Smooth
   D. Fiber

105. Which of these is a type of joint?
(*Average Rigor*) (*Skill 22.1*)

   A. Ball and socket
   B. Hinge
   C. Pivot
   D. All of the above

106. Social skills and values developed by activity include all of the following except:
(*Average Rigor*) (*Skill 22.4*)

   A. Winning at all costs
   B. Making judgments in groups
   C. Communicating and cooperating
   D. Respecting rules and property

107. Activities that enhance team socialization include all of the following except:
(*Easy*) (*Skill 22.4*)

   A. Basketball
   B. Soccer
   C. Golf
   D. Volleyball

108. Through physical activities, John has developed self-discipline, fairness, respect for others, and new friends. John has experienced which of the following? *(Rigorous) (Skill 22.4)*

A. Positive cooperation psycho-social influences

B. Positive group psycho-social influences

C. Positive individual psycho-social influences

D. Positive accomplishment psycho-social influences

109. The most effective way to promote the physical education curriculum is to: *(Rigorous) (Skill 22.6)*

A. Relate physical education to higher thought processes

B. Relate physical education to humanitarianism

C. Relate physical education to the total educational process

D. Relate physical education to skills necessary to preserve the natural environment

110. The affective domain of physical education contributes to all of the following except: *(Average Rigor) (Skill 22.6)*

A. Knowledge of exercise, health, and disease

B. Self-actualization

C. An appreciation of beauty

D. Good sportsmanship

111. A physical education instructor anticipates and prevents potential injuries, watches for hidden injuries, and takes an injury evaluation of the entire class. Which of the following strategies to prevent injuries is the teacher demonstrating? *(Average Rigor) (Skill 22.6)*

A. Maintaining hiring standards

B. Proper use of equipment

C. Proper procedures for emergencies

D. Participant screening

Visual Art

112. Engravings and oil painting originated in this country.
(Rigorous) (Skill 24.5)

    A. Italy
    B. Japan
    C. Germany
    D. Flanders

113. Which is NOT a true statement about crafts?
(Easy) (Skill 24.5)

    A. Students experiment with their own creativity.
    B. Products are unique and different.
    C. Self-expression is encouraged.
    D. Outcome is predetermined.

114. Creating movements in response to music helps students to connect music and dance in which of the following ways?
(Rigorous) (Skill 24.6)

    A. Rhythm
    B. Costuming
    C. Speed
    D. Vocabulary skills

115. The history of theatre is important at an early age Which of the following is not a vital part of the many time periods of theatre history?
(Rigorous) (Skill 27.6)

    A. Roman theatre
    B. American theatre
    C. Medieval drama
    D. Renaissance theatre

116. During the early childhood years (ages 3-5), drama and theatre experiences are especially beneficial to children because they provide the opportunity for students to:
(Average Rigor) (Skill 27.6)

    A. apply the concept of turn-taking.
    B. learn the importance of listening skills.
    C. acquire the skills needed to become a proficient reader.
    D. learn early drama skills using their five senses.

117. A combination of three or more tones sounded at the same time is called a
(Rigorous) (Skill 27.6)

    A. Harmony
    B. Consonance
    C. Chord
    D. Dissonance

118. A series of single tones that add up to a recognizable sound is called a:
     (Rigorous) (Skill 27.6)

   A. Cadence
   B. Rhythm
   C. Melody
   D. Sequence

Answer Key

1.	D	45.	D	89.	D
2.	A	46.	D	90.	D
3.	D	47.	C	91.	C
4.	D	48.	B	92.	C
5.	A	49.	D	93.	B
6.	A	50.	B	94.	A
7.	D	51.	A	95.	C
8.	D	52.	A	96.	B
9.	C	53.	A	97.	B
10.	B	54.	C	98.	A
11.	D	55.	D	99.	A
12.	D	56.	D	100.	D
13.	A	57.	A	101.	C
14.	A	58.	D	102.	C
15.	B	59.	D	103.	B
16.	A	60.	A	104.	D
17.	A	61.	C	105.	D
18.	C	62.	C	106.	A
19.	C	63.	C	107.	C
20.	D	64.	B	108.	B
21.	D	65.	B	109.	C
22.	A	66.	C	110.	A
23.	D	67.	D	111.	D
24.	B	68.	B	112.	D
25.	B	69.	B	113.	C
26.	A	70.	C	114.	A
27.	B	71.	B	115.	B
28.	B	72.	C	116.	D
29.	B	73.	A	117.	C
30.	D	74.	D	118.	C
31.	D	75.	A		
32.	C	76.	B		
33.	B	77.	B		
34.	D	78.	D		
35.	D	79.	C		
36.	B	80.	C		
37.	A	81.	A		
38.	A	82.	D		
39.	D	83.	D		
40.	D	84.	C		
41.	B	85.	A		
42.	A	86.	C		
43.	D	87.	C		
44.	C	88.	D		

Rigor Table

	Easy %20	Average Rigor %40	Rigorous %40
Question #	6,7,14,16,17,17,20, 21,28,32,39,41,55, 56,63,65,72,78,79, 87,89,90,91,104, 107,114	2,3,4,8,11,13,22,23, 24,25,26,27,33,34,42, 44,49,53,57,58,61,62, 66,71,76,81,82,83,84, 85,86,93,97,98,101. 102,105,106,110,111, 116,	1, 5, 9,10,12,15,19, 29,30,31,35,36,37,38, 40,43,45,50,51,52,64, 68,73,74,75,77,80,88, 92,94,95,96,99,100, 103,109,112,114,115, 117,118,

Rationales with Sample Questions

1. **Which of the following is not a strategy of teaching reading comprehension? (Rigorous) (Skill 1.1)**

A. Asking questions

B. Utilizing graphic organizers

C. Focusing on mental images.

D. Manipulating sounds

Answer: D. Manipulating Sounds

Comprehension simply means that the reader can ascribe meaning to text. Teachers can use many strategies to teach comprehension, including questioning, asking students to paraphrase or summarize, utilizing graphic organizers, and focusing on mental images.

2. **All of the following are true about phonological awareness EXCEPT: (Average Rigor) (Skill 1.3)**

A. It may involve print.

B. It is a prerequisite for spelling and phonics.

C. Activities can be done by the children with their eyes closed.

D. It starts before letter recognition is taught.

Answer: A. It may involve print.

The key word here is EXCEPT, which will be highlighted in upper case on the test as well. All of the options are correct aspects of phonological awareness except the first one, A, because phonological awareness DOES NOT involve print.

3. **Oral language development includes which of the following: (Average Rigor) (Skill 2.1)**

A. Listening comprehension

B. Storytelling

C. Developing vocabulary

D. All of the above

Answer: D. All of the above.

Effective oral language development includes all of the above: storytelling, listening comprehension, and an ever-increasing vocabulary.

4. **How do children make the transition from letter forms to invented spelling? (Average Rigor) Skill 2.1)**

A. Write strings of letters

B. Organize group of letters

C. Leave spaces

D. All of the above

Answer: D. All of the above.

Young children write strings of letters, organize them into groups, and then leave spaces between the groups. These are important steps in a child's early developmental stages of learning to read and write.

5.   Which aspect of language is innate? (Rigorous) (Skill 2.1)

A.   Biological capability to articulate sounds understood by other humans

B.   Cognitive ability to create syntactical structures

C.   Capacity for using semantics to convey meaning in a social environment

D.   Ability to vary inflections and accents

Answer: A. Biological capability to articulate sounds understood by other humans.

Language ability is innate, and the biological capability to produce sounds lets children learn semantics and syntactical structures through trial and error. Linguists agree that language is a vocal system of word symbols that enable a human to communicate his/her feelings, thoughts, and desires to other human beings.

6.   To decode is to: (Easy) (Skill 2.2)   *get correct meaning*

A.   Construct meaning

B.   Sound out a printed sequence of letters

C.   Use a special code to decipher a message

D.   None of the above

Answer: A. Construct meaning.

Word analysis (phonics or decoding) is the process readers use to figure out unfamiliar words based on written patterns. Decoding is the process of constructing meaning of an unknown word

7.   **To encode means that you: (Easy) (Skill 2.2)**

A.   Decode a second time

B.   Construct meaning from a code

C.   Tell someone a message

D.   None of the above

Answer: D . None of the above.

Encoding involves changing a message into symbols.

8.   **The arrangement and relationship of words in sentences or sentence structure best describes: (Average Rigor) (Skill 2.4)**

A.   Style

B.   Discourse

C.   Thesis

D.   Syntax

Answer: D. Syntax

Syntax is the grammatical structure of sentences.

9.   **Effective reading comprehension requires: (Rigorous) (Skill 2.5)**

A.   Encoding

B.   Decoding

C.   Both A and B

D.   Neither A nor B

Answer: C. Both A and B

Reading comprehension requires that the reader learn the code within which a message is written and be able to decode it to get the message.

10. **Contextual redefinition is a strategy that encourages children to use the context more effectively by presenting them with sufficient vocabulary _____ the reading of a text. (Rigorous) (3.3)**

A.   After

B.   Before

C.   During

D.   None of the above

Answer: B. Before

Contextual redefinition is a strategy that encourages children to use the context more effectively by presenting them with sufficient context BEFORE they begin reading. To apply this strategy, the teacher should first select unfamiliar words for teaching. No more than two or three words should be selected for direct teaching.

11. **What is the best place for students to find appropriate synonyms, antonyms, and other related words to enhance their writing? (Average Rigor) (Skill 3.4)**

A.   Dictionary

B.   Spell check

C.   Encyclopedia

D.   Thesaurus

Answer: D. Thesaurus

Students need plenty of exposure to the new words. A thesaurus is an excellent resource to use when writing. Students can use a thesaurus to find appropriate synonyms, antonyms, and other related words to enhance their writing

12. **Which is an untrue statement about a theme in literature? (Rigorous) (Skill 5.2)**

A. The theme is always stated directly somewhere in the text.

B. The theme is the central idea in a literary work.

C. All parts of the work (plot, setting, mood) should contribute to the theme in some way.

D. By analyzing the various elements of the work, the reader should be able to arrive at an indirectly stated theme.

Answer: D. By analyzing the various elements of the work, the reader should be able to arrive at an indirectly stated theme.

The theme may be stated directly, but it can also be implicit in various aspects of the work, such as the interaction between characters, symbolism, or description.

13. **If a student has a poor vocabulary, the teacher should recommend that: (Average Rigor) (Skill 4.1)**

A. The student read newspapers, magazines and books on a regular basis

B. The student enroll in a Latin class

C. The student write the words repetitively after looking them up in the dictionary

D. The student use a thesaurus to locate synonyms and incorporate them into his/her vocabulary

Answer: A. The student read newspapers, magazines and books on a regular basis.

The student should read newspapers, magazines, and books on a regular basis. It is up to the teacher to help the student to choose reading material, but the student must be able to choose where he/she will search for the reading pleasure indispensable for enriching vocabulary.

14. **Which of the following indicates that a student is a fluent reader? (Easy) (Skill 4.1)**

A.   Reads texts with expression or prosody

B.   Reads word-to-word and haltingly

C.   Must intentionally decode a majority of the words

D.   In a writing assignment, sentences are poorly-organized structurally

Answer: A. Reads texts with expression or prosody.

The teacher should listen to the children read aloud, but there are also clues to reading levels in their writing.

15. **All of the following are examples of ongoing informal assessment techniques used to observe student progress EXCEPT: (Rigorous) (Skill 4.1)**

A.   Analysis of student work product

B.   Collection of data from assessment tests

C.   Effective questioning

D.   Observation of students

Answer: B. Collection of data from assessment tests

Assessment tests are formal progress-monitoring measures.

16. **Which of the following is a formal reading level assessment? (Easy) (4.1)**

A.   A standardized reading test

B.   A teacher-made reading test

C.   An interview

D.   A reading diary

Answer: A. A standardized reading test.

If the assessment is standardized, it has to be objective, whereas B, C, and D are all subjective assessments.

17. **Which of the following is an opinion? (Easy) (Skill 4.4)**

A.   Subjective evaluation based upon personal bias

B.   A statement that is readily provable by objective empirical data

C.   The sky is blue.

D.   Airplanes flew into the World Trade Center on September 11, 2001.

Answer A. Subjective evaluation based upon personal bias

An opinion is a subjective evaluation based upon personal bias.

18. Which of the following is a fact? (Easy) (Skill 4.4)

A.   It's going to rain.

B.   John is a liar.

C.   Joe said he believes John is a liar.

D.   The world is going to the dogs.

Answer: C. Jow said he believes John is a liar.

The only answer that is a fact is C. Joe said he believes John is a liar. It's a fact that he said it, even though what he said may not be a fact.

19. Exposition occurs within a story: (Rigorous) (Skill 5.2)

A.   After the rising action

B.   After the denouement

C.   Before the rising action

D.   Before the setting

Answer C. Before the rising action

Exposition is where characters and their situations are introduced. *Rising action* is the point at which conflict starts to occur and is often a turning point. *Denouement* is the final resolution of the plot.

20. **Which of the following are important reasons for teaching literature? (Easy) (Skill 5.3)**

A.   Active involvement with the literature

B.   Appreciate written text

C.   Make sense of meaning

D.   All of the above

Answer: D. All of the above

Children need active involvement with the literature. Students also can understand how to appreciate written text.

21. **Which of the following is not a characteristic of a fable? (Easy) (Skill 5.3)**

A.   Animals that feel and talk like humans

B.   Happy solutions to human dilemmas

C.   Teaches a moral or standard for behavior

D.   Illustrates specific people or groups without directly naming them.

Answer: D. Illustrates specific people or groups without directly naming them.

A fable is a short tale with animals, humans, gods, or even inanimate objects as characters. Fables often conclude with a moral, delivered in the form of an epigram (a short, witty, and ingenious statement in verse). Fables are among the oldest forms of writing in human history: it appears in Egyptian papyri of c1,500 BCE. The most famous fables are those of Aesop, a Greek slave living in about 600 BCE. In India, the Pantchatantra appeared in the third century. The most famous modern fables are those of seventeenth century French poet Jean de La Fontaine.

22. **Which of the following is an example of alliteration? (Average Rigor) (Skill 5.4)**

A.   "The City's voice itself is soft like Solitude."

B.   "Both in one faith unanimous; though sad"

C.   "By all their country's wishes blest!"

D.   "In earliest Greece to thee with partial choice"

Answer A. "The City's voice itself is soft like Solitude"

Alliteration is the repetition of consonant sounds in two or more neighboring words or syllables, usually the beginning sound but not always. This line from Shelley's *Stanzas Written in Dejection Near Naples* is an especially effective use of alliteration using the sybillant *s* not only at the beginning of words but also within words. Alliteration usually appears in prosody; however, effective use of alliteration can be found in other genres.

23. **Which of the following is a ballad? (Average Rigor) (Skill 5.4)**

A.   "The Knight's Tale"

B.   Julius Caesar

C.   Paradise Lost

D.   "The Rime of the Ancient Mariner"

Answer: D. "The Rime of the Ancient Mariner"

"The Knight's Tale" is a Romantic poem from the longer *Canterbury Tales* by Chaucer. *Julius Caesar* is a Shakespearian play. *Paradise Lost* is an epic poem in blank verse. A ballad is an *in media res* story told or sung, usually in verse and accompanied by music, and usually with a refrain. Typically, ballads are based on folk stories

24. Which of the following is an epic? (Average Rigor) (Skill 5.4)

A.   On the Choice of Books

B.   The Faerie Queene

C.   Northanger Abbey

D.   A Doll's House

Answer: B. The Faerie Queene

An epic is a long poem, usually of book length, reflecting the values of the society in which it was produced. *On the Choice of Books* is an essay by Thomas Carlyle. *Northanger Abbey* is a novel written by Jane Austen, and *A Doll's House* is a play written by Henrik Ibsen.

25. The children's literature genre came into its own in the: (Average Rigor)) (Skill 5.4)

A.   Seventeenth century

B.   Eighteenth century

C.   Nineteenth century

D.   Twentieth century

Answer: B. Eighteenth century

Children's literature is a genre of its own that emerged as a distinct and independent form in the second half of the eighteenth century. *The Visible World in Pictures* by John Amos Comenius, a Czech educator, was one of the first printed works and the first picture book.

26. **A sixth-grade science teacher has given her class a paper to read on the relationship between food and weight gain. The writing contains signal words such as "because," "consequently," "this is how," and "due to." This paper has which text structure? (Average Rigor) (Skill 5.5)**

A. Cause & effect

B. Compare & contrast

C. Description

D. Sequencing

Answer: A. Cause & effect

Cause and effect is the relationship between two things when one thing makes something else happen. Writers use this text structure to show order, inform, speculate, and change behavior. This text structure uses the process of identifying potential causes of a problem or issue in an orderly way.

27. **A teacher has taught his students several strategies to monitor their reading comprehension. These strategies include identifying where in the passage they are having difficulty, identifying what the difficulty is, and restating the difficult sentence or passage in their own words. These strategies are examples of: (Average Rigor) (Skill 5.6)**

A. graphic and semantic organizers

B. metacognition

C. recognizing story structure

D. summarizing

Answer: B. metacognition

Metacognition may be defined as "thinking about thinking." Good readers use metacognitive strategies to think about and have control over their reading. Before reading, they might clarify their purpose for reading and preview the text. During reading, they might monitor their understanding, adjusting their reading speed to fit the difficulty of the text and fixing any comprehension problems they have. After reading, they check their understanding of what they read.

28. **A student has written a paper with the following characteristics: written in first person; characters, setting, and plot; some dialogue; events organized in chronological sequence with some flashbacks. In what genre has the student written? (Easy) (Skill 6.2)**

A.   Expository writing

B.   Narrative writing

C.   Persuasive writing

D.   Technical writing

Answer: B. Narrative writing

These are all characteristics of narrative writing. Expository writing is intended to give information such as an explanation or directions, and the information is logically organized. Persuasive writing gives an opinion in an attempt to convince the reader that this point of view is valid or tries to persuade the reader to take a specific action. The goal of technical writing is to clearly communicate a select piece of information to a targeted reader or group of readers.

29. **Which of the following should not be included in the opening paragraph of an informative essay? (Rigorous) (Skill 6.2)**

A.   Thesis sentence

B.   Details and examples supporting the main idea

C.   A broad general introduction to the topic

D.   A style and tone that grabs the reader's attention

Answer: B. Details and examples supporting the main idea

The introductory paragraph should introduce the topic, capture the reader's interest, state the thesis, and prepare the reader for the main points in the essay. Details and examples, however, should be given in the second part of the essay to help develop the thesis.

30. **Our borders must be protected from illegal immigrants. Which of the following does NOT support this thesis? (Rigorous) (Skill 6.2)**

A.   Terrorists can get across the border undetected.

B.   Illegal drugs flow across the unprotected borders.

C.   Illegal aliens are a drain on the American economy.

D.   Illegal aliens make good citizens.

Answer: D. Illegal aliens make good citizens.

The correct answer is D. It does not support the thesis statement. Good questions to ask to determine whether a point supports the statement are "how?" and "why?" For example: Our borders must be protected from illegal immigrants. Why? Terrorists can get across the border undetected.

31. **Which of the following are good choices for supporting a thesis? (Rigorous) (Skill 6.2)**

A.   Reasons

B.   Examples

C.   Answer to the question why

D.   All of the above.

Answer: D. All of the above

The correct answer is D. When answering "why," you are giving reasons, but those reasons need to be supported with examples.

32. Which of the following is a good definition of the purpose for an essay? (Easy) (Skill 6.2)

A.   To get a good grade

B.   To fulfill an assignment

C.   To change the minds of the readers

D.   The point of the writing

Answer: C. To change the minds of the readers.

The purpose is what you want your writing to achieve. It is based on the four forms of discourse: expository, descriptive, narrative, and persuasive.

33. Which of the following is not an approach to keep students ever conscious of the need to write for audience appeal? (Average Rigor) (Skill 6.2)

A.   Pairing students during the writing process

B.   Reading all rough drafts before the students write the final copies

C.   Having students compose stories or articles

D.   Writing letters to friends or relatives

Answer: B. Reading all rough drafts before the students write the final copies

Reading all rough drafts will not encourage the students to take control of their text and might even inhibit their creativity. On the contrary, pairing students will foster their sense of responsibility, and having them compose stories for literary magazines will boost their self esteem as well as their organization skills. As far as writing letters is concerned, the work of authors such as Madame de Sevigne in the seventeenth century are good examples of epistolary literary work.

34. **Which of the following is not a technique of prewriting? (Average Rigor) (Skill 6.3)**

A.   Clustering

B.   Listing

C.   Brainstorming

D.   Proofreading

Answer: D. Proofreading

Proofreading cannot be a method of prewriting, since it is done on already written texts only.

35. **Which is not a true statement concerning an author's literary tone? (Rigorous) (Skill 6.3)**

A.   Tone is partly revealed through the selection of details.

B.   Tone is the expression of the author's attitude toward his/her subject.

C.   Tone in literature is usually satiric or angry.

D.   Tone in literature corresponds to the tone of voice a speaker uses.

Answer: D. Tone in literature corresponds to the tone of the voice a speaker uses.

Tone in literature conveys a mood and can be as varied as the tone of voice of a speaker (e.g., sad, nostalgic, whimsical, angry, formal, intimate, satirical, sentimental, etc).

36. **Which of the following contains an error in possessive inflection? (Rigorous) (Skill 7.2)**

   A.   Doris's shawl

   B.   Mother's-in-law frown

   C.   Children's lunches

   D.   Ambassador's briefcase

Answer: B. Mother's-in-law frown

Mother-in-Law is a compound common noun and the inflection should be at the end of the word, according to the rule.

37. **Which of the following sentences contains an error in agreement? (Rigorous) (Skill 7.4)**

   A.   Jennifer is one of the women who writes for the magazine.

   B.   Each one of their sons plays a different sport.

   C.   This band has performed at the Odeum many times.

   D.   The data are available online at the listed website.

Answer: A. Jennifer is one of the women who writes for the magazine.

"Women" is the plural subject of the verb. The verb should be "write."

38. Which of the following is a valid conclusion? (Rigorous) (Skill 8.1)

A.   Based on the evidence, I believe John Jones stole the car.

B.   I suspect that John Jones stole the car.

C.   John Jones looks guilty, so he must have stolen the car.

D.   Of the two suspects, John Jones' cynical expression makes me think he's guilty.

Answer: A. Based on the evidence, I believe John Jones stole the car.

Valid conclusions are based on evidence.

History & Social Science

39. Which of the following were results of the Age of Exploration? (Easy) (Skill 9.1)

A.   More complete and accurate maps and charts

B.   New and more accurate navigational instruments

C.   Proof that the earth is round

D.   All of the above

Answer: D. All of the above

The importance of the Age of Exploration was not only the discovery and colonization of the New World, but also better maps and charts; new accurate navigational instruments; increased knowledge; great wealth; new and different foods and items not known in Europe; a new hemisphere as a refuge from poverty, persecution, a place to start a new and better life; and proof that Asia could be reached by sea and that the earth was round; ships and sailors would not sail off the edge of a flat earth and disappear forever into nothingness.

40. **What was the long-term importance of the Mayflower Compact? (Rigorous) Skill 9.1)**

A.   It established the foundation of all later agreements with the Native Peoples

B.   It established freedom of religion in the original English colonies

C.   It ended the war in Europe between Spain, France and England

D.   It established a model of small, town-based government that was adopted throughout the New England colonies

Answer: D.   Established a model of small, town-based government

Before setting foot on land in 1620, the Pilgrims aboard the Mayflower agreed to a form of self-government by signing the Mayflower Compact. The Compact served as the basis for governing the Plymouth colony for many years and set an example of small, town-based government that would proliferate throughout New England. The present day New England town meeting is an extension of this tradition. This republican ideal was later to clash with the policies of British colonial government

41. **The end of the feudal manorial system was caused by: (Easy) (Skill 9.2)**

A.   The Civil War

B.   The Black Plague

C.   The Christian Riots

D.   Westward Expansion

Answer: B. The Black Plague

The end of the feudal manorial system was sealed by the outbreak and spread of the infamous Black Death, which killed over one-third of the total population of Europe.

42. **What intellectual movement during the period of North American colonization contributed to the development of public education and the founding of the first colleges and universities? (Average Rigor) (Skill 9.2)**

A.   Enlightenment

B.   Great Awakening

C.   Libertarianism

D.   The Scientific Revolution

Answer: A. Enlightenment

Enlightenment thinking quickly made the voyage across the Atlantic Ocean. It valued human reason and the importance of education, knowledge, and scholarly research. Education in the middle colonies was influenced largely by the Enlightenment movement, which emphasized scholarly research and public service. Benjamin Franklin embodied these principles in Philadelphia, which became a center of learning and culture, owing largely to its economic success and ease of access to European books and tracts.

43. **In 1957, the formation of the Southern Christian Leadership Conference was started by: (Rigorous) (Skill 9.2)**

A.   Martin Luther King, Jr

B.   Rev. T. J. Jemison

C.   Ella Baker

D.   All of the above

Answer: D. All of the above

In 1957, the formation of the Southern Christian Leadership Conference by Martin Luther King, Jr., John Duffy, Rev. C. D. Steele, Rev. T. J. Jemison, Rev. Fred Shuttlesworth, Ella Baker, A. Philip Randolph, Bayard Rustin and Stanley Levison provided training and assistance to local efforts to fight segregation.

44. In the early 1730s, James Oglethorpe, a British Member of Parliament engaged in a campaign to bring _____ to the America. (Average Rigor) (Skill 9.2)

A.   Soldiers

B.   Farmers

C.   Prisoners

D.   Parliament

Answer: C. Prisoners

Oglethorpe presented a plan to colonize the newly available land in North America with prisoners in order to give them an opportunity to escape the horrors of prison and start over in the New World.

45. Which of the following contributed to the severity of the Great Depression? (Average Rigor) (Skill 9.2)

A.   An influx of Chinese immigrants.

B.   The dust bowl drove people out of the cities.

C.   An influx of Mexican immigrants.

D.   An influx of Oakies.

Answer: D. An influx of Oakies

The answer is "An influx of Oakies" (D). The Dust Bowl of the Great Plains destroyed agriculture in the area. People living in the plains areas lost their livelihood and many lost their homes and possessions in the great dust storms that resulted from a period of extended drought. People from all of the states affected by the Dust Bowl made their way to California in search of a better life. Because the majority of the people were from Oklahoma, they were all referred to as "Oakies." These migrants brought with them their distinctive plains culture. The great influx of people seeking jobs exacerbated the effects of the Great Depression in California.

46. The first real party organization developed soon after the inauguration of Washington as President. It included which of the following: (Rigorous) (Skill 9.4)

A.   Democrats

B.   Republicans

C.   Nationalists

D.   All of the above

Answer: D. All of the above

Washington's cabinet included people of both factions. Hamilton was the leader of the Nationalists (the Federalist Party), and Jefferson was the spokesman for the Anti-Federalists, later known as Republicans, Democratic-Republicans, and finally Democrats.

47. What was the name of the cultural revival after the Civil War? (Rigorous) (Skill 9.4)

A.   The Revolutionary War

B.   The Second Great Awakening

C.   The Harlem Renaissance

D.   The Gilded Age

Answer: C. The Harlem Renaissance

As African Americans left the rural South and migrated to the North in search of opportunity, many settled in Harlem in New York City. By the 1920s, Harlem had become a center of life and activity for persons of color. The music, art, and literature of this community gave birth to a cultural movement known as the Harlem Renaissance.   (A) The Revolution War (1776) occurred prior to the Civil War. (B) The Second Great Awakening occurred in the 1920s, but like the (D) Gilded Age (1878 – 1889), it affected the entire United States.

48. Which one of the following is not a reason why Europeans came to the New World? (Average Rigor) (Skill 9.4)

A.   To find resources in order to increase wealth

B.   To establish trade

C.   To increase a ruler's power and importance

D.   To spread Christianity

Answer: B. To establish trade

The Europeans came to the New World for a number of reasons; they often came to find new natural resources to extract for manufacturing. The Portuguese, Spanish, and English were sent over to increase the monarch's power and to spread influences such as religion (Christianity) and culture. Therefore, the only reason given that Europeans didn't come to the New World was to establish trade.

49. The Westward expansion occurred for a number of reasons, however, the most important reason was: (Average Rigor) (Skill 9.4)

A.   Colonization

B.   Slavery

C.   Independence

D.   Economics

Answer D. Economics

Westward expansion occurred for a number of reasons, the most important being economic.

50. The year 1619 was a memorable for the colony of Virginia. Three important events occurred resulting in lasting effects on US history. Which one of the following is not one of the events? (Rigorous) (Skill 9.4)

A.   Twenty African slaves arrived.

B.   The London Company granted the colony a charter making it independent.

C.   The colonists were given the right by the London Company to govern themselves through representative government in the Virginia House of Burgesses

D.   The London Company sent to the colony 60 women who were quickly married, establishing families and stability in the colony.

Answer: B. The London Company granted the colony a charter making it independent.

In the year 1619, the Southern colony of Virginia had an eventful year including the first arrival of twenty African slaves, the right to self-governance through representative government in the Virginia House of Burgesses (their own legislative body), and the arrival of sixty women sent to marry and establish families in the colony. The London Company did not, however, grant the colony a charter in 1619.

51.   The "divine right" of kings was the key political characteristic of: (Rigorous) (Skill 9.4)

A.   The Age of Absolutism

B.   The Age of Reason

C.   The Age of Feudalism

D.   The Age of Despotism

Answer: A. The Age of Absolutism

The "divine right" of kings was the key political characteristic of The Age of Absolutism and was most visible in the reign of King Louis XIV of France, as well as during the times of King James I and his son, Charles I. The divine right doctrine claims that kings and absolute leaders derive their right to rule by virtue of their birth alone. They see this both as a law of God and of nature.

52. **During the 1920s, the United States almost completely stopped all immigration. One of the reasons was: (Rigorous) (Skill 9.4)**

A.   Plentiful cheap unskilled labor was no longer needed by industrialists

B.   War debts from World War I made it difficult to render financial assistance

C.   European nations were reluctant to allow people to leave since there was a need to rebuild populations and economic stability

D.   The United States did not become a member of the League of Nations

Answer: A. Plentiful cheap unskilled labor was no longer needed by industrialists

The primary reason that the United States almost completely stopped all immigration during the 1920s was because their once much needed cheap, unskilled labor jobs, made available by the once booming industrial economy, were no longer needed. This had much to do with the increased use of machines to do the work once done by cheap, unskilled laborers.

53. **Which one of the following would not be considered a result of World War II? (Average Rigor) (Skill 9.4)**

A.   Economic depressions and slow resumption of trade and financial aid

B.   Western Europe was no longer the center of world power

C.   The beginnings of new power struggles not only in Europe but in Asia as well

D.   Territorial and boundary changes for many nations, especially in Europe

Answer: A. Economic depressions and slow resumption of trade and financial aid

Following World War II, the economy was vibrant and flourished from the stimulant of war and an increased dependence of the world on United States industries. Therefore, World War II didn't result in economic depressions and slow resumption of trade and financial aid. Western Europe was no longer the center of world power. New power struggles arose in Europe and Asia and many European nations underwent changing territories and boundaries.

54. **The belief that the United States should control all of North America was called: (Easy) (Skill 9.4)**

A. Westward Expansion

B. Pan Americanism

C. Manifest Destiny

D. Nationalism

Answer: C. Manifest Destiny

The belief that the United States should control all of North America was called (B) Manifest Destiny. This idea fueled much of the violence and aggression towards those already occupying the lands such as the Native Americans. Manifest Destiny was certainly driven by sentiments of (D) nationalism and gave rise to (A) westward expansion.

55. **Capitalism and communism are alike in that they are both: (Easy) (Skill 9.4)**

A. Organic systems

B. Political systems

C. Centrally planned systems

D. Economic systems

Answer: D. Economic systems

While economic and (B) political systems are often closely connected, capitalism and communism are primarily (D) economic systems. Capitalism is a system of economics that allows the open market to determine the relative value of goods and services. Communism is an economic system where the market is planned by a central state. While communism is a (C) centrally planned system, this is not true of capitalism. (A) Organic systems are studied in biology, a natural science.

56. **An economist might engage in which of the following activities? (Easy) (Skill 9.4)**

A.   An observation of the historical effects of a nation's banking practices.

B.   The application of a statistical test to a series of data.

C.   Introduction of an experimental factor into a specified population to measure the effect of the factor.

D.   An economist might engage in all of these.

Answer: D. An economist might engage in all of these

Economists use statistical analysis of economic data, controlled experimentation, and historical research in their field of social science.

57. **The advancement of understanding in dealing with human beings has led to a number of interdisciplinary areas. Which of the following interdisciplinary studies would NOT be considered under the social sciences? (Average Rigor) (Skill 9.4)**

A.   Molecular biophysics

B.   Peace studies

C.   African-American studies

D.   Cartographic information systems

Answer: A. Molecular biphysics

Molecular biophysics is an interdisciplinary field combining the fields of biology, chemistry, and physics. These are all natural sciences, and not social sciences

58. **For the historian studying ancient Egypt, which of the following would be least useful? (Average Rigor) (Skill 9.5)**

A.   The record of an ancient Greek historian on Greek-Egyptian interaction

B.   Letters from an Egyptian ruler to his/her regional governors

C.   Inscriptions on stele of the Fourteenth Egyptian Dynasty

D.   Letters from a nineteenth century Egyptologist to his wife

Answer: D. Letters from a nineteenth century Egyptologist to his wife

Historians use primary sources from the actual time they are studying whenever possible. (A) Ancient Greek records of interaction with Egypt, (B) letters from an Egyptian ruler to regional governors, and (C) inscriptions from the Fourteenth Egyptian Dynasty are all primary sources created at or near the actual time being studied. (D) Letters from a nineteenth century Egyptologist would not be considered primary sources, as they were created thousands of years after the fact and may not actually be about the subject being studied.

59. $\left(\dfrac{-4}{9}\right) + \left(\dfrac{-7}{10}\right) =$ (Easy) (Skill 13.1)

A. $\dfrac{23}{90}$

B. $\dfrac{-23}{90}$

C. $\dfrac{103}{90}$

D. $\dfrac{-103}{90}$

Answer: D.

Find the LCD of $\dfrac{-4}{9}$ and $\dfrac{-7}{10}$. The LCD is 90, so you get $\dfrac{-40}{90} + \dfrac{-63}{90} = \dfrac{-103}{90}$, which is answer D.

60. $(5.6) \times (^{-}0.11) =$ *(Average Rigor) (Skill 13.1)*

A. $^{-}0.616$

B. 0.616

C. $^{-}6.110$

D. 6.110

Answer: A. $^{-}0.616$

This is simple multiplication. The answer will be negative because a positive times a negative is a negative number. $5.6 \times^{-} 0.11 =^{-} 0.616$, which is answer A.

61. An item that sells for $375 is put on sale at $120. What is the percent of decrease? (Average Rigor) (Skill 13.2)

A.   25%

B.   28%

C.   68%

D.   34%

Answer: C. 68%

Use $(1 - x)$ as the discount. $375x = 120$.

$375(1 - x) = 120 \rightarrow 375 - 375x = 120 \rightarrow 375x = 255 \rightarrow x = 0.68 = 68\%$, which is answer C.

62. Two mathematics classes have a total of 410 students. The 8:00 am class has 40 more than the 10:00 am class. How many students are in the 10:00 am class? (Average Rigor) (Skill 13.2)

A.   123.3

B.   370

C.   185

D.   330

Answer: C. 185

Let x = # of students in the 8 am class and x – 40 = # of students in the 10 am class. So there are 225 students in the 8 am class, and 225 – 40 = 185 in the 10 am class, which is answer C.

63. What measure could be used to report the distance traveled in walking around a track? (Easy) (Skill 13.3)

A.   Degrees

B.   Square meters

C.   Kilometers

D.   Cubic feet

Answer: C. Kilometers

Degrees measure angles, square meters measure area, cubic feet measure volume, and kilometers measure length. Kilometers is the only reasonable answer.

64. **What is the area of a square whose side is 13 feet? (Rigorous) (Skill 13.3)**

A.   169 feet

B.   169 square feet

C.   52 feet

D.   52 square feet

Answer: B. 169 square feet

Area = length times width (*lw*)
Length = 13 feet
Width = 13 feet (square, so length and width are the same)
Area = $13 \times 13 = 169$ square feet
Area is measured in square feet. The answer is B.

65. **What is the greatest common factor of 16, 28, and 36? (Easy) (Skill 13.4)**

A.   2

B.   4

C.   8

D.   16

Answer: B. 4

The smallest number in this set is 16; its factors are 1, 2, 4, 8, and 16. 16 is the largest factor, but it does not divide into 28 or 36. Neither does 8. 4 does factor into both 28 and 36. The answer is B.

66. If $4x - (3 - x) = 7(x - 3) + 10$, then: (Average Rigor) (Skill 13.5)

A. $x = 8$

B. $x = -8$

C. $x = 4$

D. $x = -4$

Answer: C. $x = 4$

Solve for x.
$$4x - (3 - x) = 7(x - 3) + 10$$
$$4x - 3 + x = 7x - 21 + 10$$
$$5x - 3 = 7x - 11$$
$$5x = 7x - 11 + 3$$
$$5x - 7x = ^- 8$$
$$^- 2x = ^- 8$$
$$x = 4$$
The answer is C.

67. Given the formula d =rt, (where d = distance, r =rate, and t =time), calculate the time required for a vehicle to travel 585 miles at a rate of 65 miles per hour. (Average Rigor) (Skill 13.6)

A. 8.5 hours

B. 6.5 hours

C. 9.5 hours

D. 9 hours

Answer: D. 9 hours

We are given d = 585 miles and r = 65 miles per hour and d =rt. Solve for t.
$585 = 65t \rightarrow t = 9$ hours, which is answer D.

68. The following chart shows the yearly average number of international tourists visiting Palm Beach for 1990-1994. How may more international tourists visited Palm Beach in 1994 than in 1991? (Rigorous) (Skill 14.1)

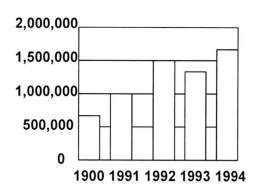

A. 100,000

B. 600,000

C. 1,600,000

D. 8,000,000

Answer: B. 600,000

The number of tourists in 1991 was 1,000,000 and the number in 1994 was 1,600,000. Subtract to get a difference of 600,000, which is answer B.

69. What is the probability of drawing 2 consecutive aces from a standard deck of cards? (Rigorous) (Skill 14.1)

A. $\dfrac{3}{51}$

B. $\dfrac{1}{221}$

C. $\dfrac{2}{104}$

D. $\dfrac{2}{52}$

Answer: B

There are 4 aces in the 52 card deck.

$P(\text{first ace}) = \dfrac{4}{52}$

$P(\text{second ace}) = \dfrac{3}{51}$

$P(\text{first ace and second ace}) = P(\text{one ace}) \times P(\text{second ace} | \text{first ace})$

$= \dfrac{4}{52} \times \dfrac{3}{51} = \dfrac{1}{221}$. This is answer B.

70. Which of the following is an irrational number? (Rigorous) (Skill 14.1)

A.   .362626262...

B.   4

C. $\sqrt{5}$

D. $-\sqrt{16}$

Answer: C

Irrational numbers are real numbers that cannot be written as the ratio of two integers, such as infinite non-repeating decimals. $\sqrt{5}$ fits this description; the others do not.

71. Corporate salaries are listed for several employees. Which would be the best measure of central tendency? (Average Rigor) (Skill 14.2)

$24,000 $24,000 $26,000 $28,000 $30,000 $120,000

A.   Mean

B.   Median

C.   Mode

D.   No difference

Answer: B. Median

The median provides the best measure of central tendency in this case, as the mode is the lowest number and the mean would be disproportionately skewed by the outlier $120,000.

72. **Which statement is true about George's budget? (Easy) (Skill 14.2)**

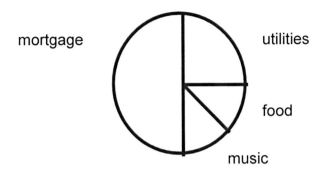

mortgage   utilities

food

music

A.   George spends the greatest portion of his income on food.

B.   George spends twice as much on utilities as he does on his mortgage.

C.   George spends twice as much on utilities as he does on food.

D.   George spends the same amount on food and utilities as he does on mortgage.

Answer: C

George spends twice as much on utilities as he does on food.

73. **Given a drawer with 5 black socks, 3 blue socks, and 2 red socks, what is the probability that you will draw two black socks in two draws in a dark room? (Rigorous) (Skill 14.2)**

A.   2/9

B.   1/4

C.   17/18

D.   1/18

Answer: A. 2/9

In this example of conditional probability, the probability of drawing a black sock on the first draw is 5/10. It is implied in the problem that there is no replacement, therefore the probability of obtaining a black sock in the second draw is 4/9. Multiply the two probabilities and reduce to lowest terms.

74. Solve for x: $|2x + 3| > 4$ (Rigorous) (Skill 14.3)

A. $-\frac{7}{2} > x > \frac{1}{2}$

B. $-\frac{1}{2} > x > \frac{7}{2}$

C. $x < \frac{7}{2}$ or $x < -\frac{1}{2}$

D. $x < -\frac{7}{2}$ or $x > \frac{1}{2}$

Answer: D

The quantity within the absolute value symbols must be either > 4 or < -4. Solve the two inequalities $2x + 3 > 4$ or $2x + 3 < -4$.

75. Graph the solution: $|x| + 7 < 13$ (Rigorous) (Skill 14.3)

A.

B.

C.

D.

Answer: A

Solve by adding -7 to each side of the inequality. Since the absolute value of x is less than 6, x must be between -6 and 6. The end points are not included, so the circles on the graph are hollow.

76. A boat travels 30 miles upstream in three hours. It makes the return trip in one and a half hours. What is the speed of the boat in still water? (Average Rigor) (Skill 14.3)

A.   10 mph

B.   15 mph

C.   20 mph

D.   30 mph

Answer: B. 15 mph

Let x = the speed of the boat in still water and c = the speed of the current.

	rate	time	distance
upstream	x - c	3	30
downstream	x + c	1.5	30

Solve the system:
$$3x - 3c = 30$$
$$1.5x + 1.5c = 30$$

77. Given segment AC with B as its midpoint, find the coordinates of C if A = (5,7) and B = (3, 6.5). (Rigorous) (Skill 14.4)

A.   (4, 6.5)

B.   (1, 6)

C.   (2, 0.5)

D.   (16, 1)

Answer: B. (1, 6)

78. 3 km is equivalent to (Easy) (Skill 14.4)

A.   300 cm
B.   300 m
C.   3000 cm
D.   3000 m

Answer: D. 3000 m

To change kilometers to meters, move the decimal 3 places to the right.

79. The mass of a cookie is closest to: (Easy) (Skill 14.4)

A.   0.5 kg

B.   0.5 grams

C.   15 grams

D.   1.5 grams

Answer: C. 15 grams

Science utilizes the metric system, and the unit of grams is used when measuring mass (the amount of matter in an object). A common estimation of mass used in elementary schools is that a paperclip has a mass of approximately one gram, which eliminates choices B and D as they are very close to 1 gram. A common estimation of one kilogram is equal to one liter of water. Half of one liter of water is still much more than one cookie, eliminating choice A. Therefore, the best estimation for one cookie is narrowed to 15 grams, or choice C.

80. **If the radius of a right circular cylinder is doubled, how does its volume change? (Rigorous) (14.5)**

A.   No change

B.   Also is doubled

C.   Four times the original

D.   Pi times the original

Answer: C. Four times the original

If the radius of a right circular cylinder is doubled, the volume is multiplied by four because in the formula, the radius is squared. Therefore, the new volume is 2 x 2 or four times the original.

81. **In similar polygons, if the perimeters are in a ratio of x:y, the sides are in a ratio of (Average Rigor) (Skill 14.5)**

A.   x : y

B.   x2: y2

C.   2x : y

D.   1/2 x : y

Answer: A. x : y

The sides are in the same ratio.

82. Find the midpoint of (2,5) and (7,-4). (Average Rigor) (Skill 14.6)

A.   (9,-1)

B.   (5,9)

C.   (9/2 , -1/2)

D.   (9/2, 1/2)

Answer: D. (9/2, 1/2)

Using the midpoint formula, $x = (2 + 7)/2$ $y = (5 + -4)/2$

83. 3x + 2y = 12
     12x + 8y = 15
     Solve for x and y.
     (Average Rigor) (Skill 14.6)

A.   All real numbers

B.   x = 4, y = 4

C.   x = 2, y = -1

D.   ∅

Answer: D

Multiplying the top equation by -4 and adding results in the equation 0 = -33. Since this is a false statement, the correct choice is the null set.

Science

84. **Carbon bonds with hydrogen by _____** (Average Rigor) (Skill 20.1)

A.   Ionic bonding

B.   Non-polar covalent bonding

C.   Polar covalent bonding

D.   Strong nuclear force

Answer: C. Polar covalent bonding

Each carbon atom contains four valence electrons, while each hydrogen atom contains one valence electron. A carbon atom can bond with one or more hydrogen atoms, such that two electrons are shared in each bond. This is covalent bonding, because the electrons are shared. (In ionic bonding, atoms must gain or lose electrons to form ions. The ions are then electrically attracted in oppositely charged pairs.) Covalent bonds are always polar when between two non-identical atoms, so this bond must be polar. ("Polar" means that the electrons are shared unequally, forming a pair of partial charges, i.e. poles.) In any case, the strong nuclear force is not relevant to this problem. The answer to this question is therefore (C).

85. Which of the following is a misconception about the task of teaching science in elementary school? (Average Rigor) (Skill 20.1)

A.   Teach facts as a priority over teaching how to solve problems.

B.   Involve as many senses as possible in the learning experience.

C.   Accommodate individual differences in pupils' learning styles.

D.   Consider the effect of technology on people rather than on material things.

Answer: A. Teach facts as a priority over teaching how to solve problems.

Prioritizing facts over problem solving is a common misconception in elementary schools. Oftentimes teachers focus on requiring students to learn and recall facts and information alone, rather than teaching them how to apply the learned facts in solving real scientific problems. In fact, problem solving is a vital skill that students need to obtain and utilize in all classroom settings, as well as their real world experiences. Choices B, C, and D all describe effective teaching strategies that exceptional teachers use in their science classrooms.

86. The Doppler Effect is associated most closely with which property of waves? (Average Rigor) (Skill 20.2)

A.   Amplitude.

B.   Wavelength.

C.   Frequency.

D.   Intensity.

Answer: C. Frequency.

The Doppler Effect accounts for an apparent increase in frequency when a wave source moves toward a wave receiver or apparent decrease in frequency when a wave source moves away from a wave receiver. (Note that the receiver could also be moving toward or away from the source.) As the wave fronts are released, motion toward the receiver mimics more frequent wave fronts, while motion away from the receiver mimics less frequent wave fronts. Meanwhile, the amplitude, wavelength, and intensity of the wave are not as relevant to this process (although moving closer to a wave source makes it seem more intense). The answer to this question is therefore(C).

87. **Accepted procedures for preparing solutions should be made with _____. (Easy) (Skill 20.2)**

A.   alcohol.

B.   hydrochloric acid.

C.   distilled water.

D.   tap water.

Answer: C. Distilled water.

Alcohol and hydrochloric acid should never be used to make solutions unless instructed to do so. All solutions should be made with distilled water as tap water contains dissolved particles which may affect the results of an experiment. The correct answer is (C).

88. **Enzymes speed up reactions by _____ . (Rigorous) (Skill 20.2)**

A.   utilizing ATP.

B.   lowering pH, allowing reaction speed to increase.

C.   increasing volume of substrate.

D.   lowering energy of activation.

Answer: D. Lowering energy of activation.

Because enzymes are catalysts, they work the same way—they cause the formation of activated chemical complexes, which require a lower activation energy. Therefore, the answer is (D). ATP is an energy source for cells, and pH or volume changes may or may not affect reaction rate, so these answers can be eliminated.

89. The transfer of heat by electromagnetic waves is called _____ . (Easy) (Skill 20.3)

A.   conduction.

B.   convection.

C.   phase change.

D.   radiation.

Answer: D. Radiation

Heat transfer via electromagnetic waves (which can occur even in a vacuum) is called radiation. (Heat can also be transferred by direct contact (conduction), by fluid current (convection), and by matter changing phase, but these are not relevant here.) The answer to this question is therefore (D).

90. Which of the following is not considered ethical behavior for a scientist?   (Easy) (Skill 20.4)

A.   Using unpublished data and citing the source.

B.   Publishing data before other scientists have had a chance to replicate results.

C.   Collaborating with other scientists from different laboratories.

D.   Publishing work with an incomplete list of citations.

Answer: D. Publishing work with an incomplete list of citations.

One of the most important ethical principles for scientists is to cite all sources of data and analysis when publishing work. It is reasonable to use unpublished data (A), as long as the source is cited. Most science is published before other scientists replicate it (B), and frequently scientists collaborate with each other, in the same or different laboratories (C). These are all ethical choices. However, publishing work without the appropriate citations, is unethical. Therefore, the answer is (D).

91. Sound waves are produced by _____ . (Easy) (Skill 20.5)

A.   pitch.

B.   noise.

C.   vibrations.

D.   sonar.

Answer: C. Vibrations

Sound waves are produced by a vibrating body. The vibrating object moves forward and compresses the air in front of it, then reverses direction so that pressure on the air is lessened and expansion of the air molecules occurs. The vibrating air molecules move back and forth parallel to the direction of motion of the wave as they pass the energy from adjacent air molecules closer to the source to air molecules farther away from the source. Therefore, the answer is (C).

92. In an experiment measuring the growth of bacteria at different temperatures, what is the independent variable? (Rigorous) (Skill 20.5)

A.   Number of bacteria.

B.   Growth rate of bacteria.

C.   Temperature.

D.   Size of bacteria.

Answer: C. Temperature

To answer this question, recall that the independent variable in an experiment is the entity that is changed by the scientist, in order to observe the effects (the dependent variable(s)). In this experiment, temperature is changed in order to measure growth of bacteria, so (C) is the answer. Note that answer (A) is the dependent variable, and neither (B) nor (D) is directly relevant to the question.

93. **Which is the correct order of methodology? (Average Rigor) (Skill 20.6)**

1. collecting data
2. planning a controlled experiment
3. drawing a conclusion
4. hypothesizing a result
5. re-visiting a hypothesis to answer a question

A.   1,2,3,4,5

B.   4,2,1,3,5

C.   4,5,1,3,2

D.   1,3,4,5,2

Answer: B. 4,2,1,3,5

The correct methodology for the scientific method is first to make a meaningful hypothesis (educated guess), and then to plan and execute a controlled experiment to test that hypothesis. Using the data collected in that experiment, the scientist then draws conclusions and attempts to answer the original question related to the hypothesis. This is consistent only with answer (B).

94. **What cell organelle contains the cell's stored food? (Rigorous) (Skill 20.6)**

A.   Vacuoles

B.   Golgi Apparatus

C.   Ribosomes

D.   Lysosomes

Answer: A. Vacuoles

In a cell, the sub-parts are called organelles. Of these, the vacuoles hold stored food (and water and pigments). The Golgi Apparatus sorts molecules from other parts of the cell; the ribosomes are sites of protein synthesis; the lysosomes contain digestive enzymes. This is consistent only with answer (A).

95. Identify the correct sequence of organization of living things from lower to higher order: (Rigorous) (Skill 20.6)

A.   Cell, Organelle, Organ, Tissue, System, Organism

B.   Cell, Tissue, Organ, Organelle, System, Organism

C.   Organelle, Cell, Tissue, Organ, System, Organism

D.   Organelle, Tissue, Cell, Organ, System, Organism

Answer: C. Organelle, Cell, Tissue, Organ, System, Organism

Organelles are parts of the cell; cells make up tissue, which makes up organs. Organs work together in systems (e.g., the respiratory system), and the organism is the living thing as a whole. Therefore, the answer must be (C).

96. **Which of the following is a correct explanation for scientific 'evolution'? (Rigorous) (Skill 21.2)**

A.   Giraffes need to reach higher for leaves to eat, so their necks stretch. The giraffe babies are then born with longer necks. Eventually, there are more long-necked giraffes in the population.

B.   Giraffes with longer necks are able to reach more leaves, so they eat more and have more babies than other giraffes. Eventually, there are more long-necked giraffes in the population.

C.   Giraffes want to reach higher for leaves to eat, so they release enzymes into their bloodstream, which in turn causes fetal development of longer-necked giraffes. Eventually, there are more long-necked giraffes in the population.

D.   Giraffes with long necks are more attractive to other giraffes, so they get the best mating partners and have more babies. Eventually, there are more long-necked giraffes in the population.

Answer: B. Giraffes with longer necks are able to reach more leaves, so they eat more and have more babies than other giraffes. Eventually, there are more long-necked giraffes in the population.

Organisms with a life/reproductive advantage will produce more offspring. Over many generations, this changes the proportions of the population. In any case, it is impossible for a stretched neck (A) or a fervent desire (C) to result in biologically mutated baby. Although there are traits that are naturally selected because of mate attractiveness and fitness (D), this is not the primary situation here, so answer (B) is the best choice.

97. Which of the following is the most accurate definition of a non-renewable resource? (Average Rigor) (Skill 21.2)

A.   A nonrenewable resource is never replaced once used.

B.   A nonrenewable resource is replaced on a timescale that is very long relative to human life spans.

C.   A nonrenewable resource is a resource that can only be manufactured by humans.

D.   A nonrenewable resource is a species that has already become extinct.

Answer: B. A nonrenewable resource is replaced on a timescale that is very long relative to human life- spans.

Renewable resources are those that are renewed, or replaced, in time for humans to use more of them. Examples include fast-growing plants, animals, or oxygen gas. (Note that while sunlight is often considered a renewable resource, it is actually a nonrenewable but extremely abundant resource.) Nonrenewable resources are those that renew themselves only on very long timescales, usually geologic timescales. Examples include minerals, metals, or fossil fuels. Therefore, the correct answer is (B).

98. Which kingdom is comprised of organisms made of one cell with no nuclear membrane? (Average Rigor) (Skill 21.3)

A.   Monera.

B.   Protista.

C.   Fungi.

D.   Algae.

Answer: A. Monera

To answer this question, first note that algae are not a kingdom of their own. Some algae are in monera, the kingdom that consists of unicellular prokaryotes with no true nucleus. Protista and fungi are both eukaryotic, with true nuclei, and are sometimes multi-cellular. Therefore, the answer is (A).

99. **What are the most significant and prevalent elements in the biosphere? (Rigorous) (Skill 21.4)**

A.   Carbon, Hydrogen, Oxygen, Nitrogen, Phosphorus

B.   Carbon, Hydrogen, Sodium, Iron, Calcium

C.   Carbon, Oxygen, Sulfur, Manganese, Iron

D.   Carbon, Hydrogen, Oxygen, Nickel, Sodium, Nitrogen

Answer: A. Carbon, Hydrogen, Oxygen, Nitrogen, Phosphorus

Organic matter (and life as we know it) is based on Carbon atoms, bonded to Hydrogen and Oxygen. Nitrogen and Phosphorus are the next most significant elements, followed by Sulfur and then trace nutrients such as Iron, Sodium, Calcium, and others. Therefore, the answer is (A). If you know that the formula for any carbohydrate contains Carbon, Hydrogen, and Oxygen, that will help you narrow the choices to (A) and (D) in any case.

100. **Which of the following types of rock are made from magma? (Rigorous) (21.5)**

A.   Fossils

B.   Sedimentary

C.   Metamorphic

D.   Igneous

Answer: D. Igneous

Metamorphic rocks are formed by high temperatures and great pressures. Fluid sediments are transformed into solid sedimentary rocks. Only Igneous rocks are formed from magma. The answer is (D).

101. **What is the most accurate description of the Water Cycle? (Average Rigor) (Skill 21.6)**

   A.   Rain comes from clouds, filling the ocean. The water then evaporates and becomes clouds again.

   B.   Water circulates from rivers into groundwater and back, while water vapor circulates in the atmosphere.

   C.   Water is conserved except for chemical or nuclear reactions, and any drop of water could circulate through clouds, rain, ground water, and surface-water.

   D.   Weather systems cause chemical reactions to break water into its atoms.

Answer: C. Water is conserved except for chemical or nuclear reactions, and any drop of water could circulate through clouds, rain, ground water, and surface-water.

All natural chemical cycles, including the Water Cycle, depend on the principle of Conservation of Mass. (For water, unlike for elements such as Nitrogen, chemical reactions may cause sources or sinks of water molecules.) Any drop of water may circulate through the hydrologic system, ending up in a cloud, as rain, or as surface- or ground-water. Although answers (A) and (B) describe parts of the water cycle, the most comprehensive answer is (C).

102. **The theory of 'sea floor spreading' explains _____ (Average Rigor) (Skill 21.6)**

   A.   the shapes of the continents.

   B.   how continents collide.

   C.   how continents move apart.

   D.   how continents sink to become part of the ocean floor.

Answer: C. How continents move apart.

In the theory of 'sea floor spreading', the movement of the ocean floor causes continents to spread apart from one another. This occurs because crust plates split apart, and new material is added to the plate edges. This process pulls the continents apart, or may create new separations, and is believed to have caused the formation of the Atlantic Ocean. Therefore, the answer is (C).

103. **Which of the following is the best definition for 'meteorite'? (Rigorous) (Skill 21.6)**

A.   A meteorite is a mineral composed of mica and feldspar.

B.   A meteorite is material from outer space that has struck the earth's surface.

C.   A meteorite is an element that has properties of both metals and nonmetals.

D.   A meteorite is a very small unit of length measurement.

Answer: B. A meteorite is material from outer space that has struck the earth's surface.

Meteoroids are pieces of matter in space, composed of particles of rock and metal. If a meteoroid travels through the earth's atmosphere, friction causes burning and a "shooting star"—i.e., a meteor. If the meteor strikes the earth's surface, it is known as a meteorite. Note that although the suffix –ite often means a mineral, answer (A) is incorrect. Answer (C) refers to a 'metalloid' rather than a 'meteorite,' and answer (D) is simply a misleading pun on 'meter.' Therefore, the answer is (B).

Physical Education & Health

104. **Which of the following is not a type of muscle tissue? (Easy) (Skill 22.1)**

A.   Skeletal

B.   Cardiac

C.   Smooth

D.   Fiber

Answer: D. Fiber

The main function of the muscular system is movement. There are three types of muscle tissue: skeletal, cardiac, and smooth.

105. **Which of these is a type of joint? (Average Rigor) (Skill 22.1)**

   A.   Ball and socket

   B.   Hinge

   C.   Pivot

   D.   All of the above

Answer: D. All of the above

A joint is a place where two bones meet. Joints enable movement. Hinge, Ball and socket, and pivot are types of joints.

106. **Social skills and values developed by activity include all of the following except: (Average Rigor) (Skill 22.4)**

   A.   Winning at all costs

   B.   Making judgments in groups

   C.   Communicating and cooperating

   D.   Respecting rules and property

Answer: A. Winning at all costs

Winning at all costs is not a desirable social skill. Instructors and coaches should emphasize fair play and effort over winning. Answers B, C, and D are all positive skills and values developed in physical activity settings.

107. **Activities that enhance team socialization include all of the following except: (Easy) (Skill 22.4)**

A. Basketball

B. Soccer

C. Golf

D. Volleyball

Answer: C. Golf

Golf is mainly an individual sport. Though golf involves social interaction, it generally lacks the team element inherent in basketball, soccer, and volleyball.

108. **Through physical activities, John has developed self-discipline, fairness, respect for others, and new friends. John has experienced which of the following? (Rigorous) (Skill 22.4)**

A. Positive cooperation psycho-social influences

B. Positive group psycho-social influences

C. Positive individual psycho-social influences

D. Positive accomplishment psycho-social influences

Answer: B. Positive group psycho-social influences

Through physical activities, John developed his social interaction skills. Social interaction is the sequence of social actions between individuals (or groups) that modify their actions and reactions due to the actions of their interaction partner(s). In other words, they are events in which people attach meaning to a situation, interpret what others mean, and respond accordingly. Through socialization with other people, John feels the influence of the people around him.

109. **The most effective way to promote the physical education curriculum is to: (Rigorous) (Skill 22.6)**

A. Relate physical education to higher thought processes

B. Relate physical education to humanitarianism

C. Relate physical education to the total educational process

D. Relate physical education to skills necessary to preserve the natural environment

Answer: C. Relate physical education to the total educational process

The government treats the physical education curriculum as one of the major subjects. Because of all of the games that we now participate in, many countries have focused their hearts and set their minds on competing with rival countries. Physical education is now one of the major, important subjects and instructors should integrate physical education into the total educational process.

110. **The affective domain of physical education contributes to all of the following except: (Average Rigor) (Skill 22.6)**

A. Knowledge of exercise, health, and disease

B. Self-actualization

C. An appreciation of beauty

D. Good sportsmanship

Answer: A. Knowledge of exercise, health, and disease

The affective domain encompasses emotions, thoughts, and feelings related to physical education. Knowledge of exercise, health, and disease is part of the cognitive domain.

111. **A physical education instructor anticipates and prevents potential injuries, watches for hidden injuries, and takes an injury evaluation of the entire class. Which of the following strategies to prevent injuries is the teacher demonstrating? (Average Rigor) (Skill 22.6)**

   A.   Maintaining hiring standards

   B.   Proper use of equipment

   C.   Proper procedures for emergencies

   D.   Participant screening

Answer: D. Participant screening

In order for the instructor to know each student's physical status, he or she takes an injury evaluation. Such surveys are one way to know the physical status of an individual. It chronicles past injuries, tattoos, activities, and diseases the individual may have or had. It helps the instructor to know the limitations of each individual. Participant screening covers all forms of surveying and anticipation of injuries.

Visual Arts

112. **The Renaissance period was concerned with the rediscovery of the works of_____ (Rigorous) (Skill 24.5)**

   A.   Italy

   B.   Japan

   C.   Germany

   D   Classical Greece and Rome

Answer: D. Classical Greece and Rome

The Renaissance period was concerned with the rediscovery of the works of classical Greece and Rome. The art, literature, and architecture were inspired by classical orders, which tended to be formal, simple, and concerned with the ideal human proportions.

113. **Which is NOT a true statement about crafts? (Easy) (Skill 24.5)**

A. Students experiment with their own creativity.

B. Products are unique and different.

C. Outcome is predetermined.

D. Self-expression is encouraged.

Answer: C. Outcome is predetermined.

Outcome is predetermined. Students should be allowed to experiment with their own creativity and self-expression.

114. **Creating movements in response to music helps students to connect music and dance in which of the following ways? (Rigorous) (Skill 24.6)**

A. Rhythm

B. Costuming

C. Speed

D. Vocabulary skills

Answer A. Rhythm

Students should be able to understand the connections made between movement and music is related by rhythm.

115. The history of theatre is important at an early age Which of the following is not a vital part of the many time periods of theatre history? (Rigorous) (Skill 27.6)

A.   Roman theatre

B.   American theatre

C.   Medieval drama

D.   Renaissance theatre

Answer: B. American theatre

American theatre wasn't included as a type of theatre in early age drama.

116. During the early childhood years (ages 3-5), drama and theatre experiences are especially beneficial to children because they provide the opportunity for students to: (Average Rigor) (Skill 27.6)

A.   apply the concept of turn-taking.

B.   learn the importance of listening skills.

C.   acquire the skills needed to become a proficient reader.

D.   learn early drama skills using their five senses.

Answer: D. learn early drama skills using their five senses.

Students in Early Childhood ages are introduced to drama and theatre using their 5 senses. Using smell, feel, sound, touch, and taste are all senses that even at the earliest ages children know and are able to relate to.

117. A combination of three or more tones sounded at the same time is called a (Rigorous) (Skill 27.6)

A. Harmony

B. Consonance

C. Chord

D. Dissonance

Answer: C. Chord

A chord is three or more tones combined and sounded simultaneously. Dissonance is the simultaneous sounding of tones that produce a feeling of tension or unrest and a feeling that further resolution is needed. Harmony is the sound resulting from the simultaneous sounding of two or more tones consonant with each other.

118. A series of single tones that add up to a recognizable sound is called a: (Rigorous) (Skill 27.6)

A. Cadence

B. Rhythm

C. Melody

D. Sequence

Answer: C. Melody

A melody is an arrangement of single tones in a meaningful sequence. Cadence is the closing of a phrase or section of music. Rhythm is the regular occurrence of accented beats that shape the character of music or dance.

Sample Essay Questions

Reading, Language, & Literature

World Literature, Important Works

Read the passage below from *The Diary of Anne Frank* (1947) and complete the exercise that follows.

Written on July 15, 1944, three weeks before the Frank family was arrested by the Nazis, Anne's diary entry explains her worldview and future hopes.

"It's difficult in times like these: ideals, dreams and cherished hopes rise within us, only to be crushed by grim reality. It's a wonder I haven't abandoned all my ideals, they seem so absurd and impractical. Yet I cling to them because I still believe, in spite of everything, that people are truly good at heart.

It's utterly impossible for me to build my life on a foundation of chaos, suffering and death. I see the world being slowly transformed into a wilderness, I hear the approaching thunder that, one day, will destroy us too, I feel the suffering of millions, And yet, when I look up at the sky, I somehow feel that everything will change for the better, that this cruelty too shall end, that peace and tranquility will return once more. In the meantime, I must hold on to my ideals. Perhaps the day will come when I will be able to realize them!"

Using your knowledge of literature, write a response in which you:

- Compare and contrast Anne's ideals with her awareness of the conditions in which she lives; and
- discuss how the structure of Anne's writing—her sentences and paragraphs—emphasize the above contrast.

Sample Response

This excerpt from *The Diary of Anne Frank* reveals the inner strength of a young girl who refuses, despite the wartime violence and danger surrounding her, to let her idealism be overcome by hatred and mass killing. This idealism is reflected, in part, by her emphases on universal human hopes such as peace, tranquility, and goodwill. But Anne Frank is no dreamy Pollyanna. Reflecting on her idealism in the context of the war raging around her, she matter-of-factly writes: "my dreams, they seem so absurd and impractical."

This indicates Anne Frank's awareness of not only her own predicament, but of human miseries that extend beyond the immediate circumstances of her life. For elsewhere she writes in a similar vein, "In times like these... I see the world being slowly transformed into a wilderness"; despite her own suffering she can "feel the suffering of millions."

And yet Anne Frank believes, "in spite of everything, that people are truly good at heart." This statement epitomizes the stark existential contrast of her worldview with the wartime reality that ultimately claimed her life.

The statement also exemplifies how Anne's literary form—her syntax and diction—mirror thematic content and contrasts. "In spite of everything," she still believes in people. She can "hear the approaching thunder...yet, when I look up at the sky, I somehow feel that everything will change for the better." At numerous points in this diary entry, first-hand knowledge of violent tragedy stands side-by-side with belief in humanity and human progress.

"I must hold on to my ideals," Anne concludes. "Perhaps the day will come when I'll be able to realize them!" In her diary she has done so, and more.

History and Social Science

Describe the rivalry between England and France

Just as they are geographically located on opposite sides of the English Channel, historically, France and England have been on opposite sides of numerous conflicts over the last few centuries.

One historical event was the Hundred Years' War, which lasted 116 years. The Hundred Years' War was not the beginning of a conflict; it was a continuation of one that had existed since the time of the first Norman Kings of England. Every king from Henry II to Edward II had engaged in warfare against French Kings on the continent since the English laid claim to the French throne. However, by 1214, the Kings of England had lost a substantial portion of their lands in France, including Normandy.

The ongoing rivalry over the years forced the Native Americans in the New World to take sides against each other in the ensuing conflicts and battles. The French and Indian War fought in North America pitted England and the young colonists against the French explorers who were laying claim to the vast lands of the Ohio Country.

When the colonists revolted against the English King in 1776, the French were willing to help the colonists fight the English.

During the War of 1812, the Americans battled Great Britain, then the world's greatest military power, especially on the high seas, while Great Britain was fighting France during the Napoleonic Wars that ultimately brought great change to Europe.

In recent history, the two countries continue to oppose each other in the latest War in Iraq, where the United Kingdom supports the United States' efforts to fight the war on terror in the Middle East, and France has provided little to no support to the United States. It would seem that if there is a conflict or global issue to be had, you will find England on one side of the table and France on the other.

Math

Solve the following problem using the diagram below:

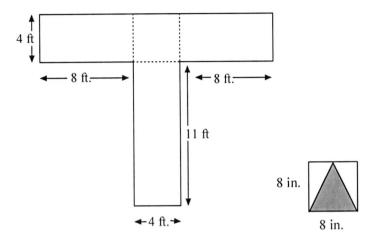

A homeowner wants to cover her foyer with 8" by 8" tiles composed of three triangular tiles of two sizes. All the tiles must be of equal size and cover the area without being cut or overlapping.

Using your knowledge of number theory and geometry:

- determine how many square tiles made up of triangles are needed to cover the area of the foyer; and
- prove that the larger, colored tiles compose exactly one-half of each square.

Sample Response

First, determine the area of each square tile. The area of a square is equal to a side squared. Since each tile is 8 inches by 8 inches, the area of the tile would be 64 square inches.

Next, determine the area of the foyer. In order to maintain the pattern, we need to determine area by section. The two ends of the top of the "T" are 8 feet by 4 feet, so each of their areas is 32 square feet. Since the tiles are measured in square inches, we need to convert the area of the foyer to square inches: 32 times 144 equals 4,608 square inches. The area of the middle section of the top of the "T" is 4 feet times 4 feet, or 16 square feet, or 2,304 square inches. The area of the stem of the "T" is 4 feet times 11 feet, or 44 square feet, or 6,336 square inches.

The total area of the foyer is the sum of the areas of each section: 4,608 + 4,608 + 2,304 + 6,336 = 17,856 square inches. To determine the number of square tiles we need, we divide the area of the foyer by the area of a tile: 17,856 ÷ 64 = 279 tiles.

To prove that the larger, colored triangle is exactly half the area of one of the square tiles, find the area of the triangle. The area of a triangle is equal to one-half the base times the height: ½(8 X 8) = ½(64) = 32 square inches. The area of the square tile is 64 square inches. Thirty-two is one-half of sixty-four. Therefore, the area of the triangle is exactly half the area of the square tile.

Rationale

The response is considered to be good because it demonstrates the respondent's knowledge of the subject matter (number sense and geometry) and addresses the specific questions asked by the test. The thinking behind the process and the derivation of the answers are fully explained in a clear and concise manner. All areas of the calculations and proof are covered.

Science

Using your accumulated knowledge, discuss the components of biogeochemical cycles.

Essential elements are recycled through an ecosystem. At times, the element needs to be made available in a useable form. Cycles are dependent on plants, algae, and bacteria to fix nutrients for use by animals. The four main cycles are: water, carbon, nitrogen, and phosphorous.

Two percent of all the water is fixed in ice or the bodies of organisms, rendering it unavailable. Available water includes surface water (lakes, ocean, and rivers) and ground water (aquifers, wells). The majority (96 percent) of all available water is from ground water. Water is recycled through the processes of evaporation and precipitation. The water present now is the water that has been here since our atmosphere was formed.

Ten percent of all available carbon in the air (in the form of carbon dioxide gas) is fixed by photosynthesis. Plants fix carbon in the form of glucose, and animals eat the plants and are able to obtain the carbon necessary to sustain themselves. When animals release carbon dioxide through respiration, the cycle begins again as plants recycle the carbon through photosynthesis.

Eighty percent of the atmosphere is in the form of nitrogen gas. Nitrogen must be fixed and taken out of the gaseous form to be incorporated into an organism. Only a few genera of bacteria have the correct enzymes to break the strong triple bond between nitrogen atoms. These special bacteria live within the roots of legumes (peas, beans, alfalfa) and add bacteria to the soil so it may be taken up by the plant. Nitrogen is necessary in the building of amino acids and the nitrogenous bases of DNA.

Phosphorus exists as a mineral and is not found in the atmosphere. Fungi and plant roots have structures called mycorrhizae that are able to fix insoluble phosphates into useable phosphorus. Urine and decayed matter return phosphorus to the earth where it can be fixed in the plant. Phosphorus is needed for the backbone of DNA and for the manufacture of ATP.

The four biogeochemical cycles are present concurrently. Water is continually recycled, and is utilized by organisms to sustain life. Carbon is also a necessary component for life. Both water and carbon can be found in the air and on the ground. Nitrogen and phosphorous are commonly found in the ground. Special organisms, called decomposers, help to make these elements available in the environment. Plants use the recycled materials for energy; when they are consumed, the cycle begins again.

XAMonline, INC. 21 Orient Ave. Melrose, MA 02176
Toll Free number 800-509-4128
TO ORDER Fax 781-662-9268 OR www.XAMonline.com

GEORGIA ASSESSMENTS FOR THE CERTIFICATION OF EDUCATORS   -GACE - 2007

PO#   Store/School:

Address 1:

Address 2 (Ship to other):

City, State Zip

Credit card number_____-_____-_____-_____   expiration_____
EMAIL _____
PHONE   **FAX**

13# ISBN 2007	TITLE	Qty	Retail	Total
978-1-58197-533-8	Basic Skills 200, 201, 202			
978-1-58197-528-4	Biology 026, 027			
978-1-58197-529-1	Science 024, 025			
978-1-58197-574-1	English 020, 021			
978-1-58197-569-7	Physics 030, 031			
978-1-58197-531-4	Art Education Sample Test 109, 110			
978-1-58197-545-1	History 034, 035			
978-1-58197-527-7	Health and Physical Education 115, 116			
978-1-58197-540-6	Chemistry 028, 029			
978-1-58197-534-5	Reading 117, 118			
978-1-58197-547-5	Media Specialist 101, 102			
978-1-58197-535-2	Middle Grades Reading 012			
978-1-58197-539-0	Middle Grades Science 014			
978-1-58197-543-7	Middle Grades Mathematics 013			
978-1-58197-546-8	Middle Grades Social Science 015			
978-158-197-573-4	Middle Grades Language Arts 011			
978-1-58197-536-9	Mathematics 022, 023			
978-1-58197-549-9	Political Science 032, 033			
978-1-58197-544-4	Paraprofessional Assessment 177			
978-1-58197-542-0	Professional Pedagogy Assessment 171, 172			
978-1-58197-537-6	Early Childhood Education 001, 002			
978-1-58197-548-2	School Counseling 103, 104			
978-1-58197-541-3	Spanish 141, 142			
978-1-58197-538-3	Special Education General Curriculum 081, 082			
978-1-58197-530-7	French Sample Test 143, 144			

FOR PRODUCT PRICES GO TO WWW.XAMONLINE.COM	**SUBTOTAL**	
	Ship	$8.25
	TOTAL	